Rhythmic Subjects

Dee Reynolds

Rhythmic Subjects

DANCE BOOKS

First published in 2007 by Dance Books Ltd
The Old Bakery
4 Lenten Street
Alton
Hampshire GU34 1HG

ISBN: 9 781852 731120

A CIP catalogue record for this book is available from the British Library

Printed and bound in Great Britain by Latimer Trend Ltd., Plymouth, UK

Contents

Illustrations

Acknowledgements

My thanks go first of all to Peter Bassett, without whose generous support I could not have carried out the initial research for this project. I am also immensely grateful to the family, friends and fellow dance scholars who have provided help and encouragement through difficult moments in the life cycle of the manuscript. A special thanks here to my husband Stephen for his very valuable advice. I also particularly wish to thank Helen Hills.

I am very grateful to the Leverhulme Foundation for a Research Fellowship, to the Arts and Humanities Research Board for a Research Leave Award, and to the British Academy for financing essential research trips and copyright payments.

I have received constructive and useful comments on drafts of the manuscript from Ramsay Burt, Petra Kuppers, Roger Smith and Linda Walker, and also from Matthew Jefferies and Gay Morris on specific chapters. Ricarda Schmidt has assisted with queries on translations from German. Thomas Rohrkrämer provided valuable bibliographical references.

I also wish to thank Sophia Lycouris and Helen Thomas for their longstanding support.

I very much appreciate the kindness and intellectual generosity of Don McDonagh and Leslie Getz during my trips to New York.

My conversations with Jonah Bokaer have been inspirational. Derry Swan, China Laudisio, Alessandra Prosperi and Maurizio Nardi gave me precious insights into the experience of dancers in the Merce Cunningham and Martha Graham Companies.

I am very grateful to David Vaughan for facilitating access to the excellent resources of the Archives of the Cunningham Dance Foundation, and to Stacy Sumpman and her predecessor, Anna Brown, for their generous assistance.

Finally, thanks to my children, Niall and Caitríona, for their example of boundless energy!

Introduction

My goal in this strongly interdisciplinary book is to show that uses of energy in movement, and their transformation, are central to dance practice and analysis. This transformation comes about through kinesthetic imagination. Kinesthetic imagination is an activity whose aim is given in movement itself, and is not fully transparent to the agent. It is both a response and an active resistance to constraining patterns of energy usage that are culturally dominant, and that shape the kinesthetic experiences and habits of individual subjects. This potential to transform uses of energy in movement places dance at the forefront of culturally significant forms of artistic practice.

Energy is connected with rhythm through expenditure and economy. Innovative dance rhythms are grounded in changes in energy expenditure through new 'economies' of energy, which can manifest the subject's resistance to constraints and transform the 'self'. Because kinesthetic imagination can be activated through virtual (e.g. empathetic) as well as actual movement, it may be experienced by spectators of dance as well as by dancers themselves.

Critical dance studies have a rich recent history,[1] revolutionised by interdisciplinary and multidisciplinary approaches, ranging from semiotics through feminism and social theory to ethnography and historical and cultural studies. Art historian and theorist Norman Bryson, in enthusiastic response to the 1992 'Choreographing History' conference held at the University of California, Riverside,[2] called for a thoroughly interdisciplinary approach to 'the body in movement'. This has been very fully achieved, with the 1990s producing an abundance of studies astounding in the quality and range of their approach.[3] The trend continues into the twenty-first century, with increasing attention to ethnic identities and to popular and hybrid forms of dance.[4]

However, despite this burgeoning of interdisciplinarity, I believe that analysis of the qualities of movement can be much more fully integrated into these approaches. Particularly in discussion of theatre dance in 'high' culture, formal and/or expressive aspects are still frequently seen as separate from social and political perspectives. For instance, in his recent (2004) study of Merce Cunningham, Roger Copeland asserts that those whom he describes as the 'race/class/gender gurus' 'vilify' the classical aesthetic criteria of 'formalism, objectivity, disinterestedness, the value of the visual'.[5] Jane Desmond, however, has argued for the need to pay 'increased attention to movement as a primary, not a secondary social text', pointing out that 'social relations are both enacted and produced through the body, and not merely inscribed on it'. She suggested that the Effort/Shape system of Rudolf Laban (1879–1958) would be a good starting point for this project, because it could provide 'an analytical system as well as a language with which to speak about the body moving in time and space'. (Effort/Shape, which will be discussed later in this book, links dynamic qualities with the shaping qualities of movement.) No one model, however, can be sufficient. As Desmond writes: 'To keep our broader levels of analysis anchored in the materiality and kinesthesia of the dancing body, we need to generate more tools for close readings, and more sophisticated methodologies for shuttling back and forth between the micro (physical) and macro (historical, ideological) levels of movement investigation.'[6]

In this book, I argue that discussion of energy is the key to linking core movement issues (the micro level) with wider cultural and theoretical contexts (the macro level). The 'self' is bound up with habitual and normative economies of energy. It is now widely accepted that the 'self' is not unified and transcendental, but is at once subject to cultural norms and open to change. Innovative choreographical practices come about as responses to cultural contexts which encourage or enforce ways of using energy that limit expressiveness. These cultural contexts are constructed through socially sanctioned uses of energy in everyday movement and behaviours, and frequently also through culturally dominant dance forms, notably ballet. When these norms are experienced as repressive, they can trigger new ways of using energy that are both choreographically creative and resistant to social norms.

I am concerned with dance as theatre art in Germany (from the early 1900s to the end of the 1920s) and the USA (from the early 1900s up to the mid-1930s, and again from the mid-1940s to the end of the 1970s) as practised by particular (now canonical) choreographers: Mary Wigman (1886–1973), Martha Graham (1894–1991) and Merce Cunningham (1919 –). These choreographers tend to conceive of energy in impersonal, universalist terms, but I show that their innovative uses of energy are stimulated by and engage with specific conditions and cultural values.

Displacements and dislocations in ways of using energy in movement actively impact upon subjective and intersubjective identities. Such effects can be produced on a physical level: directly, in the case of a dancer performing a work, or indirectly, in the case of the effects on spectators. In Wigman, Graham and Cunningham, innovative uses of energy, which resist constraints embodied in cultural norms, are grounded in vitalist values. The nature of these innovations varies according to the cultural context, as resistance is directly related to the constraints experienced.

Because of these close connections between uses of energy in movement and the constitution of subjectivity in its socio-cultural contexts, dance is uniquely important as an art form. Hitherto, no one has explored in depth the significance of uses of energy in theatre dance and performance and its subversive potential, although several recent publications have begun to highlight the importance of these issues. In *The Work of Dance: Labor, Movement and Identity in the 1930s* (2002), Mark Franko (whose valuable study, *Dancing Modernism, Performing Politics*, had already emphasised interplay between 'the aesthetic and the political')[7] discussed links between labour and dance (including 'ethnic' dance, ballet and chorus dance as well as modern dance), informed by 'the understanding of labor in the Marxian tradition as the expenditure of raw human effort in production', which 'engendered new interest in the needs and costs of human movement as well as new questions about the limits and potentials of organized energy'.[8]

In *Dances that Describe Themselves: The Improvised Choreography of Richard Bull* (2002), Susan Foster commented on the political implications of energy expenditure in rave culture: 'this immense expenditure of energy for no productive purpose, an affront to Protestant and capitalist work ethics, momentarily revitalizes wasteland spaces, subtly dramatizing the ineffectiveness of government while remaining noncompliant with civic and corporate notions of good citizenship'.[9] Felicia McCarren's *Dancing Machines: Choreographies of the Age of Mechanical Reproduction* (2003) examined analogies between human and machine movement in the Modernist period, with reference to discourses of expenditure of energy, including thermodynamics.[10] She also discussed the importance in work science of economy of gesture, and its implications for dance. This convergence of discourses on dance, energy and economy and the focus on the Modernist period has similarities with my own approach. However, McCarren viewed dance largely through other art forms, notably literature and cinema.

The word 'energy' comes from the Greek, *en* (in) and *ergon* (work), and can be defined as 'the capacity to perform work'. Biologically, it is exemplified in the use of kinetic energy while performing muscular contractions to produce movement. Thus, 'when a muscle contracts, it performs work.'[11] There is a close relationship between the use of energy to perform work and the concept of economy, viewed in modern economics as efficient 'production or action with the minimum of expense, waste and effort'.[12] Economy also has the older meaning of good management or distribution of resources, while energy is associated more broadly with 'intensity or vitality',[13] which involves sensation and/or emotion. I shall discuss energy here in terms of how it is used and experienced by human agents and spectators of movement in theatre dance. This energy is 'kinesthetic' as opposed to 'kinetic'. Both terms are etymologically related to movement (Greek *kinein*, to move). However, kinetic energy can be quantified in scientific descriptions[14] and ascribed to inanimate objects in motion, which have no experience of movement. Kinesthetic energy, by contrast, refers to energy as it is experienced by a subject.

Kinesthesia can be defined as 'the sensation by which bodily position, weight, muscle tension and movement are perceived',[15] and is central to embodied experience. Movement events that disrupt normative, habitual ways of using energy in movement and produce innovations in production, distribution, expenditure and retention of energy in the body are acts of 'kinesthetic imagination'. These acts involve a delicate balance between determinism and agency. When new movement techniques or choreographies result in changes in normative economies of energy, such changes are unlikely to be fully transparent to their initiators (here, the choreographers concerned) or to their audience, in the first instance, although they may rapidly become the objects of critical inquiry.

I connect uses of energy with rhythm through Laban's concept of 'effort', according to which movement rhythms are produced by modulations in energy expenditure. I discuss dances that I have observed in live performance and/or on video/film, situating them with reference to cultural and discursive contexts within which the works were produced and received. In particular, I focus on energy and rhythm in three main contexts: body culture and its gendering in early twentieth-century Germany; Americanism and masculinism in modernism in the USA of the 1920s; and Cold War conformism, bureaucracy and conspiracy theory. Much of my discussion is grounded in cultural and historical studies, in the history of ideas (pertaining mainly to German and American Studies), and, because uses of energy are gendered, in Women's Studies.[16]

My elaboration of kinesthetic imagination also draws on phenomenology, post-structuralism and social theory. In my *Symbolist Aesthetics and Early Abstract Art: Sites of Imaginary Space* (1995),[17] I argued that imagination can be viewed as an activity that works with sign systems to destabilise fixed meanings and representations. Phenomenology had already moved the concept of imagination away from that of an inherent power of the mind, which acted as a container for a mental image. In phenomenology, imagination was conceived in more dynamic terms, as an act directed towards an image (described as an 'intentional' act). My approach went one step further, by arguing that imagination could work with sign systems to fragment and mobilise its objects, in the manner of a kaleidoscope.

Of the critical theorists I discuss, Maurice Merleau-Ponty's phenomenological approach to embodied consciousness and Pierre Bourdieu's concept of the 'habitus' are most central to my argument about kinesthetic imagination. Kinesthetic imagination shares features of Merleau-Ponty's corporeal intentionality[18] and Bourdieu's practical sense: embodiedness, goal-directedness and lack of transparency to rational consciousness. In both corporeal intentionality and practical sense, the goal of an action/movement is already given in the action/ movement itself, but is not fully known to the agent, who is therefore a 'split' subject, and experiences otherness within the self. French poet Arthur Rimbaud famously proclaimed (in 1871) that 'I is an other'.[19] This otherness of the self, and specifically of the embodied self, is crucial to the notion of subjectivity that emerges from Merleau-Ponty's and Bourdieu's accounts, where action (such as movement) can precede conscious knowledge.

In observing and describing uses of energy in movement and in situating economies of energy with reference to wider cultural debates, I draw extensively on the Effort theory of Rudolf Laban, and on some more recent developments of his ideas in Laban Movement Analysis, notably Effort/Shape.[20] However, I do not take as my primary focus issues surrounding Laban Movement Analysis, nor do I undertake to refine it as a tool for movement description. I use some of Laban's ideas, in conjunction with elements of critical theory, as a means to further my argument that kinesthetic imagination is an activity that produces changes in habitual patterns of energy usage in the body. Effort is a useful concept because it helps to integrate the concepts of energy and economy in the discussion of movement, and because it provides a basis for conceptualising and describing changes in habitual uses of energy in movement. In the case of Cunningham, I explain how his approach to rhythm is different from Laban's. Although Effort terms continue to be helpful in analysing uses of energy in Cunningham's dance, I employ here a less descriptive vocabulary (drawn from Laban) than in my discussion of Wigman or Graham.

The origins of Laban's later theories on Effort date back to his writings in the 1920s, but it was in the 1940s that he developed fully the concept and principles of Effort analysis, when he collaborated with management consultant Frederick Lawrence in the UK to elaborate principles of movement that could lead to 'increased enjoyment of work through the awareness and practice of its rhythmic character'.[21] Laban's original German term was *Antrieb*, which would be more accurately translated as 'impulse', and his concept of 'effort' does not relate straightforwardly to uses of the term 'effort' in physics.[22] Effort analysis takes as its starting point the behaviour and experience of moving subjects. It can be applied to actions ranging from walking down the street, through physical tasks executed in the workplace, to dance performed on stage. Laban's 'effort elements' comprised both a motor impulse and an 'inner' attitude or effort/exertion. 'The impulse given to our nerves and muscles which move the joints of our limbs originates in inner efforts.' [23]

Laban analysed attitudes towards effort according to the degree of active resistance or passive yielding on the part of the mover to the 'motion factors' of weight, space, time and flow, on a spectrum ranging from 'indulging in' to 'fighting against'. It was these attitudes that produced rhythm. 'Few people realize that what they discern [i.e. rhythm] is in reality effort.'[24] Modulations in effort intensity, which brought different motion factors into play, were the core of movement rhythm,[25] and rhythm was explained as 'an alternation of stresses or more intensive effort-qualities with less intensive ones'. In this way, rhythm was linked with degrees of effort, or modulation in expenditure/economy of energy. Laban's view of rhythm was also strongly holistic. Dances were 'effort-poems', which should be informed by the 'unifying laws of harmony'.[26] He shared Isadora Duncan's fascination with rhythmic flow as an indivisible, unquantifiable force, and saw the defining characteristic of modern dance as its use of 'the flow of movement pervading all articulations of the body'.[27] There was a 'natural urge for balance and harmony', and the dancer experienced 'a strong need for unity'.[28]

However, despite his holistic orientation, Laban's ideas on effort were sufficiently flexible to be consonant with a 'split' subject, whose movement was not under conscious control. Laban argued that, even in ordinary movement, effort qualities were extremely complex, and were not wholly transparent to consciousness. 'Effort and its resulting action may be both unconscious and involuntary'.[29] For Laban, 'the richness of people's efforts consists just in the fact that their effort characteristics are an incredibly subtle mixture or compound of many degrees of attitudes towards several movement elements'.[30] This complexity defied description, as 'there exist an almost infinite number of combinations of every movement and shade'.[31] He compared the effects of effort rhythms to those of colour. 'Different combinations of efforts create different moods in the dancer, which are analogous to the moods induced by combinations of colours in all their subtle varieties.' [32] He also commented: 'We do not sufficiently realize the important effect action has on the mental state of the mover. Movement can inspire accompanying moods, which are felt more or less strongly according to the degree of effort involved'.[33]

Writing on Isadora Duncan, Laban affirmed that 'there exists in the flow of man's [sic] movement some ordering principle which cannot be explained in the usual rationalistic manner ... Movement considered hitherto – at least in our civilization – as the servant of man employed to achieve an extraneous practical purpose was brought to light as an independent power creating states of mind frequently stronger than man's will.'[34] When dancing, the dancer 'loses himself in the movement'.[35] Dancers or actors rarely performed 'a completely voluntary movement, in which every detail is premeditated and controlled'; and, paradoxically, 'only when a part of the quality of movement is, or seems to be, unconscious do we speak of a natural or true expression'.[36] In 'the art of movement', the body 'has to be carried to and fro over the threshold between consciousness and unconsciousness'.[37] For Laban, then, dancing moved the subject through a liminal realm between conscious and unconscious. Dance was not about performing steps, but about effecting radical changes in the subject through movement. This view has implications beyond those developed by Laban himself, particularly in relation to intentionality, which I discuss in Chapter 5.

Laban argued that the muscular activity of 'yielding to' or 'resisting' weight, space, time and flow produced different movement qualities, which corresponded to 'inner' attitudes towards these motion factors. For instance, flexible, expansive movements, as opposed to direct, linear ones, denoted an attitude of yielding to space by moving in different directions. Weak movements, with muscular relaxation, as opposed to forceful deployment of one's weight to make an impact on the environment, resulted from an attitude of indulgence in weight. The category of 'weight' can be confusing and is sometimes replaced by other terms such as 'pressure' or 'force'. Cecily Dell explains that '"heavy" and "light" ... describe the conditions of objects or people who are acted upon – lifted, carried, etc. – while a person who actively changes his weight quality in movement can best be described in terms of strong or light'.[38] Laban associated sustained, unhurried movement with indulging in time, while loose, unrestrained, as opposed to 'bound' movement was characterised by 'free' flow. 'A movement can be considered as bound when its prevailing attitude is the readiness to stop.'[39] He noted that 'the body and its limbs are able to execute certain dynamic nuances in movement towards certain areas in space better than towards others', and posited basic affinities between particular directions in space and dynamic qualities. Upward tendency was associated with light use of weight, downward with strength; movement across the body was linked with a direct spatial attitude, while movement outward was linked with flexibility; retreating movement was linked with suddenness, and advancing movement with slowness.[40]

Laban's work on Effort has been very extensively developed by his colleagues and successors, in the UK, notably by Marion North and Warren Lamb,[41] and in the USA by Irmgard Bartenieff, Martha Davies, Cecily Dell, Judith Kestenberg and others.[42] For my purposes, the most important extension of Laban's work is what has come to be known as 'Effort-Shape', and I shall draw on some of these ideas where they are apposite to my discussion of dance works. Lamb, who worked with Laban on assessing the movements of company managers and executives, added the term 'shaping' to the analysis in a systematic way, and so 'what came to be known in the United States as Effort-Shape analysis is a combination of Laban's concepts and Lamb's elaborations'.[43]

The concept of Effort-Shape focuses on links between dynamic and shaping qualities of movement. In Effort-Shape theory, 'the intensity of the movement in terms of space-force-time is considered as important as the form of the movement'.[44] Effort refers to 'how kinetic energy is expended in space, force and time within functional and expressive behaviour', while Shape involves the 'form given the kinetic energy or impulse'.[45] Bartenieff and Davies describe 'shaping' as 'the way the body sculpts itself in space, and gives form to kinetic energy.'[46] For Judith Kestenberg, shaping is guided by 'the reciprocal relation of body shape to the space around it'.[47] Shape comprises 'shape flow' (growing or shrinking; going away from or towards the body); directional movement; and three-dimensional 'sculpting', where the body accommodates to the space in which the part is moving.[48] Kestenberg describes the 'rhythm of shape flow' as consisting of 'alternation between growing and shrinking of body shape', which corresponds to 'modes of self-representation'.[49] She also discusses the rhythm of what she calls 'tension flow' in terms of alternations in 'sequences of fluency and restraint in the state of the muscles in various parts of the body'.[50]

There are close affinities between effort and shape. For instance, following Laban, free flow has been linked with growing, and bound flow with shrinking; indirect use of space has been linked with widening, and direct use of space with narrowing; light weight/pressure has been linked with rising, and strong use of weight with falling; while slowness has been linked with advancing, and rapidity with retreating.[51] Such affinities should not be regarded as universal, because what Laban called 'effort make-up' has significant social and cultural dimensions. Warren Lamb argued that 'the results of shape-flow changes will be affected by variables such as social status, cultural conditioning, and individual personality characteristics'. Like Laban, Lamb believed that there were observable differences between male and female movement, which were particularly manifest in shape flow. However, Lamb pointed out the cultural as opposed to the physical factors behind these differences.[52] Irmgard Bartenieff and others have used Laban's framework for cross-cultural analysis of dance and movement styles.[53]

The pioneers of early modern dance frequently espoused an ideology of the 'naturalness' of the body, but it is now widely recognised that the body itself, including its unconscious reflexes, is profoundly 'inculturated'. Each person's way of moving and of experiencing their body is formed by their past, inscribed in a 'muscular memory' that produces habits, and is itself embedded in socio-cultural contexts. In the words of theatre director and theorist Eugenio Barba: 'Each one of us is an inculturated body. He uses a daily technology of the body which derives from the cultural context in which he was born, from his family environment, from his work. This inculturation which our organism absorbs right from the first hours of our life constitutes our spontaneity, in other words a network of conditioned reflexes or of unconscious automatisms'.[54] Movement qualities embody cultural norms, which impregnate bodily behaviour through repetition and habit (whether in everyday life, in established dance forms, or indirectly through value systems encoded in dominant discourses on movement and the body) and contribute to the 'otherness' of the embodied subject. Dance occupies a broad spectrum of relationships with established conventions, ranging from conformism or straightforward opposition to more subtle relations of resistance, where certain normative qualities are retained and others altered or inflected. Even dance that is considered 'formalist', because it does not have an obvious relation to 'content' with social or political significance, can engage with and offer resistance to conventional patterns of energy usage.

Effort analysis is predicated on the belief that uses of energy in movement are open to change. According to Laban, individuals build up their own habitual ways of using effort; this can lead to imbalances in which some efforts are developed at the expense of others. As an analyst of industrial work practices, he saw his task as a diagnostic and problem-solving one, which focused on economies of energy. 'The meaning of the word effort does not only comprise the unusual and exaggerated forms of spending effort, but the very fact of the spending of energy itself.'[55] For the purpose of greater 'economy of effort',[56] which would enable individuals to perform work tasks more efficiently, it was important to redress any such imbalances by developing contrasting effort-capacities. 'A man with fine touch ... must be able to get out of his habit and predilection of making light movements and performing actions containing the effort-elements of strength with the same ease as those containing fine touch.'[57] Laban believed that training people to reach a better understanding and awareness of their own effort actions would enable them to achieve better control, and a 'proportionality of efforts' appropriate to accomplishing particular tasks, thereby conserving energy.[58] 'In general effort-training, stress is laid on the awakening of the bodily feel of the co-ordination of motion factors in complex efforts, and in sequences of them'.[59] This would have the effect of improving the mover's 'economy of energy',[60] epitomised in the 'energy-saving qualities' of rhythmic movement. It would also give to the actions 'a certain perfection', reduce frustration and produce contentment with the actions performed. [61]

Laban advocated what he called 'mastery of movement' through cultivating awareness of movement structures and of effort patterns in the body. '[We] must study the systematic order of the different types of actions resulting from the different qualities of the inner effort; thus effort control becomes possible',[62] and he stressed that 'this awareness must be achieved through practical movement experience'.[63] New uses of weight, space, time and flow (in the action of walking, for instance) could profoundly modify habitual effort patterns. Laban and Lawrence affirmed that 'it is fundamentally the awareness that man can check and alter his effort-rhythms which is needed'.[64] A major issue in any discussion of change to economies of energy occurring through movement is the acquisition of movement memory and its potential to be modified. French dance-historian Laurence Louppe declared that 'modernity in dance often consists in questioning what seems to be received or inscribed in the body'.[65] I argue that new movement techniques or choreographies, when they are sufficiently far-reaching and frequently repeated, can modify economies of energy established in dancers' bodies and alter, at a very deep level, their movement memories.

Recent work in dance ethnography has emphasised the importance of kinesthesia and of somatic awareness in movement practice as a learning and transformative experience. Anthropologist and dance ethnographer Sally Ann Ness, who draws on aspects of Laban Movement Analysis, has discussed how learning 'an unfamiliar neuromuscular pattern' necessitates also 'opening' the mind. She explained this capacity in terms of 'the dynamic mentality of one's neuromusculature'.[66] Ness described a process of 'habit change' that she experienced as a result of learning a new choreography. 'Over the weeks that passed, habit set in. The posture of everyday life disintegrated as the new patterning took over.' The physical transformation itself produced a symbolic and cultural transformation, which involved a challenge to fixed identity. 'What had been my arm became "me", and what had been "me" lost consciousness, and this transformation presented a microcosmic moment of liminality and "culture shock" '.[67] This concept closely resembles aspects of what I mean by kinesthetic imagination.

Ness, however, draws unfavourable comparisons between movement descriptions that are 'observationally weighted' and those that are 'participation-driven', and are more embodied and experiential.[68] Participation-driven descriptions are written in the first person, and express an 'embodied understanding' in which movement is felt to be 'a source of integrating relationships', which unite 'dissociated aspects of the mover's being' and connect the 'self' with the 'non-self' of the environment.[69] Here, integration is privileged over difference. By contrast, I argue that the embodied self can be experienced as 'other' to the conscious mind. My descriptions of dances will reflect the possibility that movement may be performed by a split subject, and may be experienced, by both dancer and spectator, as originating in the body or body part, rather than as the fulfilment of intentions fully known to the agent. This is the process that I believe is dramatised in Wigman's famous 'Witch Dance'. Wigman has written of her experience, through this dance, of her self as 'other', speaking of herself in the third person and designating her body and body parts with the neutral definite article: 'the body', 'the hands', etc.[70]

The use of effort actions to produce new economies of energy means resisting cultural norms inscribed in the body. The studies of power by Michel Foucault have shown how power is diffused throughout society, operating through techniques such as 'normalisation' (for instance, where 'experts in normality', such as psychiatrists, make 'judgments about normality')[71] and 'disciplinary mechanisms' or 'systems of micro-power', such as routines of physical behaviour and exercise in prisons. Foucault also described these systems as 'tiny, everyday, physical mechanisms',[72] which produce desired behaviours through disciplinary techniques working on the body.[73] These mechanisms, where 'the body itself is invested by power relations',[74] are techniques of subjectification/subjection, necessary to the production of 'subjects'.[75] As Lois McNay has pointed out, 'the concept of norm that Foucault employs is quite circumscribed',[76] and I shall construe the term 'norm' more broadly, to include 'routinized modes of behavior [in Laban's terms, effort patterns] that are so deeply inscribed on the body ... that they seem natural or normal', deriving from 'the force of tradition, collectively generated systems of values or patterns of moral action'.[77]

My concept of kinesthetic imagination as the activity of a split subject (which I discuss at more length in Chapter 5) owes much to the discourses of 'economy' and 'energy' that are commonly found in recent post-structuralist and feminist writing, but which have not hitherto been explored in relation to uses of energy in dance. These discourses have both Freudian and Marxian antecedents.[78] Foucault spoke of 'a new "economy" of power, that is to say procedures which allow the effects of power to circulate in a manner at once continuous, uninterrupted, adapted and "individualised" throughout the entire social body'.[79] Jacques Derrida expressed his objection to both structuralist and phenomenological methods largely on the grounds of their inability to take account of movement and energy as factors that could disrupt stable signifying structures, and sought an alternative 'economy' that could escape the binary opposition of 'form' and 'force' by focusing on differences which were at once topological and energetic.[80]

The economy of what Derrida calls '*différance*'[81] works against all forms of recuperation of differences into a synthetic whole. The French writer Georges Bataille proposed a concept of '*dépense*' (expenditure) of an extreme nature, which similarly critiqued recuperation of meaning through conformity to discursive norms, and also drew on discourses of economy and expenditure to critique capitalist norms. In the late 1960s and early 1970s, 'many Parisian intellectuals took up Bataille's proposal of a general economy of spending and loss', related to Marcel Mauss's *The Gift* (published in French in 1926 and translated into English in 1967),[82] which was opposed to a 'limited' economy characterised by retention and accumulation. As the critic Morag Shiach has pointed out, '*dépense*' is 'a pun suggesting both the undoing of thought and a liberal spending of energies. It would be on the side of excess'.[83] The accounts of excessive energies in '*différance*' and '*dépense*' can illuminate uses of energy in dance, as I discuss in Chapter 5.

Julia Kristeva's well-known concept of 'subjects in process', which destabilises notions of fixed identity, is predicated on tensions between free and restricted energies, and was derived from her study of avant-garde nineteenth-century French poetry, which, she argued, brought about a 'dialectisation' of the subject through conflict between the rule-bound, conventional structures of language (its 'symbolic' dimension, which encoded linguistic and social norms) and the 'semiotic', a source of pre-semantic and instinctual energies or drives.[84]

For Kristeva, the most radical avant-garde texts, through their mobilisation of semiotic rhythms, could actually modify linguistic structures,[85] although such texts also had a tendency to dispense with political and social signifieds.[86] Kristeva related the 'semiotic' dimension of literature and painting to material drives,[87] but it is only in dance and other performing arts that there is material coincidence between the embodied subject and the medium of the work itself. The modification, through kinesthetic imagination, of economies of energy encoded in habitual effort patterns, has parallels with the modification of linguistic structures discussed by Kristeva.

Closer to dance and to my concept of shifting effort-patterns in movement is the notion of 'corporeity' used by the French kinesiologist and dance theorist Hubert Godard. Godard, who has been influenced by Laban,[88] works with a mobile model of subjectivity that is derived from the body rather than from language. Godard conceives of the dancing body 'in terms of the ways in which it organizes intensity and intentionality'[89] (an 'economic' model), and he sees this organisation as cultural as well as individual in origin. 'The mythologies of the body circulating in a social group are also inscribed in the postural system and, reciprocally, the corporeal attitude of individuals becomes the medium of this mythology.'[90] The body is a 'corporeity', or an 'accumulation of corporeities',[91] rather than a unified, stable 'body-subject'. The concept of 'corporeity' (which was developed by Michel Bernard),[92] designates the body as a 'sensory ... imaginary network ... inseparable from an individual and collective history',[93] which is flexible and open to change. Godard speaks of 'the infinite quality of corporeal organization – of singular and moving geographies, comprised of and in flux'.[94] Discussing Godard, the dance historian Isabelle Launay observes: 'If each environment creates a specific corporeity, a particular movement, a particular figure cannot carry the same meaning in different epochs, to the extent that bodies and the organization of their co-ordinations are radically different, that motricity is no longer the same.' She goes on to argue that future dance history should not be so much a history of 'subjects', as a history of the processes that operate movement, which are themselves processes of subject formation.[95]

Unlike dancers (of which the choreographer may be one), spectators are not generally involved in actively performing movement.[96] They do not have to undergo the daily working regime of the dancers' training, with its concomitant fatigue and pain, but they can experience movement sensations triggered by kinesthetic empathy. 'Virtual' (anticipated or imagined) movement is itself a physical event. Hubert Godard describes as 'pre-movement' the process whereby a set of muscles contracts in anticipation of a movement to be performed by a different part of the body. For instance, if, when standing, one is asked to raise one's arm in front, the first muscles to contract are not in fact those of the arm: 'rather it is the muscles of the ankle and leg that anticipate the need for balancing the changed center of gravity that will result from the reaching arm'.[97] Modern neuroscience contends that such pre-movement starts about a quarter of a second before the main action (here, the raising of the arm) begins, indicating that pre-movement is not a localised reflex action, but rather originates in the brain, triggered by the formation of the intention to move.

It has been shown that neural pathways are 'excited' (primed for action by the transmission of electrical impulses to muscles) as a result of simply forming an intention to move, without any contraction of the muscles taking place. 'Forming the intention is enough to increase the excitability of that pathway from the brain to the muscles.'[98] Such preparation for movement was described by Merleau-Ponty as 'a certain potential for action in the framework of the anatomical apparatus'.[99] Virtual movements, where, as in Merleau-Ponty's corporeal intentionality and Bourdieu's 'practical sense', the goal is given in the action but is not fully known to the agent, are at once intentional and physical. Also, because they involve neural activity, virtual or imagined movements can be used to learn new skills, as happens when athletes repeatedly visualise correctly executed movements when learning to perform difficult manoeuvres.[100]

Kinesthetic empathy, where spectators identify with the mover and themselves experience virtual movement sensations, is often associated with a logic of 'sameness' and reduction of difference,[101] but virtual participation in the movement of another can also have a de-centring effect, accentuating the 'otherness' of self and the tension between exteriority and interiority. In Merleau-Ponty's words: 'I was first of all outside myself, in the world, with others.'[102] According to the American dance critic John Martin, through a dual process of using patterns that spectators recognise through their muscular memory, while at the same time incorporating innovative material that conflicts with this experience, dancers can set up a tension between what he called 'internal' and 'external' rhythms.[103] The dancer's movements 'retain enough of the stuff of common experience to establish an emotional association in the mind of the spectator, but ... he sets up, along with the familiar patterns, such departures from them as to give them a new cast, a new meaning'.[104]

When I discuss the dances of Wigman, Graham and Cunningham, I give particular prominence to the reactions of contemporary spectators, because they are anchored in historically situated experiences and discourses of uses of energy in movement. I draw on the writings of contemporary critics, based in part on research carried out in the Mary Wigman Archives at the Akademie der Künste in Berlin, in the archives of the Cunningham Dance Foundation in New York, and in the Dance Collection of the New York Public Library. I also discuss the writings of the choreographers, which are themselves cultural documents that elucidate the value systems underlying particular uses of energy in movement, and which can contribute to their effects.

The foregrounding of energy in the work of Wigman, Graham and Cunningham is closely linked with their espousal of 'vitalist' ideas, whose cultural contexts I examine in Chapters 2–4. In Chapter 1, 'Life rhythms: Dancing the 'body-soul', I show how attention to discourses of energy allows connections to be made between dance practices and wider cultural contexts. I examine ideas of vitalism and energy in relation to dance history, body culture and 'life reform' movements, focusing on the emergence of modern dance in Germany and America and cultivation of the 'self', particularly the female 'self'; the history of ideas and science (e.g. 'life philosophy', psychoanalysis and theories of energy); and cultural history (e.g. efficiency in modern industrial capitalism and resistance to it). I show how new understandings and practices of energy, movement and rhythm developed historically as psychophysical attempts at a naturalistic integration of body and soul.

Modern dance was rooted in practices of transforming the 'self' through kinesthetic imagination, and resisted historically specific economies of energy that assimilated human to mechanical rhythms. Wigman's dance and its reception were closely linked with body culture and with debates on vitalism, which were particularly prominent in Germany. Different economies of energy give rise to different forms of resistance, including Martha Graham's 'virile' rhythms and the radically innovative rhythmic practices of Merce Cunningham, which continue to be informed by vitalist values.

In Chapters 2–4 I look in detail at the work of Mary Wigman (1886–1973), Martha Graham (1894–1991), and Merce Cunningham (b.1919). In all three cases, I comment on contemporary behavioural norms and discourses of energy in order to connect dance practices with wider cultural contexts. I combine cultural analysis with close examination of the movement techniques and the choreographical structure of a selection of individual dances. I have chosen only dances that I have seen performed live or on video, and the descriptions are based on my own observation. My aims in including these descriptions are to help readers who may not have had the opportunity to experience live or recorded performances of the dances, and to convey something of what I mean by the 'economies of energy' that animate the dances. I draw on Laban's Effort categories of weight, space, time and flow when they can assist in describing the dancers' uses of energy. I have included a Glossary of specialised vocabulary that includes selected Laban and ballet terms, which some readers may find it useful to refer to while reading the movement descriptions.

Chapter 2 focuses on Wigman's dance of the 1920s, and also discusses interactions between German and American dance in this period. The chapter opens with a verbal account of Wigman's *Seraphic Song* of 1929. Normative containment of energies was enshrined in bourgeois behaviour codes and militaristic values in Germany, which were strongly gendered, and opposed by 'life reform' movements. The impact of World War I intensified adherence to vitalist values and resistance to imposition of spatial containment. Wigman's dance resisted containment of energies. The most striking feature of her kinesthetic imagination is the challenge to containment of body boundaries through rhythmic exchanges between body and space. Wigman's work produced a heightened sense of vitality and the permeability of corporeal boundaries.

In the 1920s, the impact of new technologies and the economic power of the USA led to a more positive view of modernity than hitherto, and to affirmation of abstract rhythms. The growth of dance-literate audiences with shared vitalist values was an important factor in the reception of Wigman's work. Her dance appealed to spectators largely through the intensity of its energies, which were felt to be life-enhancing, and were frequently described in terms of the effects of electrical shocks on the nervous system, an image also used in contemporary descriptions of technological modernity. My accounts of spectators' responses use unpublished archival material. I discuss Wigman's techniques, and how our knowledge of her teaching methods supports my argument that her uses of energy focused on connecting the body and space and on intensifying vitalist energies. I discuss how this practice challenged gender norms, and conclude with detailed analyses of *Witch Dance II* (1926), *Pastorale* (1929) and *Dance of Summer* (1929).

In Chapter 3, I move to the USA, and to Graham's work from the 1920s to the mid-1930s. I begin by describing the driving, percussive rhythms of *Steps in the Street* (1933). In the USA, the value of energy was constructed in culturally specific ways. America led the world in energy production and consumption, and World War I heightened the thirst for energy, excitement and speed, which were epitomised in New York, where Graham began to choreograph her own work in the mid-1920s. She abhorred the puritanical approach to life that had dominated much of her childhood. Puritanical constraints on corporeal expression contrasted with the energy attributed to the American 'Girl', as epitomised in the figure of the sportswoman, an influential model for American women in the 1920s and 1930s.

Graham developed new ways of using energy in movement, which enabled her dancers (exclusively female until 1938) to resist corporeal constraints embodied in normative effort patterns, notably through forceful use of weight. Her rhythmic innovations drew on the percussive energies of an aggressively masculinist and Americanist modernism, which she paradoxically appropriated for the empowerment of the female dancer. Epitomised in her 'contraction and release', Graham's kinesthetic imagination produced innovative techniques for vigorous projections of energy, which generated feelings of strength and high energy. Rhythmic tension was heightened by conflictual dynamics. As with Wigman, kinesthetic empathy based on shared experiences of energy in movement was crucial to how Graham's dance was received. Spectators accustomed to the nervous energies of contemporary urban life were kinesthetically attuned to the rhythmic economies of her dance. I draw on archival material, including early films of Graham's dances, and conclude this chapter with detailed descriptions of uses of energy in *Heretic* (1929), *Lamentation* (1930), *Primitive Mysteries* (1931) and *Frontier* (1935).

Chapter 4 focuses on Merce Cunningham's work from the 1940s up to the end of the 1970s. The chapter opens with a description of *Rune* (1959). Cunningham's dance radically displaced the basis of rhythmic structure from organic progression to fragmentation. This dislocation was motivated by the need, grounded here too in vitalist principles, to resist normative uses of energy in both choreographical and cultural contexts of the 1940s and 1950s. In this period, modern dance emphasised expression of personal emotion, partnering that displayed intimate relationships, and narrative structures grounded in progression, with dramatic climaxes (typified in Graham's work of the 1940s and 1950s). These features had parallels in social trends, critiqued by contemporary cultural commentators, towards conformism, false personalisation and misplaced intimacy, and also in a cultural climate of 'crisis saturation' that was produced by blanket sensationalism in the media and in advertising.

These trends were forcefully (and controversially) countered by the impersonality and non-progressive, dislocated rhythms of Cunningham's choreography. His methods attempted to radically erase and reconstruct movement memory, resulting in extreme concentration and amplification of energy in discrete, 'punctual' moments. This discrete approach to rhythm, based on continual 'cutting', heightened alertness to the production of differences (both in movements performed by individual dancers, and between dancers). It resisted the homogeneity promoted by social conformism and bureaucracy. I discuss *Variations V* and *RainForest* from the 1960s, and *Sounddance*, *Torse*, and *Fractions I* from the 1970s. I refer to uses of energy in *BIPED* (1999), which explores the effects of digital technologies on the boundaries of the human.

In Chapter 5, I revisit the concept of kinesthetic imagination and its relation to energy. Through discussion of kinesthesia, and with reference to Merleau-Ponty and Bourdieu, I examine in more detail the workings of kinesthetic imagination. For both Merleau-Ponty and Bourdieu, embodied action can take precedence over epistemological agency, by initiating strategies that are not fully known to the thinking subject. Similarly, kinesthetic imagination can generate unforeseen uses of energy, which are enacted in innovative movement. Kinesthetic imagination can bring about deep-seated changes to habitual effort patterns, especially in the case of dancers who work long-term with a particular choreographer. In so doing, it resists culturally coded communication, and, in the case of Cunningham, it radically disrupts concepts of rhythm based on natural paradigms.

Choreographing with digital technologies involves harnessing electronic impulses as the energy of the post-industrial, information age. These technologies can extend the boundaries of kinesthetic imagination by impacting on the human nervous system to open up new connections between senses, between individual subjects, and even between subjects separated in time and space. They also create new possibilities for interactive participation by spectators. Where such work has a visceral impact and heightens kinesthetic awareness, I argue that it resists and critiques the de-corporealising effects frequently attributed to digital technologies. New technologies can thereby enhance the reflexivity of kinesthetic imagination, on which its critical resistive potential depends. I discuss these arguments with reference to examples drawn from recent practice. Finally, I argue that dance can be experienced through the nervous system as an energetic shock, which short-circuits discursive meanings.

1: Life rhythms: Dancing the 'body-soul'

The expression of life is rhythm.
(Ludwig Klages)[105]

Dance is certainly the most highly developed expression of the body soul ['Körperseele'].
(Fritz Giese)[106]

In this chapter, I trace the historical roots of connections between modern dance, body culture, and 'life philosophy'. Preoccupations with energy and vitalism were central to the emergence of modern dance, its practice, performance and reception. Through their handling of energy in movement, choreographers evolved new movement techniques and approaches to making dances, which both engaged with and resisted uses of energy in specific socio-historical contexts. Subsequent chapters will show how this is the case in the work of Wigman, Graham and Cunningham, and, with Cunningham, will illustrate how issues of energy and vitalism continue to be at the cutting edge of innovative choreography through to the twenty-first century.

Projects to transform the self through uses of energy in movement, which were particularly developed in early twentieth-century Germany, were rooted in synergies of body culture and vitalism that provided a fertile ground for the development of new forms of dance. The impact in Germany of projects to transform the self can be said to reflect 'the enduring influence of German idealism and its notion of the perfectibility of the individual through self-cultivation'.[107] Rhythmic movement was invested with the function of restructuring the uses of energy by embodied subjects in ways that could equip them to counter the challenges to 'life' posed by conditions of modernity. In the Germany of the 1910s and 1920s, there was a striking conjunction of life reform movements (including body culture) and theoretical discourses on rhythm linked with 'life philosophy'.[108] Vitalist values and associated life-reform movements were frequently highly critical of manifestations of capitalism and bureaucracy, and combined forward-looking with conservative tendencies.[109] 'Life' came to be seen by many as a valued human attribute under threat and in need of defence against repressive social customs, as well as the assaults of industrialisation, which overwhelmed the individual. Women were regarded as having a privileged role in defending this value, and the significance of rhythmic movement was therefore strongly gendered.

1. Energy and the embodied self

It is a highly remarkable and as yet imperfectly explained fact that Germanic body culture at the end of the Wilhelmine era (1871–1918) fostered 'a mystical belief in the body as a salvational force'.[110] In many respects, the conditions of modern life – large cities, mechanisation, industrialisation, the dominance of purely quantitative exchange values – were experienced as an assault on the uniqueness of the individual and the freedom of corporeal expression. Social commentator Georg Simmel (1858–1918) wrote in 1903: 'the deepest problems of modern life derive from the claim of the individual to preserve the autonomy and individuality of his existence in the face of overwhelming social forces'.[111] The conditions of modernity also seemed to privilege quantity over quality in the interests of what critical thinkers of the Frankfurt School[112] called 'instrumental rationality',[113] in which language could be regarded as complicit. Movement, by contrast, had its own meanings, which could more easily resist appropriation and assimilation to quantifiable values.

Karl Toepfer has speculated that, in early twentieth-century Germanic body culture, 'historically unique conditions of modernity ... focused perception on the body as a source of meanings that had hitherto remained hidden'.[114] The self, whose individual 'essence' appeared to be threatened by the forces of modern life, became an object of renewed interest and scrutiny, and was reconceptualised to include the body, a site whose deepest recesses were inaccessible to the prying eye of reason. Writing in 1928, Ernst Schertel (philosopher, occultist and founder of a dance company) declared that: 'what we call the self or personality or the soul is nothing but the conscious disclosure of transactions or displacements of tensions enacted inside our bodies'.[115] It was precisely with such 'transactions or displacements of tensions' that modern dance principally concerned itself. Friedrich Nietzsche (1844–1900), a philosopher beloved of dancers, and who held dance in very high regard, saw the body as central to 'performance' of the self. In *Thus Spoke Zarathustra* (1891), Zarathustra declared: 'You say "I" and you are proud of this word. But greater than this ... is your body and its intelligence, which does not say "I" but performs "I"'; and proclaimed: 'I know how to speak the parable of the highest things only in the dance'.[116]

If the 'self' was reconceptualised to include the body, the body was also reconceptualised as 'a thermodynamic machine'.[117] Nineteenth-century work on the physics of energy influenced the writings of Karl

Marx (1818–83), as well as Sigmund Freud (1856–1939), Gustav Fechner (1801–87) and many significant thinkers of the late nineteenth and early twentieth centuries. In 1847, Hermann von Helmholtz, a pioneer of thermodynamics, delivered a groundbreaking lecture on the conservation of energy. Helmholtz's 'overarching theory of the conservation of energy', encapsulated in the first law of thermodynamics, held that 'there was a single, indestructible, and infinitely transformable energy basic to all nature'.[118] According to Anson Rabinbach, Helmholtz's ideas were influenced by German idealist philosophies of nature. They had important social implications, because they depicted both labour power and natural energy as inexhaustible.[119] Work was recast in the language of energy, which was the source of all motion and matter, organic and inorganic. '"Cleansed" of all its social and cultural dimensions and considered exclusively as a form of energy conversion, work could be applied to nature, technology, and human labour without distinction.'[120]

2. Energy Crises, Life Crises

Rabinbach argues that Helmholtz's linking of work with universal energy 'underscored the optimistic faith of science in the productive potential of the age'.[121] Later work by Helmholtz and others, which explored the implications of the 'second law of thermodynamics', dented this optimism by drawing attention to the irreversible tendency of the universe to disordered distribution of energy (increase in 'entropy'), which resulted in inertness. Scientific discourses on entropy led in the 1850s and '60s to discussions of 'decline, dissolution and exhaustion',[122] which had important implications for how human labour was perceived.

According to Marx, '"labour-power itself is energy"', which existed only in a '"living vital body"'.[123] Labour, like movement, was an 'energetic act', whose function was to add energy to the raw materials which went to make up the commodity.[124] Marx conceptualized labour power as 'a quantitative measure of the expenditure of human energy in production',[125] and accused industrial capitalism of being responsible for relentlessly mechanizing the body, requiring it to identify with '"the unvarying regularity of the automation"', and subjecting it to unnecessary fatigue. '"Factory work exhausts the nervous system to the uttermost, at the same time, it does away with the many sided play of the muscles and confiscates every atom of freedom, both in bodily and intellectual activity"'.[126]

It appeared that the cost of servicing the new processes of industrial production was physical and mental exhaustion, and subordination of human to mechanical rhythms. By the late 1890s, European medical literature reflected 'a widespread fear that the energy of mind and body was dissipating under the strain of modernity'.[127] This fear contributed towards the climate of 'cultural pessimism' in philosophy and the view that evolution was at once inevitable and inseparable from decay. Charles Darwin's *Origin of Species* (1859) suggested to many that 'blind force seems to reign, and the only thing that counts seems to be the most heedless use of power'.[128] Nietzsche wrote in 1895: 'one *must* go forward – step by step further into decadence (that is *my* definition of modern "progress")'.[129] In *Thus Spoke Zarathustra*, written in 1883–85, and published in four volumes from 1883–92, Nietzsche presented his famous view of 'eternal recurrence'. Oswald Spengler, who was influenced by Nietzsche, expounded a view of history based on biological life cycles in his immensely popular *The Decline of the West* (1918–22).

Mechanical movements mimicked those of human beings, while at the same time demanding that humans should move more mechanically. Karl Bücher noted in his *Work and Rhythm* (1896) that in machine-driven labour, where human rhythms were subordinated to machines, 'the tempo and duration of the labour is detached from the worker's will; he is chained to the *dead and yet quite living* mechanism' (emphasis mine).[130] In the words of the Dadaist poet Hugo Ball: 'Belief in matter is a belief in death ... The machine gives a kind of sham life to dead matter. It moves matter. It is a spectre. It joins matter together, and in so doing reveals some kind of rationalism. Thus it is death, working systematically, counterfeiting life. And what is more, in its continuous subconscious influence it destroys human rhythm.'[131] Fritz Lang's film *Metropolis* (1927) portrayed dramatically the physical effort demanded of workers in performing the movements necessary to operate machines, and the ways in which their own movements became 'mechanical'. In the same film, the inventor Rotwang created a robot that was intended to obviate the need for 'living workers'.

Commodity fetishism fuelled the anxiety caused by this 'uncanny' confusion of animate and inanimate.[132] In Marxist terms, commodities appropriated the energies invested in them through labour power. According to Marx, in commodity fetishism, the energy invested in commodities through labour, which had a social dimension, was translated into an abstract system of exchange value,[133] where 'the social character of men's labour appears to them as an objective character stamped upon the products of that labour'. As with religious fetishes, commodities 'appear as independent beings endowed with life'.[134]

Similarly, essayist and literary critic Walter Benjamin argued that 'the fetish Commodity ... prostitutes the living body to the inorganic world'.[135]

3. Psychophysical economies

Fears of depletion of energy through fatigue and neurasthenia[136] stimulated medical and philosophical discourses about ways of counteracting these threats, and contributed to the growth of 'body culture'. Individual freedom of expression and natural spontaneity were restricted by a work ethic that instrumentalised the body and left little scope for creativity. Writing about Germany at the turn of the century, Thomas Rohkrämer comments: 'In the interests of a disciplined, work-oriented lifestyle, desire and disgust had to be controlled; fantasy and imagination had to be dominated and directed to functional aims'.[137] Although German society in the 'swinging twenties' was far more liberal than during the Wilhelmine Empire, the respected dance critic John Schikowski lamented in 1924 that 'civilised man' had been trained to conform to repressive behavioural codes:

> Custom and upbringing have distanced civilised man – more in the north than in the south – from following natural instincts. We have been taught that it is seemly to control body-awareness, to repress the psychophysical will to expression. The countenance and gestures of the well brought-up person should betray as little as possible of what is taking place in the psyche.

These inhibitions, according to Schikowski, were 'inimical to life' ('*lebensfeindlich*'), and were extremely damaging, crippling the whole inner life of the person.[138]

According to Hans Fischer, 'modern art dance grew directly out of the coming to consciousness of the body's movement energy'.[139] This gave quite a new dimension to the notion of 'expression', which Wigman described as 'the breakthrough of unconscious spiritual [*seelisch*] processes to a state of *corporeal consciousness*' (my emphasis).[140] This 'coming to consciousness' or 'breakthrough' took place in the body itself, in a corporeal awareness that had no direct linguistic equivalent, and which challenged the reduction of knowledge to abstract concepts. Kinesthetically experienced tensions and energies could themselves bring to 'corporeal consciousness' ideational and/or emotional charges, which remained unspecific in terms of particular thoughts or feelings.[141] If the 'self' was indeed constructed, as argued by Ernst Schertel, by a 'conscious disclosure of transactions or displacements of tensions enacted inside our bodies', then the very enactment of these transactions or displacements and their effects on consciousness constituted what we now call the 'subject in process' (see Introduction).

Sociologist Norbert Elias has said of constraining behavioural codes in court societies that: 'body management norms became *internalised*. Instead of being imposed from outside, through the threat of sanctions, codes of behaviour became adopted partly at a subconscious level'.[142] It is significant that the rise of modern dance coincided historically with that of Freudian psychoanalysis, and it is hardly coincidental that both took shape during a period of German thought when, in sociologist Bryan Turner's words, 'the suppression of the life of the body by the mind was seen to be one source of the alienation of human beings in a rational capitalist system'.[143] Freud famously believed that 'the ego must be understood as a bodily ego',[144] and in *The Ego and the Id* (1923) he presented 'a startling, enigmatic account of the structure and form of the ego as a corporeal projection'.[145] Published in 1930, just at the end of the decade when German modern dance, at the peak of its development, had been exploring new modes of subjectivity through the 'body-soul'[146], Freud's *Civilisation and its Discontents* proclaimed the opposition between the instinctive desires of the individual and the restrictions imposed by communal living, which had long been a key aspect of his thinking.

Influenced by the psychophysicist Gustav Fechner and the physiologist Ernst Brücke, Freud explored libido as a quantitative and energetic concept.[147] His specific focus on sexual energy raises issues with which I am not concerned here, but his combination of economic and energy-based models to explain the formation of subjectivity has parallels with 'economies of energy' in movement, where repetition, habit and interaction with external stimuli have similarly formative functions. Freud conceptualised the 'ego' as 'a mass of pathways in which psychical energy is bound'.[148] The energy of the 'life drive' needed to be contained by flowing along pathways that were familiar to it (through repetition and habit) in order to constitute an 'energetic system which gives the subject boundaries'.[149] Freud described the distribution and regulation of energy in 'economical' terms, and believed that the organism needed to protect itself against excessive stimulation and excitation.[150] One means by which the nervous system could regulate accretion of excitation was 'by discharging it by an appropriate motor reaction'.[151] Although he later developed the use of the talking, rather than the moving, cure, in his early work with hysterics, Freud posited as crucial in interpreting the hysteric's symptoms 'an understanding of the emotional and libidinal investment obtaining between the subject and her (or his) body',[152] which was responsible for diverting energy.

This interpretation of the psychophysical economies of energy of individual subjects had significant parallels with contemporary accounts of capitalist economies.[153] Critiques of the effects of early capitalism, notably those of Georg Simmel, also emphasised fears concerning stimulation. The subject's integrity and control were threatened by an excess of products on offer, which 'places demands before the subject, creates desires in him, hits him with feelings of individual inadequacy and helplessness'.[154] The individual was overloaded with 'continuous stimulation' by 'a thousand superfluous items'[155] from which he could not escape. In his famous essay, 'On some motifs in Baudelaire' (1939), Walter Benjamin discussed in Freudian terms the shock effect triggered by the excessive energies at work in the world of 'big-scale industrialism',[156] produced, for instance, by advertising and traffic, which caused 'nervous impulses' to 'flow through [individuals] in rapid succession, like the energy from a battery'.[157]

4. Reform movements

The multifarious 'life reform' movements in Germany which originated during the nineteenth century and came to prominence in the first two decades of the twentieth century aimed to bring about changes in social life. The term 'life reform', which first appeared in Germany in the 1890s,[158] refers to a loose grouping of social movements, including 'body culture' movements and dance, which aimed to counteract the nefarious, energy-depleting and life-threatening effects of modernity by reconnecting with idealised, 'natural' rhythms, of which the body was the repository.[159] Like psychoanalysis, dance explored the body as 'a source of meanings that hitherto had remained hidden'.[160] Wolfgang Graeser (1906–28), who was a protégé of Oswald Spengler, regarded dance as the highest form of body culture, and identified 'the "id" within us' with 'the rhythm of life itself'. This rhythm was embodied in the pulsebeat of the blood, of which the heart was 'the central driving motor', and felt directly through breathing. However, Graeser criticised psychoanalysis on the grounds that 'its ultimate aim was to domesticate the body and adapt it to the life-draining demands of ... rationalism'.[161]

So-called life reformers believed that healthy attitudes to the body would overcome stultifying moral codes and lead to a transformation of the whole person. In the face of industrialisation and city life, they aimed to bring modernity closer to 'nature', and focused on issues such as diet, clothing (dress reform), living conditions and health. According to Friedrich Landmann, a Wilhelmine reformer: 'Lifestyle reform is above all reform of the self; it has to begin with one's own body and in one's own home'.[162] The 'reform' agenda in Wilhelmine Germany involved a broad spectrum of social backgrounds and ages, and included both women and men. Rhythmic gymnastics and dance and their associated 'reforms of the self' were dominated by women.

Not surprisingly, the leaders of these movements – including Rudolf Laban and Mary Wigman – were from the educated middle classes. Rudolf Laban (1879–1958) was born in Hungary, the son of an Austro-Hungarian general. Laban was a dancer, teacher and choreographer, as well as a movement theorist. He is perhaps best known for his invention of the dance notation named Labanotation, but he is also widely considered to be the founder of expressive dance (*Ausdruckstanz*), and he pioneered the popular phenomenon of 'movement choirs'. Laban saw the choirs, which flourished in Germany in the 1920s, as fulfilling a crucial social need for 'celebratory community action'.[163]

According to a teacher associated with the Wilhelmine youth movement, the life styles imposed on young people were a complete denial of corporeal existence, and the mission of the young generation was to be 'the bearer of the principle of embodiment, of body awareness'.[164] The way to discover one's true self was through physical experiences, such as hiking, dancing and nude bathing. Interestingly, despite the rise of interest in, and public discussion of, sexuality,[165] the cult of the body did not give rise, within the youth movement, to a revolution in sexual mores: on the contrary, the body as the source of 'self' was a sublimated, desexualised body. The bohemian, artistic life reformers, on the other hand, many of whom banded together in colonies[166] in an attempt to forge autonomous new life styles, rejected conventional sexual restrictions. These groupings encompassed a wide political spectrum, united by the common factors of return to nature, search for self and valorisation of the body.

Despite the massive upheaval and repercussions in Germany of World War I (see Chapter 2), many Wilhelmine figures lay behind life reform issues usually associated with Weimar culture, and cultural historian Matthew Jefferies suggests that 'in purely cultural terms, the period from the 1890s to the 1930s is perhaps best viewed as a single entity'.[167] Nietzsche's ideas exerted a strong influence on the development of life reform movements in Germany,[168] and the re-valorisation of the human body that reached its peak in 1920s German body culture followed the spirit of his call for a 'transvaluation of all values', including the hierarchy of soul and body.

5. Vital women

The new 'body culture' was of particular significance for women, who were accorded a privileged position as somehow closer (as 'primitives' were) to embodied existence than were their male counterparts. To many, rhythmic gymnastics and dance, rather than politics, appeared to open a new path for women. Although the vogue for body culture and the accompanying craze for rhythmic gymnastics were liberating for women and gave them greater status, a further consequence was that women were often cast in a traditionally facilitating and even redemptive role, rather than being encouraged to achieve personal self-fulfilment:

> The rhythm movement made socially acceptable what women had previously been able to enjoy only behind closed doors. Their 'nature', increasingly repressed by the civilising process, was now valued, as earlier in the Romantic movement of the nineteenth century, as the redeemer of the human race, damaged by civilisation.[169]

Mothers were seen as having a special duty to maximise their physical and psychological health.[170] In the case of Rudolf Bode (1881–1971), essentialism in gender terms was linked with racism. Bode was a member of the National Socialist party from 1922, and drew up Nazi guidelines for dance in 1933 (see Chapter 2). He declared in 1923: 'The freeing of the German soul from the chains of intellectual violation is the decisive event that we await from a true German body-training ... We also call on women to assist in this.'[171]

By contrast, the writer Rudolf von Delius (whose championing of Wigman will be discussed in the next chapter) understood the implications of the need for women's input as undermining the 'universality' of male culture. Delius considered that men were alienated from the earth, whereas women held sense and spirit in equilibrium through 'internally contained rhythm'.[172] Culture was a construct of male reason, and was significantly different from how women would have made it.[173] Woman was in a state of evolution, and was as yet less developed than man. Delius held that women had a creative potential that was distinct from men's, and that needed to be expanded in order for women to be autonomous, and to create a complete world. The time had now come for women to develop independently of men. 'The whole of human culture, for thousands of years, is a purely male culture ... *Masculine experience is only a particular, thoroughly one-sided type of experience* ... Women must now put their women's world in place as a necessary complement.'[174] Delius even saw this necessity for women to become creative as 'the great crisis of our time'.[175]

Although some aspects of gymnastics, notably its more goal-oriented approach to movement, distinguished it from the values of the early modern dancers, the vision of dance as the culmination of the liberation of the female self through the body would have been unthinkable outside the wider context of physical culture, in particular of new forms of gymnastics that appealed particularly to women. There was a gradual turning away from emphasis on strength and on exercises using static poses towards expression and movement.[176] Rudolf Steiner invented an approach to movement which he called 'eurythmy' and described as an art form.[177] Rudolf Bode invented his own system of rhythmic gymnastics, calling it 'expressive gymnastics'. There were close links between rhythmic or expressive gymnastics and dance.[178] Schikowski argued that the 'rhythmic exercises' practised in rhythmic gymnastics, which were closely related to dance, would have the effect of freeing not only the body, but also the soul, from 'crippling constraint'.[179] Wigman believed that although gymnastics was not an art form, dance and gymnastics should not be enemies, because gymnastics was the necessary basis for dance.[180] She described how she 'devised an entirely natural system of rhythmic gymnastics which came to be known as *Tanz Gymnastik*'.[181] The Dorothee Günther School, founded in 1924, was entitled 'School for Gymnastics, Rhythm and Artistic Dance', and gave rise to a dance group in 1930.[182]

Rulebound, goal-oriented movement based on strength and epitomised in sport tended to be seen as 'male'. It contrasted with rhythmic, expressive movement epitomised in dance and seen as 'female'. Dance that arose out of the body's 'movement impulse' could be purely rhythmic and expressive of the 'body-soul', free of external goals. According to writer and critic Hans Fischer (1876–1945), whereas male beauty was determined by 'goal-conscious energy', female beauty was 'not linked to purposefulness: it exists for itself'. In man, body and soul were separate: in woman, the body and soul each 'live through and in the other'.[183] Goal-oriented movement, which 'is directed from the brain, neither needs nor knows rhythm'.[184] Fischer wrote in 1928: 'If the body culture of sport brings man to the heights of the beauty of strength, the body culture of dance brings woman to the peak of expressive beauty.'[185] The new German dancers, according to Fischer, as well as being female artists ('*Künstlerinnen*') were also 'pioneers of a new body awareness'.[186] This 'new body awareness' provided release from bourgeois behavioural norms. John Schikowski declared that expressive body movements brought about a 'wonderful feeling of liberation and purging', because they broke through repressions and inhibitions. This feeling reached its zenith in dance, where spiritual experience could be expressed through rhythmical movement.[187] Dance was seen as a source of the kinds of experience that had been lost to modern 'man': a rhythmic, kinesthetic dimension of movement, which opened up new ways of performing the self and of 'talking without words'. 'Making the body talk, but without words: that was the aim of the "new dance" in the Germany of the Twenties.'[188]

The new gymnastics owed a great deal to the multi-faceted work of the Frenchman François Delsarte (1811–70), actor, singer, and teacher of oratory and music. Delsarte developed a system of exercises that were intended to increase the emotional depth of the actor's gestures, and had international repercussions on the world of physical education and dance.[189] Delsarteans placed a high premium on 'life' and 'energy'. 'Vitality, encouraged through "energising" exercises, was the name for life force, both in movement and personality.' Repose itself was seen as 'the luxuriant energy of inner calm', which was 'a necessary balance for the constant high-energy business of modern life'.[190] Not surprisingly, given the cultural positioning of women in relation to the body, most students of gymnastics in Germany and the USA were women. In the USA as in Germany, physical culture emphasised 'self-improvement', and many of its practitioners focused their attention particularly on cultivation of the female 'self'.[191]

The Swiss Emile Jaques-Dalcroze (1865–1950), who had studied under Delsarte, was probably the most famous inventor of rhythmic gymnastics, or '*rythmique*'.[192] He founded his Institute for Applied Rhythm at Hellerau, near Dresden, in 1911, and soon had 500 pupils, almost all women. Hellerau was a planned community and the first garden city in Germany, modeled on the vision of the Deutsche Werkbund. There were significant similarities between Dalcroze's ideas and Isadora Duncan's, and Dalcroze had planned 'a joint venture to illustrate her ideas in conjunction with his', but this plan was never realised.[193] By 1912, private schools using Dalcroze's method existed throughout Germany and in Stockholm, Paris, London, Geneva and St Petersburg. In 1926, a major Congress on Rhythm took place at the Jaques-Dalcroze Institute in Geneva.

Dalcroze believed that the arts of moving and of making music were intimately related. Despite the importance he attributed to the role of the muscular sense in rhythm, he held that corporeal rhythms could not operate independently of music. 'Music is the only art, directly founded on dynamics and rhythm, which is capable of giving style to bodily movements, while permeating them with the emotion which has inspired it and which it in turn inspires.'[194] He was criticised (notably by Rudolf

Laban and Mary Wigman) for this subordination of movement to music, and for adopting an over-mechanical approach to the body. For Dalcroze, rhythm was also the basis of a utopian social vision. He declared: 'I want to raise rhythm to the status of a social institution and prepare the way for a new style ... which will become the product of the soul of all inhabitants'.[195] Modern life had imposed patterns of moving that had become embedded in our muscular memories, and had caused us to lose touch with natural rhythms.

> We feel ourselves checked in motor expansion by habits of poise and gait which constitute the technique of conventional good manners. This technique has been built up throughout the ages by the special conditions of the locality inhabited by man, by his clothing and occupation, by the whole of the social customs and laws which repress his individual temperament.[196]

What Dalcroze called 'the gymnastics of hygiene and athletics' could 'restore to the body a number of natural rhythms which it was thought had been utterly lost'. However, it was also necessary to combat the 'disorder' and 'disharmony' that resulted from 'nervous oppositions' between bodily and mental rhythms; this Dalcroze saw as the task of rhythmic gymnastics.[197]

In the USA as in Germany, vitalist thinking and concerns with the embodied 'self' influenced the growth of physical culture. America in the 1890s was seized by a physical fitness craze, which, as in Germany, affected women in particular.[198] Positivism was frequently rejected 'in the name of a vitalist cult of energy and process'.[199] Geneviève Stebbins, who studied under Steele MacKaye in New York and popularised her own version of the Delsarte system, worked with eclectic vitalist ideas ranging from Bergson's '*élan vital*' to Havelock Ellis's *The Dance of Life*.[200] The crucial belief underlying all the new gymnastic systems was that the self was centred in the body, and that one should therefore, in Bess Mensendieck's words: 'first discipline the body ... It is important for the destiny of nations and of humanity, that one should start culture from the right point – not the soul, as was the fatal superstition of priests and half-priests, but the body'.[201]

The cultural historian Jackson Lears writes of the stifling morality in *fin-de-siècle* America, and the humdrum existence that made 'intense experience – whether physical or emotional' seem a 'lost possibility'.[202] Neurasthenia, whose victims were plagued by 'a paralysis of the will', was the illness of the age, especially prevalent in metropolitan areas and among the middle classes. Lears argues that its prime cause was *embourgeoisement*: stifling social conventions that forced repression of feelings. A more common contemporary explanation was based on an economic model of energy. The remedy for exhaustion of productive energies 'at precisely the moment when economic development had moved into high gear' was prudent conservation, which meant exerting even more control over energy expenditure. However, the turn of the century saw a reaction in the form of newer style, 'abundance' therapies, which 'paralleled the growing fascination with economic abundance among the educated bourgeoisie' and advocated tapping into the 'great everlasting currents of psychic energy' in the unconscious, as 'a wellspring of psychic strength'.[203]

The dance historian Ann Daly has aptly characterised Isadora Duncan's early dances as being about 'the self in formation', and described Duncan as a 'dancing "subject-in-process"'.[204] Duncan was an avid reader of Nietzsche, and Karl Federn, who wrote the preface to the German translation of Duncan's *The Dance of the Future* (1929), declared that Duncan's dance revealed '[the] striving after unmediated expression of true life in opposition to convention and tradition'.[205] She revolted against repressive puritan culture, and declared in 1922 that 'if my art is symbolic of one thing, it is symbolic of the freedom of woman and her emancipation from the hidebound conventions that are the warp and woof of New England Puritanism'.[206] Duncan's 'dancer of the future' was a vision of a 'glorious harmony' of body and soul in a woman who 'will dance the body emerging again from centuries of civilized forgetfulness'.[207]

German gymnastic associations proliferated, and Duncan received what Daly describes as 'probably her most significant formal physical training' from the Oakland Turnverein.[208] As in Germany, awareness of the body favoured the development of new forms of dance and meant that audiences were attuned to an unusual extent to the subtleties of movement rhythms, thereby facilitating a process of kinesthetic empathy with dancers' rhythmic tensions and releases of energy. According to Augustin Duncan's second wife, Marguerita, Duncan's audiences found in her dancing a 'release for [their] own impulses of expression': 'in watching her we had a sense of satisfied longing'.[209] For Duncan, natural rhythms, epitomised by the motion of waves, through which 'all energy expresses itself',[210] were a model of harmony for human movement and emotions. Duncan believed that artist and dancer could transcend particularity and finitude by revealing 'the great movement which runs through the universe'.[211] According to her, this meant that dance should be 'no more nor less than a human translation of the gravitation of the universe'.[212] The rhythms of nature, idealised as harmonious and unifying, were a paradigm for dance. 'The movements should follow the rhythm of the waves: the rhythm that rises, penetrates, holding in itself the impulse and the after-movement; call and response, bound endlessly in one cadence.' The 'profound rhythm of inner emotion' was not frenzied, but 'unfolds with a gentle slowness', and the true dance, which was controlled by this rhythm, was 'an expression of serenity'.[213]

6. Theorising vital rhythms

Life philosophy or 'vitalism' was not a school, but rather a category loosely applied to a range of philosophers. The German term '*Lebensphilosophie*' can be traced to Friedrich Schlegel's *Lectures on the Philosophy of Life* (1828). Philosophers Friedrich Nietzsche (1844–1900), Wilhelm Dilthey (1833–1911) and Henri Bergson (1859–1941) are widely cited as key figures in 'life philosophy', but representatives of fields as diverse as Romanticism (Friedrich Schlegel, 1772–1829; F.W.J. von Schelling, 1775–1854), phenomenology (Max Scheler, 1874–1928) and existentialism (Søren Kierkegaard, 1813–55) are sometimes included under this umbrella. I shall not attempt to give an overview of life philosophy here. My concern is rather to highlight the importance for dance of a vitalist espousal of 'life' as 'the highest value', where 'life' is defined as 'a process of perpetual and dynamic flux',[214] and to emphasise the function of rhythmic movement in intensifying 'life feelings' and linking life philosophy with body culture.

Belief in the body as the locus of formation of 'self' was predicated on rhythm as a synthesising force, capable of linking body and mind. These views were in part inherited from Romanticism, and impacted strongly on different art forms in this period,[215] but were given new impetus by the linking of rhythm with discourses of energy and economy. The perception of 'life' as a value under threat from 'lifeless' matter meant that the body required conscious cultivation – as in 'body *culture*' – in order to preserve and enhance the 'life force' within the individual. Rhythm took on new significance through association with a psychophysical life force: at its most extreme, rhythmic movement which linked mind and body was indistinguishable from life itself, since, as the German Romantic poet Novalis had suggested, 'life is perhaps nothing other than the result of this union [of body and soul].'[216]

The scholar and writer Fritz Giese (1890–1935) defined what he called the 'body-soul' in dynamic terms: '"body-soul" is first and foremost a motor phenomenon'.[217] The rhythmic movements of the dancer's body constituted a model for the ideal artwork, which, by contrast with commodified objects, was animated and 'liberated' by the creator's energy. According to Rudolf von Delius: 'Art is liberating. The material world receives my will, sucks the spiritual energies of the creator into itself, is free matter'.[218] The artwork, 'like the living', was 'permeated by spirit'.[219] The temporality of organic rhythm was 'no longer understood as linear, objectively measurable, but as dependent on individual movement rhythm',[220] whose projective temporal structure set it apart from 'the inorganic realm'. Simmel wrote:

> Life – and especially its intensification in consciousness – contains its past history within itself in a more immediate form than does any morsel of the inorganic world. At the same time, this historical element circumscribes its future ... in a manner which is without analogy in the inorganic realm ... The inner necessity[221] of organic evolution is far profounder than the necessity that a wound-up spring will be released. While everything inorganic contains only the present moment, living matter extends itself in an incomparable way over history and future.[222]

For life philosophers and practitioners of rhythmic movement informed by vitalist values, the most central characteristics of rhythm were its psychophysical character, its indivisibility and resistance to quantification, its openness to the future and to change, and its capacity for self-renewal, all of which could have the effect of enhancing 'life awareness'. It was argued that rhythm could not be accounted for in objective, quantifiable terms because it was dependent on the active participation of the perceiver. Willy Drost wrote in 1919 that 'rhythm is not a quality of the object, but is first created by the apprehending subject'. Drost also believed that 'movement sensations are connected with sensations of vitality'.[223] According to Hans Fischer (1928): 'rhythmic movement only ever arises out of the play of living forces, because rhythm is thoroughly bound to organic life and its course'.[224] Some, such as Ludwig Klages (1872–1956) and Theodor Lipps (1851–1914), placed more emphasis on the psychical aspects of sensations of vitality. For others, such as Karl Groos, the physical sensation of being 'organically swept away' was said to precede that of 'spiritually living with [*miterleben*]'.[225] Similarly, for Richard Müller Freienfels, music must be translated into motor experience in which 'the whole human organism is put into a state of excitement', which was also an excitement of our 'life awareness'.[226]

Germanic body culture was directly linked with philosophical discussions of rhythm, notably through Rudolf Bode, who was strongly influenced by the theory of rhythm propounded by Ludwig Klages. The direct influence of Klages's ideas on Bode[227] exemplifies the very close connection between the valorisations of rhythm in 'life philosophy' and in body culture, and between discursive and corporeal practices. Klages, frequently described as a 'life philosopher', was a renowned graphologist, and his 1917 textbook on writing and character was widely read in the 1920s and 1930s. As a graphologist, Klages was interested in how rhythm was manifested in the expressive power of line, and his ideas about an 'artistic education for the body' were similar to Rudolf Laban's.[228]

Klages acknowledged the influence of Lipps, his former teacher, on his study of graphology.[229] According to Lipps, '*Einfühlung*' (literally, 'feeling into') meant that, through a process of transference, a subject could experience an inanimate object (e.g. line or colour) as a living being.[230] '*Einfühlung*' involved an inner mimesis,[231] where the subject identified with the object by projecting subjective dynamism onto it. A line, for instance, could be perceived as moving when the dynamism of the act of perception was transferred onto the line itself. 'The straight line runs, extends or stretches itself from A to B or from B to A, or from the middle to both sides. It does the one or the other, *depending on my observation*. If it is vertical, it rises up or sinks down.'[232] Klages said that 'an experience of movement lies at the basis of every apprehension of line', and he substantiated this assertion by referring to expressions such as 'the path "goes", "bends", "rises", "sinks", "twists"'.[233] For Klages, when we apprehend a line in this dynamic way, instead of giving it a name and conceptualising it as an object of thought, we '*experience* its *character*'.[234]

Both Klages and Lipps saw subject and object as connected through movement, and both considered the experience of this connection as irreducible to quantitative analysis. Moreover, in this dynamic interchange, it was often the 'object' that took the active role. In Lipps's description of '*Einfühlung*' involving colour, it was the colour that exerted a 'pull'. Similarly, Klages spoke of 'columns that *seize the viewer* into the heights', and of 'the almost frightening upwards momentum of all movements' in cathedrals, where 'the absorbed spectator is *seized upwards and led away* from the earth'. This shared dynamism of subject and object implied the notion of virtual or imaginary movement. In his 1925 book *Perception Theory* [*Wahrnehmungslehre*], to which Klages contributed the preface, Melchior Palagyi spoke of 'virtual movements', and elsewhere of 'phantasmatic movements'. 'We are able to "live ourselves into" a movement, without having to complete this movement in reality. I call these kinds of life processes ... *imagined movements* or also *phantasmatic movements*'.[235]

Klages attempted to establish a very clear distinction between rhythm, which was holistic and unequivocally aligned with organic life, and rulebound movement, as epitomised in the machine, which destroyed rhythm.[236] This opposition between rhythm and '*Takt*' (measure, or beat) was symptomatic of a more general difference, which separated what Klages called '*Geist*', or 'intellect', from 'life'. Klages appropriated key aspects of Nietzschean thought. His irrationalist categories of 'elemental ecstasy' and 'erotic rapture' were derived from Nietzsche's *The Birth of Tragedy*, which sought, as Klages put it, to penetrate 'through the limits of individuation into the life of the elements'.[237] For Klages, the thinking that characterised *Geist* was responsible for separating off and glorifying the bourgeois individual, who was obsessed with ends and goals. Like Nietzsche, Klages believed it was necessary to escape from one's ego, and concurred with the sage in one of Goethe's poems that 'you have to kill off the ego in order to open the gate of life'.[238]

For Klages, true rhythm, epitomised in the motion of the wave, was an indivisible totality. The closest markers of measure here were the peaks and troughs of the waves, but because of the constant motion of the waves they could not be perceived as clear divisions. The rhythm of the waves was to be felt in the transitions between these states. While *Takt* was merely repetition, rhythm was also renewal – in other words, rhythm projected beyond the present. He continued: 'Everything in organic life renews itself, nothing repeats itself; repetitions can be calculated, renewals can only be evaluated'.[239] For Bode (following Klages), genuine rhythm was a continuum, based in time: 'spatial rhythm does not exist without temporal rhythm'. In rhythm, time and space could not be separated: 'indivisibility is the hallmark of rhythm'. By contrast: 'All rules, all *Takt*, all ordering is based on the dissection of what is living through understanding.'[240] Whereas *Takt* was an abstract category, rhythm was an experiential function of time and space.[241] Rhythm was inseparable from life itself. Max Merz, director of the Elizabeth Duncan School, cited both Klages and Bode, and aligned *Takt* with 'dead machines', but rhythm with 'live bodies'.[242]

Bode quoted Klages: 'The expression of life is rhythm, the expression of the mind is the replacing of rhythm by the rule of law'.[243] For Bode, natural movements 'arise in instinct, in feeling or in gravitation', as opposed to controlled movements, which were 'guided, mentally directed movements'.[244] The best example of natural, rhythmic movement in the body was swinging: this movement originated in the centre of gravity and emanated outward, involving the entire body, 'and at the same time stimulates a swinging rhythm of the soul through relaxation and contraction'.[245] Bode argued that 'in our civilised life, will is being expressed through the extremities, and not through the entire body', and that 'the civilised man of today works and moves always with the exclusion of the trunk of his body'.[246] He criticised the system of rhythmic gymnastics created by Jaques-Dalcroze, his former teacher, which he saw as too mechanical. He spoke of a 'general confusion between rhythm and regulation', which, he said, dominated his time, an illusion that he credited Ludwig Klages with dispelling.[247] In fact, similarly to Klages, Dalcroze described rhythm as 'the animator of bodies', while measure was 'merely the regulator',[248] and argued that meter 'was maintained only through reasoning' and '[developed] the power of control'.[249] However, Bode accused him of placing too much emphasis on *Takt*, and of equating rhythm with 'the mere metrical repetition of movements',[250] thereby confusing 'dead' meter with 'living' rhythm.[251]

It is now clear – never clearer in the English-speaking world than since the publication in English of Lilian Karina's and Marion Kant's *Hitler's Dancers* in 2003[252] – that there were close affinities between aspects of rhythm valued by life philosophy and body culture, and pernicious racist notions that came to the fore under Nazism. At issue here is not only the extent to which particular individuals did or did not collaborate with the regime (a question beyond the scope of my study), but also whether the values they espoused were themselves suspect. Where rhythmic attributes are regarded as racially and/or biologically defined rather than inculturated, they are 'essentialised' and predicated on exclusion of 'foreign' elements. In 1920, Laban stated that 'the soil shaped animal nature and brought forth biological differences, which determined racial characteristics'.[253] He defined 'niggers' as 'a less developed species of humanity, nearer to animals than to (white) human beings'. In a text of 1935, he made extensive links between race and ways and forms of moving. 'For Laban, "racial criteria" characterised dance movements, in particular "rhythm" but also "body posture" and the "way the extremities" are used.'[254] These criteria allegedly made it possible to distinguish German dance from other movement styles.

Such essentialist and elitist attitudes informed the vitriolic attitude towards jazz dance expressed by Laban and others. Laban declared in 1928 that jazz dance was 'nigger dance, jewified and spoiled by Americanization'.[255] As Ann Daly has discussed, Isadora Duncan also reviled jazz and ragtime, which she associated with 'African primitives'. The uncontrolled 'spasms' or 'paroxysms' of the African-inspired modern dances were incompatible with the moral order espoused by Duncan, which was ostensibly 'natural' but was in fact a harmonious ideal of

Nature 'gleaned from the Greece of Botticelli and the natural theology of Haeckel'.[256] Duncan's 'natural' body was a construct, which excluded what she described as 'the sensual convulsion of the Negro'.[257] What counted for Duncan as rhythmic was movement that followed the idealised natural paradigm offered by the waves (also cited by Klages), which was harmonious and controlled, reflecting, as Daly argues, values that were at once white and middle-class.[258]

7. Rhythmic values and critiques of capitalism: Regulating economies of energy

Rhythmic values cannot be separated from particular subject positions, marked by gender, class and race. Ann Daly has argued convincingly that Duncan's 'nature' was in fact already artistically ennobled (her 'natural body' was really a 'civilized body'),[259] and that her rebellion against puritanism and the oppression of women mobilised rather than contested the values of 'high' culture. 'She used strategies of difference and exclusion, exploiting the conventional distinctions between high and low'.[260] Duncan enlisted classical aesthetic values of beauty and grace in the service of her art. When particular aspects of rhythm cultivated in white, Western societies have been elevated to a falsely universal status, other rhythmic forms (e.g. jazz) have been denigrated and excluded. As with Rudolf Bode's guidelines for German dance, which were designed to express 'the healthy energy of the people' and prescribed fixed differences between male and female rhythms, such exclusions were predicated on essentialist, unchanging economies of energy.[261]

The new discipline of sociology situated the valorisation of rhythm in a socio-economic context. It was in the early twentieth century that sociology became established as a discipline, and it is doubtless not coincidental that society should have become self-reflexive at a time when traditional communities were giving way to new and unstable groupings. Max Weber (1864–1920), who used the term 'sociologist' to describe himself and is regarded as one of the discipline's founding fathers,[262] formulated a view of 'instrumental reason', which strongly influenced thinkers of the Frankfurt School. Weber saw 'instrumental reason' (like Klages's *Geist*) as a negative, reductive influence that led to 'disenchantment'. The effects of instrumental reason were epitomised in capitalism and bureaucracy, which emphasised calculability, efficiency, predictability and control of uncertainty. This could be seen, in Rick Roderick's words, in:

'the progress of industrialization, the urbanization of social life, the increase in the areas of social life subject to rational decision procedures such as private law, economic activities, and bureaucratic control, the bureaucratization of administration and the expansion of bureaucratic authority, the radical devaluation of tradition and the destruction of traditional forms of life, the rise of cultural secularization and the consequent "disenchantment" of the world.' [263]

Instrumental reason was also manifested in the 'rational application of technology to production'.[264]

The use of machinery in industrial production and its effects on the movements of workers stimulated the desire to establish the supremacy of organic human rhythms. Franz Hilker spoke in 1925 of the problem of how to 'subordinate the unbroken working motion of the machine to our rhythmic living motion'.[265] The concept of labour power as energy and links between expenditure of energy and fatigue led to a search for 'the most beneficial methods of organising the expenditure of energy – both muscular and "nervous" – so that the resources of both the individual and society might be properly deployed.'[266] Unlike machines, human workers were subject to fatigue, and needed rest. French physiologist Etienne-Jules Marey (1830–1904) and Italian physiologist and education reformer Angelo Mosso (1846–1910) attempted to establish the dynamic laws of fatigue, and agreed that the 'law of the least effort' characterised 'the tendency of all organic life to find the shortest path to its goal'.[267] In 1894, the anthropologist and psychologist Guillaume Ferrero argued that a certain degree of immobility was necessary to restore energy, and that the need for rest was evidence of 'the law of the least effort' in human psychology. For Karl Bücher, rhythm was the principle that regulated the economy of energy in the working body,[268] conserving energy through repetition and through 'the substitution of automatic movements for those of the intellect and will'. Rather than being externally imposed (e.g. by machines), rhythm should derive from the body, and workers should themselves be able to 'determine the tempo of their bodily movements'.[269]

Rhythmic movement, then, was associated with energy conservation, making of rhythm itself an 'economical' principle. However, the value of 'economy' could also be mobilised for capitalist interests. Fatigue or, at its most extreme, the inability to act (as in neurasthenia) could be seen as a form of resistance to the work ethic, while economical use of energy through rhythmic movement could increase work efficiency and raise levels of productivity, thereby recuperating 'rest' in the interests of capitalist production. The most famous example of movement study in the service of industry was the work of F.W. Taylor (1856–1915). In the years following World War I, Taylorism became very popular in Europe with social theorists and politicians on the left and with artists, writers and architects. Later, as the utopian aura of American productivity was undermined, Taylorism came to appeal more to conservatives.[270] Taylor studied what he called 'motion economy', and took into account 'such non-linear and unmechanical factors as work-rhythms, balance, muscular groupings, fatigue, and "rest minutes"'. He developed 'a system of *work cycles*, each involving a whole network of movements and pauses, allowing the worker to produce the greatest work output with the least amount of strain'.[271]

Whereas Taylorism instrumentalised movement in order to further the aims of industrial production, Rudolf Laban's ideas on effort, developed in the 1940s in collaboration with Manchester management consultant Frederick Lawrence, outlined a non-instrumental economy directed at freeing up the energy expended in movement from subordination to the ends of commodity production, in order to enhance workers' life experience. Although they aimed to improve workers' performance by redressing 'unbalanced personal effort',[272] Laban and Lawrence were critical of what they saw as 'the inhibition of the freedom of movement and its degradation to the role of a means of production only'. This was 'a grave error which results in ill health, mental and bodily discord and misery, and thus also in a disturbance of work'.[273] They argued that 'modern working habits' frequently created 'detrimental states of mind from which our whole civilisation is bound to suffer if no compensation can be found'.[274] Through enhancing 'effort rhythms', which, in pre-industrial times, had been the basis of 'working actions' as well as of different art forms and of 'movement and behaviour in everyday life', it would be possible to free movement from subordination to the mechanical rhythms of industrial production and to recuperate the 'rhythmic vitality' and the 'living, driving force of man', which had been 'directed into mechanical devices', and 'left without articulate expression'.[275]

Laban and Lawrence discussed the function of rest in terms of the time necessary to allow the muscles and nerves to recover from fatigue, which meant elimination of waste material and the 'building up or feeding of new muscle tissue which can be used in the following exertions'. They pointed out that rest in the sense of complete cessation of activity, or inertia, should be distinguished from relaxation, in which some effort was present, but in which recovery could also take place. Well-regulated rhythmic movement could achieve the right balance between exertion and relaxation. It was therefore less fatiguing, but also more 'pleasant', because 'its energy-saving qualities are felt by the operator' and because 'it gives to the actions a certain perfection'.[276]

This focus on enhancing the mover's experience was important for dance. In *Modern Educational Dance* (1948), Laban commented on the connection between 'modern work research' and dance: 'a new conception of the elements of movement based on modern work research has been introduced into dance tuition'.[277] According to Laban: 'Modern dance from its early days has emphasised the importance of rhythmic swinging movement, in which a relatively relaxed phase of movement is compounded with a relatively stressed phase. An effort to attain lightness and buoyancy is made in a rhythmical interchange with an effort of weighty strength.' He continued: 'It was ... soon discovered that the time rhythm of a movement and the shape of its path through space are just as important for the right proportion between exertion and relaxation as that between the changing degrees of its strength'.[278]

Effort rhythms regulated alternating restraint and discharge, conservation and expenditure of energy, which corresponded to different attitudes towards the 'motion factors' of weight, space, time and flow. Metrical beat (referring to the duration of a movement rather than the speed with which it was executed) was not an intrinsic part of effort-rhythm, though it could be related to it. Laban noted, for instance, that in a sequence involving transition from a 'pressing' motion (direct, strong, sustained) to 'gliding' (direct, light, sustained),[279] the time element in effort terms remained the same (sustained), but that 'in relation to a metrical beat one of the two combined actions might be of shorter duration than the other'.[280] In an early text, Laban emphasised that dance rhythm was 'not time-duration divided by accents, as one tries to interpret this concept in music'. He described rhythm as 'a change between waxing and waning of the manifestations of force between tension and release ... which subjects all movement to a kind of pulsation, to breathing'.[281] These self-generating dynamics made the rhythms of dance independent of music. According to Fritz Böhme: 'true absolute dance is without music ... for it receives its motor impulse from the original sources: the body and space'.[282]

In *Effort*, Laban and Lawrence also emphasised the capacity of embodied subjects to bring about changes in their effort patterns. Although it was difficult to intervene in 'involuntary effort-habits enforced upon man by inheritance or acquired under the constant weight of outer circumstances', they argued that even such 'dimly felt habits' could be made conscious and open to change if 'the person subjected to such habits learns to think in terms of effort'.[283] I shall discuss in Chapter 5 the extent to which such habit changes are possible, and the risks of apoliticism in focusing on resistance and change at a kinesthetic level without taking sufficient account of frameworks of power. But first, in the chapters that follow, I want to look at how the movement techniques and choreographies of Mary Wigman, Martha Graham and Merce Cunningham brought about changes in uses of energy which both reflected and actively resisted culturally normative effort patterns, and which, in Cunningham's case, radically subverted conventional notions of rhythm, in the interest of vitalist values.

1. Mary Wigman in *Seraphic Song*, 1929

2: Opening rhythms:
Spatial energies in Mary Wigman

Besides the motion of bodies in space there exists motion of space in bodies.
(Laban)[284]

Almost everything that is said about space can also be applied to energy, since energy comes from space.
(Wigman)[285]

The most striking feature of kinesthetic imagination in Wigman's work is the challenge to containment of body boundaries through rhythmic exchanges between body and space, which resist culturally normative containment of energies and spatial restriction. The relationship between body and space is dramatised in the rhythmic alternations of shape flow (opening-widening and closing-narrowing) in *Seraphic Song* (1929). It is enacted in violent form in *Witch Dance II* (1926), and eroticised in *Pastorale* and *Dance of Summer* (1929), which will be discussed later in this chapter. Wigman's uses of energy challenged compartmentalisation of the body and emphasis on peripheral movement at the expense of the whole body, which were associated both with ballet and with effort patterns imposed by working conditions in industrialised societies. She succeeded in combining these holistic uses of energy with extreme formal precision in individual body parts, thereby mediating between aspects of the discourse of vitalism, on the one hand, and instrumental reason, on the other.

Seraphic Song, *from* Swinging Landscape, *1929*[286]

There is no visible set for this solo, other than the backdrop, which is dark in the film. The lighting from downstage[287] left, which provides a focus throughout, casts bold shadows. The dance is very short (less than two minutes). Wigman wears a striking costume of shiny fabric (probably silk), which catches the light as she moves. A circular cape draped over her shoulders falls in soft, scalloped folds, and the hemline of her hip-hugging skirt clearly reveals her feet and ankles. (See Illustration 1, and pictures in **The Language of Dance.**)[288] *This dance has a musical accompaniment: a plain, soft, almost ethereal score for piano and glockenspiel by Hanns Hasting. Wigman's dominant effort is light, free flowing and indirect/flexible. Movement permeates her whole body and is continuous, with no breaks. Shaping is predominantly rounded and curving, with an extraordinary degree of precision and attention to detail. The relationship between body and space is* *dramatised through contrasts between shape flows of opening-widening and closing-narrowing, associated with contrasts between effort qualities of rapid and sustained movement. For much of the dance, Wigman's eyes are closed, evoking focus on an inner space, which interacts with external space through her 'opening' movements.*

The dance begins:

The opening of this short dance is very slow and solemn. With arms held at shoulder level, bent at the elbows, and with the palms of her hands touching as if in prayer, Wigman inclines in a very slow curtsey and rises again, her head tilted slightly back, opening and lengthening her upper body in a pose that suggests adoration (in keeping with the 'Seraphic' of the title), her eyes apparently closed. She steps forward, and curtsies more deeply. As she rises, her head again tilts back. She steps forward and swings backward from the hips, arms swaying forward and back and from side to side, with palms still touching. Stepping forward, she curtseys to stage right and then left. Still facing the audience, she moves backwards to upstage centre, with a noticeable increase in pace. Here, right leg crossed behind, she rests her 'praying' hands on her left hip. Now she steps forward, and her movements continue to speed up as her hands part and her arms open with undulating movements and free flow of energy, in a full embrace of the surrounding space.

[...] With her body in an open position, arms held wide, displaying her fingers, Wigman moves with increasing rapidity in a circle to her left, in a series of long steps. As she comes full circle, she inclines forward from the hips, while her arms move fluidly from the elbows, with hands bending sinuously from the wrists, fingers separating and curving expressively. The climax of the dance comes with the final closure of the body. Arms still apart, Wigman very slowly hollows her whole body, bending her torso from the hips, increasing the plié in both legs till she is in a semi-sitting position, her gaze focusing on the extended fingers of her right hand. As if on a hinge, she folds down her torso towards her thighs, with her right forearm and right thigh drawing ever closer until they finally meet and her body closes, bringing the dance to completion.

1. German and American contexts

The emergence of new forms of dance in both Germany and the USA represented a radical departure from the ballet tradition. It was thought that ballet trained the body to perform types of movement that accentuated the damage being done to natural ways of moving by living and working conditions in industrialised capitalist societies. Rudolf Bode's description of the detrimental impact of 'civilised life' on balanced, rhythmic movement through over-emphasis on the extremities to the detriment of 'the trunk of [the] body'[289] was similar to contemporary critiques of ballet. According to John Schikowski, ballet training focused on certain parts of the body (legs, feet) at the expense of others (the upper body, the arms and hands), whereas what was needed was 'a new kind of artistic dance ... which is based on the *harmonious training of the whole body*',[290] in order to counteract the 'cramping' and 'atrophy' which were a direct result of 'the unhygienic lifestyle and workstyle of the capitalistic age'.[291]

By contrast with ballet, where the torso was held still while the limbs, in particular the legs, performed sequences of movements that formed part of the ballet vocabulary, in modern dance the body moved as an organic whole, as in nature. Unlike ballet, where the roles of choreographer and company director were a male preserve, the modern dancers, who were almost exclusively women, choreographed their own work and performed either solo or in small companies, frequently composed entirely of women.[292] The movement styles of modern dance were not drawn from pre-existing vocabularies: rather, the choreographers created their own vocabulary, which challenged stereotypical, idealised images of women encoded in Romantic ballet, where the ballerina appeared to defy gravity. Like Duncan, who attributed a metaphysical status to dance, Wigman aimed to establish a new field, that of modern artistic dance, which would be radically different from ballet but would also be a 'high' art, superior to popular dance performances, where dance was treated primarily as entertainment and dancers' bodies were presented as decorative and seductive objects for the audience's delectation. What was at stake was at once the establishment of modern dance as a high art form and the role of women dancers as serious artists. Wigman's group-dances from 1923 to 1928 included only women; although she had some male students, none were involved in the performances.

There were close parallels between the German and North American contexts in which modern dance took shape. Isa Partsch-Bergsohn, author of *Modern Dance in Germany and the United States: Cross Currents and Influences*, was a student of Kurt Jooss, and knew Wigman. She also studied at the Julliard Dance School Division and went on to teach dance in the USA. Partsch-Bergsohn affirmed:

> I see Modern Dance, in spite of its considerably different forms in America and Europe, as a single radical rebellion of young dancers against nineteenth-century formalism ... Studying Modern Dance on both sides of the Atlantic Ocean convinced me that there is a commonality in the way the body serves as the primary source of invention, producing the disharmony, asymmetry and countertensions of Modern Dance.[293]

Duncan performed extensively in Europe, where she was seen by Laban and Wigman, and Ruth St Denis created a sensation in Europe on her tour in 1906. Expressive dance (*Ausdruckstanz*) was the name by which the dance practised by Laban, Wigman and their followers came to be known, and is a term used with reference to 'a wide range of quite distinct styles'.[294]

Wigman's *Ausdruckstanz* was holistic in that the entire body was involved in the movement of each part, and the impetus for each movement was derived from the preceding one. Like Duncan's performance, Wigman's enactment of what Ann Daly has called 'the drama of kinesthetic force'[295] deflected the spectator's attention from her body as a visual object. Unlike Duncan's dance, however, *Ausdruckstanz* frequently involved attacks on conventional beauty, which further undermined the archetypal 'feminine' as encoded in ways of moving that reflected social ideals of womanhood and 'body images' imposed on women. In 1916 Wigman saw Duncan dance, and claims to have found it 'horrible'.[296] Her own aesthetic, influenced by Expressionism, belonged to a more iconoclastic era.[297] By contrast, Laban, who became Wigman's mentor, saw Duncan perform in Paris during his stay there from 1903 to 1907, when she danced in the salon of the Comtesse de Greffulh and in the studio of Madame Madeleine Le Marre,[298] and later wrote of Duncan that she 'reawakened the sense of the poetry of movement in modern man'.[299]

In turn, European dancers would themselves exercise a significant influence on the aesthetics of American modern dance. In 1929, Harald Kreutzberg (1902–68) and his Wigman-trained partner Yvonne Georgi spent a full year on tour in the USA. Wigman herself toured in North America three times between 1930 and 1933, and her student Hanya Holm (1893–1992) arrived in the autumn of 1931 to direct the New York Wigman School, which became very influential. In 1933, the Ballets Jooss (directed by Laban's former student, Kurt Jooss) gave its debut performance in New York. The first critic who wrote on dance in *The New York Times*, John Martin, who had studied modern theatre in Europe, played a vital role in promoting appreciation of European modern dance in the USA. Martin, whose role in relation to modern dance in many ways resembled that of Clement Greenberg in relation to modernist painting (see Chapter 3), championed Wigman as an 'outstanding practitioner' of 'Expressionistic dancing', whose basis in 'metakinesis' made it 'the purest manifestation' of modern dance.[300]

Martin was directly influenced by Theodor Lipps's theory of kinesthetic empathy, which he discussed in *America Dancing*.[301] Following Lipps, he argued that we can experience even inanimate objects in terms of our own bodies, projecting our own motor responses onto them. He appears to have been referring to Lipps's term, 'inner mimicry' when he stated that 'this faculty for transferring to our own consciousness those motor experiences which an inanimate object before us could undergo if it were capable of undergoing conscious experiences, has been aptly termed "inner mimicry"'. Although 'inner mimicry' did not involve actual movement, it was a muscular experience. 'Psychologists have discovered changes in the postural condition of the muscles in response even to shapes, though there is no outward movement of any kind visible.' Such motor experience left traces – 'paths' – in the neuromuscular system, which, Martin argued, were closely associated with emotions. Sensory experience could have the effect of 'reviving memories of previous experiences over the same neuromuscular paths', and also of 'making movements or preparations for movement'.[302]

All art forms were based on motor experience, which was the substance of dance. 'Thus essentially dance is at the root of all the arts, and every art creation comes into being first in terms of that body movement which is the stuff of dancing.'[303] The experience of watching dance was grounded in the kinesthetic sense, and in the spectator's capacity to experience what Martin called 'kinesthetic sympathy' with the dancer:

> When we see a human body moving, we see movement which is potentially produced by any human body and therefore by our own ... through kinesthetic sympathy we actually reproduce it vicariously in our present muscular experience and awaken such associational connotations as might have been ours if the original movement had been of our own making.[304]

Response to dance combined sensory and emotional experience, which took precedence over rational understanding, and provided a paradigm for the arts. 'It is useless to approach any work of art with the notion that it must be understood before it can be responded to. Understanding is a process of rationalization after the experience.'[305] These premises correspond very closely to those of German dance critics influenced by 'life philosophy'.

Despite the many connections and similarities between German and American dance, however, it was in the interests of both Germans and Americans to emphasise their distinctive national roots, which could lead to putting nationalist values in the foreground. The drive to make modern dance acceptable in the United States in the 1930s encouraged emphasis on American identity and themes. Especially from the mid-1930s, the reputation of German dance in the USA was tarnished by its Nazi associations, and by the adverse effects of the Nazi regime on the creative development of German dance artists. Wigman's North American tours were successful, but also controversial. In an article published in the American journal *The Dance Magazine of Stage and Screen* in 1931 (a few months after Wigman's first American tour) entitled 'What dancers think of the German dance', Ruth St Denis conspicuously avoided mentioning Wigman by name, but her remarks and rhetorical questions (such as 'Why return to the primitive and the savage?') left no doubt as to her conclusions. The dancer Louise Brown was more direct: 'a series of ugly and grotesque poses does not constitute an evening of dancing'.[306]

During the 1930s, Wigman's style became less challenging as a result of her attempts to conform more closely to Nazi ideals of femininity[307], and her 1935 book *German Dance Art [Deutsche Tanzkunst]* revealed the influence of National Socialist ideas. Articles in Louis Horst's *Dance Observer* in 1935 criticised both Wigman's and Laban's compliance with the Nazi regime.[308] Also, American audiences (including John Martin) were not impressed by Wigman's group work on her 1932–3 tour. Martin continued to champion Wigman as a solo dancer, declaring in 1939 that 'with Wigman the dance stands for the first time fully revealed in its own stature'.[309] However, Martin now 'essentialised' (Susan Manning's term)[310] the national characteristics of both German and American dancers, insisting that the traditions were separate, and denying Wigman any influence on the development of American dance. 'Wigman is too nearly contemporaneous with the American leaders to have influenced them in any tangible way'.[311]

2. Wigman's beginnings

Wigman is widely regarded, in Karl Toepfer's words, as 'the greatest dance artist Germany has yet produced'.[312] Although there was feverish experimentation with rhythmic movement and dance in Germany in the early years of the twentieth century, it was not really until the inter-war years that modern dance became established in Germany and Central Europe. Gertrude Bodenwieser, the famous Viennese dancer,[313] gave her first solo recital in 1919, the same year in which Wigman embarked on her first German tour. Wigman was tutored by Laban and worked closely with him, but she developed her own distinctive style. This was quite different from the neo-Grecian, lyrical movement of a Duncan, which evoked Art Nouveau, or the romantic exoticism of Ruth St Denis. Unlike Laban, Wigman believed that modern dance must make a complete break with ballet.

Marie Wiegmann (1886–1973) grew up in Wilhelmine Germany (1871–1918), the birthplace of many of the intellectual and social currents described in the previous chapter. In 1918, Laban would advise her to use 'Mary Wigman' as her stage name. Factories, businesses and commercial firms were thriving: by 1913, the pattern of German trade was that of 'a highly developed capitalist economy'.[314] Imperial Germany, ruled by Prussia, was a conservative, patriarchal society, heavily influenced by military values, with strong gender divisions between the female domains of '*Kinder, Kirche, Küche*' ('children, church, kitchen') and the male cult of the army officer, who was 'the prototype of what the ideal German [male] was meant to be'. The system of universal conscription meant that most men spent long periods in the army. Middle- and upper-class German men 'chose to be tightly dressed with almost military discomfort'; schools and universities made much of military uniform and ritual, and military values were firmly instilled in German youth.[315] As Hubert Godard has argued (cited in the Introduction), 'the mythologies of the body circulating in a social group are also inscribed in the postural system and, reciprocally, the corporeal attitude of individuals becomes the medium of this mythology.'[316] The emphasis on containment of individual boundaries, where the body was separated from space, constituted a normative attitude, which was resisted by the opening of the body to space in Wigman's dance.

Middle-class women were expected to conform to the norms of marriage and motherhood, but change was in the air. By 1900, when Wigman was fourteen, the first grammar school for girls had opened in Hanover, and universities began to open their doors to women. As industrialisation intensified, the employment of women increased, and by the 1890s most working-class women worked outside the home, for reasons of financial necessity. For Wigman and others of her class, work represented a lifestyle choice that was not always open to them. Wigman wanted to become a doctor, but her parents did not want a 'bluestocking' in the family. Instead, she was allowed to learn languages, and study in England.[317] But she could not reconcile herself to the domestic destiny expected of her, and later broke off two engagements, in 1904 and 1908. In 1908, she heard about Jaques-Dalcroze, and attended a demonstration of his rhythmic gymnastics in Amsterdam. Shortly afterwards, she saw a performance in Hanover by the famous Wiesenthal sisters (Bertha, Grete and Else) from Vienna, with their characteristic mixture of 'Strauss waltzes with the lightness of ballet and the directness of "Greek" dancing'.[318]

In 1910, when she was twenty-three, Wigman learned that Jaques-Dalcroze was moving to Dresden and was enrolling students, who could gain a teaching qualification. This offered her the opportunity of financial independence; and against the wishes of her mother, she left for Dresden. Although she was able to break away, and was later reconciled with her family, her independence as a creative woman was not compatible with the demands of home and family as they were constituted at that time. Later, in 1916, Wigman would write in her diary about two irreconcilable longings: one leading to 'humanity, existence as a woman' and the other leading to 'loneliness and dance'.[319]

Early modern dance, pioneered mainly by women, was closely associated with the growing independence of women, without which it could not have materialised. Like Duncan, Wigman was a keen reader of Nietzsche, and took inspiration from his writings (see later, p.53). Nietzsche exerted a powerful influence on German feminism. Lily Braun (1865–1916) was a Social Democrat who envisaged 'female liberationism ... as a heroic Nietzschean act of self-creation', which would result in 'the release of women's creative powers in all spheres of life'.[320] These sentiments were similar to those of Wigman herself, and of sympathetic commentators, such as Rudolf von Delius, who saw dance as the realm where women could best realise their creative powers. Nietzschean iconoclasm was taken further by the most prominent Nietzschean feminist in Germany, Helene Stöcker (1869–1943), who founded the so-called 'New Morality', which called for a 'reform of sexual ethics' and critiqued conventional morality and sexual life-denying asceticism.

According to Delius, it was men's duty to facilitate women in the creation of a female world, 'in order to recognise the female friend on an equal footing'.[321] Because Delius saw the female self as closely bound up with the body,[322] the way to create a new female self was through cultivating the body. 'Woman wants to form and purify her own soul, and she achieves this by taking her body in hand.'[323] Female beauty lay not in superficial appearances, but in the manifestation of spiritual force in the body.[324] This process was fully realised in expressive dance. 'She [woman] concerns herself with her own self, and since for woman her body is the closest material for formation of the self, so the new woman makes her body an expression of herself: she dances.'[325] However, Delius perceived a potential conflict between female autonomy and woman's enslavement to the sexual instinct, which necessitated a 'subordination of sexual nervous excitation in a predominant human feeling [*Menschenge-fühl*]'.[326] Only then could the female dancer become a self-sufficient person: 'The dancer forms herself and thereby also becomes spiritually complete. She is now a world reposing in itself. Centre, circle, swinging, closed being'.[327] She no longer existed simply for men, but on her own account. 'The dancing woman is with herself. She has her body entirely for herself.'[328] For Delius, this placed her at the forefront of women's struggles: 'The dancer now stands in the front row of the fighters for women's freedom. For through the shaping of inner life she reaches the pure, genuine self'.[329]

3. Wigman and dance

Wigman's decision in 1910 to study rhythmic gymnastics with Jaques-Dalcroze brought her to Hellerau, a melting pot of innovative 'life reform' and artistic ideas. Hellerau was also close to Dresden, which was the centre of the Expressionist painters' group, *Die Brücke* (The Bridge). Wigman visited exhibitions of Expressionist painting, and was attracted to the 'wild forms, the strident colours, the unrestrained drive to communicate'.[330] She heard talks by Oskar Kokoschka, the Expressionist painter and playwright, and music by Igor Stravinsky, Arnold Schönberg, Alban Berg and Anton Webern. In 1913, she worked on a production with the theatre director Max Reinhardt, and became acquainted with the Expressionist painter Emil Nolde and his wife Ada, with whom she developed a lasting friendship, and who told her about Laban. In the same year, she went to the community at Monte Verità, above Ascona, the small village on the Lago Maggiore in Switzerland where in the summer months Laban ran a 'School for the Arts', which gave him the opportunity to 'try out his growing belief that everyone should dance, could dance, and that a renewed form of community dance should be sought'.[331] Like Laban, Wigman could not accept Dalcroze's refusal to separate corporeal from musical rhythms, and she had begun composing dances without music. She was enthralled to discover Laban's 'free dance', where the musical accompaniment, usually limited to percussion instruments and gongs, had the function of supporting, rather than leading, the rhythms of the dance.

Wigman wrote in her diary:

> Almost all our modern dancers, male and female, embody music, dance what is foreign when they could perhaps create something original. To become free of music! That's what they should all do! Only then can movement develop into what we all hope from it: free dance, pure art.[332]

In order to stay with Laban, she turned down the offer from Hellerau of running a new school for rhythmic gymnastics in Berlin, and was soon given teaching responsibilities, first at Ascona and then in Munich, where Laban opened a school in 1913. The Schwabing district in Munich, where

Laban settled in 1910, was home to a bohemian group of artists and intellectuals, including the Expressionist painter Wassily Kandinsky (1866–1944), co-founder with Franz Marc in 1909 of the 'Blue Rider' group of painters.[333]

It was Laban who first gave Wigman the idea of becoming a professional dancer.[334] At her first professional engagement in Munich in 1914, she performed her solo, *Lento*, and the first version of her famous *Witch Dance*, which received thunderous applause. Already she had captivated Rudolf von Delius and the Expressionist writer and dance critic Hans Brandenburg, who would be among her most enthusiastic and influential supporters. After war broke out, Laban and Wigman could no longer work in Munich, and went to Zurich, where Wigman moved in Dadaist circles. In 1916, she gave her first 'dance evening' in Zurich, when she danced to Zarathustra's 'Dance Song' from Nietzsche's *Thus Spoke Zarathustra*, which was her favourite book. She also read works by Ludwig Klages.[335] Wigman's first appearance on a real stage, in Zurich's Pfauentheater, was in June 1917. Responses were mixed, with praise for her expressive qualities, but with some commentators criticising her lack of beauty and charm. She often danced without music, and sometimes used recitations.

That summer, Wigman went with Laban to Monte Verità, where she worked on new dances, and gave her first solo dance evening in Zurich in the winter. This was the first of her dance 'cycles', entitled *Ecstatic Dances*. Here, the overall structure was based on contrasts between dark, 'demonic' dances – which used movements of wild turning and crouching, crawling postures – and 'festive' dances, with flowing, trance-like, gliding movements. A photo of the section *Sacrifice* from *Ecstatic Dances*[336] shows a strong oriental influence, with emphasis on profile, angled limbs, and detailed, stylised gestures of the fingers similar to the *mudras* of Indian dance.

Early in 1919, after the war was over and she had recovered from illness, Wigman experienced her first major success, when she performed a programme that included *Ecstatic Dances* in the Alpine town of Davos in Switzerland. The Expressionist painter Ludwig Kirchner, who may have seen her dance in Davos, became very interested in the new dance, and felt a strong affinity with Wigman, with whom he later became closely associated. He wrote in 1926:

> I feel that there are parallels [with my work], which are expressed in her dancing in the movement of the volumes, in which the solitary movement is strengthened through repetition ... M[ary] W[igman] instinctively took much from modern pictures, and the creation of a

modern concept of beauty operates just as much in her dancing as in my pictures.[337]

Even before the outbreak of war, conventional aesthetic canons had come under attack, notably from Expressionist quarters. Kandinsky felt that modern life was full of 'questions and premonitions and omens – hence full of contradictions'. Writing in 1912, he referred to 'clashing discords, loss of equilibrium, "principles" overthrown, unexpected drumbeats, great questionings, apparently purposeless strivings, stress and longing (apparently torn apart), chains and fetters broken (which had united many)', and declared: 'opposites and contradictions – this is our harmony'.[338] Conventional notions of beauty were replaced by the criterion of 'internal necessity'. Kandinsky declared:

> Just as in music or in painting, there exist no 'ugly' sounds and no external 'dissonance' … every sound or concordance of sounds is beautiful (= purposeful), provided that it arises from internal necessity, so too in ballet we will soon be able to sense the inner value of *every* movement, and inner beauty will replace outer beauty.[339]

The war intensified this iconoclasm. As Wigman declared: 'War has changed life. Revolution and suffering tended to destroy and shatter all the ideals of prettiness'.[340]

Following the war, the value of 'life' took on new meaning. Wigman later referred to the destruction wrought by the 'mechanically working war machine'.[341] Expressions of longing for heightened intensity of 'life' in the 1920s need to be seen in the context of this experience of technologically mediated mass destruction, as well as of the conditions of modernity discussed in the previous chapter. Dianne Howe refers to the impact on Wigman of 'the death and destruction of World War I, its resulting uncertainties of existence, and the mechanization and dehumanization of the world'.[342] Wigman later described the 'ghastly terror of ultimate aloneness' evoked by the sight of the 'forgotten cemetery of the German soldiers', and recounted that her dance *The Face of Night*, which formed part of the 1929 cycle *Swinging Landscape*, was inspired by the sight of this cemetery.

Post-war conditions also affected experience of space. The Great War had expansionist aims, and was supposed to gain territory for Germany. Instead, it led to defeat, loss of territory and humiliation. In the words of the American dance writer Elizabeth Selden, evoking in 1929 the rise of German modern dance in the 1920s:

People burdened beyond human reason were struggling for space, struggling to free themselves from a limitation which erected inexorable walls around their country, their very lives; they lived like inside a wall; their freedom to move was gone. To move meant all.[343]

Similarly to the containment of bodily boundaries through the influence of military-style dress and deportment in pre-war Germany, the experience of spatial restriction in the post-war period was countered by Wigman's exploration of spatial energies both inside and outside the body.

After the war, in 1919, Wigman performed in Munich and Berlin. In the same year, her performances in Hamburg and Dresden were resounding successes. In 1920, she set up a dance school in Dresden, and the following year founded the Mary Wigman Chamber Dance Group, which gave its first concert in Dresden, followed by a tour which was 'an artistic and financial success',[344] and established Wigman as a major figure in the German dance scene – even as 'the greatest German dancer'.[345] By 1925, the view represented by the dance critic John Schikowski was not untypical: '[Wigman] has, for herself, achieved the ultimate aim of art. The peak on which she stands is unattainable for all others.'[346]

Wigman's bourgeois background, coupled with her later links with artists and intellectuals, including the psychiatrists Hans Prinzhorn[347] and Ludwig Binswanger, and her association with the bohemian community at Ascona, which attracted a glittering panoply of writers and artists,[348] placed her in a position of cultural strength. Herself a member of the educated middle classes, she associated with others who, like her, rebelled against the values of their own class. Artists and critics frequently moved in the same circles. Hans Brandenburg, who wrote on Wigman and Laban, had collaborated with Laban at Ascona in plans for a performance, which was prevented by the outbreak of war. According to Wigman's biographer Hedwig Müller, the 'propagandistic' intervention of Lasar Segall, a painter, and the art critic Will Grohmann (a friend and supporter of Wassily Kandinsky and Paul Klee, and who would later become known as a leading authority on their work) was a crucial factor in securing Wigman's success in Dresden in 1919:

The hall is full right down to the last seat, Will Grohmann and Lasar Segall have been good propagandists and have drummed up *a public open to modern and Expressionist art*. In the newspapers announcements had appeared in which Mary Wigman was advertised with a citation from the novelist Otto Flake: 'she realises an idea, a task. Dance is for her a religious art'.[349]

The quasi-religious aura of Wigman's dancing resonated with the desires of a society in need of values to fill the void left by the war.[350] 'The loss of a sense of coherence and order were characteristic of Weimar culture.'[351] The Wilhelmine Empire had been destroyed by the war, and the Versailles treaty, which humiliated Germany, decimated the economy and undermined political stability. According to Richard McCormick, 'Germany's dominant order – symbolized by the Kaiser and the aristocratic-military caste he represented – was deposed in 1918, beginning a chaotic period of revolution, counter-revolution, and hyperinflation that would take four years to "stabilize"'.[352] Inflation destroyed middle-class savings, the new democracy undermined the old system of social status, and consumerism and mass culture overturned traditional values. Women were granted voting rights under the Weimar constitution of 1919. They increased their participation in education, in white-collar jobs and in the caring professions and the civil service, leading to accusations from conservatives that they were endangering 'the family, population growth, and the future of German society itself'.[353]

Unlike performances by the satirical dancer Valeska Gert (1892–1978), Wigman's dances did not require spectators to reflect on social or political problems. Even her group dances did not engage with social questions. 'Social critique was not to be found in Mary Wigman's dances. They gave no pictures of social conditions, but rather images of experience motivated by personality.'[354] According to Hedwig Müller and Patricia Stöckemann, focus on the 'self' in dance was in part a reaction to the devaluing of the individual under the Wilhelmine Empire, an authoritarian state that had been dominated by aristocratic and upper-middle-class values. Preoccupation with the 'self' also provided a refuge from social problems for those who felt powerless to influence the state.[355] By playing out or performing conflicts in and through the energies of the dancing body, without a wider frame of reference, dance could encourage the view that movement alone provided a paradigm for individual and social harmony, an apolitical approach that would have dangerous implications in the light of the emergence of National Socialism. Müller notes that critics on the left in the Weimar Republic regarded Wigman with some suspicion, and her 'life-philosophical dance understanding' was seen as aligning her with the educated middle classes.[356] In Berlin, Wigman was supported by the critic Artur Michel, who wrote for the liberal middle-class *Vossische-Zeitung.* Laban was supported by Fritz Böhme, a dance teacher and critic who leaned heavily towards metaphysical idealism and mysticism[357] (and would later work for the Nazis), writing in the national-conservative *Deutsche Allgemeine Zeitung*, while the left-liberal *Berliner Tageblatt* favoured Gert and the jazz dancer Josephine Baker.

Gert, who never achieved the same level of success as Wigman, accused her of becoming the 'national dancer' by virtue of fulfilling the needs of the educated German middle classes. Gert set up an opposition between the kind of dance that she herself saw as authentic, which was based on 'living out drives', and artistic dance, which involved 'sublimating drives'. She complained of Wigman's devaluation of erotic and frivolous dance and her championing of what Gert regarded as a false intellectualism.[358] Sublimation of erotic impulses indeed formed part of the appeal of the new artistic dance. The educated middle classes found in this dance an engagement with existential dilemmas that was lacking in more popular forms such as jazz dance, which was very much in vogue in the 1920s. In *Artistic Dance* [*Der Künstlerische Tanz*], published in 1922, the critic Werner Suhr referred to the importance attributed to the sexual drives by Schopenhauer and Freud, and argued that these drives could be 'ennobled', as happened in artistic dance. It was not necessary that 'strong, sexual tensions and exercises should be discharged in a physical passion': artistic dance was 'always a spiritual experience, since the female creator has already animated/spiritualised her senses ... the public ... experiences the transformation along with the female dancer'.[359]

However, Wigman's enactment of subjectivity was more complex than Suhr's account indicated, because it involved shifting traditional gender categories, and also explored a new openness of the body to space. According to Richard McCormick, Germany's post-war crisis was not only social, political and economic, but also a crisis of the autonomous bourgeois (male) subject. This subject had hitherto been predicated on a model of closure and individuation, with quasi-military discipline, which the tragic fiasco of the war and its aftermath, including the breakdown of old hierarchies and enhanced rights for women, had seriously undermined. 'A new order of modern social, gender and sexual identities threatened more traditional concepts of identity.'[360] On the one hand, this provoked insecurity and reactionary attitudes. The 'blurring and confusion of traditional categories of identity' led to attempts to 'conceal any deviation from traditional norms for gendered behavior'.[361] On the other hand, the undermining of closed models of subjectivity, epitomised in tight clothing and the repression of spontaneous physical behaviour, opened the way for new possibilities and experimentation with what Isabelle Launay has described as 'the virtualities of a body liberated from its socialised and aesthetic state', through 'a disturbance that produces "play" in corporeality, abolishing the unity of a stable body ... a "blocked" body'.[362] Wigman's kinesthetic imagination explored openness and permeability across boundaries between body and space, and her challenges to gender norms were enthusiastically received by many critics.

4. Germany in the Twenties: Technology and abstraction

It was in the 1920s that Wigman achieved resounding success in Germany. This was also a period of very rapid social and economic change, which brought about shifts in attitudes, notably to technology. Germany of the so-called 'golden Twenties' experienced a dramatic improvement in economic stability and prosperity, triggered by the Dawes Plan of 1924. It saw itself as sporty, dynamic and progressive, and looked for a model to the USA, with its image of riches and freedom, its skyscrapers and jazz rhythms. In 1923, Henry Ford's autobiography was published in Germany. The fact that it immediately became a best-seller was indicative of a fascination with the USA and its new technologies. Ford's mass production methods, which provided jobs and allowed large numbers of people to own cars, seemed to bring Utopia close to reality. Indeed, 'America became the model not only of technological reason but also of an ideal society in which all people were both rich and equal'.[363] The aesthetic of so-called New Objectivity was characterised by greater formalism and geometrical abstraction, which contrasted with the visionary qualities of Expressionism.

This shift was exemplified in the evolution of Bauhaus ideology. In the early 1920s, the architect Walter Gropius, director of the avant-garde Bauhaus school of art and design (which he founded in Weimar in 1919), distanced it from its allegiance to its original motto, 'Art and craft – a new unity' and its 'preoccupation with the individual and his cosmic integration'. Instead he redirected it towards a new aim, 'Art and technology – a new unity', and a new field of activity, contemporary design for industrial production.[364] Forms were designed to be economical and adapted to their function. The aesthetic of the new design-oriented approach was pragmatic, and was aimed at mass production and economic success during the years of prosperity that preceded the Wall Street Crash. Some Bauhaus artists, such as Oskar Schlemmer, were suspicious of the effects of mechanisation and loss of individuality. Wassily Kandinsky, Paul Klee and others also maintained a metaphysical perspective, attributing a 'cosmic' dimension to their work and its rhythms. For instance, Kandinsky regarded the circular form, which was very characteristic of his paintings in the 1920s and figured in titles such as *Circle within a Circle* (1923), as suggesting 'a link with the cosmic'.[365]

Increasingly, however, pseudo-religious, mystical approaches were regarded as passé. Magdalena Droste reports that at the Bauhaus in 1921 'many in the theatre workshop supported the mechanisation and standardisation represented by Americanism', while Lothar Schreyer's primitivistic and pseudo-religious approach to theatre was unpopular.[366]

Wigman's work in this period successfully combined features typical of New Objectivity with those of expressive dance. The 1913 prospectus for Laban's school in Munich, at which Wigman taught, had emphasised the potential for everyone to 'recognise, strengthen and control his life's rhythm' in order to resist the 'triumph' of 'technology and formal expedience'.[367] Much later, in 1931, Wigman wrote positively about connections between machine rhythms and dance:

> We live in what is known as the 'Machine Age'. However paradoxical it may seem, I believe there is a certain connection between what we call the machine and what we call dancing … If we consider that behind the machine stands the primeval force of rhythm: that every machine represents a tamed rhythmic force; if we also remember that rhythm is the source of the dance, then we certainly have a connecting link, a common basis, for these seemingly unconnected forms of present-day life.[368]

The more positive approach to technology in the 1920s brought a forward-looking, modern dimension to the more nostalgic 'vitalism' of the pre-war years. 'What fascinated the dancer in mechanical rhythms corresponded to the life feeling of the time: hectic, full of changes and turning around itself.'[369] This 'life feeling' was also in tune with jazz dance, which had been criticised by exponents of natural rhythms for its mechanical polyrhythms that fragmented the body.[370] Instead of following the unifying principle of involving the whole body in 'swinging' rhythms, jazz dance followed the dividing principle of combining different rhythms in different parts of the body. 'It demands the isolation of particular parts of the body, for instance the legs, so that the knees kick in and out, the legs make "x"s and "o"s, while the hands, the trunk and the head perform different movements.'[371] Jazz was also associated with mass culture and with Negro 'primitivism'. Interestingly, Wigman was open to the rhythmic possibilities of social dance, including jazz. She said in 1925 that the rhythmic basis of modern dances corresponded to contemporary sensibilities and held potential for the future of dance:

> The rhythmic music that is really the point of departure for the newer social dances has indeed got possibilities of development which perhaps

cannot be fully perceived at the present time. I am even convinced that, in the near future, jazz music will give rise to a great number of rhythmic stimuli, which will give life to quite new dance forms. Underlying all modern dances is an immense, almost elemental, *original* rhythm, which coincides perfectly with the sensibility of our times ... I hold the foxtrot along with the shimmy to be the most excellent expressions of our contemporary sensibilities.[372]

As earlier with *Ausdruckstanz* and the frequently decadent world of nightclubs and cabarets, in the 'Golden Twenties' there was virtually no contact between artistic dance and the popular world of the glamorous reviews, which starred performers like Josephine Baker and the Tiller Girls. Radically different dance forms prospered side by side, with perhaps as many as twenty different dance performances at a weekend in Berlin alone.[373] New developments in artistic dance were closely related to New Objectivity, which led in dance, as in other art forms, to a more functional, technically oriented and abstract approach. 'Expression through clear, simple structure was the principle that dominated art and architecture in the framework of New Objectivity in the mid-nineteen-twenties.'[374] Wigman's *Scenes from a Dance Drama* (1923–4) comprised several sections with geometrical titles, such as 'Circle'. She was acquainted with the ideas of Kandinsky, who taught at the Bauhaus from 1922 to 1933. Although her own work was very different, she was sympathetic to the choreographical experiments of Oskar Schlemmer (1888–1943). She attended a performance of Schlemmer's famous *Triadic Ballet* in Dresden in 1923, and later wrote to him that she regretted that such work could not be seen more often, concluding: 'For your creations, apart from their pure aesthetic value, are a stimulus and a signpost for the whole modern mode of representation [*Darstellungswesen*].'[375] In 1927, Wigman and Laban sat with Schlemmer on a committee organised to initiate a Dance Congress.[376]

Schlemmer's choreographic experiments were often criticised by his contemporaries: 'his dancers, encased in geometrical forms or body-concealing costumes, were [seen as] dehumanized and mechanistic'.[377] However, as the critic Anna Kisselgoff points out: 'ironically it was Schlemmer – who supposedly concealed the human figure in his theater – who stressed the role of the human figure in theoretical writings more than any other Bauhaus artist and who emphasized it in his own paintings'.[378] Debra McCall, who restaged Schlemmer's dance pieces in New York in 1982, affirmed that:

[Schlemmer] felt he could liberate the dancer with masks and costumes ... he could abstract the dancer and create new eternal symbols to represent the new technological age ... he was ultimately a humanist and he foresaw the great advantage that technology could bring to the theater.[379]

Schlemmer emphasised the importance of mechanisation as an 'emblem of our time', but stressed that the result was 'our recognition of that which can *not* be mechanized'.[380] Several Bauhaus productions by Schlemmer and his students critiqued mechanisation and technology. In his piece *Figural Cabinet,* Schlemmer parodied 'progress and the worship of technology'.[381] He used shape-distorting costumes to bring about 'the transformation of the human body, its metamorphosis'.[382] He explored what he called the 'laws of space' applied to the human form, giving rise to 'ambulant architecture', and the 'functional laws of the human body in their relationship to space', which brought about a 'typification of human forms', resulting in the 'marionette'.[383] He also employed gestural symbolism. His aim was not to mechanise the human figure, but rather to call into question the boundaries of the human and expand its possibilities.

Schlemmer's exploration of abstract and experiential relations between the body and space had close similarities with Laban's approach, and Elizabeth Mauldon has pointed out that 'both Laban and Schlemmer ... attempted to order and fuse the organic and geometrical worlds'.[384] Schlemmer's use of the mask to transform the individual into the 'universal and timeless' has been compared with Wigman's.[385] Another less well-known but important dancer who explored the possibilities of 'machine' rhythms, with ultimately metaphysical tendencies, was a former student of Wigman's, Vera Skoronel (1906–32). Skoronel saw her 'abstract dance' as a development from and an intensification of Wigman's 'absolute dance'. It was a world of 'fantastic and yet clear structure ... inflamed with superpersonal ecstasy'. Skoronel concentrated on repetitions of basic, monotonous movements, which she called 'machine [*maschinelle*] movement'. She declared that machine movement was not related to machinery or technology: it aimed rather to:

transform the human body into an instrument that no longer conforms to human characteristics, but that from a mysterious centre of gravity sets the limbs in motion and brings them into the purest harmony of a sphere, which no longer expresses anything and has no contents. A different harmony from the one that counted for centuries as a Greek ideal, which brought man and nature into beautiful, wholesome [*gesundschön*] harmony.[386]

Like earlier modern dance, these experimental forms, which drew on mechanical rhythms and were closely related to contemporary technological developments, were influenced by aspirations towards metaphysical harmony. Such aspirations, and the association of rhythm with life forces and energies, sometimes with quasi-mystical connotations, contributed towards the image of modern dance as an absolute art form, similar to abstract painting in terms of its independence from representational content and from other art forms, and in its direct, psychophysical effects on spectators. Wigman declared:

> The absolute dance is independent of any literary-interpretative content; it does not represent, it is; and its effect on the spectator who is invited to experience the dancer's experience is on a mental-motoric level, exciting and moving.[387]

Hans Brandenburg commented in 1921 that the content of Wigman's dances was not personal feelings, but rather 'a general, elementary and regular space symbolism, which was indicated by designations such as "Swing", "Sign", "Centre"'.[388] In its self-proclaimed freedom from 'undancerly' elements, the concept of absolute dance was typically modernist. (On modernism, see Chapter 3.) It was crucial to Wigman and Laban that the body could produce its own 'music' in the form of rhythmic movement, without the need for instrumental accompaniment. According to Wigman:

> the purest fulfillment of the dancerly conception of space is absolute dance, which, free from concepts external to dance, free also from music, mirrors the experience of inner, spiritual turbulence in the space-dominating dance composition.[389]

5. Reception of Wigman's dance

Both the context of body culture and the intellectual climate of life philosophy were crucial factors in the positive reception of Wigman's dance. Wigman saw her 'ideal spectator' as actively participating in a shared dynamism with the dancer. This experience of kinesthetic empathy was predicated on shared kinesthetic histories and discourses on rhythm and the body. For Wigman, dance was based, not on conceptual knowledge, but on lived experience, and was not a straightforward expression of definable feelings. 'We don't dance "feelings"! They are already much too clear-cut, too distinct. We dance the changes and fluctuations of *states of mind*.'[390] These fluctuations of states of mind were inseparable from corporeal rhythms, which themselves formed a kind of 'body music'. Writing in 1922, novelist Frank Thiess compared the emergence of dance based entirely on rhythmic movement, which could not be interpreted by the understanding, with painting that did not rely on depiction of objects.[391] The rhythmic relationship between body and space could both replace narrative content (as found in ballet) and render music superfluous as an accompaniment. In Fritz Böhme's words: 'logically consistent absolute dance is without music ... for it receives the motor impulse from the primary sources: the body and space'.[392] Wigman performed some dances in complete silence, while others were accompanied by spare, evocative percussion or piano music; her favourite instrument was the gong.

Already in April 1914, a programme note for Wigman's second public performance under the auspices of the Laban School in Munich, in which she presented seven dances without music, affirmed the priority of 'corporeal movement and its laws' and of sensitivity to spatial rhythms over music and 'pantomime':

> Dance without music or with rhythmic accompaniment, which adapts to the movement of the body and its laws, is a necessary consequence of the development of modern dance art. The movement sequences and structural forms, which today are also freer, more independent, and are not products of dance that is dependent on musical rhythms, have emerged, not from a pantomimic, but from a spatio-rhythmic perception.[393]

In the 1920s, critic after critic described, with astonishment, the 'body music' of Wigman's movement: '[she is] the creator of a new music, whose instrument is the human body';[394] 'the rhythm of her limbs is music';[395] her dance is 'music without music, perceived rhythm, audible plastic art';[396] 'no longer dance coming from the music, but music coming from the dance'.[397]

In 1923, Eric Vogeler declared of Wigman's *Chaos*:

> Pain, fear, menace, terror, despair, indignation – it is all that, and it is not all that, because it is not in the least pantomimic, it is only dance, pure dance, absolute dance. Flow and radiation, movement, moving

limbs, moved, fluctuating, endlessly pure and tense, constantly varied, expressive forms, playing musically against each other in an unheard-of appassionato.[398]

This musical quality was frequently linked with a much-remarked-on characteristic of Wigman's dance, which I also highlighted in my commentary on *Seraphic Song*: an extreme precision and attention to detail, such that even the smallest, apparently most insignificant parts of the body became rhythmic and expressive. The numerous contemporary commentators who espoused the values of 'life philosophy' regarded this extraordinary animation of each part of the body through movement as a manifestation of the vivification and 'spiritualisation' of the body. Artur Michel wrote that the unique characteristic of Wigman's art was 'the polyphony of the movements (which simply does not tolerate any limb not "joining in", that any part-gestures remain expressionless, unformed, but every limb, every gesture shows its own positive movement character!).'[399] Oskar Bie wrote of a 'spiritualisation of matter', Fritz Böhme of a 'spiritualisation of the corporeal'.[400] According to another reviewer, 'the fire of a demonic self-forgetting and searching for self flows through the corporeality of her body and causes it to announce the spiritual'.[401] Fritz Böhme, who was among Wigman's most effusive admirers, saw her as 'the priestess of a *new life*, a clear, aim-conscious, strong, living life',[402] and a 'mediator of *life-enhancing energies*'.[403]

Commentators' experience of the effects of Wigman's dance was mediated by their exposure to technology, particularly electricity, which caught the public imagination especially through 'the shock techniques of electric advertising', as discussed by Janet Ward in *Weimar Surfaces*.[404] As argued by Simmel and Benjamin, modern urban and working environments subjected people to unprecedented levels of stimulation, which Benjamin too described in terms of electricity ('like the energy from a battery').[405] On the one hand, this stimulation was energising, and enhanced 'life feelings'. Writing in 1922, the Expressionist architect Bruno Taut used an electrical metaphor to evoke the vitalism of technological modernity: 'if you do not plug yourself into advertising as the new "current of life", then you will effectively switch yourself off from the creative possibilities of modernity'.[406] On the other hand, excessive stimulation could lead to paralysing effects of 'shock', unless subjects were able to protect themselves by reducing levels of stimulation. According to Freud, one way to parry effects of excessive shock was through the production, resulting from exposure to 'a series of minor stimuli and shocks', of a protective layer or shield.[407] In dance, the production of shock effects through motor stimulation could be artistically performed.

In his book on Mary Wigman (1925), Rudolf von Delius wrote of a spiritual/emotional [*seelisch*] tension or energy, which, in 'strong', creative people, overflows into art works that 'assail' the receiver with an 'electrical *energy wave* [*Kraftwelle*]'.[408] Another critic also compared the effect of the rhythms of Wigman's dancing to electricity: 'the rhythms of this dancer generate *impulses like sparks*, which *electrify* the heart of the spectator ... Mary Wigman is a great artist'.[409] Discussing Wigman in 1928, Rudolf Lämmel, a physicist who also wrote on dance, declared:

> I consider it possible that from such a mental tension, of which only the inspired dancer is capable, an *energy current* radiates, which *grips and excites* similarly tuned souls, in the way that a radio receiver is touched by the space waves of a transmitter.[410]

A reviewer of a performance by Wigman in 1922 (who cited Rudolf Bode approvingly) described its effects in terms that graphically evoke a dramatic experience of kinesthetic empathy:

> It grips one right into one's physiology. It twitches the nerves. Pulls at the muscles. One feels whirled away, swept off. One feels like jumping up, participating, throwing oneself in, whirling around ... The 'human' [*menschliches*] surges here and there. Physical-spiritual [*Körperseelisches*].

He continued that the only way to understand this kind of performance was through 'a transformed body, a new body, and muscular awareness'.[411]

Through its artistic shaping of nervous stimuli, Wigman's dance contributed to the creation of this 'transformed' body and muscular awareness. Artur Michel said of 'absolute dance', which he saw as the creation of Laban and Wigman:

> in it [absolute dance] we experience for the first time a dance that ... springs from primary movement impulses. We encounter for the first time the phenomenon that the modern person searches for – and finds – in dance: an *artistically shaping expression* for his present energies, nerves and objectives, his shocks, his mental tensions and releases.[412]

Wigman described the desires of spectators (with whom she identified herself through her use of 'we') to participate imaginatively in dance on both physical and mental levels: 'We want to participate in experiencing and suffering, want to be swept along and carried away'.[413] She evoked a performance situation where the spectators themselves lived out a 'process of transformation' taking place in the dance: 'a completely other world ... in which we no longer take part merely as spectators, but in which – by virtue of the process of transformation which we experience with the dancer – we are drawn in, *full of life*, with the dancer'.[414] According to Wigman, 'dance is the expression of *heightened awareness of life* ... Dance is a single rhythmical swinging or flowing ... illuminated corporeality, animated form'.[415]

For Laban, too, movement was 'the great integrator ... the vehicle which concerns the whole man with all his physical and spiritual faculties'.[416] He declared that: 'the rhythm of movement ... excites *our sense of vitality*'. Dance 'does not speak through the intellect to the heart as does the spoken word; it speaks directly to our hearts, and afterwards perhaps also to the brain, or intellect. Dance is ... *vibrant life itself*'.[417] John Schikowski wrote: 'dance is the art form that can make the strongest impressions, because in it the essence of all art, rhythm, stirs not only the soul, but in the same way also the body'. Such rhythms were psychophysical [*körperseelisch*].[418] Wigman affirmed that 'the true dance, the dance artwork, demands that the person's spirit, his whole "I" vibrates in every one of its movements, shines through and spiritualises each movement'.[419] Psychophysical rhythms were not seen as purely personal, but as participating in 'the vivifying and ordering force that pulsates through the whole cosmos'.[420] Dance, according to Wigman, was 'space, symbol; finitude formed, penetrated, constructed with infinity'.[421]

Dancers and critics alike attested to the role of 'corporeal awareness', fostered by experience of active participation in rhythmic gymnastics and dance, in producing a kinesthetically aware dance-going public. Hans Brandenburg pointed out in 1913 the importance for the spectator of being kinesthetically aware:

One wants ... to transform the public from passive spectators into inner participants. But the spectator can only really participate actively when the most complete and most concentrated optical impressions urge him to inner participation, *provided that he also possesses a trained corporeal awareness*.[422]

The existence in Germany of audiences for dance who were attuned to corporeal rhythms and who were frequently themselves dancers led Wigman to remark in 1925: 'The time is past when one could charm a public with a little *pointe* technique and lovable smiling. Today's public are themselves dancers, to some extent colleagues, and see much more critically'.[423] This meant that the public could respond more directly to the rhythmic language of dance, as she later claimed:

> The body means something more and something different to the young person of this generation. He knows of his body as a corporeal existence and experiences it in all its rhythmically conditioned manifestations. Therefore this generation also understands the dance that has been born from it and the language spoken by this dancer, without detours and intellectual translation.[424]

Direct experience rather than abstract analysis was seen as primary. 'Where knowledge of things ends, where only experience is law, there dance begins.'[425]

The powerful impact of the new dance was predicated upon a shattering of rational boundaries, through the staging of a liminal body which, in Laban's words, hovered on 'the threshold between consciousness and unconsciousness',[426] and whose effects were experienced by spectator as well as performer. These effects centred on an experience described as 'tension' [*Spannung*] and its release [*Ab/Entspannung*] or 'discharge' [*Entladung*]. In 1909, in *Revolution in the Theatre*, Georg Fuchs, director of the Munich Künstlertheater, wrote that 'the aim of the stage is ... to excite and then to discharge an excessive tension ... While we are compelled by the suggestion of rhythmic forces to experience the events on stage with the performer, we ourselves also finally experience the greatest intensification of our being'.[427] Wigman described a state of ecstasy, in which knowledge and experience were indistinguishable, and which manifested itself in 'a heightened tension, an intensification of one's whole being'. She continued: 'the inner charge, which one experiences, longs for expression ... in the person who has the gift of dance, this [rhythmic force] discharges itself as movement'.[428] Wigman's method was based on improvisation using this corporeal awareness, and was a '*Technik*' in the German sense of 'a method for experiencing and structuring movement', rather than a 'technique' in the American sense of 'a codified movement vocabulary'.[429]

6. Rhythmic exchanges in the space-body:
Tension and release

Kinesthetic imagination in Wigman's dance did not involve an active body moving through a passive space, but rather a dynamic interaction of forces in body and space, a projection and reception of 'tension' and 'release'. 'Energy comes from space',[430] and the dance experience consisted in those intensely lived and yet ungraspable moments of 'fully realised being', the experience of 'inner charge', the heightened tension and energy that the dancer generated and embodied, and its discharge in movement. This experience was at once an intensification of being and a loss of individual selfhood. In Wigman's words, the creative person:

> turns back in on himself, in order to lose himself in one greater than himself: in the immediate, indivisible being. Like lightning, perhaps just for one second he is caught up and flooded with the wave of the great current of life, which extinguishes him as an isolated existence and makes him a present of participation in the whole.[431]

These comments indicate the paradoxical status attributed to the individual, who was seen as exercising a quasi-religious function of mediating contact with the great 'stream of life', yet destined to be extinguished in the process. The interactive relationship between body and space in Wigman's dance was frequently conceptualised by contemporaries in this quasi-mystical manner. In fact, Wigman's ideas on this subject went back at least to her early enthusiasm for Nietzsche. Her view of the creative person as being in touch with the 'current of life' was close to Nietzsche's belief in the 'creative being of the earth, of life itself', and the possibility of 'an act of sympathy or empathy with the flowing movement of the unending current of life'.[432]

According to Laban, the dancer 'transposed' external impressions into a 'corporeal-mental/emotional-intellectual tension feeling'.[433] Wigman used the term 'condensation' or *Verdichtung* (the same word as for linguistic 'condensation', applied to metaphor) to describe this creative 'work' of the dancer, which staged the act of moving as the result of an empathetic (and even amorous) penetration of the dancer's body by space. 'The dancer becomes the soul of space, the receiver of the spatial vibration, which in him condenses into inner movement and releases itself from the body through momentum [*Schwung*].[434] Although in German the opposite of '*Spannung*' (tension) is '*Entspannung*' or '*Abspannung*', one also frequently finds as a contrast to '*Spannung*' the word '*Entladung*' or '*Ausladung*', denoting not only a 'release', but also a 'discharge' or 'offloading' of tensions. Tension is a muscular stretching that constrains and builds up momentum, which is then released in *ausladende Kraft* (discharge energy/force) or *Schwungkraft* (literally, swing/vibration-energy/force), which is in turn projected into and embodied by space: 'the corporeal swing/vibration that is transmitted to space becomes space swing/vibration'.[435] Dance consisted in this rhythmic alternation between the extremes of *Spannung* and *Entladung* in body and space. Artur Michel described Wigman's dance as 'striding from tension to release and to new tension'.[436] This economy of energy was self-generating and self-renewing.

Whereas muscular tension typified the body in ballet, *Schwung* and *Impuls*, which were movements produced by releases of tension, were innovations of the dance developed by Laban and Wigman. The so-called movement scales that Laban evolved[437] were based on such 'swinging' movements. '*Schwung*', which designates a rhythmic, swinging movement in which tensions are discharged, and which integrates the whole body, was a key term in accounts of Wigman's dance. Michel evoked the 'productive tensions of the body ... which express themselves, discharge, regroup and retransmit'.[438] Wigman referred to 'swinging energy' as 'the weak, or offloading energy',[439] which derived from relief/discharge rather than tension. She said of 'swinging dances' that 'their being is the eternally flowing' and that their rhythm was spatial rather than temporal: 'they are not metrically, but spatially bound'.[440] Hans Fischer compared *Schwung* to a current that flowed softly through the whole body. 'Impulses' similarly involved the whole body, but they were stronger discharges, or rather, in Fischer's words, 'unleashings', which pushed the body in a particular direction. Fischer regarded Wigman as 'decidedly the greatest artist of dancerly unleashing', and credited her with movement inventions based on the countering of unleashing by a powerful movement of 'gathering in', on freed versions of the pirouette (performed in ballet with tensed muscles), on rotating and circular forms (for which she was famous), and on the loosening of all limbs and joints through an all-over vibration technique.[441]

What Wigman called the 'inner charge', the 'climax of the flow of energies', the 'rhythmic force', which 'pulsated' through the dancer did not begin and end with the boundaries of her body, but was affected by, and affected, the surrounding space. Kinesthetic imagination repositioned space, not as a passive container for the dancing body, but rather as itself a space-body [*Raumkörper*][442] which became an active partner in the dance. Wigman recounted:

In the centre of space [the dancer] stands, eyes closed, feels how the air weighs on her limbs. The arm rises, groping jerkily, cuts through the invisible space body ... Then space grasps for her ... The great invisible, transparent space spreads itself undulating formlessly; a raising of the arms alters, shapes it.[443]

It is significant that Wigman expressly stated that the dancer's eyes were shut: sensory awareness was here grounded inside the body, in tactile and kinesthetic sensations.

In his article of 1924 on 'Absolute Dance', Artur Michel emphasised that 'every corporeal tension is [directed] into space, [is] the expression of a relationship to space' and spoke of a 'discussion of the body with space'. *Spannungen* (tensions) were therefore experienced as a function of space itself as well as of the body.[444] According to Laban, 'all movement tends into space, both the space around us and the space within us', and 'spatial directions combine into tensions and sequences of tensions'.[445] David Kuhns has compared the importance attributed by Wigman to space as a medium with Expressionist acting techniques:

Just so [as in Wigman], in theatrical Expressionism the emphatic visual gestures in scene design and lighting – together with the bold strokes and accents of characterisation and dialogue, costuming, and make-up – stimulated, indeed forced, the actor to 'feel' the performance space and be shaped by its textures and rhythms.[446]

In a video on Mary Wigman technique, Helmut Gottschild,[447] who stresses that what he is teaching 'is not a Mary Wigman class, it's what I'm doing, [but] it's deeply rooted in her', demonstrates very graphically what the exchange of the body with space involves. He tells his class: 'taking from the space and receiving from the space: that constant giving and receiving is the dance'. He emphasises that the body does not end at its physical boundaries, and encourages the class to experience their bodies in terms of energy that can extend beyond these boundaries. For instance, they are asked to 'imagine energy draining into the ground through the soles of your feet: concentrate just on that energy'. Later, the students are asked to 'allow the energy to reverse and come back up into the body'. When on the floor, a movement of 'allowing the knees to lift away from the ground' is accompanied by an instruction to 'feel that you can touch your skin from the inside and gradually allow the energy to rise ... open every pore of the skin ... some of the energy gets out around your body, so your body is an inch or two larger than your skin'. Only at this point are the dancers instructed to open their eyes, and even then, they are asked not to focus their gaze. 'Open the top of your head and let the energy rise all the way up into the ceiling – try to touch the ceiling through the top of your head.' They are encouraged to experience 'a very open body, ready to give and ready to receive'. The relationship to space is based on this exchange of energy, and also on touch. 'You really want to feel that space around you.' 'Empty' space has volume and substance: 'your arms are resting on top of the space'. Contact with the floor is a sensual, tactile experience, emphasised in a movement where the feet gently pad the floor before resting on it.

Isa Partsch-Bergsohn's account of Wigman's classes also emphasises the importance Wigman attributed to tactile sensations and their permeation of the entire body:

> She used images from nature to arouse tactile sensitivity, not just peripherally or in the extremities, but as a specific translation of the tactile experience of hands or feet into the whole dance instrument. Studies in different textures formed an essential part of her improvisation classes ... Wigman's vision was first of all tactile.[448]

Laban, too, emphasised the tactility of space:

> The primary pleasure of dancing is the contact with space pure and simple. The essence of pleasure is touch, and beauty arises when the soul is able to return to its first contact with the silent space. It is a home-coming in which the dancer contacts space. Space loses its shapelessness, it finds its embodiment in shape. The hands caress a shape of space in writing it in the air.[449]

As Fritz Böhme wrote, Laban's concept of dance, like Wigman's, was based on body-space, 'because he [Laban] did not divide the two principal components of movement, the human body and movement space, but understood them as a reciprocally penetrating, regularly combined unity'.[450] It was as if the dancer (and the spectator) had found in space an imaginary body, and the exchange between the dancer's body and this newly-found partner, which Laban referred to as a 'home-coming', had all the intimacy of lovers' caresses, or, even more fundamentally, of a pre-natal relationship to the maternal body, a pre-conscious source of life.

7. Performing self-transformation

Wigman consciously used movement to construct her body as both 'self' and 'other', beyond conscious control, creating dynamic forms whose force in turn directed the dancer. 'Her body draws a circle into space ... a secret power emanates from this circle and directs the feet ... a living circle this dancer is, subject to the very law conjured up by herself! ... Driven by an alien force, the feet rush along the painful circle'.[451] A documentary video[452] shows her teaching one of the movements for which she is most famous: spinning on the spot. We see a close-up of a student performing this movement, bending as if thrown somewhat off balance by gravity. When Wigman demonstrates, however, the turning impulse becomes self-generated and sustained, as if impelling the body rather than being produced by it, and she succeeds in communicating this difference to her students.

Wigman described the sensation involved:

Fixed to the same spot and spinning in the monotony of the whirling movement, one lost oneself gradually in it until the turns seemed to detach themselves from the body, and the world around it started to turn. Not turning oneself, but being turned, being the center, being the quiet pole in the vortex of rotation![453]

The 1917 programme *Ecstatic Dances* contained a section called *Temple Dance*, where, as Wolfgang Schumann recounted:

For seven minutes she spun round and round on the same spot with heroic energy, intensifying the concentric circle with a whirling spiral of her arms and hands. The spectators were drawn as if by hypnotic power into the very vortex of the dance. That Wigman in this barbaric dance relied not on inspiration but on technique is borne out by the words of her pupils who told me that after strenuous discipline over a period of three months they were able to approximate her whirlpool dance for only three minutes. When they complained she said: 'What is three months? Work for three years and try again.'[454]

In contrast with many postmodern dancers, Wigman did not put reflexivity to the foreground in her dances,[455] but it emerges clearly in her writings, where she reflected upon her process of artificially constructing a dramatic build-up of tension and intensification of energy in movement. Speaking of the preparation of *Witch Dance*, she recounted: 'I ... *worked myself up* into a rhythmic intoxication', and described her horror on catching sight of her image in the mirror: 'there she was – the witch ... I shuddered'. Her body seemed to take on a life of its own: 'my hands pressed themselves clawlike into the ground ... I had the sensation of being full to the point of bursting and near desperation ... something ... forced the body time and time again into a sitting or squatting position'.[456] A close associate of Wigman's said that, in performing *Witch Dance*, she was able to 'experience the full spectrum of self and (while performing it) she was both falling in love with and being scared of (the power of) the work'.[457] In 'The Circle', Wigman referred to 'the *self-created* madness',[458] and she said of the end of *Totenmal* (1930): 'with a deep breath I could release myself from the *self-imposed* spell'.[459]

In his review, 'The solo dancer Mary Wigman' (1927), Fritz Böhme described Wigman's 'expression of intensified being, *consciously* searching for means of intensification through movement, which lead to dissolution of self, to the elementary experience of liberation from individuation'.[460] In a 1927 lecture, Wigman explained her process of producing altered corporeal consciousness in herself:

> When I stretch out my arm and slowly tense its muscles, this purely corporeal event changes in the next moment to something quite different. I *feel*, how under the effect of this tension and exertion, a feeling of energy penetrates me, which is not confined to the arm, but fills the whole body evenly ... I feel how this energy, *which I have generated*, takes possession of me beyond my will, how I myself become the container of my own energy.

Wigman's expenditure of energy on opposing free flow through muscular tension in turn produced a movement sensation of heightened energy and 'life'. In the same lecture, she described how 'only through the purely muscular function does a large, strong feeling of life awaken in me'.[461]

Kinesthetic imagination here produced a split subject, on the threshold between conscious and unconscious, 'subject' and 'object', 'self' and 'other'. This process took its most extreme form when the dancer used a mask, as described by Wigman:

> Always then, when the urge to produce form itself triggers a process of splitting, when fantasy reveals an image and being of an *apparently* alien form, which is like a part-self released from its whole-self, the dancer is compelled to change his form.[462]

The creative process was conceptualised here in terms of energy and transformation, where the dancer was 'compelled' to move by a seemingly 'other' power. This formation of 'otherness' from within the self, where the impulse to move was experienced as coming, not from the conscious will, but from an external/unconscious force, was itself a consciously willed performance, an 'event' which could also be enacted by the spectators who participated kinesthetically in the performance. By analogy with psychoanalysis, where subjects find 'catharsis of affect through speech', and 'perform their own minor tragedy through the verbalization of the unconscious wish',[463] both dancer and spectator could here enact, through actual or empathetic virtual movement, 'the breakthrough of unconscious spiritual [*seelisch*] processes to a state of *corporeal consciousness*'.[464]

8. Subverting feminine subjectivity

Wigman's challenge to normative boundaries of embodied human, and specifically feminine, subjectivity, discomfited some spectators. As discussed in the previous chapter, women's self-realisation through practices of 'body culture' was frequently regarded, not as an end in itself, but rather as a means to redeeming a humanity that had been distanced from nature through modern living conditions. Rudolf Lämmel declared: 'woman is the form of man closer to nature ... dance appears to be the original domain of the woman, a kingdom in which she is the "stronger sex"'.[465] Hans Fischer in fact claimed that 'all Modern Dance, which found its climax in [Wigman's] performances, was women's work. Men can dance only with a cultic or ethical purpose in their minds; they cannot achieve absolute dance'.[466]

According to Hans Brandenburg (1919), the dance movement was women's 'veritable emancipation, far bolder and more radical ... than women's entry into politics'.[467] Wigman's much-celebrated 'demonic' performances, epitomised in *Witch Dance II* (1926), as well as conveying a strength and superhuman power that totally subverted images of graceful femininity, performed the function of making audiences feel they were in touch with primitive, life-giving forces. In this role, she could be seen as a saviour of her age, fulfilling a typically feminine function. Fritz Böhme declared that 'Mary Wigman is for us the priestess of a new life, a clear, aim-conscious, strong, living life'.[468] Another critic wrote of Wigman's use of masks: 'Only insofar as the dancer succeeds in existing in pure dance, does she desire to exist at all ... The last remainder of bourgeois, of empirical existence itself is negated. Here dances no I and no You, no describably physiological or psychological entity. Here dances an It.'[469]

However, critics also made frequent references to the gender neutrality of Wigman's dances and their lack of eroticism, which disrupted male spectators' expectations of the 'feminine'.[470] 'Wigman makes absolutely no attempt to create an impact as a woman, to mix the dance with naïve eroticism ... her world is not beauty as an end in itself ... but the demonic, the nightside, the horrible'.[471] 'Certainly her art comprises ... austerity, almost manliness. It is not a spectacle for those looking for entertainment ... Her gestures are meaningful without favours for herself or others.'[472] Rudolf Delius reported that the unerotic nature of Wigman's dances caused consternation among critics for whom female eroticism was crucial to dance. The conclusion was sometimes drawn that 'Mary Wigman is not a proper woman ("there must be a disorder, the erotic is lacking, one sees here the type of the 'man-woman'")'.[473] He wryly recounted the effect on male spectators:

> Oh, I think the poor creatures are disappointed. Their snouts don't find their usual fodder. After all, dance must be risqué: this exhibition of sexual characteristics is indispensable. Normally the [female] dancer takes care almost to beg for recognition of her charms. And if the man says 'she is beautiful', then the dance has been successful.[474]

However, dancers such as Anita Berber, who had a strong erotic appeal, faced the problem of not having their art taken seriously, and sometimes even aroused the audience's rage because 'the dance was "provocative" while the dancer remained unavailable'.[475]

The impact of Wigman's dance in challenging norms of femininity would later be sufficient to draw the wrath of the Nazis. According to the Nazi guidelines for dance drawn up by Rudolf Bode in 1933, dance movement should be clearly gender-coded. Whereas men's dance should foreground 'stamping and striking rhythms' and emphasise the deployment of energy as resistance in the conquest of body weight through 'jumping', in women's dance, energy should be deployed as an 'expression of swinging powers', and woman's 'deeper anchoring in the rhythmical circulation of all happening' should be revealed in 'free, floating movements'.[476] In the 1930s, Wigman would in fact make attempts to conform to Nazi expectations of dancers' 'feminine' role. Susan Manning has described how Wigman reinforced gender differences, introduced men, in relation to whom women's identities were defined, and even staged 'traditional images of women as revalued by Nazi ideology'.[477] Her movement style in a dance of 1934 was described by Artur Michel as 'an immensely easy and elastic whirling'.[478] However, her dance was nonetheless finally outlawed by the Nazis on the basis that it was too 'philosophical'. Joseph Goebbels declared in 1937: 'I have prohibited the philosophical dance of Wigman, Palucca [a student of Wigman's] and others from taking centre stage. Dance must be buoyant and must show beautiful women's bodies. That has nothing to do with philosophy'.[479] In fact, by this time, her dance was much less philosophical than formerly, but Goebbels's statement clearly points up that the 'feminine' was firmly relegated to a marginal status, serving men's erotic desires and excluded from the realm of enquiry into the 'universal'. This ancillary status was strongly contested by Wigman's dances up to the end of the 1920s.

9. Witch Dance II, *1926*

Wigman's solo performances of the 1920s are the only works that survive on film, and that can therefore be observed and commented on directly. A large number of dances that have not been recorded, including group dances and choreography of the 1930s and later, have been extensively discussed and described in Susan Manning's *Ecstasy and the Demon*, which is an indispensable source for Wigman scholars. However, despite the obviously mediated nature of film representation, the fact that even an imperfect record exists on film means that we do have access to images of Wigman in performance. Wigman herself was of the opinion that the future of dance lay in group work rather than solos, but it was in the solos that she explored most fully the dialogue of the body with space. The documentary video, 'Mary Wigman, 1886–1973', contains footage from several solos, including *Witch Dance II* (1926) and *Seraphic Song, Pastorale* and *Dance of Summer* from the 1929 dance cycle *Shifting Landscape*.[480] Fortunately, there are marked contrasts between these dances, which enable us to observe very different facets of Wigman's art.

By the mid-1920s, Wigman's choreography had become more abstract, angular and stylised[481], but without losing the energy and excitement of *Ausdruckstanz*. *Witch Dance II* of 1926, a reworking of a much earlier version of 1914, is probably her most famous dance today, and is an extreme example of her 'demonic' style. It was influenced by Wigman's interest in the art of the Far East, and incorporated features from Javanese and Japanese cultures. The critic Ernest Scheyer wrote that 'the mask [designed by Victor Magito], at first perhaps frightening to the western beholder, stilled the wildness of the gestures, controlled them, making

2. Mary Wigman in *Witch Dance II*, 1926

them impersonal and universal'.[482] The rhythms are indicative of controlled conflict between impulses to release and to contain energy.

In effort terms, we see here a conjunction of the forceful use of weight combined with a direct use of space, rapidity and bound flow. Flow is frequently blocked through tautness and through enclosed body positions (crossing of legs, closure of arms). The playwright and novelist Rudolf Bach, who was a strong supporter of Klages's views on rhythm,[483] published a detailed description of the dance in 1933,[484] including the opening and concluding sections, which are not recorded in the filmed version. Bach frequently referred to instances of both categories of movement delineated by Bode in his Nazi guidelines of that year as 'feminine' and 'masculine' respectively: swings [*Schwünge*] and strikes [*Schläge*], including repeated 'strikes of the claw-hand'.[485] Stamping, similarly gendered by Bode as 'masculine', is also prominent in this dance.

The filmed section lasts for just under two minutes. At the beginning, the dancer is seated on the floor and remains rooted to the spot, with legs bent at the knee and held together. Later the knees open, with the soles of the feet still touching, and in the very dramatic last part, the seated body moves along defined pathways, both linear and circular, while remaining on the floor. The movements are alternately fast and convulsive and slow and trancelike, as if the figure is possessed. (Bach describes a swinging sequence later in the dance, first from side to side and then from front to back, whose momentum brings the figure to her feet, in a 'violent swing'; but this part has not survived on film.) There is no sense of meandering or free extension into space – in effort terms, the use of space can be described as narrow. The only musical accompaniment is from percussion instruments – three gongs, drum and cymbal – and some passages are performed in complete silence.

At the start, the figure is masked, dressed in rich brocade, seated on the ground with bent legs, knees together, facing the audience. Suddenly, the arms shoot tensely and violently up and down three times (the right arm fully extended); the head jerks and the fingers gesticulate, grasping greedily at space (see Illustration 2), and then 'the arms perform powerful circular swings in countermovement', before the hands, which Bach compares to 'claws', 'pounce down on the knees like birds of prey'.[486] (Wigman in fact believed that hand movements 'can become the essence of the expression of the dance ... The sensations of the hand go into the entire body'.[487]) The seated figure remains in the same position on the floor, and the only extensions into space at this point in the dance occur in the arm movements. The violent upward projections of the arms are accompanied by loud drumbeats, combining kinesthetic with sound effects to suggest that space itself is a material entity which the body is fighting against, attempting to release its energy and 'break out' of its confines.

Weight is strongly and actively projected into the surrounding space, as the torso rocks twice in a circular motion from left to right, while the neck and head perform jerking, upward movements, again accompanied by sharp drumbeats. With each of the two staccato beats, the knees, which were slightly apart, are brought together suddenly, 'closing' the body. Then the body slowly begins to open up: the hands clutch the knees and prise them apart, while the feet are still touching each other. The torso now rocks again twice, in movements coming right from the pelvis and circling more widely than before, each finishing with a jerking of the head and neck that coincides with a strong drumbeat, again suggesting that space is being 'struck'.

By contrast, there follows a slow sequence, performed in silence, whose dynamics are characterised by free flow and light use of weight. We see here an opening of the body to the right side, with a rotation of the hips, where, in contrast with the previous rapid grasping movements of the arms and legs, the body is more relaxed. Here it is as if the figure is communicating with space and internalising external forces. At one point, the dancer's hand momentarily touches her mouth, a gesture which, in her notes on the dance, Wigman referred to as an injunction to 'keep the secret', associated with 'the enigmatic Sphinx'.[488]

Then the arms are raised, fingers gesticulating as at the outset, and the percussive beat is heard again as the arms cross over, the hands crash down on the knees with great force and the head protrudes forward. The impact, still stunning for the twenty-first-century spectator, of this disturbingly violent sequence of movements is heightened by its seemingly involuntary character, where the body appears to be possessed by external forces. Now, still seated, with feet together and with open knees, the whole body begins to move forward, the torso rocking from side to side, with the hands descending on alternate knees, coinciding with the percussive beat. The legs are now extended as the figure advances, 'thrusting one leg out, crashing it into the ground then dragging the body up to that leg, then repeating the movement with the other leg'.[489] The figure advances purposefully and menacingly towards the spectator. Bach refers here to powerful swinging movements in the crossed arms, where the left hand repeatedly grasps and releases the right knee and vice versa. These swings become progressively larger, extending further into space and producing an increased sense of opening and projection of energy as the movement speeds up. Bach associates the head movements here with the action of striking, describing them as disjointed and jerky. On the seventh beat (out of a total of fourteen), the right arm is lifted up and out over the left arm.

Still seated, the figure then propels itself in a circle, with increasing speed, again producing a sense of extraordinarily heightened tension, where the energy built up in the circular movement is centripetally contained, at the same time as being forcefully projected into the floor. The body 'pivots around holding onto ... [the] ankles, lifting one leg at a time then stomping down, shoving the foot onto the stage'.[490] This very strong use of weight produces an extremely powerful projection of energy. Drumbeats are accompanied by staccato stamping of the feet, creating a strong sense of violent resistance to enclosure.

In effort terms, what is perhaps most striking in this filmed section of the dance is the projection of energy through strikingly forceful use of weight, producing strong shocks in the body and appearing to indicate a loss of control, but executed with a predominantly bound flow indicative of muscular tension and restraint. The effect of menace is heightened by sudden increases of speed, as when the figure advances towards the audience. The combination of violent energy (expended in extending movements with forceful use of weight and increases in speed) with restraint (manifested in bound flow, direct use of space and precision of detail) produces tension between release and control. As discussed in the Introduction, Effort-Shape analysis takes account of elements of both 'effort' and 'shape', between which certain correlations can be posited. 'There is a relationship between the spatial fluctuations of shape flow [the continuous change in the form or spatial relationship of body parts either towards or away from each other] and the way kinetic energy is discharged in effort flow.'[491] For Kestenberg, muscular modulations are linked with libidinal energy flows. She notes that 'in observation of movement patterns one finds an affinity between "growing" of body shape and free flow of tension (smoothly running, continuous processes) and an affinity between "shrinking" of body shape and bound flow of tension (interruptive processes)', where the former is 'conducive to the outward discharge of libido' and the latter 'seems best suited for the discharge of aggression inward'.[492]

In *Witch Dance II*, we experience rhythmic alternation of shape flow between shrinking (crouching, closure of the knees) and growing (extension of the arms and legs) of body shape, which is not accompanied by comparable fluctuations between 'bound' and 'free' flow. The shooting movements of the arms, the thrusting movements of the head and the beating of the feet on the floor combine forceful use of weight with suddenness and a direct attitude to space, and are 'interruptive' actions performed with predominantly bound flow. Outward discharge of energy takes place in a manner that also controls energy flow, thereby avoiding what Kestenberg describes as 'feelings of deflation, collapse and emptiness', which frequently follow 'abrupt decrease of tension'.[493] This also contributes to the feature noted by Manning that 'the gestures contain more energy than they release', and that even at the end, where the dancer has risen to her feet and danced with fierce intensity (see the account by Rudolph Bach), 'the masked face rears up to confront the spectator' but 'the dance has not exhausted the potential energy of the *Gestalt*'.[494]

Wigman's *Witch Dance II* placed the spectator in the position described by Georg Fuchs (see above): 'while we are compelled by the suggestion of rhythmic forces to experience the events on stage with the performer, we ourselves also finally experience the greatest intensification of our being'.[495] The ground was well prepared, both in terms of movement experience and of intellectual disposition, for spectators to be kinesthetically aware and to empathise with the subversive uses of energy enacted in Wigman's dance. The wild, grotesque elements which so appealed to her contemporary spectators were described in terms of 'primitive',[496] 'demonic'[497] forces, and 'madness beyond the human'.[498] According to Rudolf Bach, *Witch Dance II* possessed an 'uncanny intensity',[499] where demonic features were combined with the carefully crafted precision that also astounded spectators of Wigman's work – its stylised, ritualised qualities, its clearly orchestrated repetitions, and the extreme precision of the gestures, notably in the movement of the fingers. Hands and feet attracted particular attention. 'And what trembles and flashes in the whirling feet: this glowing, fervent feeling flows also in the incessantly playing hands which vibrate right down to their fingertips, which announce independent life.'[500] 'Her hands – flashing announcers of spiritual storms, and every trembling, swaying, sinking down, tightening of her body can cry, smile, scream, lament, forgive. Never before has anything like this been seen in a dancer.'[501] The combination of these qualities inspired Felix Emmel to attempt a reconciliation of the terms 'life' and 'intellect' [*Geist*], which life-philosophers had firmly opposed. Having referred to the polarisation of these terms in Germany, he declared that Wigman's dance was 'completely given over to that hidden force we call "life"', but then went on to evoke the clarity, precision and logic of her work, arguing that her dances combined the contrasting attributes of 'intellect' and 'life', and should therefore be called 'intellectual-vital [*geistvitale*] dances'.[502]

A great deal has been written on 'primitivism' and associated appropriation of performance elements from other cultures, both with reference to Wigman in general and to *Witch Dance II* in particular.[503] The construction of the witch figure involved such appropriations and also raises issues concerning archtypal, essentialising presentations of 'woman' through the witch figure, which have been discussed by Manning and Banes. According to Manning, '*Witch Dance II* threatened to redefine Woman as the Demonic, albeit in a way that celebrated rather than denigrated her otherness'.[504] In this dance, the mask, whose features are markedly Asian, is in fact recognisably female. Interestingly, Wigman said of the mask that its 'features were my own translated into the demonic'.[505] The filmed version of the dance shows that the way in which Wigman draped her body with the rich brocade famously described in her *The Language of Dance*[506] left her bra very visible. Markers of femaleness, then, were deliberately present, although markers of conventional femininity (delicacy, grace, etc) were absent or subverted. As I have indicated, *Witch Dance II* is an excellent example of rhythms that crossed the boundaries established by the Nazis between essentially 'male' and essentially 'female' styles of dancing.

Wigman's refusal to conform to normative images of the feminine also had implications for normative *human* images. A review of a 1926 programme that included *Monotonie I* and *Witch Dance II* referred to 'uncanny visionary power', 'ghostly blackness', and 'infernal demonry'.[507] Reviewing *Celebration II*, Fritz Böhme referred to 'dark demonry'.[508] Wigman's figure appeared to transgress categories of the 'human': 'sometimes there is no longer any reminder of the human form'; 'one cannot compare her with anything human ... one can never say what it means, any more than one can say what it means when the wood, blowing, bends in the storm!'[509] Arnim Knab described Wigman's face in *Dream Form* as an 'incarnation of creature-like suffering, not a human head', while her gestures in *Witch Dance II* were inspired by a 'madness beyond the human'.[510] Rudolf Delius recounted that, after a visit by Wigman, he found himself asking: 'Who was it? A person? A woman? I didn't really know. But certainly a demon. Or, an element like fire and wind'.[511]

This subversion of the 'human' is entirely compatible with misogynist images of woman as less than fully human, closer to 'primitives' and animals than men. Bach referred to Wigman performing in *Witch Dance II* in impersonal terms as 'the form', and described her movement towards the spectator as 'an almost reptile-like dragging'.[512] However, what emerges in the effort-shape rhythms of *Witch Dance* is not a caricature of 'primitivism' objectified as an inferior 'other', but rather an embodiment of indomitable, inexhaustible and yet artistically controlled energy, which inspired both fear and respect in male spectators, despite their knowledge that the dancer was female. In a review of November 1927, John Schikowski wrote: 'horror makes us tremble'.[513] Rudolph Bach's references to 'a formidable tension' and to the dancer's 'quite mysterious smile'[514] in *Witch Dance II* make it clear who appeared to be in control.

The image of madness which is often evoked in connection with this dance (for Schikowski it 'touches the border of insanity', and Bach said of the ending of *Witch Dance II* that the mask stared at the spectator 'in frozen frenzy')[515] is also ambivalent, in that this too could be construed as essentialising, indeed demonising, a facet of woman perceived as dangerous to men and constructed as alien and 'other'. However, the deliberate staging of madness can be viewed as an empowering strategy all too often reserved for male artists. As Whitney Chadwick has argued in her study of women artists associated with Surrealism:

> Adopting madness as a creative pose for men and viewing it as a subject for scientific and poetic inquiry when it occurs in women ... renders simulated madness a source of man's creativity, real madness a source of woman's. The man's is active, the woman's passive, powerless, and at the mercy of the unconscious.[516]

I referred above to Wigman's description of dancing a circle, which evokes an artistic experience of *constructed* 'madness': 'To become the centre herself, and then from there to destroy the *self-created* madness'.[517] Delius, who recognised that women had creative potential different from men's, found in Mary Wigman a supreme example of the creative woman:

> Woman became a creator. A new unknown world rises up: a woman's world, which until now slept enchanted in the unconscious ... Mary Wigman is creative. A woman, who forms great art from the material of her body. She is no longer conformity to manhood. Sovereign woman.[518]

Vera Skoronel defended Wigman against accusations of 'masculinity' based on her capacity for strong leadership:

> ... the view that she is a 'man-woman', academic-masculine-intellectual. These terms, coined by men and therefore emerging directly from the principle of masculine predominance, are in themselves already more than naïve ... Genius stands above gender and must be universal, must be human in itself, with everything available to it and disposing of all spiritual-intellectual domains.[519]

10. Performing Alternative Femininities
– Swinging Landscape

The widespread equation of the feminine with the erotic and the subordination of the erotic to the interests of the male spectator appeared to preclude a style of dancing that presented a subject who was both autonomous and 'feminine'. Parody or satire (notably as practised by Valeska Gert) could seem the only empowering 'feminine' alternatives to the extremes of sublimation or titillation. Wigman's diverse practice, however, also delineated a role for the female dancer that refused objectification and marginalisation, while affirming sexual difference in recognisably 'feminine' terms. In 1929, three years after *Witch Dance II*, she performed a dance cycle entitled *Swinging Landscape*,[520] a series of solos inspired by a summer trip to France, which inaugurated a new phase of her work. In several of the dances in this cycle there is a striking conjunction of individuality and universality, described by Böhme as 'a figure of being that is superpersonal and yet formed in personal movement'. Böhme also commented on a new coming-together of subjectivity with reflections of the external environment.[521] The programme note by Wolfgang Schumann (a critic, and a supporter of Wigman) referred to 'a graspable, nameable fantasy figure' as a departure from the earlier 'general, indeterminate excitements and streams of experience'.[522]

Here, by contrast with Wigman's earlier, purely percussive accompaniments, recognisable and repetitive melodies by Hanns Hasting were played on a variety of instruments, and their ephemeral and haunting qualities form an evocative background to the dances. In certain solos of this cycle, notably *Seraphic Song*, *Pastorale* and *Dance of Summer*, Wigman achieved the feat of visibly dancing as a woman, evoking a positive femininity which was also perceived as 'impersonal', thereby resisting marginalisation in terms of a specifically feminine 'other'. Other solos in this series were closer to the dark impersonality of *Witch Dance II*. Wigman described *Storm Song*: 'The feet race across the floor, chasing the body in wide curves through space, as though whipped by the winds, driven by the storm. Blindly, the body throws itself into mercilessly hammering rhythms'.[523]

Pastorale, also known as *Pastorale I*, is the fourth section of *Swinging Landscape*. Wigman's movements are extraordinarily light, flexible and flowing throughout, with gentle gradations between sustained and sudden effort qualities. Here, by contrast with *Witch Dance II*, the relationship with space is playful and erotic rather than aggressive. Wigman moves as if both caressed by, and caressing, the surrounding air, and as if traversed by 'the rhythm of wave and tide'.[524] The dance lasts for four minutes. Its overall structure is circular, with the first and third sections, where the dancer is lying on the ground, contrasting with the central section, where she moves around the stage with great lightness and speed.

As the dance opens, we see the dancer lying on the ground, which Wigman's own commentary describes as a beach, where she is soaking up the sun. She lies parallel to the audience, facing stage right. Movement begins in the fingers of the right hand and gradually extends to the whole hand and then to the entire arm and to the left arm, which move upwards and downwards, away from and towards the body. The dancer's attitude to space, as seen in the fluttering, vibrating movements of the fingers and the curving shapes and extraordinarily fluid undulations of the arm movements, is indirect/flexible, while her use of weight is extremely light. 'The slightly raised arm swung to and fro in the air without resistance, the fingers moved playfully in the rhythm of wave and tide'.[525]

Each phrase melts imperceptibly into the next: there is no interruption to the flow, which is extremely free. Effort and shape-flow qualities combine to produce a sense of relaxation and well-being, particularly in the light, free-flowing qualities of the arms, which lead the body as they rise and stretch. According to Kestenberg, 'Low intensity of tension, combined with growing in length (stretching, rising, straightening), is conducive to engaging good humor and optimism in free flow'.[526] The raising and lowering of the arms creates a rhythmic alternation between growing and shrinking, suggesting an exchange between inner and outer space similar to exhalation and inhalation, as if the body itself had become permeable.

Following the upward movement of the arms, the dancer rises to a sitting position, and subsequently (her body still extended parallel to the audience, facing right) she arches her back in a high curve, leaning on her extended left arm, with her right arm stretching in a vertical line towards the sky, hand open. Her head is thrown back in a gesture of abandon, while she maintains perfect balance. In terms of shaping, in this remarkable pose (which will be repeated in this section, and again just before the end) the body is open to and in contact with/supported by the earth beneath, while also opening onto and rising towards the sky. Then, the dancer rises gently and effortlessly to her feet, and moves gaily and exuberantly around the stage, executing sideways 'fan kicks' similar to Martha Graham's.[527] She twirls in circles, the full skirt of her dress billowing around her. Here, the undulating, curvaceous flexing of arms and fingers is amplified by the flowing curves of the fabric. The gentle piping flute, which plays a recurring, lightly sounding tune, heightens the sense of sensual entrancement, which becomes more and more intoxicating as the pace of both movement and music quickens. Gradually, the speed decreases, and, in a reversal of the opening sequence, increasing slowness coincides with a lowering of the body, which finishes in a prostrate position, motionless and completely relaxed.

Like *Seraphic Song* and *Pastorale*, *Dance of Summer* is characterised by very evocative, extraordinarily sinuous movements of the fingers, hands and arms, which are also very clearly shaped. Piano music, light and hypnotically repetitive, heightens the spellbound effect, where sound, touch and movement are linked. *Dance of Summer* is two minutes long, and also has a circular structure, with the most dynamic section at the centre. Wigman is again wearing a dress with a full skirt, this time with a mid-calf hemline in front, revealing the movements of her legs and feet (although, frustratingly, the camera frame rarely includes them).

The movement begins very slowly, spreading through the body, starting from a static, kneeling position, with the dancer facing the audience as her torso sways, first right and then left, leading to movements of each arm and hand (including fingers) in turn, then of both arms. Wigman wrote that 'as if touched by a soft summer's breeze, the dance had a transparency in everything physical, through which eroticism filtered like a butterfly'.[528] Kneeling on her left knee, with right leg bent, and facing stage right, Wigman commences a series of extraordinary undulating movements, with seamless energy, in free flow. Still on the spot, she sways back and forth, her whole body curving as her head is thrown back while her right arm opens upwards and her left arm downwards, with bent wrists. Against the dark background, she forms stunning silhouettes, which evoke the sculptural qualities of Indian dance, for instance as in statues of Shiva.[529] (See Illustration 3.) Rising to her feet, she then moves along circular pathways, executing a dance that she described in her own words as a 'tango, whose features ... were so far reduced that its remaining effect was a finely organized rhythmic vibration'.[530] The dance nonetheless retains a tango-like flamboyance in its thrusting movements and dramatic contrasts between speed and stillness. As in *Pastorale*, we witness here both the 'birth' and the 'death' of the dance, where the end reflects the beginning, as movement is gradually reduced until the dancer is seated, with only her right arm moving, and then only her right hand, before becoming completely still.

Because Wigman's persona in *Pastorale* and *Dance of Summer* did not visibly transgress gender norms, these works did not arouse comment and controversy as did her 'demonic' dances. Here, however, was a subtle and yet powerful transformation of the erotic, which was not sublimated, denied or instrumentalised, but was rather expanded beyond the sexual to encompass desire and sensuality as ends in themselves, experienced

3. Mary Wigman in *Dance of Summer*, 1929

through interaction with the 'space-body'. I discussed above Laban's description of the dancer's relation with space and the role of tactile sensation in Wigman's kinesthetic imagination. Wigman's costumes played an important role in her interaction with space. Her descriptions of the ways in which she felt her costumes enveloping and enclosing her, 'clinging tenderly' to her and responding to the warmth of her body, while also shaping and magnifying her movements and carrying them into space ('it rippled with the fast rhythmic movements of the feet and surged about the wide swinging gestures') indicate that the costumes functioned as a kind of mediating membrane through which the body and space could interact.

She described vividly her own tactile experience of the costumes while she danced *Pastorale* and *Dance of Summer*. In *Pastorale*, the costume was 'very wide and spread about the relaxed figure lying on the floor like the valve of a shimmering shell. It clung to the body. It rippled with the fast rhythmic movements of the feet and surged about the swinging wide gestures'. (See Illustration 4.) Of *Dance of Summer*, she wrote: 'how I loved the costume of this dance, its silken velvet clinging so tenderly to me – golden yellow like a ripening field atop the finely woven silken brocade which rustled faintly when touched by the warmth of the body'.[531] This tactile, synesthetic intimacy was sensual and erotic, independently of any sexual partner. Wigman recalled being asked of *Dance of Summer*: 'Who is the lucky one?' which prompted her to affirm that the dance was indeed a love song, but was dedicated, not to one person alone, but to the summer itself.

Wigman's foregrounding of kinesthetic (and here synesthetic) rather than primarily visual appeal encouraged the spectator to respond through kinesthetic empathy rather than through objectification of the dancer as an erotic female figure. Moreover, the comments of critics cited above show that Wigman succeeded in *Swinging Landscape* in evoking an impersonal dimension embodied in a female persona, thereby challenging the exclusion of feminine subjectivity from the 'universal'. By contrast with later work, where her attempts to accommodate Nazi guidelines led to stereotypical feminine roles, in these solos Wigman demonstrated the possibility of 'dancing as a woman' whose subjectivity was not defined in relation to a male 'other', but rather in relation to a 'space-body'. The relationship between the body and space enacted by Wigman's kinesthetic imagination can be conceptualised in terms of 'reversibility' of body and world. In his late work, the philosopher Maurice Merleau-Ponty developed the idea of 'dehiscence', which opens a space in the body between seeing and being seen, touching and being touched, and which means that 'things pass into us as much as we pass into things'.[532] In Wigman's

4. Mary Wigman in *Pastorale*, 1929

dance, kinesthetic imagination opened up the individuated subject to rhythmic exchanges with the space-body: 'Let us listen to the pulsebeat of our own heart, to the whisper and murmur of our own blood, which is the sound of this space.'[533]

3: Virile rhythms:
Empowering energies in Martha Graham

Virile gestures ... are evocative of the only true beauty ... ugliness may be actually beautiful, if it cries out with the voice of power. *(Graham)*[534]

My dancing is just dancing. It is not an attempt to interpret life in a literary sense. It is the affirmation of life through movement.

Its only aim is to impart the sensation of living, to energize the spectator into keener awareness of the wonder of life; to send the spectator away with a fuller sense of his own potentialities and the power of realizing them, whatever the medium of his activity. *(Graham)*[535]

Martha Graham's rhythmic innovations drew on the percussive energies of an aggressively masculinist and Americanist modernism, which she appropriated for the empowerment of the female dancer. She developed new ways of using energy in movement, which enabled her dancers (exclusively female until 1938) to resist the constraints on corporeal expression that she associated with the puritanical approach to life. Graham's kinesthetic imagination was grounded in vigorous projections of energy, with much emphasis on direct movement and forceful use of weight, producing feelings of strength and high energy. Conflictual dynamics heightened the rhythmic tension. Spectators accustomed to the nervous energies of contemporary urban life were kinesthetically attuned to the rhythmic economies of Graham's dance.

Steps in the Street: *Devastation – Homelessness – Exile*, 1936.[536]

There is no set, and the lighting, from stage right, is low. Silent darkness reverberates to the sound of footsteps. Women (the reconstructed version has twelve dancers in all) enter from both sides of the stage. They walk backwards, in opposite directions, forming lines which cross contrapuntally. They wear long dark dresses with full skirts which show their ankles, feet and arms. Each torso twists to the left, the left arm bent at an acute angle under the chin, with neck and head also angled to the left. Their steps are stiff and slow, in staccato rhythm, with bound flow and strong use of weight. The ball of the foot 'stabs into the floor before it lowers through the metatarsal arch to the heel'.[537] The dancers turn, and repeat the movement in reverse. The principal dancer, her torso now facing stage right but her head turning to face the audience, tenses her upper body and focuses her gaze intently on her left hand, held next to her face. Then, in a sudden, startling movement, she swivels to face stage left, thrusting both arms above her head and opening them out to the sides, while her right leg extends behind her, showing a strongly flexed foot. At the same moment, a chord crashes out from the silence: the opening of the insistently percussive score,[538] *whose strident beats are strikingly reminiscent of Stravinsky's **Rite of Spring**.*

[...] Alone on stage, the principal dancer stands still, arms raised, body tensed, beating her left foot in an insistent down–up movement. She is joined by a group of six women who enter from stage left, forming two 'vertical' lines of three extending backwards from downstage to upstage. They perform vigorous leaps, pushing off from the floor with both feet. Then five dancers enter leaping from stage right, forming 'horizontal' rows of three (upstage) and two (downstage). This configuration of six and five produces a highly dynamic visual balance and asymmetry across the stage, with one group sometimes staying still while the other leaps on the spot. Starting with the group on the left, the dancers begin to exit to stage left, wheeling around along a curving trajectory, with an extraordinary traveling step, whose shaping qualities are remarkably evocative of a swastika. Bending forward on the left knee, which forms an angle, while kicking the right leg up behind, forming another angle (think of a slightly rotated swastika), they forcefully swing torso, head and neck forward and down. Their right arms (fully visible to the audience) are raised and bent at the elbow, and their left arms lowered and also bent. Having lunged fully forward and down, they spring back up, and then down again, in a rapid swinging motion, while they continue to travel forward, leading with the left foot, to exit stage left.

The dance continues.

1. Wigman and Graham: German and American energies

As previously discussed, there were significant parallels and connections between the German and American contexts within which modern dance took shape. Delsartism was influential in the United States and specifically at the Denishawn School, where Martha Graham was a student. Ted Shawn in fact wrote a book on Delsarte.[539] In the USA, physical education was the most important route through which the 'new' dance established an institutional foothold. Following World War I, progressive methods in education, including physical education and dance, gained in popularity. The philosopher and educational theorist John Dewey (1859–1952), whose ideas on body–mind connections and the possibility of changing habits of behaviour were affected by his first-hand experience of the Alexander technique, enjoyed widespread influence in the first decades of the twentieth century.[540]

The well-known dance educationalist Margaret H'Doubler, a former student of Dewey's, 'explored dance rhythm as a tool to open new psycho-physical experiences', and 'raised the esteem of dance in higher education all over the United States'.[541]

H'Doubler introduced dance as a credit course into the physical education programme at the University of Wisconsin. By 1921, she had designed the first comprehensive dance curriculum in American higher education. Martha Hill, a young educator who was a Graham dancer for a time, also advanced the cause of dance in colleges and universities throughout the USA. According to Walter Terry, 'Hill literally took over the whole Atlantic seaboard and, eventually, through her own college pupils, exerted her influence at universities on the Pacific seaboard'.[542] It was she who led the Bennington School of Dance which began at Bennington College in Vermont in 1934, and which provided an important forum for young choreographers (notably Graham, Hanya Holm, Doris Humphrey and Charles Weidmann).

The extent of the direct influence of German on American dance has long been disputed. Graham and her dancers saw pictures of Wigman in books brought back from Austria and Germany by Graham's pianist and mentor, Louis Horst. According to Gertrude Shurr, one of Graham's early dancers, in her early teaching at the Anderson-Milton School (1926–7), when she was beginning to develop her own approach, Graham drew on what she had seen in these pictures.[543] Horst later recounted: 'We began to hear about what Mary Wigman was doing in Germany. She, we were told, thought of dance as an independent art, one that could come into being and exist without music.' I described in the previous chapter how independence from music was a major issue in early modern dance, and the significance of Graham's exposure to this idea should not be underestimated. Horst continued: 'When Martha Graham created *Frontier* she choreographed the entire dance to counts. After she showed me the dance, I wrote the music to the counts she gave me. We used the same procedure with *Primitive Mysteries.*' With other composers, 'she outlined the action, or a mood, and set the duration of the section'. Sometimes adjustments would have to be made, but 'the fact of starting with the dance is important, because the dance should be the centre of interest, the point of tension'.[544]

In the mid-1920s, Ronny Johansson, a Swedish-born dancer who had trained in Germany, came to the Denishawn School. Gertrude Shurr described how: 'Roni was the first one we ever saw do any what's called European Modern Dance. She danced with Mr Shawn and Miss Ruth in the company, and of course I was invited and Martha was invited to watch ... we'd never seen such free dancing'.[545] Later, in 1928, Horst was the pianist for Harald Kreutzberg, one of Germany's leading 'expressive' dancers, who made a great impact in New York.

Thanks to Horst (who had studied in Vienna in 1925), Graham was also exposed at an early stage to a wider range of cultural influences from Europe, notably modern music and art. Speaking of Graham's early dancers, Shurr affirmed that 'because of Louis all of us were introduced to a tremendous knowledge of art'.[546] Horst recounted: 'Mostly I became interested in modern music and played a lot for her [Graham]. I'd buy Hindemith and Bartok for her. Then we began to go and look at all the modern art paintings and we bought books. There was a little bit about Wigman in German books, but when we were looking for new ideas we always had to turn to painting. We could see the way things were going.'[547] Horst's comment, 'we could see the way things were going', suggests that they had a definite strategy in mind, in terms of anticipating contemporary trends in art. However, it seems that Graham was also spontaneously enthused and excited by modern art.

She later recalled how, when she was working with the *Greenwich Village Follies* (1923–5), one of the stops when they toured was Chicago. 'I remember going into the Art Institute one afternoon. I entered a room where the first modern paintings I had even seen were on display – Chagalls and Matisses – and something within me responded to those paintings. I saw across the room a beautiful painting, what was then called abstract art, a startling new idea. I nearly fainted because at that moment I knew I was not mad, that others saw the world, saw art, the way I did. It was by Wassily Kandinsky, and had a streak of red going from one end to the other. I said, 'I will do that someday. I will make a dance like that'.[548] She was also impressed by the Expressionist artists Käthe Köllwitz and Ernst Barlach. The dance critic and scholar Deborah Jowitt remarked that Graham's solo of 1930, *Lamentation*, 'resembles Köllwitz in theme and intensity of expression, and also bears a sculptural resemblance to Barlach's *Russian Beggar Woman*'.[549]

It is striking that Graham was so impressed by, and consciously took as a model, an abstract painting by Kandinsky. Wassily Kandinsky, leader of the Blue Rider group, is widely credited with having made the first abstract painting.[550] The vision of matter as energy and a belief in the kinesthetic properties of visual forms and colours were central to Kandinsky's move towards abstraction. He affirmed that scientific discoveries that called the solidity of matter into question were a crucial factor in influencing this move. The concept of matter as energy promoted by atomic physics challenged notions of the solidity and indissolubility of objects and pointed to possible connections between matter and the dynamics of 'inner' consciousness.[551] Kandinsky's friend and collaborator in the Blue Rider, Franz Marc, declared that 'the theory of energy was a more powerful inspiration to us than a battle or a rushing torrent'.[552]

Kandinsky predicated his pictorial composition on the notion that colours and forms were not purely static, visual entities, but also contained potential dynamism. Visible colours and forms contained 'tensions', which were inner 'forces' or capacity for movement. This movement was attributed to colours and forms through kinesthetic empathy, and remained virtual. Through rhythm, which was 'the absolute law of composition', pictorial composition at once activated and orchestrated tensions.[553] For Kandinsky, 'the content [of the picture]... is not a literary narrative, but the sum of the emotions aroused by *purely pictorial* means'; or, in other words, 'what the spectator *lives*, or *feels*, while under the effect of the *form and colour combinations* of the picture'.[554]

This determination to communicate through the tensions produced by the material form of the medium itself and to assert independence of other art forms, in particular literature, was typical of 'modernist' art. (The equivalent move for literature was the avoidance of literal or denotative content.[555]) The 'affirmation of life through movement' was the foundation of Graham's dance, and she aimed to affect the spectator directly through kinesthetic sensation, rather than through conceptual or narrative content, which she described in terms of an 'attempt to interpret life in a literary sense' (see the epigraph to this chapter). 'It is my hope that audiences will eventually stop seeking the literary meaning in my dancing, stop transmitting the significance of movement into word sequence.'[556] She declared that: 'when people make the mistake of reading literary meanings into dance movements, they are simply confusing different arts.'[557]

Ernestine Stodelle's description in 1929 of the reaction of audiences to Graham's solo, *Dance*, indicates precisely this kinesthetic response, and uses physical and emotional terms remarkably similar to the discourses of German dance critics speaking about Wigman. 'Brutally sparse, the dance took on the dimensions of an impassioned exhortation, involving audience and dancers in the same kinesthetic excitement. One was lifted, one was swung, one was spiraled into the ether of space and lost in the intangibles of sensation.'[558] In 1974, Deborah Jowitt wrote that '[Graham's] earlier pieces can make you cry because, although you've never in your life seen movement like that, you feel that something in your blood and your bones performs at times inside you with the same reckless force.'[559]

According to the critic Clement Greenberg, whose article 'Modernist painting' acquired canonical status (and subsequently notoriety) for definitions of modernism in the visual arts, 'modernism used art to call attention to art', and 'the task of self-criticism became to eliminate from the effects of each art each and every effect that might conceivably be borrowed from or by the medium of any other art. Thereby each art would be rendered "pure"'.[560] The new dance, in eschewing 'literary' content and establishing its independence from music, corresponded to Greenberg's criteria of modernism.[561] However, Greenberg's character-isation of modernist painting was restrictive in its assertion of the purely optical nature of pictorial space. The quintessentially modernist phenomenon of abstraction in painting was in fact strongly influenced by perception of matter as dynamic and by the desire to produce rhythmic forms that functioned kinesthetically, rather than purely optically, as Greenberg claimed. 'Whereas the Old Masters created an illusion of space into which one could imagine oneself walking, the illusion created by a Modernist is one into which one can only look, can only travel with the eye.'[562]

By contrast, Kandinsky expressed a desire to '[let] the viewer "stroll" *within the picture*'.[563] The model for this activity was his experience of visiting ornate peasant houses in the province of Vologda. 'I shall never forget the great wooden houses covered with carvings ... They taught me to move *within the picture*, to live in the picture.'[564] Kandinsky's spectator, then, was invited to respond to the picture, not on a purely optical level, but through projected movement, a 'motor intentionality',[565] comparable to kinesthetic response to dance.[566]

Kinesthetic empathy based on shared experiences of energy in movement was central to how Graham wanted her dance to be received, and, as with Wigman, her technique and choreography challenged normative uses of energy. These norms were culturally specific in both cases, as were the concepts of energy upon which her resistance was predicated. I have argued that Wigman's espousal of 'life' as a cultural and artistic value was very much in tune with vitalist discourses and body culture practices, which strongly influenced reception of her work. Her dance produced feelings of intensification of being, leading to a breakdown of boundaries of self, and challenging bounded and gendered notions of the subject. In Graham's America,[567] the cultural value attributed to 'life' and 'energy' had some influences in common with German culture, notably psychoanalysis and Bergsonian vitalism. But if energy could be described, in the words of Ann Douglas, as 'the premier commodity, ethos and aesthetic of the modern era', and if the modern era was characterised by 'a trust in energy as surplus life and a worship of energy as force', this was tied up, in the USA, with factors that constructed the value of energy in culturally specific ways.

In 1890, America led the world in energy consumption. This was a marker of its productivity potential, which grew at staggering speed, exceeding, by the 1920s, that of all the other Great Powers combined. The war was a factor in this development: it 'revved up the dizzying pace of change and reinforced acceleration itself, the trademark of American life, as the most valuable asset any society could possess'.[568] The war also triggered an 'energy rush', and generated an 'excitement [that] left its participants afraid of nothing but boredom'.[569] The thirst for excitement and the fast pace of change were factors in attracting Americans to New York, whose population doubled between 1910 and 1930, and where Graham went to live when she was hired by the Greenwich Village Follies in 1923. Contemporary urban rhythms constituted a kinesthetic experience that Graham shared with her audiences, and that could form a basis for empathetic response to the hard-edged, tense rhythms of her dance. The new movement techniques that she evolved in New York in the 1920s were inseparable from urban life. 'The modern dance is couched in the rhythm of our time; it is urban and not pastoral. It is broken and the body falls into angles, which are percussive segments of a circle – the circular movement arrested.'[570]

The environment of New York, which to many distilled the essence of American modernism, was aggressively masculine. Art historian Wanda Corn recounts that photographer Alfred Stieglitz (married to painter Georgia O'Keeffe) thought that cityscapes were an inappropriate subject for a woman, given how much 'the city had become a male subject and how much it was tied to machine age advocacy. In the mid 1920s he [saw New York] ... as a mean and hostile marketplace, masculine in its aggressive streetlife and phallic in its skyscraper figurations.'[571] Characteristics that might now be dubbed 'macho' were central to a trilogy of modernism, 'Manhattanism' and Americanism. These included an unsentimental, ruthlessly economical pursuit of the 'truth', epitomised in the prose of Ernest Hemingway, who wrote: 'Write one true sentence. Write the truest sentence that you know ... that and no more'. In a letter of 21 March 1925, Hemingway boasted that his prose was 'so tight and so hard that the alteration of a word can throw an entire story out of key'.[572] Tightness and hardness were entirely characteristic of the effort qualities of Graham's early work, whose vector of energy projection from inside to outside corresponded with contemporary Americanist and masculinist discourses, and constructed a paradoxically 'masculinist' feminism, predicated on rhythms of empowerment.[573]

As with Wigman, Graham's kinesthetic imagination capitalised on new freedoms open to women, and engaged powerfully and critically with restrictive norms (in Graham's case, this meant above all the constraints characteristic of 'the puritanical concept of life'),[574] but with very different results. Both resisted the marginalisation of the feminine as 'other' and forcefully dislodged the male 'universal'; in Wigman this involved developing effort-shape qualities predicated on opening the body to rhythmic exchanges with space. In Graham, however, it meant putting the female dancing body at the centre of 'aggressive' modernism, developing movement qualities that could integrate, energise and actively strengthen and empower female embodied subjects. In what follows, I shall address uses of energy in Graham's work up to the mid-1930s, which developed a conflictual dynamics, with hard-edged, angular and dissonant qualities, very far removed from the flowing rhythms based on idealised natural paradigms that I discussed in Chapter 1. During this time, all Graham's dancers were women. After the first man (Erick Hawkins) joined the company in 1938, her work altered, and her use of Greek mythology in the 1940s brought further changes. These issues are beyond the parameters of my present discussion, though I shall discuss some aspects of Graham's later work in Chapter 4.

2. Denishawn

Like Wigman, Graham came from a middle-class family. Her father was a psychiatrist, and she said that in a way her first dancing lessons were watching the 'strange involuntary movements' of one of his patients.[575] He famously told her that she could not hide wrongdoing: her movements would give her away, because 'movement doesn't lie'. The body, then, could betray one's secrets. The belief that 'movement never lies' was one that Graham held throughout her life, and she responded to the threat of involuntary revelation of the inmost self through movement by taking control of this potential of the body to short-circuit repression of feelings. She observed closely the minutest links of movement with emotional states, in order to be able to enact these states at will. This meant engaging in a very deliberate construction and staging of emotional effects, which empowered the (female) moving subject.

Graham described the Presbyterian church of her childhood as 'so intellectual, so without the livingness of the body and the child-life that it became a kind of dread'. Dance, by contrast, was a celebration of the 'miracle' of the body.[576] Her great-grandmother, on whom she modeled the Ancestress in *Letter to the World* (1940), was a formidable woman, who 'at home always sat upright in a tall wooden chair, hands clasped on her lap', and 'tried to make proper young ladies out of all of us'. This meant becoming a 'wife': 'we were brought up to be young ladies, with the plan that one day we would be wives. What else was there except a wife? You were supposed to marry and have children and so on.'[577] She was strongly attracted to 'the glamour, the glory, the pageantry and regality' she attributed to the Catholic Church, which had been her father's religion, but, she said, 'it was the Presbyterian Church that assumed authority over our lives, as it was my mother's and grand-mother's church', which to her was 'a dark, rather sinister place'.[578] When she was fourteen, the family moved to California, a move that Graham experienced as a liberation, declaring that 'no child can develop as a real Puritan in a semi-tropical climate'.[579]

Although Graham described her family as 'strict religionists who felt that dancing was a sin' and who 'frowned on all worldly pleasures',[580] her father agreed to take her to see Ruth St Denis perform in spring 1911. It was indicative of the educational opportunities open to middle-class women that Graham's father hoped she would attend Vassar College, which was famous for its sporting activities and where there was active support for the suffrage movement. An 1896 edition of the *New York Journal* featured a picture of the Vassar basketball team in action: typifying 'the surge of energy the [American] Girl embodied',[581] the players were depicted as both conventionally feminine and physically strong and assertive. Sport was a crucial arena for women, as Lois W. Banner notes: 'Aside from film stars, the most prominent women in the United States in the 1920s and 1930s were sportswomen'.[582] Having seen St Denis, Graham dreamed of becoming a dancer, which her family considered too unorthodox, but she was permitted to enroll in the Cumnock School of Expression in Los Angeles in 1913. Her father died unexpectedly in 1914, but her mother ensured that she could continue her education. When she was twenty-two, Graham attended summer school at Denishawn, the dance school founded by Ruth St Denis and Ted Shawn in California in 1915, and the following year she became a student and then a performer in the company, where she stayed until 1923.

Denishawn choreography was highly exotic, adopting influences from a wide range of cultures, and its curriculum was very eclectic. Based on the 1918 brochure, Deborah Jowitt recounts that 'courses were offered in basic technique, Delsarte, oriental dance, Egyptian dance, ballet, Greek dance, creative dance, music visualisation, plastique, geisha, piano, French and crafts'.[583] While at Denishawn, Graham performed 'Javanese, Chinese, Spanish, Indian, Japanese, Aztec pieces'.[584] She once referred to Isadora Duncan and Ruth St Denis as 'a double matriarch',[585] but never emphasised the significance of Ted Shawn's influence on her development. However, it was Shawn rather than St Denis who trained Graham as a performer, and a letter from Graham to Shawn written in 1923 indicates the extent to which she acknowledged her debt to him.[586]

Later, she would be very critical of Denishawn, referring to its 'weakling exoticism of a transplanted orientalism',[587] but she recognised its importance in providing her with a thorough training.

This included costume: at Denishawn, Graham learned to sew costumes, and became skilled in manipulating costume fabric as part of her dancing. Doris Humphrey (1895–1958) and Charles Weidman (1901–1975) were at Denishawn at the same time as Graham, and also left to work independently. Humphrey went on to become a major and influential choreographer, who situated 'the core of all movement' in 'fall and recovery ... that is, the giving into and rebound from gravity', which was epitomised in walking.[588] Humphrey's techniques were also based on economies of energy, especially in relation to weight. Henrietta Bannerman notes that '[her] ideas on succession and flow, suspension and rebound are the building blocks on which current release technique is founded'.[589] However, Graham would go on to develop a technique more fully codified than any of her contemporaries, including Humphrey.

3. New Beginnings

Graham's characteristically radical modernist style took shape in the mid- to late 1920s. Shurr recounted that Graham left Denishawn because she wanted to find an American kind of dance.[590] In her autobiography, Graham said that she was forced to join John Murray Anderson's Broadway revue, the *Greenwich Village Follies*, for financial reasons, because her family was in difficulties when her father's estate was embezzled after his death. It was not until she went to teach at the Anderson-Milton School and the Eastman School in 1925 that she began to develop her own technique and choreography. Shurr described how '[Graham] had to find a technique because she couldn't pay Denishawn to use theirs ... she had very little to teach ... did everything eight times ... she found techniques when she started to do her own dances'.[591]

At this time, there was no clear separation between choreography and technique classes: the classes were a laboratory where Graham worked out technical solutions to choreographic problems, which meant that the technique fed the choreography and vice versa. Graham recounted her first experiences of teaching:

> The first morning I went into class I thought, I won't teach anything I know. I was through with character dancing. I wanted to begin, not with characters, or ideas, but with movement. So I started with the simplest – walking, running, skipping, leaping – and went on from there. By correcting what looked false, I soon began creating. I wanted

significant movement. I did not want it to be beautiful or fluid. I wanted it to be fraught with inner meaning, with excitement and surge. I wanted to lose the facile quality ... Gradually, as I was able to force out the old, little new things began to grow.[592]

Drawing on accounts given by dancers from this period, Alice Helpern describes Graham's style. 'A strong spatial attack was characteristic of Graham's movement. Space was used to the maximum. Movements were conceived with tremendous breadth, width and height; they covered all levels from the floor to the air.'[593] The famous practice of 'contraction and release' began at that time, when, in Gertrude Shurr's words, Graham was 'experimenting with what happened to the torso when breathing in and out', and instructed the dancers to feel their 'inner skeleton', and 'the projection of going outward'.[594]

We found that upon the exhaling of breath, the skeleton or bones of the body moved: the pelvic bone tippled forward, the cartilage of the spine allowed the spine to stretch and curve backward, and the shoulders moved forward, always retaining the alignment of shoulder over hip, while never lowering the level of the seated position. When the breath was inhaled, the skeleton resumed its original position, moving to that position in the same order as in the contraction: hip, spine, shoulders ... The muscles return to their original position upon the release. This is the anatomical movement of the contraction and release. The anatomical count for this was: hip (1); spine (2); shoulders (3) ... Martha wanted to give us the feeling of the depth of movement. We were not to be two-dimensional.[595]

For the dancers, the act of moving was a holistic one, which integrated the internal and external 'architecture' of the body; and for the audience, seeing movement meant also perceiving the processes and forces that impelled it. 'Contraction and release is about initiating movement, propelling the body through space.'[596] As the critic Walter Terry said, 'the Graham technique ... was based on the concept of the body as a breathing instrument that could be seen'.[597] Whereas Wigman's classes were based on improvisation, classes in Graham technique were much more 'defined and detailed'.[598]

At the Eastman School, Graham was still not free to develop dance in the way she wanted to, as an innovative art form. Dance was viewed primarily as entertainment (vaudeville, minstrel shows, ballroom competitions, social dancing), and the only dance accorded the status of an art form was ballet, which was associated with Europe. At Eastman, 'they did not accept that the dance was not going to go into the Eastman Theatre as a revue, like Radio City, but was going to be developed as an art'.[599] Dorothy Bird's autobiography paints a vivid picture of the scant respect with which female dancers and the dance form itself were treated in the world of vaudeville. The battle to establish modern dance as an art form coincided with the battle to establish female dancers as artists,[600] and it was important for Graham to cultivate the image of herself as an artist. She proudly recounted how, when the 'girls' of the 'Follies' were subjected to (routine) police inspections for modesty, she was exempted on the grounds that 'she's art'.[601] 'Martha's men' looked up to her and regarded her as an 'artist' and a 'genius'. Louis Horst, whose support was vital to her early career, declared: 'I am her wall. An artist needs something to lean against.' Erick Hawkins proclaimed, 'I knew when I saw *Frontier* that a genius was at work.'[602]

Graham began to expand her teaching experience, and in 1926 she borrowed a thousand dollars to enable her to make her debut concert recital at the 48th Street Theatre in New York. Her early concert dances were derivative of the Denishawn style, and contained ritualistic elements that were comparable to Wigman. For instance, *Scène Javanaise* (1926) displays an exotic costume, profile pose and sculpting of arms, wrists and finger gestures similar to those commented on in the previous chapter. (See Illustration 5) A pose from *Désir*, 1926, also shows parallels with Wigman's style (use of the torso, drapes, closed eyes and upwardly angled face), as exemplified in a very similar pose in Wigman's *Dance into Death* (1931). (See Illustration 6) However, Graham's costume is noticeably sparer, and the image emphasises pared-down lines (curves and verticals), which create an almost two-dimensional effect; Wigman's pose is less geometrical, and her reflective costume falls in full and textured folds, with contrasting areas of light and shadow. (See Illustration 7) Rapidly, notably in *Revolt* (1927) and *Immigrant (Steerage/Strike)* (1928), Graham's style evolved towards a hard-edged, modernist and self-consciously American mode which was very far removed from the ornate exoticism of Denishawn. (See Illustration 8)

Deborah Jowitt has described how Graham transformed features of Egyptian and Far Eastern styles and 'ended up with something startlingly expressive of all our illustrious Western dilemmas'.[603] She achieved this particularly by using conflictual dynamics and an emphasis on effort, both within individual bodies and in the group. Graham said: 'I did not dance the way that people danced. I had what I called a contraction and release. I used the floor. I used the flexed foot. I showed effort. My foot was bare. In many ways I showed onstage what most people came to the

5. Martha Graham in *Scène Javanaise*, 1926

6. Martha Graham in *Désir*, 1926

7. Mary Wigman in *Dance into Death*, 1931

8. Martha Graham in *Immigrant*, strike scene, 1928

theatre to avoid.'[604] Her evolution of a more hard-edged style was in tune with the difficulties of the Depression years. In Jowitt's words:

> its distortions and conflicts were expressive of the political and social unrest, its emphasis on strength and action symbolically relevant to the activism of the day ... you feel something of the same impulses molding the blunt but shapely prose of Ernest Hemingway, the polished primitivism of e.e. cummings's poetry, the bleak dissonances in the music of Henry Cowell or Wallingford Riegger.[605]

As is well known, however, this 'symbolic' link with social reality was not sufficient for many contemporaries, who criticised the lack of explicit political involvement in Graham's dance.[606]

4. Energy, politics, memory

On the whole (with the notable exception of her outspoken opposition to fascism), Graham did not overtly concern herself with politics. The political indifference of the 'moderns' in the 1920s reflected wider social attitudes, and 'though the suffragists had won the vote in 1920, their daughters, most experts agreed, disdained to use it'.[607] The 1930s saw a radical change in this attitude, triggered in part by the crash of 1929 and the depression that followed. Particularly in the early 1930s, with the founding of the Workers Dance League in 1932, 'those who did not overtly align themselves with the proletariat were regarded as defending bourgeois ideology'. This category included Graham, until the Workers Dance League became the New Dance League in 1935, and adopted a platform against 'war, fascism and censorship'.[608] Graham's commitment to these causes reduced the ideological distinctions between 'bourgeois' and 'revolutionary' dance.

Discussing American dance of the 1930s, Mark Franko argues for a distinction between the 'affect' produced by 'successful metakinesis' (John Martin's term denoting 'the physical transfer of feelings across bodies'), which 'universalized the personal and essentialized the irrational' (processes which Franko attributes to Graham's dances), and the 'emotion' produced by 'radical' (left-wing) dance.[609] Graham's universalisation of the personal meant 'vacating the place of a historical and historically bounded self', although as Franko's has argued, this supposedly 'universal' self was in fact linked with nation.[610] By contrast, the 'socially specific emotions' of radical dance did not deny personal agency, but created a new awareness of the self as social and class-bound as well as personal. 'Affect leads to nation; emotion leads to class.' Franko regards this acquisition of class awareness as an 'emotional event' in itself, which consolidates his view that 'the labor of dance is emotion'.[611] However, Graham's dance also involved the 'labour' of creating a new awareness of self, by modifying and foregrounding effort in order to intensify energy levels and produce effects of empowerment that were closely linked with gender.

Graham's work of the 1920s and 1930s focused on reconfiguring familiar effort patterns (especially through forceful use of weight) and production of movement sensations (especially feelings of strength). Her movement was elliptical, percussive and characterised by 'bound flow'. Rather than creating an impression of weightlessness as in ballet, now tension, conflictual dynamics and effort were highlighted as the principal material of the dance. Deborah Jowitt remarked in 1977 that 'Graham, until very recently anyhow, wanted her movement performed with tremendous tension. One set of muscles inhibited or restricted another.'[612] (See, for instance, Graham's pose in *Immigrant (Steerage/Strike)* (1928): Illustration 8.) According to Marie Marchowsky: 'in movement across the floor, as in walking or running, the body had to appear to be pushing through a heavy mass, much like the pressure confronted when walking through water'.[613] Cecily Dell noted that:

> in terms of dynamics, Graham movement made visible the gradations of tension that are part of modern experience. Where movement had been light, effortless, Graham introduced strong, often direct movement and bursts of quickness, often accompanied by a boundness of the energy that created high intensity dynamics.[614]

Movement was deliberately heavy and earthbound, using weight as a dramatic force. Bird recounted: 'Martha told us that when we move, the audience must feel the muscles thrusting against the resistance of our weight.'[615] There was a great deal of emphasis on floorwork and the expressiveness of the torso. Falls replaced leaps, and turn-out gave way to parallel legs and feet, which flexed as they rooted into the earth.

Graham conceived of individual corporeal space as interacting with American topographies, themselves conceptualised in corporeal terms and inscribed in individual and collective movement histories. In *Dancing Modernism, Performing Politics*, Franko argued that Graham's 'creation of the dancing self strictly out of one's own body' was predicated on American social and topographical space.[616] Graham described dance as having 'an awareness, a direct relationship to the *blood flow* of the time and country that nourishes it'.[617] As was also strongly indicated by the title of her biography, *Blood Memory*, Graham was keen to emphasise corporeal links with the past, including collective ones based on shared ancestry. She stated:

> for all of us, *but particularly for a dancer with his intensification of life and his body*, there is a *blood memory* that can speak to us. Each of us from our mother and father has received through their blood and through their parents and their parents' parents and backward into time ... How else to explain those instinctive gestures and thoughts that come to us.[618]

Graham believed that 'training, technique ... can awaken *memory of the race* through *muscular memory of the body*'.[619]

There are clear implications here concerning the shaping of embodied subjectivity through personal and racial histories, which Graham envisaged as being played out in her choreography. 'There are always ancestral footsteps behind me, pushing me, when I am creating a new dance, and gestures are flowing through me. Whether good or bad, it is ancestral. *You get to the point where your body is something else* and it takes on a world of cultures from the past'.[620] She described being with the Penitentes, a Hispanic-Native American sect of the Southwest, and seeing a mother manipulating a baby's feet in the ways in which their dancers manipulated their feet. 'When this child grew older he would not have to learn the dance. He would already know it. It would have become a part of his memory and entered the rhythm of his blood'.[621]

As Franko has pointed out, it was rhythm that forged the link between past and present. 'Rhythm is the term for Graham that translates the archaic past into the contemporary present'.[622] It is doubtless not unconnected with her view of the importance of 'ancestors' that Graham took immense pride in her own ancestry. She recounted that when she and her sister Geordie were dancing with Denishawn, a dance magazine 'ran a cover story claiming that Geordie and I were not direct descendants of Miles Standish [who arrived on the *Mayflower*], but Romanian immigrants. Geordie and I arrived at their office like bats out of hell.'[623] Graham's emphasis on her own American ancestry went hand in hand with staunch defence of other races and ethnic backgrounds,[624] and she was very outspoken in her opposition to Nazism. Nonetheless, her strong sense of corporeal connection with the past was a force for conservation rather than innovation, where rhythmic awareness in the present was also envisaged as a reactivation of the past.

5. Techniques of power

For Graham, rhythm was an integrating, empowering force in dance. Her view of rhythm privileged integration over difference and memory over forgetting. Problematically, she considered 'Negro' dance as 'a dance to forgetfulness', inferior to 'Indian' dance. 'The Negro dance is a dance toward freedom, a dance to forgetfulness, often Dionysiac in its abandon and the raw splendor of its rhythm – it is a rhythm of disintegration.' By contrast, 'the Indian dance [was] for awareness of life, complete relationship with that world in which he finds himself: it is a dance for power, a rhythm of integration'.[625] She felt a strong affinity with the Penitente sect of New Mexico, whose culture and rituals she was strongly attracted to, and saw 'primitivism' as closely allied with modernity. Graham herself aimed to 'energize the spectator into keener awareness of the wonder of life; to send the spectator away with a fuller sense of his own potentialities and the power of realizing them' (see the epigraph to this chapter).

This energising focused on the nervous system, whose importance had been ignored in the puritanical tradition.

> The puritanical concept of life has always ignored the fact that the nervous system and the body as well as the mind are always involved in experience ... Primarily it is the nervous system that is the instrument of experience ... In life, heightened nerve sensitivity produces that concentration on the instant which is true living ... Spontaneity ... is due largely ... to a technical use ... of nervous energy. Perhaps what we have always called intuition is merely a nervous system organised by training to perceive.

Paradoxically, spontaneity on stage was not 'natural', but was rather the result of training and technique, which produced the 'nervous, physical and emotional concentration' necessary for 'action timed to the present moment'.[626] Spontaneous movement required the body instantly, without conscious reflection, to reactivate learned, past experience. This reactivation was not merely repetition, because the very fact of fusing these temporal dimensions was itself a performative act, which '[freed] the body to become its ultimate self'.[627]

Graham's refusal of stereotypically 'feminine' emotion and decorativeness and her espousal of stereotypically 'masculine' strength were bound up with the tendencies in her work towards formalism and impersonality. These tendencies may have been influenced by a desire to avoid pigeonholing as a 'feminine' artist, as happened to her contemporary, the painter Georgia O'Keeffe. The popularising of Freudian psychoanalysis in the 1920s encouraged the view that men and women had different psyches as well as different bodies, and different ways of expressing themselves. 'Men spoke in thrusting forms; women spoke through curves. Men were cerebral; women were emotional.'[628] O'Keeffe's art was judged in relation to the sex of its producer. Paul Rosenfeld declared in 1922 that 'essence of very womanhood permeates her pictures'.[629] The work for which O'Keefe is still best known, her flower paintings, although highly stylised, were regarded as typically feminine, suggestive of female anatomy, and contributed towards her categorisation in essentialist terms as a 'female artist'. Graham refused both the symbolism associated with the female dancer – 'I did not want to be a tree, a flower, or a wave'[630] (one is reminded here of such illustrious predecessors as Loïe Fuller and Isadora Duncan) – and a specifically female image. 'In a dancer's body, we as audience must see *ourselves* ... something of the miracle that is a human being, motivated, disciplined, concentrated'.[631]

Most commentators align Graham with feminism. The Popular Library edition of Don McDonagh's biography carries on the back cover a quote from the *New York Times*: 'The most militant feminist who ever lived and the most talented ... Martha Graham emancipated both women and the dance!'[632] More cautiously, Marcia Siegel described her as 'an early if undeclared feminist, so early that she couldn't entirely shake off society's expectations for her, or the armor of guilt, conflict, repressed violence that society reserves for its female mavericks'.[633] According to Mark Franko, 'Graham was *not* emotivist precisely because she *was* feminist and purposefully avoided identification with the feminine as powerless'.[634] Graham herself was insistent that she never wanted to be a 'women's liberationist'. Her explanation for why the movement of the 1970s did not interest her was that she had 'never thought of herself as inferior'. To a woman who assumed she must have had 'girlfriends', because she was 'such a strong female figure', she retorted: 'It is impossible. I have no interest in women. I like men.'[635]

As Lynn Dumenil observes: 'the new psychology of sexuality [in the 1920s] made close relationships between women suspect as homosexual. It became increasingly common ... for popular observers to analyze militant feminists as repressed lesbians.'[636] The negative attitude towards 1970s feminism that Graham expressed in *Blood Memory* was probably linked with her unwillingness to identify either with an 'inferior' gender position or with lesbianism. However, she did assert her right as a woman to sexual fulfilment independently of procreation, and emphasised that in relationships (with the exception of Erick Hawkins) she was always the one in control.[637] In the 1920s, the aspect of emancipation that interested most women was sexual liberation, facilitated by the availability of birth control, which was widely used, especially by the middle classes.[638] Because, in Graham's work, 'so much of the movement comes from a pelvic thrust' (she would sometimes admonish students that they were not moving sufficiently from their vagina), her technique was associated with expression of (female) sexuality.[639] Graham was outspoken about her rejection of conventional morality. Indeed, she insisted that her dancers should be sexually experienced, and is reported to have told them: 'I won't have any virgins in my company. I don't care if you have to stand on a street corner and get a man.'[640]

Graham's valorisation of 'masculine' movement qualities and their appropriation for women are problematic in terms of feminisms that emphasise and valorise feminine difference.[641] However, the association in her work between powerful movement and female sexuality was a potent one, to be further developed in her later work, which drew on Greek mythology. Her choreography of the 1920s and 1930s continues to have extraordinary impact today in terms of the sheer strength and forcefulness conveyed by her all-female dance group, which refused any marginalisation of women into the position of 'other' to a male universal. The 'popularity of showing off bodies as powerful mechanisms', which Elizabeth Kendall suggested may have favourably influenced audience reaction to the forcefulness of Graham's dancers,[642] affected women as well as men, and was an important element in European myths of the 'American woman'.[643] The power of Graham's female dancers to influence today's audiences was attested by Henrietta Bannerman, reviewing the *Radical Graham* programme at the Edinburgh Festival in 1996. 'It was clear from the overall response that Graham dance still has a relevance for today's audiences, particularly in the dances that feature the self-sufficiency and empowering of the female.'[644]

However, contemporary critical response to the 'defeminisation' of Graham and her dancers was frequently negative, or at best ambivalent. Don McDonagh has drawn an evocative thumbnail sketch of the early Graham dance troupe:

Graham ... deployed a squad of strong, powerful women who pounded the earth, rebounded from it, and strode rather than glided across it. She created dances that launched these women like battering rams against the stage conventions of her day. Glamour was definitely out. No-one dieted. No-one wore make-up to heighten the color of the flesh. Instead, the dancers put on dead-white and made a mask out of the face. To emphasise the look, they layered dark shadow under the eyes.

The mouth was a gash of red, the hair drawn straight back and held firmly in a net.[645]

Such provocativeness sparked off extreme responses, ranging from wild enthusiasm to parody, caricature and scorn, including that of Lincoln Kirstein (writer, and founder with George Balanchine in 1934 of New York City Ballet and the School of American Ballet). According to Kirstein:

[Graham's] subject-matter ... is stark, earth-ridden, gaunt, inward-eyed woman. It is not feminine since it has neither amplitude or richness ... Her jumps are jolts; her walk, limps and staggers; her runs, blind impulsive gallops, her bends, sways. Her idiom of motion has little of the aerial in it, but there is a lot of rolling on the floor.[646]

The subversiveness of Graham's approach to normative patterns of energy usage in everyday behaviour regarded as appropriate for young women, especially young women from sheltered, puritanical backgrounds, is forcefully conveyed in Dorothy Bird's autobiographical account of her time with Graham. Here we learn how Graham reprimanded her dancers for being too polite ('You are all much too polite. You must break this habit of extreme politeness.'), encouraging instead 'fierce energy' and creating effects of 'conflict and insolence'.[647] More than once Bird affirms that Graham's choreography allowed her to experience previously repressed emotions. There was a strong sense of release as far as the performers were concerned. 'The fierce energy Martha sought was finally there. Its liberating surge charged through me. No longer were we graceful little Greek sylphs; we were down-to-earth women with powerful feelings.'[648]

Graham emphasised the importance of combining 'intense energy' with 'clarity of purpose'. Bird exemplifies this by citing Graham's transformation of the 'German-style swings' which she had learned in Ronny Johansson's class at the Cornish School. Graham incorporated into the basic swing motion a whiplash movement of the arms, and a powerful forward lunge, telling her students: 'if you ... fling yourselves forward into the lunge with sufficient power, the life force in each of you will burst forth ... this force is powerful enough to break a large rock!'[649] Bird described this as a regeneration of 'movement that had been brought to us from the Old World into a creation with an American sense of power, freedom, and energy'.[650]

Power for Graham was an aesthetic value, which she wanted her dancers to acquire. 'They [students] come with all sorts of conventional notions of prettiness, graceful posturing, and what not. My first task is to teach them to admire strength – the virile gestures that are evocative of the only true beauty. I try to show them that ugliness may be actually beautiful, if it cries out with the voice of power' (see epigraph to this chapter). Graham rejected gendered movement that made dance 'a sign of essential differences between men and women',[651] where virility was the exclusive property of men, as in Ted Shawn's hypermasculine choreography for his all-male troupe, Shawn and His Men Dancers. Empowerment of women through modification and control of habitual uses of energy in movement were central to her training. As Marcia Siegel argues, 'Graham gave to these early dancers the gift of power through body image.'[652] Bird declared: 'I embraced the new body image that was being created, not feminine or masculine, but a strong, vibrantly active, independent, disciplined human figure.'[653] Henrietta Bannerman comments on Graham's early technique, as demonstrated by Bonnie and Dorothy Bird in a film made at Bennington College in 1934, saying that 'the overall approach ... shows athleticism, attack and flow, and this quality comes from a *deep sense of physicality* produced through the rigors of the Graham training of the time'.[654] Through this training, the dancers' effort patterns were altered, with lasting effects on movement memory.

Dorothy Bird recalls the dancers' exploration of the rhythm of sobbing, where they experimented with and varied learned movements familiar to many (which Bird had been taught to suppress), until the new movement material was internalised. 'The experience was like that of eating something new. You tasted, swallowed, then digested. The memory was part of you from then on.'[655] She describes Graham's training in 'intense energy directed at a purpose', where:

> powerful down–UP preparation was followed by a sudden, violent release from the centre into a wide aggressive lunge on half-toe with arms still and straight like a spear. Impelled by hip thrusts, the movement lurched from one side through centre to the other side ... The heel kept up its insistent beat on the floor, down–UP, down–UP. This went on and on, relentlessly, frenetically, centre-left-centre-right, until the brutally heavy, crushing feeling of power was fully established in our *muscular memories*.[656]

For the bold walk in *Primitive Mysteries*, the dancers practised walking in the surf at Long Island. 'When we returned to the studio we could draw upon the distinct *muscular memory* we had absorbed through thrusting our whole body forward against the surf, then being dragged back by the undertow.'[657] Not only did her dancers perform powerful actions, but they became aware of their muscularly generated 'feeling of power'.[658]

Performance of emotion was empowering, rather than sentimental or enfeebling. Graham's use of the face as a mask, through make-up and impassive expression, liberated the dancer from identification with her usual persona. Bird recounts that after Graham had made her up, she looked into the mirror, 'and looking out at me was a strange, strong, daring person. No one would ever recognize me.'[659] Emotion was provocatively withheld from the audience: the dancers were warned not to show feelings in their faces. In Mark Franko's words: 'emotion was not encoded in the work, but in the audience's reception of the work'.[660] In this way, the dance itself was active and performative, corresponding to Graham's ideal of American art as 'masculine and creative rather than imitative'.[661] Movement quality also conveyed pent-up energy. 'The thrust of the energy was to be held in, intensified, never totally given out.'[662] Dorothy Bird reports Graham's instructions to 'abstract a stamp – don't hit the floor', and to 'segment: do a beautiful circle and cut it in this angle'.[663] Graham told her dancers: 'the objective is to trigger the audience to continue the percussive movement after it is cut off', and Bird affirmed that 'the percussive quality was important to create a harsh but exciting impact, which projected a feeling of strength of purpose and high energy'.[664]

Some critics were disturbed by this approach. Stark Young commented unfavourably on the 'stubborn elimination' of feeling in Graham's early work, and Edwin Denby was critical of what he saw as Graham's overemphasis on 'visual definition' instead of 'shading, continuity and breath', stemming from her desire to 'keep a dance constantly at the tension of a picture', which he saw as indicative of Graham's lack of confidence in her ability to 'communicate her tension directly to the body of anyone in the audience'. For Denby, Duncan was superior in this respect.[665] John Martin defended Graham, however, on the basis that she expected active participation from her audiences, and he aligned her work with other modernist art forms.

Miss Graham has developed a style that has much in common with modern painting and sculpture. It is economical of means ... strong of accent, and consequently distorted. It credits its audience with the ability to respond to esthetic impulses and never stoops to platitude or explanation. When it has furnished the suggestion, the onlooker is counted upon to supply the completion of the experience in his own receptiveness. For the same reasons, therefore, that modern music and painting have had such an uphill road to travel in the winning of public sympathy, Miss Graham's dancing seems ludicrous and obscure to those who use dance recitals as a substitute for bridge parties and backgammon.[666]

Fragmentation was a central feature of Graham's style. She declared that:

There is a 'break-up' in the body sometimes, as there is a break-up in sound, or a break-up in color to intensify the look of a flower on a canvas, or a face. You see not only the line of the face, you sometimes see the hidden forces that have made that face and in a way that is for me the reason for what is called contemporary dance.[667]

Her instruction to 'segment' curves and to arrest movements before their completion, and the emphasis in her technique on bound flow, run counter to the organicist views of rhythm discussed in Chapter 1, epitomised by Klages's and Duncan's paradigm of the movement of waves, where transitions between peaks and troughs occur within a single, indivisible flow. Siegel describes what she calls '*echt*-Graham of the earliest vintage' in terms of:

the sculptural designs on the body, the *controlled flow* of movement that is often *cut off before completing its path*, the flexed-footed, straight-legged jumps where the body pushes its energy into the ground, the violent, angular thrusts into stillness. All of this has a severe, monolithic intensity that even today we find strange and ascetic, and purifying.[668]

In Graham's work, empowering the embodied female subject meant concentrating and channelling energy from inside to outside, so that the dancer was seen and felt by the audience to have an impact on the surrounding space, shaping it in accordance with her intention. Gertrude Shurr reports that Graham told her dancers that they had to 'feel the inner skeleton of the body ... the projection of going outward'. They had to 'not just hop, skip and jump, but move on a stationary base and carve, carve a space for yourself, she would say'.[669] In Graham technique, movement is always initiated from the centre of the body, the pelvis (the centre of weight) and the torso, and carried outward to the extremities. Graham recounted in an interview in 1973 that it was movement which I was naming and it was movement taking breath which I called 'release', and 'contraction' which is squeezing it out. It was built on the breath, with the body as a breathing instrument that you can see, see breathing ... the phrase is a word that originally meant 'breath-length' ... I still use the phrase as the metric count.[670]

Jane Dudley explained in a 1997 interview with Henrietta Bannerman that:

you have to let your breath forcibly out through your teeth and feel how the spine pushes outwards and lengthens (contracts) and then breathe in and see what your back does as you stretch your spine upwards (release). The thing that makes your breath come out is the pressure from the abdominal muscles and your ribs through your teeth.[671]

Graham said that, although the actions of contraction and release were derived from the breathing mechanism, they could be performed as a muscular activity alone. 'These two acts, when performed muscularly only, are called "release", which corresponds to the body in inhalation, and "contraction", which corresponds to exhalation.'[672] She believed that 'energy is the thing that sustains the world and the universe. It animates the world and everything in it ... It begins with breath. I am sure that levitation is possible. I am not speaking mystically, I am speaking practically.'[673] In her study of connections between yoga and Graham's contraction and release, Eileen Or pointed out that in yoga 'the act of inhaling is negative or passive, since we are merely receiving the life-element of *prana*. Exhaling, on the other hand, is positive and active, because "we are giving, radiating", distributing the energy we have taken in to all parts of our bodies'.[674]

Initiation from the centre is exemplified most dramatically in contraction and release, where the torso 'contracts', tenses and hollows when the dancer exhales, and 'releases' when air returns to the lungs. Through this technique 'everything started from the gut', and 'in [Graham's] early dances, the effect this had on the audience was both exciting and exhausting'.[675] Through contraction and release, movement is felt and seen as being initiated inside the body and moving purposefully outwards to impact upon surrounding space. For instance, Alice Helpern explains that 'the arms ... are never flung aimlessly, but are lifted from the back with the palms facing the body center before extending into space'.[676] In a tribute to Graham in 1976, Agnes de Mille referred to the 'nervous vitality' of her technique:

> Graham thought that effort was important since, in fact, effort is life, and that the use of the ground was vital ... And because effort starts with the nerve-centers, it follows that a technique developed from percussive impulses that flowed through the body and the length of the arms and legs, as motion is sent through a whip, would have enormous nervous vitality. These impulses she called contractions.[677]

By organising energy through concentration and projection outwards, Graham technique intensified sensations of vitality and reversed the tendencies towards repression and containment of emotions that characterised the puritan tradition, which figured strongly in her background. Critics frequently referred to Graham's American pedigree, and Bird confessed to being shocked at Graham's suggestion of sexual inhibition underlying the character she played in *American Provincials*, as a betrayal of the puritan tradition coming from a 'direct descendant of Miles Standish'.[678] But hostility to the repression associated with the puritan tradition, particularly repression of sexuality and spontaneous physical behaviour, was a major cultural trend in the 1920s, influenced in part by Freudian psychoanalysis. 'The young men and women of the period ... decided that any force was evil that stood in the way of a full, wholesome primitive expression of natural impulses.'[679]

In *The American Mind in Action* (1920), Harvey O'Higgins wrote of puritanism: 'The instincts were not merely to be prevented from impelling to sinful action; they were to be stopped from getting into the conscious mind, as sinful thoughts; they were to be dammed up in the subconscious mind, with all their undrained energy and all their unrelieved tension.'[680] Graham overtly opposed puritanism in well-known works such as *American Document* (1938), and *Appalachian Spring*, with its 'specter of Puritan fanaticism and repression in the role of the Revivalist'.[681] Marcia Siegel commented on *Deaths and Entrances* (1943): 'The artist struggling to get liberated from the Puritan's body *is* Graham ... She seems ... always to be grappling with the confinement versus the security imposed by tradition, the disastrous results of trying to conceal one's nonconformity, and the bliss of being able to give in to a higher authority'.[682]

6. Americanism and masculinism

The shared movement experience that encouraged Graham's spectators to respond to her dance on a kinesthetic level was predicated in large part on the 'nervous energies' of contemporary urban life and on the empowering effects for women of energetic rhythms. Sophie Maslow, one of Graham's early dancers, said in a panel discussion that she always associated Graham, in contrast to Duncan, with 'city life'. Graham had 'an uncanny way of feeling the times and what was happening around her', and 'the nervous energy, the tall buildings, the sirens of ambulances and the continual racket that goes on – her kind of thing came out of that'.[683] Whereas the urban space of New York was gendered as masculine and phallic, Graham assimilated its rhythms to the bodies of her female dancers. She even used the image of a skyscraper in order to convey to her dancers in some detail how their bodies functioned as a 'human building', and asked them to imagine analogies between parts of their own bodies and the skyscraper edifice. She included references to hips and breasts, and gave the instruction: 'feel your breasts held high'.[684]

Graham's views were inseparable from her championing of American modernity, which defined itself in large part as both anti-European and pro-masculine:

Fatuous in our adoration of all things European, we gazed longingly at the fruits of a tired culture, while Europe smiled and reached past us to help itself to the wine of our land; its monstrous vital rhythms, crude, glowing colors, dynamic economy of gesture, and that divine awkwardness which is ever a part of what is vital, fresh and masculine in the arts.[685]

Many American artists and writers were ambivalent about 'the machine and its potential for dehumanizing culture', although they recognised that 'it embodied the essence of a distinctly modern American culture'.[686] Graham, however, insisted that the only effect of machines on modern dance was to produce a change in tempo. 'The dance today does not express a machine. How can man be a machine or imitate a machine? There has been a change of tempo brought about by the machine. We can only express this tempo.'[687] Graham asserted that there were fundamental differences between European and American attitudes to machines, and branded the European approach as overly sentimental.

To the European the machine is still a matter of wonder and excessive sentimentality ... But to the American sentimentality for the machine is alien ... The dancer of America ... no longer considers protests against the mechanization of life. He sees the machine as one of the many products of human skill, and then considers its work.[688]

Graham's aesthetics of rhythm combined qualities of 'Americanness' and masculinity. She declared that: 'America's great gift to the arts is rhythm; rich, full, unabashed, virile.'[689] This association of America with virility was not peculiar to Graham, but was linked with broader cultural tendencies. Aggressively masculinist tendencies in American modernism have been seen as a reaction against a 'feminisation' of culture in the Victorian era, whose 'ideology of domesticity elevated the serene and self-possessed woman over the striving and ultimately self-defeated man'.[690] The generation of intellectuals dubbed by Gertrude Stein the 'Lost Generation' and described by Elaine Showalter as 'a community of men' who tended to be dismissive of women, were determined to create 'a new and vital American artistic culture, free of the complacency and repression of the Victorian tradition'.[691] Some Victorian matriarchs were formidably assertive figures who have been dubbed 'Titanesses'.

According to Ann Douglas, American psychiatrists frequently observed that 'the mother usually appeared to be by far the more significant figure in the mind of the patients they were treating', and accordingly adopted a matriarchal focus.[692] Douglas characterises (American) modernism itself as a matricidal backlash against the all-powerful figure of the Victorian matriarch, arguing that 'the slaying of the Titaness, the Mother God of the Victorian era, was the most important instigation of the modern urban era'.[693] Moreover:

> the daughters of the Titaness were as instrumental in overthrowing her as her sons. The modern American women who aided the male writers, psychologists and theologians in the masculinisation process were at least as eager as their male peers to seize the liberties of adventurous autonomy, creative and vigorous self-expression, sexual experimentation, and full exposure to ethnic and racial diversity, liberties that had been even harder to come by for women than for men.[694]

The preoccupation with 'Americanism' had its roots in several factors, notably debates concerning mass immigration. The first Quota Act was passed in 1921, and in 1924 the National Origins Act was passed. Dumenil argues that 'ethnicity provided the major focus for cultural conflict in the 1920s', and that there was an 'implicit assumption' on the part of 'old-stock Americans' that there had existed in the past a homogeneous society based on democracy and equality, but which was dominated by 'native, Protestant, middle-class Americans'.[695] This nostalgic vision of the past was aggravated by the realities of a society that was increasingly industrialised, urbanised and heterogeneous, especially in ethnic and racial terms, and which encouraged a revalorisation of American cultural heritage. Revisionist artists and critics sought in the art of the American past models for contemporary creations. American furniture and decorative materials were exhibited in museums, and collections of American folk art were assembled.[696]

Bonnie Bird commented in relation to Graham's early work that 'there was a kind of cultural nationalism that was very, very important at this time', and she referred to 'this whole business of identifying *who* you were through *where* you were, and this business of the architecture of the country, the kinds of nervous tempos of people'.[697] Graham was keen to assert both the specifically American character of her dance and accompanying music, and its independence from German dance:

> [My dance] must be recognized as American either through its subject matter or through a tempo, rhythm and attitude toward space which is peculiar to America ... I have consciously chosen woodwinds, bass and percussion as best suited to the expression of the American idiom. America has a characteristic percussive beat, a rhythmic richness and excitement from rhythmic interplay rather than a richness of melodic line ... Isadora Duncan and Ruth St Denis danced in Germany before the name of von Laban was known ... The American dance today is in no sense German.[698]

Graham's confident assertion of America's leading role in defining the new dance and its emancipation from conformity to European codes was part of a wider trend towards affirmation of a distinct American cultural identity, specifically in terms of its independence from European models. 'In the 1920s ... identity for modernists ... was based on definitions of Americanness. The issue was whether America had a useful identity separate, and different from Europe.'[699] Uncovering the heritage of the American past also raised the question of how to reconcile past and present. The painter Charles Sheeler (1883–1965) succeeded in bringing together old and new values. The second Stieglitz circle, a small group of artists known for its elitism and its 'mystical, vitalist and nationalist rhetoric', used the term 'American' as a brand name.[700] Initially they were opposed to the machine age and to features of life in large cities, epitomised by New York. The photographer Alfred Stieglitz (1864–1946) and the writer Paul Rosenfeld (1890–1946) believed that 'the artist must stand critically outside industrial culture'.[701] The novelist Waldo Frank (1889–1967), a member of the Stieglitz circle, wrote of New York's 'iron rhythm', claiming that the people who had created the city were less alive than the city itself. 'Life that should electrify their bodies, quicken them with high movement and high desire is gone from them. And if you seek that life, look to slashing stone that stands above them.'[702] By the mid-1920s, however, these artists sought to reconcile modern and antimodern tendencies by vitalising technology and 'animizing the modern material world'.[703] (Note here similarities with the values of 'life philosophy'.)

It was in fact European (especially French) artists in exile whose imaginations were fired by the urban landscapes of New York and who first articulated its significance for a new artistic future, no longer dominated by a European past. They were interested mainly in the most modern features of New York, which corresponded to their own constructions of 'America'. The Dadaist artist Marcel Duchamp (1887–1968), who had moved permanently to New York in 1915, exhorted his new countrymen to recognise the superiority of American over European paradigms. 'If only America would realize that the art of Europe is finished – dead – and that America is the country of the art of the future.' American art critics revelled in this shift of perspective, proclaiming that New York was now 'the art capital of the world', and that 'for the first time European artists journey to our shores to find that vital force necessary to a living and forward-pushing art'.[704]

By contrast with Europe, America (in other words, the United States, conflated with New York, particularly Manhattan) was seen as young, unfettered by its past, and forging into the future. 'By 1920, the *new* New York of skyscrapers, bridges and bustling crowds had come to be a *big* subject for artists on both sides of the Atlantic, so intimately tied had it become to their self-conception as moderns.'[705] New York was a 'focal point' for 'the fusion of modernity and nationalism'.[706] Movement and dynamism could be conveyed as much through the formal structures of painting as through overtly dynamic subject matter, and the urban modernity of New York became a catalyst of abstraction. Once in Manhattan, the French painter Francis Picabia (1879–1953) 'set about making a series of abstractions based on street energy, jazz, and the city skyline'. He declared that he wanted to find abstract equivalents for New York's 'stupendous skyscrapers' and 'breathless haste'.[707]

In itself, the 'elevation of technological principles' was a factor in 'the promotion of 'masculine' as opposed to 'feminine' values';[708] the adoption of technological (as in Graham) as opposed to natural (as in Duncan) paradigms already tipped the balance in favour of masculinist aesthetic values. Because of its female-dominated past, dance was more vulnerable than other art forms to the stigma of 'effeminacy'. Hence Graham's lament that 'we [have not] yet entirely succeeded in ridding men of the grotesque notion that the art of dance is essentially effeminate'.[709] The cultural move in the mid-to-late 1920s (in which Graham and O'Keefe participated) away from the urban environment as a locus of inspiration and towards 'primitive', elemental sources in the South-west was part of 'a backlash against ... both Manhattan-centrism and Europhilia in the arts'.[710] These seemingly contrasting sources (the 'urban' and the 'primitive') held fundamental characteristics in common, particularly in terms of economy of means, a central modernist concept. Graham perceived both moderns and 'primitives' as 'masculine'. She declared that 'the heritage of the Indian dance, with its intense integration, our activity, the power and sweep of our perpendicular architecture – these do not speak of things effeminate'.[711]

7. From Heretic (1929) to Frontier (1935)

Heretic (1929), Graham's first choreography with her Dance Group of Twelve, is striking above all for its extreme economy and intensity, which extend from the costuming (a simple white dress for Graham and dark tunics for the rest of the other dancers), through the music (a simple Breton tune repeated eleven times) to the choreography for the whole group.[712] This dance, which lasts for 26 minutes, explores the gradual and relentless crushing of a nonconformist individual (Graham) by a domineering (puritan?) group. (See Illustration 9) There are three sections, in each of which the women form a wall that defeats the effort of Graham, the outsider, to break through it. The dance ends as the outsider falls to the ground, vanquished.

Tension is created largely by the tempo and weight of the movement and the counterpoint of individual and group. The dancers move in geometrical shapes, sometimes splitting into asymmetrical formations performing contrasting movements: for instance, two or three groups of dancers confronting the single Graham figure, where the groups form different heights, in bending, standing or leaning positions. A great deal of emphasis is placed on weight: in a frequently repeated movement, the members of the group, stiffly erect and with folded arms, feet together, rise on their toes and descend rapidly and heavily onto their heels. The group's use of raised arms with clenched fists creates a sense of strength and menace, enhanced by the lighting design, which produces long shadows. (Similar effects were used in German Expressionist performances, and had also been exploited by Loïe Fuller.)

Transitions between postures are abrupt, creating an automated, machine-like effect, which heightens the feel of relentless ruthlessness. Anger as well as despair is suggested by the muscular tension and twisting

9. Martha Graham in *Heretic*, 1929

movements of the principal figure and by the clenching of her fists. She conveys a strong sense of contained intensity, like a coiled spring. Although it was not until later that Graham fully developed her technique of the 'spiral fall', her fall to the floor here, starting with her back to the audience and falling with a twist in her torso, is similar to Jowitt's description of Graham's adaptation of the 'twist' between the direction of the feet and that of the upper body in Egyptian friezes. 'In her famous fall sequences, she arrived at a position in which the arms opened in one direction, while the knees remained pressed together, hips averted from the focus of the reaching arms. An agonized and somehow reticent posture.'[713] Here Graham falls, starting with her back to the audience and developing a twist in her torso as she sinks downwards on a contraction, but the tension is released as her body suddenly crumples, and she lies on the ground. Bannerman notes that at times in *Heretic*, 'Graham uses the contraction principle to show a deeply hollowed torso and in the context of the group's menacing solidarity this strong, concave body design signifies the Heretic's vulnerability.'[714] In the 1986 reconstruction of *Heretic*,[715] where Takako Asakawa performed the principal part, Asakawa's movement appears both more peripheral and more superficially dramatic than in Graham's performance, where the movement clearly emanates from the lower torso to the peripheries, and which is both understated and intense.

Already in *Heretic* we can see clearly the predominant 'effort' characteristics of Graham's dance, as described by Billie Lepczyk:

> Looked at through the Laban perspective, the suffering and struggle within the soul of Graham's dancing figure is visualised through an investment of energy that stresses the elements of bound flow, strength, sudden and direct ... the dynamics are reflected throughout the whole body, which magnifies the projection of emotion.[716]

It is notable that these effort attitudes all involve a high degree of active resistance to the motion factors of space, weight, time and flow. Graham said that 'every place [a heretic] goes *she goes against* the heavy beat and footsteps of those she opposes'.[717] In *Heretic*, the weight element is particularly marked in the movements where the dancers repeatedly descend heavily onto their heels. The percussive quality of the movement is emphasised by the predominance of bound flow, with frequent use of contractions, and by the rhythms of the very simple, repetitive tune.

Lamentation was a solo for Graham, premiered in 1930, accompanied by a spare, sombre piano score by Zoltán Kodály. The costume, of lavender stretch jersey, was designed by Graham herself and encased the whole body, with only face, neck, hands and feet showing. For the first part of this short solo (less than two minutes long), the dancer is seated on a bench (the only prop), where she makes slow bending and circular stretching movements. She gradually rises to a near-standing position, and the final movement consists of her fully extending her right arm upwards and then 'closing' her body by lowering her arm to the floor, with torso leaning forward and knees bent. Here, flexible, expanding movements, which denote a passive 'yielding' to space, are impossible because of the constraints imposed by the tube of jersey that sheaths the body, and which the dancer resists with her thrusting gestures. The notion of making breathing (an 'inner' function in both anatomical and emotional terms) visible in the movement of contraction and release takes on a new dimension, where the dancer, whose feet are firmly rooted to the ground for most of the dance, stretches the fabric of her costume into folds as she strains to move inside it. This artificial 'skin' performs a function that our real skin cannot: it is a membrane that expands and contracts in rhythms of effort shape, in accordance with inner tensions.

Lamentation[718] is an extraordinarily 'sculptural' dance, with strong emphasis on qualities of 'shaping'. May O'Donnell, one of Graham's early dancers, said of *Lamentation*: 'You couldn't move very much, but you could get dynamic oppositions of lines, of pull in the body and the tensions of lines that made it – like a piece of sculpture.'[719] Marcia Siegel refers to Graham's exploitation of 'the tensions that can be created when the body works against itself, twisting into dissonant shapes or defying the stabilizing centre of gravity'.[720] Here these tensions are enacted in the fabric itself. 'The minute she starts to move, the tube gets pulled into diagonals that cross the center of her body; as she tugs asymmetrically in opposition to the rounded forms of her back, her head, her arching rib cage, the jersey converts the energy of stress and distortion into visible shapes and lines'.[721]

Lepczyk points out the importance of the 'cube' orientation to *Lamentation*, and notes that:

> in Graham's style, the baseline is mobile. It is based in the diagonals and their peripheral connections of the eight diagonal pulls that form the geometric model of the cube ... The diagonal tensions hold the most drama of all spatial pulls because ... each diagonal pull consists of vertical, horizontal and sagittal tensions.[722]

Lamentation is an extremely tactile dance: not only does the foregrounding of the fabric suggest touch, but the dancer touches her own face with the fabric in an evocative but ambiguous gesture. Her face, however, is completely impassive throughout. Again, there is a deliberate withholding of emotion from the audience, with the performer in control.

Primitive Mysteries (1931) is undoubtedly the most acclaimed of Graham's early works. The programme notes described it as 'literally a celebration of the coming of age of a girl. It has its beginnings in the adoration of the Virgin as experienced in the Southwestern, Spanish-American culture.'[723] (See Illustration 10) It premiered in February 1931, and received thirty-two curtain calls. John Martin reported in the *New York Times* on 8 February 1931: 'at the conclusion of her *Primitive Mysteries* ... the majority of the house burst into cheers. It was not just a scattering of 'bravos' ... but was the expression of a mass of people whose emotional tension found spontaneous release'. Gertrude Shurr, one of the original dancers, declared that '[Graham] generated a light around her. The audience all stood up, they yelled, they screamed. It was just a tremendous thing.'[724] In the *New York Herald Tribune*, Mary Watkins described *Primitive Mysteries* as 'the most significant choreography which has yet come out of America ... it achieves a mood which actually lifts both spectators and dancers to the rarefied heights of spiritual ecstasy'.[725]

Jack Anderson affirmed that: 'Indeed, if I were asked to name what I considered the greatest single work by an American choreographer, I would probably answer *Primitive Mysteries*, a dance which miraculously balances restraint and rapture.'[726] *Primitive Mysteries* has all the intensity and spareness of *Heretic*, but with greater subtlety and complexity.

> Again, the ensemble delineates geometric structures in space to frame a lyrically vulnerable but valiant heroine – the Virgin ... But in the formations of *Primitive Mysteries*, the line is now richly augmented by the circle, and both vocabulary and detail of design are greatly expanded. The splendor of the piece lies in the way the structural formality just barely contains the emotion and thus intensifies it.[727]

The dance, which is twenty-two minutes long, and in three parts ('Hymn to the Virgin', 'Crucifixus' and 'Hosanna'), for Graham and her Dance Group of Twelve, is highly ritualistic.[728] The musical accompaniment is a simple score by Louis Horst, for flute, oboe and piano. Graham (or the dancer playing this part) wears a white flowing dress, while the other dancers are in dark blue. In each of the three sections (the dancers leave and enter again for each one) the dancers form and re-

10. Martha Graham in *Primitive Mysteries*, 1931

form into different configurations, creating contrapuntal, moving patterns, which act as a foil to the soloist, a regal figure, who moves with authority. The contrapuntal formations are especially noticeable in the ceremonious entrances and exits. For instance, when the dancers first enter, they form an open 'square', with the row of dancers furthest from the audience forming a horizontal line and two other rows extending towards the audience, forming vertical lines, with Graham in the centre. They all walk slowly and purposefully in the same direction (from stage left to stage right), but the lines move at different speeds.

For the second entrance, the dancers again walk on in horizontal and vertical rows, but then the angles of the rows change to diagonals, which move in different directions, creating an effect akin to an abstract painting in motion, or to moving architecture. In the third entrance, the dancers begin by walking from stage left to stage right, in two horizontal rows composed of five dancers, while Graham walks in the centre, with one other dancer beside her. Direction and pace change when the row of five nearest to upstage, and also Graham and her companion, turn to face the audience and move quickly forward, while the row nearest the front turns away from the audience and walks upstage.

These processions are performed in silence, and 'all have halting rhythms and a weightiness to them', where the dancers walk on a contraction, and 'take one step and then pause, then step again with the same foot'.[729] I referred above to Bird's description of training for this walk, at Long Island: 'thrusting our whole body forward against the surf, then being dragged back by the undertow.'[730] The manner of executing the walk foregrounds the effort element of weight as pressure or force. The movement style, as well as the absence of men, denotes female self-sufficiency and strength, especially in repeated sequences where the dancers perform powerful weighted leaps and circle around Graham, gradually getting faster, with swinging rhythms, heavy leaps and sometimes loud footfalls. The body weight is projected strongly forwards and downwards through the leg, while the arms are immobilised. These sequences have been eloquently described by Bannerman:

> Travelling in a circle with the supporting leg in a low *plié* and torso bent forward, the dancers unfold one leg and spring onto it. The arms are held to the back of the body with the elbows pushed back ... The jump gathers speed gradually until the dancers are leaping or running quite fast around the stage in a circular pathway. The event is extraordinary in terms of primitivism and power and may have been borrowed or adapted from the Mexican-Indian dance vocabulary.[731]

Graham herself is the focus of attention throughout the dance, appearing at the centre of the formations and leading the other dancers' movements. The dancers split into groups, who wait for Graham to approach before performing their movement sequences. In the first part, groups of dancers use their arms to 'form a halo around her behind her head'.[732] (See Illustration 10.) At one point they form two lines where she passes down the centre, and they bow as if in homage. Here it is as if her movements control theirs – they move in direct response to her, with highly ritualised arm gestures. The entrances and exits are very ceremonious and slow, but other parts of the dance are fast, even frenetic at times. In the final section, Graham performs a remarkable duet with one of the group, which ends with a climactic pose resembling some images of Shiva, where the crowned Virgin, standing, raises her arms, while the other dancer raises her arms in a sitting position behind her.[733]

Siegel remarks that in this dance 'the women ... act out the grief and compassion and exaltation without male intermediaries to do it for them or delineate the forms of their worship'.[734] Graham has taken here the daring option of using clearly 'feminine' (as marked by full-skirted dresses and loose hair) figures to enact generic human and even divine roles. Interestingly, to my knowledge this aroused no opposition, perhaps because it was so successful as to go almost unnoticed. It does not even appear at all incongruous when, in the 'Crucifixus' section, Graham's role evokes the crucified Christ. Apart from the titles of the sections and some basic symbolism, the 'ritual' element is itself generic. As Susan Manning has said: 'Ultimately no allegory can account for the plot. *Primitive Mysteries* became the abstraction of religious rituals'.[735]

The 'Primitive' in the title is extremely significant. On the one hand, it signalled a desire to return to the roots of ritual, its most elemental and universal forms. At the same time, this 'primitivism' was also modern, in that America itself was a nation then forging its own cultural identity. 'For we, as a nation, are primitive also – primitive in the sense that we are forming a new culture.'[736] The Penitente sect of New Mexico (see earlier) had been converted to Catholicism in the seventeenth century, but had also retained aspects of their own rituals. In 1931, Martin hailed *Primitive Mysteries* as the first 'genuine masterpiece of white man's dance created under Indian influence'.[737] Recent accounts have been more critical of this association. According to Dixon-Stowell:

> There was no authentic replication of Native American culture in this work. The ritual quality of the dance was set up by the processionals; by Horst's score – based on Native American themes; by the stark,

narrow, dark blue dresses of the 'novitiates' in contrast to the stiff, wide, white, cake-like gown of the Virgin; and by the ritualized gestures in the choreography – including the positions of the Virgin's hands and arms in angular, stylized poses, and the thumping feet of the chorus.[738]

On the other hand, Ramsay Burt argues that Graham (unlike Denishawn) did not conceal differences, but was open about the modern, Western origins of the piece, and that 'through her seriousness, [Graham] expresses a great respect for what she imagines to be Penitente mores, although she undoubtedly misrepresented these by mediating them in assimilationist terms'.[739] Most interestingly, he notes that Graham experienced 'a life-long affinity between her own puritan sensibility and the extreme asceticism of these Native Americans', and that she created her own modern equivalent of the ritual elements of tension and 'possession' through the rehearsal and performance processes.[740]

It is paradoxical that Graham should have been drawn to a movement practice whose ascetic base had affinities with the puritanism of which she was so critical. In *Primitive Mysteries*, however, a Protestant austerity is combined with a Catholic sensuality and ceremony. Moreover, asceticism is expressed in ritual movement itself, rather than privileging the mind at the expense of the body and the nervous system, as Graham argued was the case in the puritan tradition. Movement training could heighten nerve sensitivity and produce a 'concentration on the instant' in which the past was mobilised in the present through the activation of corporeal memory. Performance was itself a ritual, involving the repetition of previously choreographed movements, stored in muscular memory. Graham wanted her dancers to develop their awareness of the changes that occurred in the body in different states of emotion,[741] and to learn to recognise and interpret the 'language' of the body. She explained:

> You experiment, you find out, and then it tells you what it means. The movement gives you back very often the meaning. You don't start 'I will express anger', or 'I will express grief'. You move in such a way that it gives you back anger or grief.[742]

The performance of a movement could in itself evoke emotion. 'I allow the form of the dance to give me back the certain emotional quality which goes with it. I do not put myself consciously into that mood before the dance'.[743] Here, Graham recognises that the moving subject is 'split', not fully in control of the effects that movement will produce. Her belief that movement could inspire moods is similar to Laban. 'We do not sufficiently realise the important effect action has on the mental state of the mover. Movement can inspire accompanying moods, which are felt more or less strongly according to the degree of effort involved'.[744] This movement–expression relationship was choreographed, not improvised: it could be repeated without any loss of effect, and, once the right movement was found, it must be repeated exactly. 'I must be very sure of all my movements. If my hand goes in one place one day it must go exactly the same place next day ... One remembers such movement with one's body particularly.'[745] Graham demanded perfection from her dancers, in whom she inspired both adoration and fear, and whom she subjected to considerable physical hardship. The extreme tension felt by the audience in *Primitive Mysteries* was in fact integral to the performance situation of the dancers themselves.[746]

The 'primitive' power of *Primitive Mysteries* was a quality Graham wanted to appropriate for herself as a female American dancer in Manhattan. The directing of energy towards external space closely paralleled Americanist discourses, in particular the America of the pioneers and their experiences of 'carving out space'. John Martin associated American dance with 'the impulse of a civilization that has cut its way through wildernesses, both physical and mental, to shape its environments according to its own concepts'.[747] The pioneer figure Graham evoked in her solo *Frontier: American Perspective of the Plains* (1935) played to Americanist discourses by looking to a different source of modern-day American identity, which was very much in vogue at the time. Frederick Jackson Turner's essay, 'The significance of the frontier in American history' (first delivered as a lecture in 1893, and published in volume form in 1920), which argued that the frontier typified what was most distinctive about America, had become extremely popular. Graham's programme notes declared that '*Frontier* ... is a tribute to the vision, and independence of the pioneer woman ... The movement, completely at one with the decor's widening horizon, evokes the feeling of distance, loneliness and courage. *Frontier* is an American classic.'

During the Depression era, the American Western frontier was a powerful image, which 'provided one of the most concrete and appealing depictions of American cultural identity in the theatrical arts'.[748] Evocations of the frontier drew nostalgically on 'the image of an indefinite range of unclaimed territory with unlimited natural resources [which] characterized the American view of the Western terrain'.[749] They also drew on the American ideal of individual freedom, personified in the frontiersman, an ideal whose attractions had been increased by the growth in the 1920s of an anonymous, corporate environment.

A modern-day equivalent of the frontiersman was the pilot Charles A. Lindbergh, who in 1927 became the first person to fly the Atlantic alone. 'Writers lionized the flyer for representing the American past of the frontier and the rugged individual. The fact that he flew alone was central to this celebration.'[750] However, the image of the frontier also became a focal point for many intellectuals who were critical of the ideology it represented,[751] and the Depression exacerbated criticism of American ideals as having failed in their goals. Graham's *Frontier* did not address these criticisms, and is an almost entirely celebratory dance, whose evocative power is greatly enhanced by the stage décor, designed by the sculptor Isamo Noguchi. Hindman notes that 'Graham's costume was abstract and suggestive rather than authentic Pioneer attire',[752] and in fact the dance as a whole can be viewed as an exploration of the experience of a frontier in general, rather than in a specific historical context. Walter Terry wrote: 'It was everyone's frontier, for Martha Graham was dancing *about* us as well as *for* us. This was not only a frontier but a threshold.'[753]

Graham wrote in 1937 that 'all of life today is concerned with space problems, even political life. Space language is a language we can understand. We receive so much of sensation through the eye.'[754] On one level, *Frontier* is an exploration of the structuring of space through movement.[755] Noguchi's décor uses a small fence centre stage, and behind it a rope forms a v-shape, which touches the ground in the middle and extends to the far upper corners of the stage in both directions, suggesting infinite expansion as well as division of space. According to the designer Rouben Ter-Arutunian:

> The basis of any decor for the dance is space. Dancers move essentially on the stage floor, but the audience is far less aware of the floor than of the comparatively large space in height, mostly in the back of the stage, and to the left and right of it, against which the movement is visually inscribed. This is the area that the designer is most concerned with, and whatever he places on the stage floor has to relate to this large, often permanently visible, high plane.'[756]

Graham's movement interacts closely with the lines of these objects. For instance, with both arms fully extended above her head, she stands on her right leg in front of the fence and bends her torso to her right, thereby forming a horizontal line parallel to the fence. This line is continued by her left leg, which is raised and extended parallel to the fence. At one point, positioned at the centre of both the fence and the acute angle formed by the ropes, she stands on her right leg with her left arm fully extended and raised above her head, fingers also extended, so that her body forms a vertical line that bisects the v-shaped angle formed by the ropes. At the same time, her left leg is extended and raised to the side to form a diagonal line, which exactly parallels the diagonal of the rope on that side.[757]

During the course of the dance, which lasts for five and a half minutes, Graham moves away from the fence and returns to it three times. On the second occasion that she moves away, she performs a leaping sequence that is even more vigorous and expansive than the first time, and which becomes overtly playful and girlish as she runs and skips with her arms behind her back, flouncing her shoulders. However, the music changes with what Marcia Siegel, in her excellent description of this dance, refers to as 'a mournful suggestion of a hymn tune',[758] and this is the cue for the movement to metamorphose into tiny mincing steps, traced in a square, before she returns to the fence and the fanfare sounds again. For the third time she moves away, she combines curving gestures with very vigorous, abandoned and exuberant jumping, until once again the 'hymn' tune interrupts, causing her to revert to small steps, this time also performing a cradling gesture with her arms, as if rocking a baby. Her return to the fence again marks a change of mood; and as the fanfare sounds in a triumphal climax, she sits on the fence and brings one fist down to clasp her knee, 'as if she were hammering in a stake'.[759]

Effort-shape rhythms here are based on contrasts between the growing of body shape combined with active and 'direct' attitudes towards space, and shrinking of body shape combined with more passive moments of 'indulgence' in space, characterised by meandering movements. Siegel speaks of the contrast between 'large, straight, circular movements, and small, twisting, adaptable movements'.[760] The contrasts of movement qualities, music and mood also correspond to those between the exploration and conquering of new spaces, in which the pioneer woman participated, and her repression by puritanical religion and by pressure to bear numerous children.[761]

Graham wore a long, plain pinafore with a very full skirt, which fell in heavy folds. The extremely vigorous movements that she performed (for instance, the beating up and down of her extended left leg and right arm, and her 'fan kick', where her leg flies out to the side) convey a sense of confidence and strength. Referring to her dance *Hérodiade*, Graham later described the action of a woman throwing her leg across a chair as an act of possession,[762] and in the opening of *Frontier*, the woman's attitude as she dances with the fence (which can also be seen as a *barre*) evokes precisely this sense of taking possession, which is confident, strong and joyful, accompanied by Horst's fanfare for a small wind ensemble. Some of the movements are quite 'unladylike', such as the splaying open of her legs when she returns to the fence and leans against it, rocking from side to side with almost sensual pleasure, and the scissors movement she performs with her legs while sitting on the ground.

Her energetic structuring of the space through movement connotes conquest, and it is striking that the agent of this conquest is a woman. Once again, Graham succeeded in conveying a female persona who was both feminine and assertive, female and representative of a male constituency, a 'frontierswoman' who encapsulated the (legendary) experience of the 'frontiersman'. The female dancer's body itself became a spatio-temporal frontier where the (mythical) American past was assimilated in the present, and where interior (individual) space interacted with external (geographical) space, as her gaze into the distance evoked the vastness of the American plains.

As is often the case, reconstructions of the dance brought about marked changes, closely linked here with costuming as well as movement. In the version danced by Graham, the heaviness of the costume lends substance and solidity to the movements that it literally shapes, or sculpts, in space, a substance that enhances the sense of strength conveyed by the dance. In the 1964 version, danced by Ethel Winter,[763] the skirt of the pinafore is slightly shorter, and is in a lighter fabric. The costume becomes a little more elaborate in each reconstruction - here the sleeves are slightly puffed, rather than being simply full, as in the 1935 version. In the 1974 version, danced by Janet Eilber,[764] the skirt has a large stripe around the bottom, and the sleeves are puffed. The 1985 version, performed by Peggy Lyman at the New York State Theater,[765] is even more different, in terms of movement as well as costume. The gestures are loose and large-limbed, fluid and lyrical, and the fabric of the costume is silky and flowing, creating an overall effect of theatrical glamour, far removed from the plain, simple strength of the first version.

Graham's appropriation of 'virile' qualities for her female dancers was a daring, challenging move, which came directly out of her experience as a woman and a dancer in the first decades of the century. Her 'economies of energy', with their foregrounding of effort and aggressive, thrusting rhythms, emanating from deep within and projected outwards with clearly defined spatial focus, intersected closely with the innovations of her modernist counterparts in other art forms. But, as a choreographer and dancer, Graham's modifications to habitual patterns of energy usage were not confined to the canvas or the page, but affected physical behaviour. Her technique trained her dancers in the use of nervous energy, which, she asserted, was the fundamental instrument of experience, and which had been 'ignored' in 'the puritanical concept of life'. This training enabled them to generate 'fierce energy' and release it into space, showing their audiences powerful performers whose 'heightened nerve sensitivity produces that concentration on the instant which is true living'. [766] In the 1920s and 1930s, the dancers' bodies were heavier than now, with a stronger attack, and it is therefore all the more striking that this work still carries such impact today. In Marcia Siegel's words: '[Graham's] was fierce female power, dionysiac joy that was neither provoked nor licensed by gazing males. Energy of such dynamism could be dangerous even today, which is probably why you don't see it much.'[767]

4: Punctual rhythms:
Life energies in Merce Cunningham

Dance technique is the disciplining of one's energies through physical action in order to free that energy at the desired instant. For the disciplined energy of the dancer is the *life-energy* magnified and focused for whatever brief fraction of time it lasts.
(Cunningham)[768]

Dancing provides an amplification of energy that is not provided any other way, and that's what interests me.
(Cunningham)[769]

Cunningham's kinesthetic imagination radically displaces the ground of rhythmic structure from organic progression to fragmentation. This move may be regarded as a rupturing of rhythm, even as a dehumanisation of movement.[770] However, Cunningham's new approach to rhythm triggers alertness to production of difference, and results in extreme concentration and amplification of energy. Modulations in effort intensity give way to combinations of movement qualities based on abrupt transitions and juxtapositions, e.g. sudden shifts from rapid to sustained movement (or contrasts of both taking place together), and from flexible to direct movement (or again, juxtaposition of these contrasting elements). His work also explores undecidable[771] moments, e.g. where movement appears to inhabit stillness and vice versa, and where off-balance weight-shifts displace the boundaries between maintaining and losing equilibrium.

This approach to movement represented a radical break with rhythmic practices inherited from both ballet and modern dance. The emphasis on rapidity and lightness and the separate articulation of different body parts resembled aspects of classical ballet, but the flexibility of the spine, which is at the core of Cunningham's movement style, was completely foreign to ballet, as was the dislocation of ballet vocabulary. Cunningham's rhythmic innovations were grounded in vitalist principles, which involved reacting against characteristics of modern dance that were prevalent in the late 1940s and 1950s. Modern dance's emphasis on personal expression and on partnering representing intimate emotions had parallels in contemporary social trends of false personalisation and misplaced intimacy, as discussed by contemporary cultural commentators. These features were forcefully (and controversially) resisted by the objectivity and 'coolness' of Cunningham's choreography.

Rune (1959)[772]

Performed at the Opéra Garnier in Paris, January 1998, twelve minutes into the dance, which lasts for a total of twenty-five minutes. Music is by Christian Wolff. Costumes for the 1998 version by Mark Lancaster (dresses in muted colours for the women, leotards and tights for the men).[773]

Random snapshot:

Despite the classicism of certain individual elements, the asymmetrical distribution of the dancers on the stage and their apparent lack of connection with each other (at this moment in the piece), the unconventional arm positions of the dancers in arabesque and the flexibility of the torso create a decidedly unballetic feel. We see in this dance frequent tiltings of the body and jumps executed at odd angles, which explore undecidable space between maintenance and loss of balance and between movement and stasis.

Four dancers on stage, two standing in arabesque.[774] However, the arms are out of alignment, so that, unlike in the ballet position, there is no 'unbroken line ... from the fingers of the front hand to the toe of the extended foot'.[775] A third dancer stands facing the audience, with a very open body, legs turned out, with feet about 12 inches apart (as in second position), with one arm fully raised and the other slightly raised, palm facing the body (as in demi-seconde). A fourth dancer, facing the audience, moves rapidly across the stage from stage left to stage right, with fast, regularly paced turns and shifts of weight from one foot to the other. This dancer's body opens and closes alternately, and explores different directions in space: it bends and folds as he turns, then opens as he straightens and rises, with his left arm extending to form a half-circle above his head (as in third position en haut), and his right leg and arm raised and extended to the side. As he raises and curves his left arm, his whole torso bends and inclines in this direction, and his right leg rises further.

Enter suddenly a fifth dancer from upstage left, in a rapid run similar to everyday movement, except that his legs move very fast while his arms are quite static. This dancer[776] uses a movement vocabulary similar to that of the fourth one, and advances towards the audience downstage left; but his movements are characterised by extreme speed, light use of weight, irregularly distributed pauses and bound flow, which produce a sense of contained energy. During this time, the other four dancers each perform unrelated movements, and the spectator has to choose which part of the stage to focus on, as the resulting complexity is too great to encompass at once. Attention is thereby both fragmented and intensified. Gradually, the movements synchronise, and four and then six dancers move together in unexpected unison and symmetry, before the distribution changes again.

The dance continues.

Merce Cunningham is now in the extraordinary position of having a choreographic career that has moved into its eighth decade (his first piece, *Unbalanced March*, was performed in 1938), but which is still ground-breakingly innovative. Rhythm had traditionally been based on a projective temporal structure, where 'each new direction is indicated in the preceding one', and each movement anticipated movements to come, thereby synthesising past, present and future.[777] For Klages, rhythm was holistic and grounded in temporal projection and renewal. By contrast, in Cunningham's work, rhythm as a holistic, indivisible flow of energy, which had been held to resist definition in quantitative terms, was fragmented.[778] Rhythm as indivisible flow had been systematically challenged by techniques of segmenting and cutting in Graham's work. Cunningham took this challenge further through a fundamentally punctual approach to movement. The interconnectedness of past, present and future was contested, and constant and sudden changes in space, weight, time and flow made for maximum unpredictability.

Cunningham's way of using energy combines rigorous structure with incalculability. Unlike traditional rhythm, it does not prepare the spectator for the moves that are coming next, but rather constantly takes one by surprise, producing an extreme concentration of energy in each particle of movement, which is continually being broken down. Indirect attitudes to space are often combined with direct, focused attitudes, where the dancers appear to be moving with urgency towards a goal, which suddenly shifts location. According to the dance scholar and kinesiologist Hubert Godard, 'Cunningham never stops cutting, directions in particular'.[779]

The dancers' effort attitudes are stimulated directly by the choreography itself. For instance, the relatively rapid or sustained quality of a movement in Cunningham's dance is likely to be primarily a function of the number of movements choreographed within a particular segment of time, which determines how long each movement can last. Cunningham sees rhythmic structure as based on division into segments of time, 'in which anything can happen in any sequence of movement event, and any length of stillness can take place'.[780] In Valerie Preston-Dunlop's words, '[Cunningham] is not concerned with acceleration and slowing down, but with the duration of a phrase in seconds and half-seconds. Neither he nor his dancers colour the movement over and above what has to be done in that duration'.[781] As Cunningham said recently, 'it is not a question of going fast or slow, but of putting more or less in'.[782] If many movements need to be performed within a short space of time, this will produce an effort quality of speed and a sense of urgency associated with 'fighting against' time, which is a direct effect of the choreography itself. According to Cunningham: '[The fact that] you have a certain amount of activity to do within a certain amount of time creates a kind of urgency.'[783] Also, the sequences and juxtapositions of movements in his choreography frequently involve complex combinations of effort elements that would be unthinkable outside those particular movement configurations, and which can be quite 'unnatural'.

In many respects, then, Cunningham's work would appear to reject the 'vitalist' character of rhythmic movement and to be aligned with the very tendencies which were regarded by the proponents of rhythm discussed in Chapter 1 as 'inimical to life', including classical ballet. However, his punctual approach to rhythm embodies vitalist values for his own era and cultural context. His work aims to focus and magnify 'life-energy' for a 'brief fraction of time' (see the epigraph to this chapter). 'I prefer the moment I'm in. That's the one where I'm alive. When the next one comes along, I hope to be alive in that.'[784] In a nutshell, as the dance critic Joan Acocella put it, Cunningham's dancing is 'to begin with, a celebration of energy. Cunningham is a vitalist'.[785]

Cunningham says, 'Certainly everybody including dancers can leap, sit down and get up again, but the dancer makes it apparent that the going into the air is what establishes the relationship to the air, the process of sitting down, not the position upon lying down, is what gives the iridescent and *life-quality* to dancing.'[786] He claims that 'there is an ecstasy in dance beyond the idea of movement being expressive of a particular emotion or meaning. There can be an exaltation in the aura that the freedom of a disciplined dancer provides that is far beyond any literal rendition of meaning'.[787] The function of technique is not to exhibit virtuosity for its own sake, nor to give the opportunity for 'willful and rhapsodic self-expression', but rather to enable the dancing body to become 'a channel to the source of energy'.[788]

The issue of expressiveness in Cunningham's early work, or rather the alleged lack of it, provoked heated controversy, and continues to be contentious. Cunningham has described dance as a source of energy that precedes emotions. 'In the nakedness of its energy [dance] is a source from which passion or anger may issue in a particular form, the source of energy out of which may be channeled the energy which goes into the various emotional behaviors.'[789] Mark Franko has argued that the expressive content of Cunningham's early work consisted in the dancers' experience of his choreography. Despite its negation of narrative structures, the choreography preserved the agency of individual dancers, and expressed the subjective 'drama' of their movement experience.[790] Franko maintains that Cunningham thinks of movement as a 'reaction to a physical rather than to a spiritual reality, to energy rather than to the soul'.[791] This view is supported by Gus Solomons's statement (Solomons danced in the company in 1965–68) that for him, 'doing the movement fully' meant generating emotion, 'but the emotion had nothing to do with some intellectual fantasy, it had to do with the physical feeling the choreography gave me'.[792]

As is the case for Wigman and Graham, in Cunningham's work dance is itself a source of energy. In both Wigman and Graham, energy was frequently intensified by combining potentially contradictory effort qualities, such as strong outward projection executed with bound flow (either used continuously or in order to cut movements off before completion). Conflicts between free discharge and containment or curtailment of projected energy through bound flow increase tension and maintain high levels of potential (unexpended) energy. Cunningham uses bound flow to a far greater extent than either Wigman or Graham, frequently combined with strong resistance to time, in the form of very rapid movements. He also cultivates more complex contrasts in effort qualities, such as combining direct and flexible use of space, both in the bodies of individual dancers and in groups of dancers. In fact, except for a few early pieces, all of Cunningham's choreography is for groups, and dynamics are created largely by fluctuating group structures. The distribution of groups and partners is constantly changing, with dancers alternating between unison and separate movements, and between solo work and different group configurations within a single piece.

Cunningham has embraced the potential of digital technologies for dance, and his use of computers and of 'motion capture' techniques has led to 'uncanny' effects of confusion between human and cyber identities, which recall the issues raised by uses of machinery in industrial production described in Chapter 1. The paradox that Cunningham's work comprises characteristics formerly regarded as 'inimical to life' reflects the fact that there is no so-called 'primordial ... experience of living [the human body]',[793] as this experience evolves according to material circumstances, and changing economies of energy give rise to new modes of resistance. The 1940s and 1950s were formative and decisive years for this work. Climates of homophobia, conformism, false projections of intimacy and determinism were among the factors that favoured the development of movement strategies through which embodied identities became at once more fluid and flexible and more autonomous and private. They also fostered the use of 'chance' methods, which asserted the value of objectivity, punctual energies and surprise over subjectivism, linear progression and predictable structures. I shall discuss these cultural factors in some detail below, before moving on to look at uses of energy in examples of Cunningham's work from the 1950s to the 1970s.

1. Post-war blues: Discrete dance, corporate conformism and tyranny of the 'self'

The positioning of gay men in USA culture at what was a formative period for Cunningham is likely to have been a significant factor in the evolution of his work, in terms of increasing the attractiveness of inscrutability over the expressive qualities that were held in high regard by dance critics. His choreography is frequently extremely sensuous, but not erotic: partnering and lifts tend to remain within conventionally heterosexual models, but with a focus on formal patterning rather than erotic charge, and without any hint of homoeroticism.[794] Composer John Cage was Cunningham's personal and professional partner until the Cage's death in 1992. They were always very discreet about their relationship, never referring to it in public, apart from a notorious jokey remark by Cage to the effect that 'I do the cooking, and Merce washes the dishes'.[795] Lack of tolerance for homosexuals was in evidence even at Black Mountain, the experimental community and liberal arts college that functioned in North Carolina from 1933 to 1956.[796] The long list of major figures in the USA art world associated with Black Mountain includes Cunningham, Cage and painter Robert Rauschenberg (the Merce Cunningham Company's resident designer from 1954 to 1964). After 1950, attitudes at Black Mountain became more liberal, but this was a gradual process.

From early on, John Cage had connected musical and social systems, asserting in 1937 that 'Schoenberg's method is analogous to modern society, in which the emphasis is on the group and the integration of the individual in the group',[797] and the social content of his thought grew in importance during the 1960s. Much of Cunningham's work also has implications on this level, and in fact his career started with more overt links with social issues, through texts which he composed himself. Despite his reputation for apoliticism, key features of Cunningham's uses of energy, notably his dislocated and constantly changing rhythms, were resistant to social trends in post-war America, with its influences from corporate culture, as discussed by contemporary cultural analysts.

In Cunningham's first independent concert with Jean Erdman in 1942 (see section 6 below), one of the duets, entitled 'Credo in Us', was a clear 'satire on contemporary American mores'.[798] The programme note for this piece included an extract from a text that was spoken as part of the performance. It was written by Cunningham, in a pseudo-Joycean style, but fictitiously accredited to the French Surrealist magazine *Minotaur*. In 1944, Cunningham wrote *Four Walls*, which he described as 'a dance-play lasting an hour'. David Vaughan recounts that:

To a contemporary newspaper writer, it was a one-act play dealing with 'a certain type of American family life'; a weak but loving mother, a silent father, their rebellious son and daughter, and the daughter's ineffectual fiancé ... The opening stage directions say, 'One should feel the rigid pattern of a family set by years of time, particularly in the parents, and the complete subservience to it.'[799]

Contemporary commentators and cultural historians of post-war American society have drawn attention to increasingly problematic relationships between the individual and social units such as the family and, in particular, the normative behaviour patterns of corporate culture, which promoted conformism and false intimacy, and restricted 'natural energies'. According to the scholar Daniel Belgrad, 'political and economic leaders of the post-war period equated America's national interest with the stabilization of the corporate-liberal system'.[800] Paul Goodman, who taught at Black Mountain, condemned 'the ways in which *natural energies* are absorbed, sublimated, and verbally gratified in our corporate industrial states'.[801] In 1955, Cunningham staged some dances for production by the Living Theatre of a play by Paul Goodman, *The Young Disciple*, and again in 1959 for his *The Cave at Machpelah*.[802]

Writing in 1950, David Riesman established a contrast between inner- and other-directed society, according to whether it required more than outer conformity to established norms. The inner-directed person had internalised the voices of authority, and obeyed their 'internal piloting'.[803] But according to Riesman, 'contemporary metropolitan America' was a society where 'other-direction is the dominant mode of insuring conformity ... other-direction is becoming the typical character of the "new" middle class – the bureaucrat, the family employee in business, etc.' Riesman argued that this trend was linked with the growth of service industries and the mass media, which promoted an other-directed approach through a message that 'implies constant need of approval by others'.[804] The desire to conform was causing people to 'lose their social freedom and their individual autonomy in seeking to become like each other'.[805] On this view, even Cold War attitudes to Russia were linked with other-directedness: 'on the international scene the focus is on what the significant others, in this case the Russians, are doing'.[806] Diffusion of information by mass media had the effect of atomising, personalising – or rather 'pseudopersonalising' – political events.[807] Paul Goodman contrasted unfavourably 'role', which depended on 'the interpersonal expectation of the others' with 'identity', which 'was defined by its task, mission, product'.[808]

William Whyte, in *The Organization Man* (1956),[809] also criticised the corrosive effects of conformity produced by a corporate-driven culture. He defined three core characteristics of this social ethic: 'a belief in the group as the source of creativity; a belief in "belongingness" as the ultimate need of the individual; and a belief in the application of science to achieve the belongingness'.[810] Whyte emphasised that it was not only organisations themselves that were the problem, but also the individual's seduction by them and his ensuing complicity. 'The group is a tyrant; so also is it a friend, and *it is both at once* ... unless the individual understands that this conflict of allegiances is inevitable, he is intellectually without defenses ... For ultimately his tyranny is self-imposed ... He is intimidated by normalcy'.[811]

Richard Sennett, writing in 1974 about advanced industrial society, argued against the belief that society was 'meaningful' only when converted into 'a grand psychic system'. Sennett spoke of an 'obsession with persons at the expense of more impersonal social relations'. This produced a blurring of the boundaries between public and private life, and 'leads us to believe community is an act of mutual self-disclosure and to undervalue the community relations of strangers, particularly those which occur in cities'. He argued that 'masses of people are concerned with their single life histories and particular emotions as never before; this concern has proved to be a trap rather than a liberation'. There was an expectation of 'intimacy' – which connoted 'warmth, trust, and open expression of feeling' – throughout the range of our experience, and the failure of 'the world outside', the 'impersonal world', to meet this expectation, led to the view that it was 'stale and empty'.[812] Like Whyte, Sennett evoked the twin actions of tyranny and seduction to explain what he called 'the sense of claustrophobia which oppresses so many people today'. He argued that the real tyranny was that of the self, which, 'as both secularity and capitalism arrived at new forms in the last century ... came to define social relations'. The self 'became a social principle', and 'at that point, the public realm of impersonal meaning and impersonal action began to wither'. The inherited problem was 'the effacement of the *res publica* by the belief that social meanings are generated by the feelings of individual human beings'.[813]

The tyranny of intimacy was 'the measurement of society in psychological terms'. This misplaced intimacy had distorted our understanding of the purposes of the city, as 'the instrument of *impersonal* life, the mold in which diversity and complexity of persons, interests and tastes become available as social experience'. The city should be 'the forum in which it becomes meaningful to join with other persons without the compulsion to know them as persons'.[814] In fact, Sennett's 'intimacy' can be seen in terms similar to Riesman's 'other-directedness', in the sense that the latter involves seeking the approval of a personalised 'other', and therefore leads to similarly misplaced projections of 'personality' onto the outer world. Sennett argued that an important consequence of loss of self-distance (which he dated from the nineteenth century) was the undermining of the ability to 'play'. 'The self of motivations intervenes in an intimate society to block people from feeling free to play with the presentation of feelings as objective, formed signs.'[815]

Another manifestation of pseudo-personalisation in bureaucratic culture is the prominence of conspiracy theories. Peter Knight argues that: 'during the twentieth century, and since the foundation of the CIA in 1947 in particular, American politics has increasingly relied on clandestine means to pursue its goals, and a bureaucratic culture of secrecy has come to be taken for granted'.[816] According to Timothy Melley, conspiracy theories are linked with 'a pervasive set of anxieties about the way technologies, social organisations, and communication systems may have reduced human autonomy and uniqueness'.[817] Conspiracy theories are attractive in this context because they make it possible to de-anonymise undesirable forces at work in society by (falsely) identifying agents at their source. Melley has pointed out the close similarities between Vance Packard's *The Hidden Persuaders* (1957), which identified advertisers and others as guilty of manipulating behaviour through unconscious persuasion, and J. Edgar Hoover's *Masters of Deceit* (1958), where, similarly to the Cold War, communism was identified as 'a revolutionary "conspiracy" with extraordinary powers'.[818]

By contrast, Cunningham's kinesthetic imagination resisted tendencies to conformism and pseudopersonalisation by foregrounding differential and impersonal energies. In his choreography, identity was not 'other-directed', because the dancers were not dependent on any other dancer as a central focus: rather, each dancer functioned as a separate centre. The relationships between dancers were constantly changing, and were structured by the choreography's impersonal, dislocated rhythms, rather than by emotional dynamics or personal choices, resisting false intimacy and the 'tyranny of the self'. Not only were partnering and the formation of groups subject to constant change, but individual dancers' energies remained very self-contained. Also, the deterministic mentality characteristic of conspiracy culture was challenged through the role of chance (see section 5 below) and the associated undermining of linear narrative. Constant 'cutting' produced high excitement and con-centration of energy, and replaced rhythmic progression towards a climax. The celebration of play (following the Dadaists) in certain pieces (e.g. *Variations V*, which will be discussed below) also resisted the determinism of the unconscious and the invasive probings of psychoanalysis.

Although Cunningham is insistent that 'dance is not social relation-ships', he concedes that 'it may influence them'.[819] He sees art as 'a practice zone for living',[820] and envisages the function of his dance as emancipatory, in terms of providing a model for the separateness of individuals and their interaction as a group. Vernon Shetley argues that: 'in the polity whose first principle is the individual ... a sudden impulse of unification may appear, but that impulse competes with those that make for separation and individuation, and Cunningham privileges neither the centripetal nor the centrifugal moment.'[821] According to Cunningham:

> each [dancer] in the company is a soloist, and in a given dance we may act sometimes separately and sometimes together ... It is an anarchic process of working ... each person and the work he does is independent, and he acts with the others, not competitively, but complimentarily [sic] ... Each person, observant of the others, is allowed to act freely.[822]

Cunningham's treatment of each individual dancer as a 'centre' often creates the sense that each dancer inhabits a very private world. Of *Summerspace* (1958), he commented that his work with individual dancers may be 'what gives the dance its sense of beings in isolation in their motion along with the sense of continuous appearance and vanishing'.[823]

According to Shetley, 'Cunningham finds a liberating potential in flux; each dancer traces a unique route through the course of the dance, freely entering into group activity, just as freely as stepping out as a soloist'.[824] Cunningham affirms his belief 'that life is constantly changing and shifting, that we live in a democratic society, and that people and things in nature are mutually independent of, and related to each other'.[825] In an interview given in 1998, he spelled out his attitude to politics:

> Our way of working is political, but not overtly so, rather in the way we work together ... We have traveled all these years with separate individuals, each one doing their work; I don't tell the musicians what they have to do, nor they me, and it's the same with the artists. For me, this is political movement ... I never talk about it because I'm not an activist. And I think that all governments, whoever they are, are only motivated by greed and power.[826]

In a telephone interview with me in April 2004, in the context of a discussion of the events of 9/11, Merce commented: 'governments are impossible, the President certainly is'.[827]

2. Forgetting habits: Dance and play

There are significant similarities between the aspects of post-war American society I discussed above and the manifestations of 'instrumental reason' in bureaucratic procedures and goal-oriented behaviour that I outlined in Chapter 1. The irreverent defiance of artistic and social conventions embodied in the playful mood and ironic distance of Dada as it was manifested from 1916 to 1922, first at the Cabaret Voltaire in Zurich, and then also in Paris and New York and later in several German cities, offered ways of resisting conformism, other-directedness and misplaced 'intimacy'. In the late 1950s, the controversial term 'neo-Dadaism' was coined to designate art that was made in the USA between the abstract expressionist period and pop art, and which had significant similarities with historical Dada. 'Artists' use of chance as a compositional method, their interest in performance and other ephemeral manifestations, and their challenges to the conventional exhibition, distribution, and commodification of art all reflect major shifts effected by Dada.'[828]

Another link was the use of everyday materials. Cage, in Jill Johnson's words, 'idolised' Marcel Duchamp (the most famous Dadaist and inventor of the idea of the 'readymade'), whom he had known since the 1940s (and with whom he loved to play chess). Rauschenberg's famous erasure in 1953 of a drawing by Willem de Kooning could be seen as a typically 'dadaist' gesture. He, Jasper Johns and Allan Kaprow were the first artists to be designated as neo-Dadaists. Cage appears to have been the source of Rauschenberg's knowledge of Dada,[829] and he was the main link between Dada and the activities of the Fluxus group of New York artists in the 1960s.[830] However, exasperated by 'another superfluous label', Cage exclaimed: 'If they say I'm neo-Dada, I'll arrange somehow to free myself from that category', and mischievously went on to affirm his attraction to abstract expressionist painting.[831]

Cunningham's working methods, which were closely related to neo-Dadaism, exemplify kinesthetic imagination as an open-ended process of learning and habit change. One way in which expressiveness (as opposed to self-expression) and distancing can be combined is for the artist to enter into a dialogue with the physical properties of the medium, where, as in Cunningham's work, 'the dance assumes an expressive character that derives from the choreographer's materials – the dancers' bodies'[832]

– or, in painting, a dialogue with the medium of paint, as in abstract expressionism. Paul Goodman (cited above) saw the learning process whereby 'the work of an artist becomes unpredictably new to him as he handles the material medium'[833] as a model for healthy experience.

The dance scholar Roger Copeland has long argued that, rather than being allied with abstract expressionism, Cunningham should be seen as moving away from 'inner' experience, which, in the world of dance in the 1940s, was epitomised in Graham's work of that period.[834] However, it should be noted that the dialogue with the medium in abstract expressionism was not entirely unmediated, but involved elements of distancing and reflection. In fact, Daniel Belgrad has disputed the similarity, advanced by Stephen Polcari, between Graham's work in the 1940s and abstract expressionism, on the grounds that her work of this period was heavily dependent on narrative, and was lacking in the self-reflexivity found in abstract expressionism.[835]

Cunningham's desire to break personal memory patterns through the use of chance methods in choreography (see section 5 below) is paralleled in Paul Goodman's aim to 'wrest the expressive body out from the net of habit'.[836] Cunningham once said of his way of working: 'I ordinarily start with myself; not always, it may be with one or two of the dancers. But then out of this the action begins to assume its own proportions, and other possibilities appear as the dance proceeds.'[837] He has also referred to the role played by 'slips of the foot, rather than slips of the pen' in the choreographic process.[838] Clearly, Cunningham seeks in his dance (as Cage did in his music), to make discoveries that are centred in embodied movement itself, through a process of kinesthetic imagination that promotes self-distance and play rather than self-revelations of an emotional nature. 'I think I am an explorer. My life has been spent with movement, with steps. There are always more if one is lucky enough to find them. You sometimes try to act like a tourist outside, looking at something rather than being so concerned with your own ideas.'[839]

This also meant taking the dancers themselves as a starting point. Since the early days, Cunningham has choreographed work with particular dancers in mind. According to Marianne Simon, one of his earliest dancers:

> Merce was most attentive to the way he used the material he had, which was the dancers. It was my impression during that early period in the fifties, that he gave us things to do that were based on who we were and how we moved individually. Furthermore, he made movements for us that were a bit beyond what we could do, so that we had to grow around them. Yet his dances were criticized as being abstract and

dehumanized. I thought they were extraordinarily personal, because they had to do with who we dancers in the company were, how we moved, what our quality of movement was.'[840]

Early Cunningham dancer Carolyn Brown affirmed that Cunningham 'uses everything that a dancer brings', and Kristy Santimyer, a recent member of the company, said that Cunningham made parts that 'used dancers' weaker sides'.[841] Cunningham has always been keen for his dancers to discover their own way of doing his movement, and he expects it to look different on different dancers. (This is not of course to be confused with improvisation, where the dancers can take the initiative in inventing their own movement.)

3. New directions in dance

Cunningham's primary interest, as he has explained on countless occasions, is in movement itself. Although he has no objection to spectators finding specific meanings in his work – indeed, he makes the point himself that human movement is unavoidably expressive – he is adamant that his starting point is the body.

> There's no thinking involved in my choreography ... I don't work through images or ideas – I work through the body ... If the dancer dances – which is not the same as having theories about dancing or wishing to dance or trying to dance – everything is there. When I dance, it means: this is what I am doing.[842]

Dancers who performed in Cunningham's early works have contested these disclaimers, saying that although Cunningham refused to disclose what his group dances were about, or denied that they were about anything, they 'knew better'. The dancers would make up 'elaborate stories about what was actually going on', which made Cunningham laugh, but 'didn't bother him so long as they didn't intrude on his sense of dynamics and timing'.[843] Remy Charlip commented: 'Particularly in his solos, what he danced was directly in touch with his feelings and had immediate emotional content.'[844]

Carolyn Brown said that Cunningham's 1944 solo, *Root of an Unfocus*, 'seemed to tell a story, to be *about* something. (Merce denies this ...)'.[845] She advocated scepticism about the Cunningham 'dogma'. 'You shouldn't believe everything that is said to you ... You have to dig around to find out that there are other things going on in the work besides chance. That's the dogma, I know, but look deeper.'[846] Of *Septet* (1953), she said that it 'has a very definite story', with named sections, and that Cunningham had been planning to use appropriate sets, but 'Cage's influence – to have no stories and no narrative – obliterated all that early history of the piece'. She continued: 'now, I think *all* of his dances (and I'm not talking only about through [sic] my time there) are about something beyond "just the steps"', but added: 'it's not important either that we knew it or that the audience knows it'.[847] Marcia Siegel argued in 1970 that 'a Cunningham dance *is* a theatrical entity', and drew attention to the importance of the mood of individual pieces: 'each piece usually has an overall sensibility that is apparent to everyone'.[848]

Cunningham likes to tell the story of *Winterbranch* (1964), which was performed in different parts of the world, and was interpreted in wildly diverse ways depending on the context. He frequently comments gleefully on these divergent interpretations, which included race riots and nuclear war: 'Everybody was drawing on his own experience, whereas I had simply made a piece which was involved with *falls*, the idea of bodies falling.'[849] *Root of an Unfocus* (1944), which he later admitted 'was about fear – one of the predominant things in my life',[850] was also the first piece Cunningham made with John Cage where dance and music were substantially independent of one another. The speeds and accents within the dance phrases were unrelated to the musical beat. Dance and music were linked only through a time structure. 'It was divided into time units, and the dance and the music would come together at the beginning and the end of each unit, but in between they would be independent of each other'.[851]

For Cunningham, the thematic content of *Root of an Unfocus* was of less importance than the way in which the content took shape through the dance's time structure, but he noted that 'this was the thing everybody missed'.[852] In his account, there is a clear progression from the first part, where the solo figure is the object of external aggression ('it is as though there is something attacking him in some way'), to confrontation with this fear, culminating in 'the realization that the fear is in yourself'. The structure facilitated the expressive dimension in that it did not impose a return to an earlier point in time, as in an 'A-B-A' structure: 'the idea which comes with A-B-A – that you do the A, then do the B, and then you go back comfortably to the A again.'[853] The dance 'began in conscious awareness of something outside the individual, and after its passage in time ended with the person crawling out of the light. The time structure allowed for this in a way that I felt more conventional structures, [e.g.] theme and variations, ABA, would not.'[854]

As can be seen from articles published in *Dance Observer* at the time, the period of the mid-to-late forties was marked by considerable uncertainty about the future direction of modern dance. By the mid-1940s, there was insecurity about dance's over-reliance on expressive symbolism, and a sense that a less personal approach was needed, but also a reluctance to conceive of the value of dance works in terms other than 'expressive' and 'theatrical' (in the realist, psychological sense). There was, however, a marked emphasis on 'universality'. In a 1945 article, dance educationalist Margaret H'Doubler referred to 'expressive forms in dance' that were 'embedded in muscle tension, and in the tensions arising from stresses in structure itself', and she declared that 'modern dance is the contemporary phase of dance in its evolution towards its destined goal of greater universality'.[855] In 'Grace and clarity', published in *Dance Observer* in 1944, John Cage criticised modern dance as being too insecure and too dependent on the personalities and physiques of individual leaders. He argued for the importance of 'clarity of rhythmic structure', whose function was 'universal', rather than 'private' (objective rather than subjective). In a similar vein, Cunningham later said of modern dance in the 1950s that 'it was almost impossible to see a movement in the modern dance during that period not stiffened by literary or personal connection'.[856]

Cage argued that in ballet, by contrast with modern dance, the most important attribute was clarity of rhythmic structure.

> It may seem at first thought [sic] that rhythmic structure is not of primary importance. However, a dance, a poem, a piece of music ... occupies a length of time, and the manner in which this length of time is divided first into large parts and then into phrases (or built up from phrases to form eventual larger parts) is the work's very life structure.

By 'grace', Cage meant a 'play with and against the clarity of the rhythmic structure'. He singled out for criticism the structure of Graham's then recent work, *Deaths and Entrances* (1943), while praising early works such as *Frontier* as 'magnificently moving and clear'.[857] However, these early works were no longer innovatory in contemporary terms, and while Lois Balcom, writing in 1944, praised *Primitive Mysteries* as 'kinetically ecstatic' and 'visually luminous', she also expressed the opinion that the 'starkness' of Graham's early work (as exemplified in *Primitive Mysteries* and *Lamentation*), was experienced by contemporary audiences as eloquent, and even 'romantic'.[858]

In the 1940s, Graham's work was widely regarded as embodying the qualities most valued by dance critics – humanity, psychological depth, theatricality – and would move further in this direction in the late forties and fifties, with her intensely introspective and dramatic works based on Greek mythology. Her psychological realism and profound emotional impact on the spectator were highly praised. Writing in 1945, Robert Sabin described *Appalachian Spring* (1944) as 'a touching picture of human relationships, timeless and yet very real'. He found in Graham a 'higher virtuosity in which power and brilliance of technique are completely subservient to the artist's communication',[859] as shown in her inflection of rhythm and cadence in the movement of the young woman in *Appalachian Spring*, which evoked an 'inner change' from youth to maturity. He felt that *Mirror Before Me* 'actually does purge the spectator with pity and terror'.[860] However, criticisms were also voiced of Graham's over-reliance in her more recent works on theatrical props and literary symbolism. Nik Krevitsky had high praise for Isamu Noguchi's set in *Night Journey* (1947), but found it 'intrusive rather than intrinsic to the work'.[861] Richard Lippold, reviewing a Graham programme in 1946, was critical of her 'over-occupation with symbol in *Dark Meadow*' (1946), and commented on the need for her to direct expression 'away from the probing of personal frustration'.

This criticism was juxtaposed with praise of Cunningham's dancing in Graham's works, which re-focused attention on movement:

> Merce Cunningham's 'March' [in Graham's *Letter to the World*, 1940] has become a classic, and his solo, to his own choreography, in *Appalachian Spring* [Graham,1944], brings new life to a piece whose backward-looking is indicated in its sub-titled explanation [*Ballet for Martha*], and he restates here a faith in the magic and power of movement itself.[862]

Reviewers of Cunningham's early performances were frequently very enthusiastic about his dancing, but bewildered by his choreography, which they found hostile to their values. Commentators tended to equate assault on psychological expressivity with the undermining of a fundamentally 'human' interiority.[863] Robert Sabin, writing in *Dance Observer* (May 1944) supported Cunningham's belief in dance as 'an independent means of expression with its own laws and objectives', and felt that he could become 'an artist of the highest rank', but only on condition that he 'get more humanity into his dancing'. He was impressed by the solos, *Root of an Unfocus* (described by Mary Phelps in 1946 as 'fast, energetic and conflicted')[864] and *Totem Ancestor* (1942), which he characterised as 'psychological studies of a penetration truly amazing in so young a dancer', but he maintained that Cunningham needed to 'put more "theatre" and more warmth and variety into his work' if he wanted to appeal to a less specialised audience.[865]

Cunningham began choreographing in 1938, but first made his name as a dancer, rather than a choreographer, in Graham's company, which he joined in 1939. Encouraged by Cage, he performed an independent programme in 1942, together with two other Graham dancers (Jean Erdman and Nina Fonaroff), first at Bennington College, Vermont, and later in New York, with Cage writing the score for *Credo in Us* (a duet with Jean Erdman) and *Totem Ancestor* (a solo, first performed in New York). He performed with Erdman again in 1943, and in 1944 he gave his first joint concert with John Cage, from which he says he dates his beginning, and in which they experimented with new time structures and dissociation of music and dance, which would continue to be central to their work.[866] The influence of Cage's thinking, especially on the use of chance in composition, led Cunningham in a more avant-garde direction, away from traditional theatre, and his espousal of broadly neo-Dadaist ideas put his work into a very different category from that of other dancers at the time, and much closer to musicians and painters, who constituted his main following in the early days.[867] This situation made it difficult for Cunningham to be accepted in the dance world, but also meant that he was well placed to offer radically new directions in dance.

4. Chance and energy

Cage began to use chance operations in his musical composition at the beginning of the 1950s, first with his own charts, based on the 'magic square', in which he replaced numbers with sounds and 'groups of sounds',[868] and subsequently drawing on the *I Ching*, or *Book of Changes*, to which he was introduced by the composer, Christian Wolff. 'He drew up charts for such elements as tempo, duration, kind of sound, and dynamics, then made choices among them by tossing coins, as when obtaining oracles from the *I Ching*.'[869] Composing directly onto magnetic tape encouraged working with temporal structure in terms of segments of time. 'The measurement of the magnetic tape is in inches – a spatial measure, that is, rather than metric beats in time, as traditionally in music'.[870] Cunningham said: 'I know for me one of the things that changed my thinking about time very much was electronic music, because I suddenly realized that I couldn't count in the way that I had counted conventional, metrically arranged music.'[871] The abrupt transitions between very different types of sound stimulated him to think about how to effect the rapid transitions between radically different movements for which he has become famous.[872] He also recalled that 'one of the reasons I began to use random methods in choreography [was] to break the patterns of personal remembered physical co-ordinations.'[873] Remy Charlip referred to Cunningham's 'conviction that it's possible for anything to follow anything else ...the resultant experience being *free and discovered rather than bound and remembered.*'[874]

Cunningham's use of chance methods involves first preparing 'elaborate charts for such elements as body parts, directions, the duration of movements, and the order of choreographed sequences. Then he composes a dance by selecting elements from the charts through arbitrary means. These include coin-tossing, dice-throwing, or hexagrams from the *I Ching*.'[875] These methods are used to determine variables such as 'the locations of the dancers, the speed with which phrases are performed, the order in which the steps are combined, the number of dancers who might appear in a sequence'.[876] His first application of chance methods in determining the order of chronological sequences was in *Sixteen Dances for Soloist and the Company of Three* (1951). The choreography was concerned with what Cunningham called 'expressive behavior, in this case the nine permanent emotions of Indian classical aesthetics, four light and four dark with tranquility the ninth and pervading one', and the order of these sections was decided by tossing a coin.[877] In *Excerpts from Symphonie pour un homme seul* (1952), choreographed to music by Pierre Schaeffer with the collaboration of Pierre Henry, and composed directly onto magnetic tape, chance procedures were used to choreograph everyday gestures, which allowed amateur dancers to participate. 'Historically, *Excerpts from Symphonie pour un homme seul* marked the first time everyday gestures were used in performance simply as movement – that is to say, without mimetic significance.'[878]

In *Suite by Chance* (1953), sequences of movements were also constructed by chance methods. Remy Charlip recounted in 1954 that 'for this dance, a large series of charts was made numbering body movements of various kinds ...; a chart numbering lengths of time ...; a chart numbering directions in space'.[879] In a few dances of the late 1950s and early 1960s, Cunningham used elements of indeterminacy or open form, where the dancers themselves exercised a degree of choice.[880] Usually, however, as David Vaughan has stated, 'Cunningham has preferred to use chance not in the performance of his choreography but in its composition'.[881] Unlike music, in dance there are risks of injury if unexpected collisions take place on stage. Performance is regulated by the patterns generated by chance procedures, which are both highly structured and unpredictable.

Cunningham's emphasis on breaking with remembered patterns and on dislocating expectations of progression introduced a radically fragmented approach to rhythmic structure, which brought into play different ways of experiencing time, encouraging a flexible attitude to the future as well as freedom from the past. 'In life, if you decide on something, the next minute it has changed. If you count on anything, it doesn't work. So you have to put yourself, it seems to me, in a situation in which you don't count on anything, and then deal with whatever arises.'[882] Cunningham's undermining of progressive linear structures was in keeping with experience of time in contemporary culture, as epitomised for him by 'the whole way that television presents things, the fact that you can change it by switching channels, so that you don't have a logical continuity'.[883] In 1952, he expressed his dissatisfaction with modern dance's reliance on musical structures characterised by 'theme and variation, and associated devices – repetition, inversion, development and manipulation'. Experience of 'crisis saturation' in contemporary life meant that notions of progression and climax had become less meaningful.

> There is ... a tendency to imply a crisis to which one goes and then in some way retreats from. Now I can't see that crisis any longer means a climax, unless we are willing to grant that every breath of wind has a climax (which I am), but then that obliterates climax, being a surfeit of such. And since our lives, both by nature by the newspapers [sic], are so full of crisis that one is no longer aware of it, then it is clear that life goes on regardless, and further that each thing can be and is separate from each and every other, viz: the continuity of the newspaper headlines. Climax is for those who are swept [sic] by New Year's Eve.'[884]

(Compare Riesman's critique of the mass media announcing 'a world crisis and a new toothpaste with similarly breathless voice'.[885]) This lack of hierarchy also applied to relations of cause and effect. Cage declared in 1961: 'That is the real situation: that everything causes everything else. In other words, it is much more complicated than our scientists like to admit'.[886] The ubiquity of crisis and of cause and effect removed the rationale for privileging some examples over others, as in conventional narrative structures. As noted in *Dance Observer* in 1954, for Cunningham, continuity 'is thought of as being the continuum of one thing after another, rather than being related by psychological or thematic or other cause-and-effect devices.'[887]

Cunningham understands 'continuity' as a sequence of events without hierarchising, deterministic factors. For instance, the programme note for *Un jour ou deux* (1973) stated that: 'there are no predetermined characters and there is no prearranged story, so the characters of the dance become the characters of the individual dancers themselves, and *the story is the continuity of the events as they succeed one another*'.[888] Time here is non-hierarchical, and change is dissociated from progression. All moments have equal value, instead of being subordinated to climactic points. By employing chance means in the choreography, 'the presence of a continuous metric beat is largely eliminated in the dancing, since the tempo is changed so often that the sense of a particular tempo disappears.'[889] Moreover, rather than acquiring significance through its relation to past and future, each present moment of movement can be broken down into a complex set of relationships to a number of events that are happening at that moment, but which, because they exceed the perceptive capacity of the spectator, also 'split open' the moment by making the spectator aware of what he or she is unable fully to register.[890]

This can happen even in solo performances, but it is accentuated in Cunningham's group works by decentred use of stage space, in which different groupings of dancers perform unconnected movements simultaneously. This treatment of space, where the central point for each dancer is where they are located at a given moment, also reinforces the autonomy of individual dancers, a characteristic that counters pressures towards conformism and hierarchical bureaucratic structures. According to Vernon Shetley, 'one of the notable difficulties in setting [Cunningham's] work on dancers trained in other techniques is getting them to overcome the gravity exerted by center stage'.[891] In Cunningham's collaborations with other artists, music, décor, lighting and movement can be juxtaposed in the same space at the same time, without previously defined connections. These strategies have the effect of demanding from the spectator what Cage called 'polyattentiveness', which can be defined as 'the simultaneous apprehension of two or more unrelated phenomena'.[892]

Cage was profoundly influenced by his study of Indian music and philosophy with Gita Sarabhai, and by Dr T. Daisetz Suzuki, who lectured on Zen Buddhism at Columbia University in the late 1940s. Cunningham also attended some of these lectures, as Vaughan reports, 'when rehearsals allowed', and 'his ideas about structure, like Cage's, were increasingly influenced by these Eastern philosophies'.[893] Among the principles Cage adopted from Suzuki was the relinquishment of external frameworks to measure 'the life of things', in favour of a recognition that 'each thing is at the center'. 'Therefore, there is a plurality of centers, a multiplicity of centers. And they are all interpenetrating and, as Zen would add, non-obstructing.'[894] He was also inspired by Suzuki's principle of 'non-dualism'. 'You don't revert to a duality of figure and background, or determinacy and indeterminacy, etc. You remain *between* one and two. You can't choose, because everything comes at once. There is temporal simultaneity.'[895]

This world-view is non-hierarchical. In Cage's words, as reported by Francine du Plessix Gray:

> No value judgments are possible because nothing is better than anything else. Art should not be different than life but an act within life. Like all of life, with its accidents and chances and variety and disorder and only momentary beauties. Only different from life in this sense: that in life appreciation is passive like listening to a sound complex of bird, waterfall and engine, whereas in art it must be a voluntary act on the part of the creator and of the listener.[896]

Each sound should be heard for itself, rather than as part of a hierarchical, organised rhythmic structure.

> When you listen to sounds that share a periodic rhythm, what you hear is necessarily something other than the sounds themselves. You don't hear the sounds – you hear the fact that the sounds have been organized. Zen cultivates this flowing back towards non-organization, that is, towards sounds as such, in and for themselves.[897]

Cunningham's use of chance methods in composition (complemented since 1991 by the use of the computer program LifeForms)[898] led to complex and unexpected combinations and sequences of movement, whose execution required from the dancers a complete concentration and intense alertness to the present moment. 'This attention given the jump … makes it clear that each act of life can be its own history: past, present and future, and can be so regarded, which helps to break the chains that so often follow dancers' feet around.'[899]

Discussing Cunningham's early work, Charlip recounted how he would make a chart of, for instance, possibilities for the head ('"look down", "look up", "look to the right", "look to the left", "turn back"'), arms ('in second, fifth and parallel') and body placements ('twisting, bending, stretching').

Then Merce tossed coins at the charts. He might get a head looking up while the torso was turning while the arm was moving back ... Merce was able to do amazing moves, where you'd be heading in one direction with your body and suddenly your leg would be whipping you around in another direction.

He continued: 'For the dancer, the challenge was always to do completely what he'd given you, down to the last syncopation, pinky, or whatever. That was really quite difficult and kept us so busy we didn't have time to think about anything else.'[900] According to Marianne Simon: 'what we projected was exactly what the movement was and nothing else'.[901] Cunningham emphasised the importance of performing each movement in itself, with maximum precision. He aimed to combine complete awareness with complete detachment: 'Our ecstasy in dance comes from the possible gift of freedom, the exhilarating moment that this exposing of the bare energy can give us. What is meant is not license, but freedom, that is, a complete awareness of the world and at the same time a detachment from it.'[902]

Cunningham sees the use of chance methods in composition as giving access to a source of energy that transcends the individual. In 1978, he affirmed: 'when I choreograph a piece by tossing pennies – by chance, that is – I am finding my resources in that play, which is not the product of *my* will, but which is an energy and a law which I too obey.'[903] He wrote in 'The impermanent art' (1952): 'The feeling I have when I compose in this way [by chance] is that I am in touch with a natural resource far greater than my own personal inventiveness could ever be, much more universally human than the particular habits of my own practice.' Dance is a primal 'source of energy', and it is 'the blatant exhibiting of this energy, i.e. of energy geared to an intensity high enough to melt steel in some dancers, that gives the great excitement'.[904] The 'raison d'être' of dance is the liberation of energy through 'physical action'. Energy is released through 'a whipping of the mind and body into an action that is so intense, that for the brief moment involved, the mind and body are one'.[905] It is 'just this fusion at a white heat' that gives 'the look of serenity and objectivity that a fine dancer has'.[906]

5. Energy fields and unpredictable events

Carolyn Brown remarked astutely in 1968: 'The desire to absent one's ego from the work, to allow the work to be itself, is of course a paradoxical one. The work will not come into existence on its own; it must be initiated ... by choosing to make a work by chance one makes a choice, one asserts one's ego.'[907] However, the unpredictability of the impersonal chance method results in an openness to immediate experience, which is at the core of the 'culture of spontaneity' discussed by Belgrad in the book of that name. This was exemplified in cultural practices that emphasised the spontaneous creative process, including abstract expressionist painting; the writing of William Carlos Williams, Charles Olson and the Beat poets; gestalt therapy; bebop jazz; and Zen. Belgrad discusses the importance for the avant-garde, in the late 1940s and through the 1950s, of the 'energy field' model, which was inspirational for Cunningham:

> As opposed to the atomistic individualism of classical liberalism, the energy field model of human experience defined it as emerging from a 'field of force' that was prior to any individual identity ... The avant-garde's most important source of the 'field' model of social relations was twentieth-century physics, which defined objects as events constituted by a field of energy in space-time ... modern (Einsteinean) physics ... viewed the energy field as primary, and the 'objects' in it as complicated perturbations of that field.[908]

In 1963, Cunningham choreographed *Field Dances*, and Jasper Johns named one of his pictures *Field Painting*. Cunningham still likes to cite Einstein's statement 'There are no fixed points in space', which inspired the title of his 1986 dance, *Points in Space*.[909]

Belgrad sees Cunningham's decentred use of space as evidence of his 'reliance on an aesthetic of the energy field'[910]. The abstract expressionist painters Barnett Newman and Robert Motherwell (who visited Black Mountain in 1945) and the poet Charles Olson (who taught at Black Mountain, and studied dance with Cunningham) saw 'energy' as central to their work. The philosopher Alfred North Whitehead (whose lectures Motherwell attended) posited the fundamental unity of all forms of energy, including the physical and the emotional. He gave centre stage to the body, and stated that 'the energetic activity considered in physics is the emotional intensity entertained in life'.[911] Against Freudian notions of a libidinal economy with finite energy, Goodman favoured a model where spontaneous expenditure of energy led only to more energy. Goodman's text on this topic, 'The Emperor of China', was published by the avant-garde magazine *Possibilities*, jointly edited by Robert Motherwell, Harold Rosenberg and John Cage from 1947–8.

'Chance' methods, rather than starting from the psyche and projecting its dynamics onto the outer, public sphere, start from an impersonal structure in order to generate different and unpredictable ways of moving, necessitating from the dancer an intense alertness and concentration in the present, and from the spectator a complex and multilayered perception and openness to the unexpected. The unusual degree of independence of dance and music in Cunningham's work, where dancers frequently hear the music for the first time at the premiere, means that they have to rely more than usual on an internal sense of timing, as well as being extremely alert to each other. They have to concentrate on the movement to the exclusion of frequently distracting and unfamiliar external stimuli, such as very loud music or bright lights. This approach counters attitudes of passivity, boredom and 'never being present in one's action', ascribed by Sennett to some white-collar workers.[912]

The physical key to openness to change in movement is flexibility of the spine, and Cunningham's model here is 'the animal', who 'makes [the spine] his physical conscience'. The arms and legs are 'the spine's extensions', so that speed comes, not from 'the feet or arms twiddling at some fantastic tempo', but from 'the diligence with which the spine allows the legs and arms to go'.[913] Speaking of the evolution of Cunningham's technique, Carolyn Brown said that 'the real goal was to develop speed'.[914] The spine is almost a living entity in itself, which 'can coil and explode like a spring, can grow taut or loose, can turn on its own axis or project into space directions'. This is the source of the effect, frequently produced by Cunningham's dances, of continuity in change, where extremely rapid and unexpected adjustments of speed and direction, combined with shifting distributions of weight without definitive metrical accents or breaks, create high levels of alertness in spectators as well as in dancers. In Cunningham's words:

> If one uses the torso as the moving force itself, allowing the spine to be the motivating force in a visual shift of balance, the problem is to sense how far the shift of balance can go in any direction and in any time arrangement, and then move instantaneously towards any other direction and in other time arrangements, without having to break the flow of movement by a catching of the weight, whether by an actual shift of weight, or a break in the time, or by other means.[915]

Earle Brown stated that Cage 'uses chance as a means to remove his own memory and the memory of the musicians from the process, in order for them all to make an almost pure event'.[916] As is well known, the notion of an 'event' was the basis of a new departure in performance, which became popular in the 1960s. Cunningham also used the term for the first time in 1964 to designate a performance consisting of excerpts from full-length works, put together in a new sequence, which could be performed in non-conventional spaces.[917] Cage credited the influence of the Zen text, *Huang Po*, along with that of Antonin Artaud and Marcel Duchamp in his creation, in 1952 at Black Mountain College, of the prototype of a new kind of theatrical event. '"All fused together into the possibility of making a theatrical event in which the things that took place were not causally related to one another – but in which there is a penetration, anything that happened after that happened in the observer himself."'[918] This performance, which combined poetry (Charles Olson, Mary Caroline Richards), painting (Rauschenberg), music (David Tudor on the piano, Rauschenberg playing recordings) and dance (Cunningham) has been seen as a precursor of what in the 1960s would be called 'happenings', following *18 Happenings in 6 Parts* by Allan Kaprow (who had studied with Cage), which was presented in 1959. The defining feature of a 'happening' for Michael Kirby (writing in 1965) was that it must contain a number of discrete elements, with an alogical structure, by contrast with the more minimalist 'events' staged by the Fluxus group. 'The Happening contains several, most often sequential, compartments, and a variety of primary materials.'[919]

6. 'Political movements'

Jill Johnson linked the 'destructive urges' in the Fluxus group – 'destroy art (a tool of the government), make way for life (a free commodity of the people)' – with the contemporary political situation in the early 1960s:

> The world was not at war in 1962, but there was tremendous unrest and discontent around the globe. There was a Cold War. And there was the Bomb, which hung over populations like fleets of lethally charged dirigibles threatening to fall when some man in a suit pushed a button. In America there were race riots, and politicians gathering momentum to start the very unpopular war in Vietnam. Drugs of ecstasy and oblivion were reaching deep into society, and the women's movement was taking root. And scarcely forgotten were the repressions of the 1950s, when the American government sponsored Communist witchhunts, homosexual purges, and demands for uniformity in general.[920]

Cage's response to the world situation in the 1960s was both anarchistic and utopian. He is quoted in Marshall McLuhan's and Quentin Fiore's *The Medium is the Massage*: 'One must ... give up illusions about ideas of order, expressions of sentiment, and all the rest of our inherited aesthetic claptrap ... They [I Ching] told me to continue what I was doing, and to spread JOY and revolution.'[921] In addition to having the influences already mentioned, Cage was an admirer of Henry David Thoreau (who believed that 'that government is best which does not govern at all'),[922] Marshall McLuhan and particularly Buckminster Fuller. Cage stated in 1963: 'the work and thought of Buckminster Fuller is of prime importance to me. He more than any other to my knowledge sees the world situation – all of it – clearly.'[923] He later said of Fuller: 'I believe that I am completely faithful to his ideas.'[924]

Fuller, who is usually described as an architect but thought of himself as a practitioner of 'comprehensive anticipatory design science',[925] joined Black Mountain College in 1948, and appeared that summer in a play by Eric Satie with dances by Cunningham and music by Cage. He inspired a painting by Johns, entitled *Map, after Buckminster Fuller's Dymaxion Airocean World*, which later formed the backdrop to Cunningham's solo, *Loops* (1971).[926] Fuller was an extraordinarily maverick and prolific inventor and writer, who believed that 'making the world work is an invention initiative and not a political responsibility and is only solvable by a world design revolution'.[927] Asked in 1976 about the main points of Fuller's most important solution, Cage spoke of the need to see to the physical problems of the world by regenerating the 'utilities', and universalising the benefits of technology. 'We should reach a stage where machines free us from work ... We must let technology act, let it be.'[928]

The focus on 'utilities' rather than politics meant prioritising practical functions over issues of property or power. USCO, a group of avant-garde artists, emphasised their agreement with Fuller's view that what mattered was 'not how can we get something but how can we make it work'.[929] Technology played a crucial role in utopian visions of the future, including the extension of the human senses and of the human brain through information technology. Marshall McLuhan famously proposed the view, supported by Cage, that 'we have through electronic technology produced an extension of our brains to the world formerly outside of us'.[930] For McLuhan:

> all media are extensions of some human faculty – psychic or physical. The wheel ... is an extension of the foot. The book is an extension of the eye ... clothing, an extension of the skin ... electric circuitry, an extension of the central nervous system.[931]

McLuhan's description of the function of the media was in fact very close to avant-garde perceptions of the function of art. There was a broad consensus among practitioners and critics favourable to new forms of theatre that their function was to enhance perception. According to Cage, 'the obligation – the morality, if you wish – of all the arts today is to intensify, alter perceptual awareness and hence, consciousness'.[932] Kostelanetz wrote that 'the most profound purpose of the new theatre, then, is initiating a multiply attentive perception that enables us better to perceive ... the structure and order of events in space-time – to comprehend ... our multiply transforming, discontinuous environment'.[933]

McLuhan argued that electronic technology had changed people's relationship to time, propelling them into a complex and constantly shifting present which blocked out the past, rendering memory problematic. 'You now have everything at once. You don't move on from one thing at a time to the next thing. There is no more history; it's all here ... Speed, huge speed-up, means there's no more past ... no more history.'[934] Speaking in 1970, Cunningham asserted his belief that:

> there has been a great opening in the last few years, all due to McLuhan's idea about the visual world. People can look at dancing now ... Through television, people have become more accustomed to relating to a visual image; since dance is visual, it's not such a desperate effort any more.[935]

However, although he welcomed the fact that McLuhan had changed 'accepted ideas about logic and logical discourse ... from linear to field', Cunningham argued that 'dance has kinesthesia, and McLuhan's point about the tribal vision and the use of other senses must include this'.[936]

The sheer quantity and variety of works choreographed by Cunningham make it impossible within the framework of a single chapter to discuss a representative sample. In my selection below of examples from the 1950s to the 1970s, I have included only pieces that I have been able to see in performance and/or to which I have had access on video. Although Cunningham's work constantly increases in complexity, and incorporates contemporary influences and moods (e.g. the playfulness and focus on technology characteristic of the 1960s in *Variations V* [1965]), in these examples we also see how his kinesthetic imagination consistently fragments rhythm through abrupt changes and striking juxtapositions of effort patterns.

7. *The 1950s* – Lavish Escapade *and* Rune

Lavish Escapade (1956) already has a very typical Cunningham 'look'. (See Illustration 11)[937] It was subtitled *An Adventure into an uncharted territory*, and was the second in Cunningham's trilogy of solos to music by Christian Wolff (*For Piano II*). The score is random and percussive. 'Cunningham himself knitted the costume, a kind of union suit in multicolored stripes with one very long leg. The chance possibilities even included changes in the costume.'[938] Cunningham explained that he used chance procedures here for movements of various parts of the body, and even for the eyes, eyebrows and mouth. 'Very often, you did something slow with your arm, for example, and something rapid with your feet – but the arm had to do something large against this – and this set up a kind of opposition. It was physically very difficult for me.' He said that in this dance, 'getting from one thing to another ... was in itself part of the drama, because just to do that was so intense'.[939] There is no choreographic equivalent of musical meter, with phrases comprising clear breaks or accents, composed of progression leading up to a climax. Changes, most notably of speed and of direction, do not follow a predictable pattern, and take place without transitions.

In *Rune* (1959) (see also the description at the beginning of this chapter), the spare, striking score by Christian Wolff creates a sense of randomness which seems curiously planned, evoking Cunningham's description of painters who imitate 'the way nature makes a space and puts lots of things in it, heavy and light, little and big, all unrelated, yet each affecting all the others'.[940] Although music and dance are structurally independent, the choice of composers is not arbitrary. The music generally plays an important role in stimulating a mode of attention similar to that required for the dance, whose combination of complex choreography, performed with very focused attention, and lack of progression along the lines of a conventional narrative or teleological musical structure, produces the sense of a hidden, mysterious purpose. For Siegel, *Rune* is characterised by 'gravity and intensely concentrated energy', and its 'archaic, almost desolate mood' is reinforced by Christian Wolff's score.[941] The independence of dance and music heightens the dramatic impact of occasional apparent synchronisations.

The movement vocabulary is extremely varied, with elements of balletic elegance and grace (e.g. the use of extensions and jumps), but also with typically Cunninghamesque awkward postures, flexed feet and stiffness, which have the effect of binding energy flow even while movement is taking place. As Vernon Shetley has pointed out, 'awkwardness implies effort, so the exploration of that register of movement presupposes the rejection of effortlessness as a goal'.[942] Typically, extreme speed can be

11. Merce Cunningham in *Lavish Escapade*, 1956

12. *Rune*, 1959. Left to right: Viola Farber, Remy Charlip, Marilyn Wood, Judith Dunn, Merce Cunningham, Carolyn Brown,

combined with bound flow, producing what the choreographer James Waring referred to in 1957 as the quality of 'energetic life in containment' that was to be seen in Cunningham's early solos, including *Lavish Escapade*.[943] Siegel comments that: '*Rune* seems to have a lot to do with stillness, with condensing energy instead of spilling it out'.[944] The complexity of this effect is increased when contrasting effort elements are combined in different parts of the body.

The movement Cunningham originally choreographed for himself in *Rune* has a very distinctive quality, typical of Cunningham's solos (here these qualities are also taken up by the other male dancer, and by one of the female dancers), of nervous, almost jittery energy, which at times penetrates the whole body. Rapid movements of the head, which turns in different directions, produce a sense of intelligent alertness and flexibility. This quality characterised Cunningham's personal style from his very first recital in 1944, as remarked on by Edwin Denby: 'His torso can turn on its vertical axis with great sensitivity, his shoulders are held lightly free, and his head poises intelligently.'[945] At the same time, the irregular, pulsating vibrations of the very fast rhythms, combined with emphasis on looking in different directions, produces a sense of watchfulness, perhaps indicating a potential danger. Treatment of the stage space is decentred and spare, making the spectator aware of the physical presence of space, and the 'open' structure is accentuated by the lack of a clear ending when the curtain goes down. *Rune* was the first work to have no fixed order, though the complexity of the movement meant that new orders had to be rehearsed before each performance, and this proved so time-consuming that Cunningham ultimately abandoned it.[946]

8. The 1960s – Variations V *and* RainForest

Variations V was performed in 1965 in New York, and a film version (50 minutes long) was made in Hamburg in the following year.[947] This is a quite extraordinary piece, at once of its time (in the spirit of 1960s 'happenings') and late postmodern in its fragmented and fragmenting energies. The set is very 'busy', with a variety of objects and technical equipment on stage, including multiple screens. There are six dancers, three men and three women. They wear basic leotards and tights, over which the women sometimes wear dresses of their own choosing. The piece has a playful, absurd, iconoclastic (neo-Dadaist) flavour, with actions such as potting and repotting a plant with detachable plastic leaves, riding a bicycle and doing a headstand taking place alongside virtuosic, high-speed dance, performed with classical precision and clarity.

There is also a strong sense of mediation and fragmentation produced by technology. In the background are numerous screens, and six projectors project a moving patchwork of constantly changing images across the back wall, spilling over the boundaries of the screens. These are a collage of film images from unrelated contexts – footage of the dancers that had been previously taken and later altered (including, according to Cunningham, his feet blown up and looking like elephants), along with 'still shots and shots from movies, a montage of contemporary scenes, automobiles, a man in space, nature, buildings'.[948] The intermedia artist Nam June Paik played a role in manipulating these images. In addition, coloured slides were projected apparently at random, sometimes the right way up, sometimes not.[949] Because they change so quickly and appear in the background, they tease the eye and draw attention but never stay long enough to be fully looked at. Moreover, in the film version some images also appear as a filter between the viewer and the dancers, including some abstract patterns that look like computer-generated images, so that it becomes quite difficult to follow the live performers on stage. The soundtrack of music by John Cage is intrusive.

13. *Variations V*, 1965. Front left to right: John Cage, David Tudor, Gordon Mumma. Rear left to right: Carolyn Brown, Merce Cunningham, Barbara Dilley.

The number of different things happening at any given moment makes it impossible to take everything in fully. (This is true on screen as well as on stage.) For some contemporary spectators, this was irritating; for instance, Noel Goodwin complained that 'the work diffused the spectator's attention over too wide an area instead of concentrating it on one focal point after another'.[950] The score is loud and aggressive, so that overall one has a sense of sensory bombardment. Finally, the camera frequently cuts (sometimes very briefly) to images of various technical installations – tape-recorders with revolving tapes, electronic sound equipment – so that one is constantly aware of the role of technology as a mediating element in the performance. In fact, the overwhelming presence of technical installations, and the rather official, besuited appearance of the musicians/technicians, produce an impression of the dominance of technology.[951]

Variations V even experimented with the use of technology to enable the dancers to trigger sounds through their movements. There were two sources of such sounds: a series of twelve poles, placed all round the stage, which were sensitive to a dancer's presence within a radius of 4 feet, and a series of photoelectric cells. The plant (described by Clement Crisp in the *Financial Times* as 'the loudest aspidistra in the world')[952] carried a cartridge microphone, and Barbara Dilley put on her head a towel with a contact microphone attached, and then stood on her head. Ultimately, it was the musicians who determined the effects, and the correlation between movement and sound was not obvious to the audience, although Don McDonagh said that Cunningham's final cycle-ride around the stage managed 'to break all of the magnetic fields, changing the sound and visual décor rapidly as the curtain comes down'.[953]

Kerstin Evert has suggested that the effects of technology in *Variations V* are very similar to McLuhan's famous idea of the 'global village' as 'a worldwide electronic network in which geographical differences are erased. In *Variations V*:

> Signals triggered by light barriers or motion sensing systems activate recorders and short-wave radios, which then randomly select programs from various parts of the world and bring these into the performance space ... By connecting the movements of those dancing in the artificial space of the performance with the worldwide space outside, *Variations V* serves as a model of the electronic network comprising the *global village*.[954]

The overall effect of the combined elements is extremely stimulating and exciting. Much of the dancing is high-velocity, contrasted with everyday actions (including walking and sitting) performed at normal speed. In McDonagh's words, 'it is an all-stops-out pacing which contrasts strongly with the deliberately casual walking episodes'.[955] This piece exudes pleasure in fracture, with no sense of nostalgia or desire to predict the next move. The spectator needs to be open to multiple stimuli and to the possibility of anything happening next, which means deploying one's faculties fully in the present, without trying to make links with the past or to project preconceived notions into the future. The dancers themselves appear fully concentrated and absorbed in their movement, doubtless owing in part to the potentially distracting nature of the very loud sounds exploding around them.

In 1967, the critic Clive Barnes wrote in *Dance and Dancers* that 'Cunningham is currently regarded as the most respectable of the American avant-garde. Indeed, he holds something of the position in American dance that Picasso holds in international painting.'[956] The

Company had an extended New York season for the first time when they appeared at the Brooklyn Academy of Music in 1968, with a programme that included *RainForest*, which had been premiered earlier that year.[957] It also included *Walkaround Time*, with a solo by Cunningham that purportedly referred to Duchamp's *Nude Descending a Staircase*.

RainForest presents an extraordinary world of movement behaviour, which has recognisably human but also some non-human (mainly animal-like) qualities, as indeed the title suggests. (See Illustration 14) There are six dancers: three men and three women. The dance lasts for twenty minutes, and has five sections. The dancers wear flesh-colored leotards and tights, which Jasper Johns had cut and ripped with a razor blade. David Tudor's music (*RainForest*) is strangely evocative of animal noises in a rainforest. The dance opens on a striking set, where helium-filled balloons, designed by Andy Warhol, float around and above the stage. The opening movement sequences are extremely slow, and reflect the dreamlike floating quality of the balloons (through which the dancers move). There is even a spacelike, 'moonwalking' quality to this movement, and the film sequences contain images of astronauts. Although Armstrong would not set foot on the Moon until a year later, the possibility of walking on the Moon had been on the agenda for several years.[958] The use of the floor for sliding, crawling and rolling movements produces strongly animalistic connotations, as does the sight of Cunningham, near the beginning of the dance, crouched on his hunkers, rather like a four-legged creature on its hind legs.[959]

Also near the beginning, in the background we see another male dancer (Albert Reid) standing, intermittently performing curious twitching movements with his hands and fingers, and moving his arms in a robot-like fashion. The nervous quality of this movement has associations that are at once animal-like and technological. Marcia Siegel comments that the dancers in *RainForest* seem 'poised between their humanness and some nonhuman existence that could be either animalistic or artificial'.[960] There is a wide variety of travelling steps and positions that are not typical of human movement and postures. Some movements are similar to actions such as walking, running and skipping, but with unfamiliar elements, e.g. off-balance use of weight, abnormally fast execution, extreme stiffness and strange, awkward angles. At the same time, heterosexual dramas are enacted which clearly do have human connotations. Indeed, there is some very conventionally gendered pairwork in this piece, with manipulation and carrying of female dancers by male partners, and there are clear suggestions of competition between males for partnership with the females, e.g. as Albert Reid advances

14. *Rainforest*, 1968. Left to right: Merce Cunningham, Barbara (Dilley)
Lloyd and Albert Reid

towards the 'couple' of Merce Cunningham and Barbara Lloyd. (See Illustration 14)

The movement is performed with great intensity and sense of purpose, and is mostly tense, light, fast and seamless, but it is sometimes punctuated by 'slashing' actions, where speed and flexibility are combined with strong use of weight.[961] The tempo alternates very dramatically between extreme rapidity and very slow motion, replacing modulation with rhythmic dislocations and concentration of energy. The execution of small, rapid, darting, tightly controlled movements in quick succession figures prominently in the female role in a duet near the end. In effort terms, the predominant movement qualities here are light, indirect, fast and bound, involving a high degree of energy expenditure on resistance to weight, time and flow. At the end, the energy is picked up and further amplified in an extraordinary solo by Cunningham, where his whole body is saturated by tiny, jabbing gestures, as if animated by a series of electrical currents that move his body in different ways all at once, while at the same time he projects a strong sense of intensity and controlled concentration. This movement juxtaposes direct effort attitudes to space (individual 'jabbing' movements) with indirect attitudes (movement into different directions in space), a combination that produces rhythmic dislocation. Relationships between the dancers are at times close, at times distant, but never invasive: communication is of a purely physical kind, and does not involve signaling inner emotions through facial expression. There is a strong sense of the dancers' alert awareness of each other, combined with a grounded centering in their own execution of the movement, over which they are in control.

This choreography resists conformism, and exemplifies characteristics of what Sennett (see above) saw as a salutary response to the growth of misplaced intimacy and the effacement of an impersonal public realm: a recovery of self-distance and the ability to play. (Some dances of the 1950s and 1960s are overtly playful, notably *Antic Meet* [1958] and *How to Pass, Kick, Fall and Run* [1965].) A potential narrative based on relationships between the dancers, which clearly involve sexual tensions, never crystallises. Instead, the complexity of the movement and its rhythmic dislocations convey a high degree of excitement, particularly in the nervous energy of Cunningham's final solo.

9. The 1970s – Sounddance *and* Torse

The 1970s were an important transitional period. In 1972, after nearly twenty years, Carolyn Brown left the company. Her departure marked a 'profound change'.[962] According to Meg Harper, it prompted

Cunningham to 'test the physical limitations of his dancers'.[963] From 1973 to 1975, most of the company's performances were Events or lecture-demonstrations. It was not until 1977 that the Company would have its first Broadway season, at the Minskoff Theatre, and Arlene Croce was prompted to ask in *The New Yorker* in 1975: 'What kind of dance capital of the world is it which confines the presentation of a new Merce Cunningham work to his downtown loft studio?'[964] In the meantime, Cunningham was developing an interest in making dance for video, and in 1974 he and Charles Atlas participated in the making of a two-part programme for CBS Camera Three, *A Video Event*, directed by Merrill Brockway, which included a company class with rehearsal of movement later seen in *Sounddance*, and also an excerpt from this 'new piece' (which did not yet have a name).

Cunningham made *Sounddance* after he returned from 9 weeks working at the Paris Opéra, where he choreographed *Un jour ou deux*. He recounted:

'The work [at the Opera] had been so difficult, and trying, that when I got back to my own dancers, it was like an explosion, a tremendous release. I felt like doing something vigorous, fast, complex ... The rehearsal room at the Paris Opera had been very small. I felt like doing something in the same type of space, something compact, in which to keep up the energy level constantly.[965]

In Part I of *A Video Event*, he described *Sounddance* as 'a packed scene of activity, and perhaps it comes from my interest in the way life looks under a microscope, where it exhibits itself so feverishly'.

Sounddance was first performed as a work in progress in 1974, and was staged in Detroit in 1975 and New York in 1977.[966] It is eighteen minutes long, for ten dancers. The costumes by Mark Lancaster were 'light yellow and grey, his decor across the back is tent-like and sand colored'.[967] David Tudor's score, *Toneburst*, was fast and frenetic. Even by Cunningham's standards, this was an extraordinary piece, which created quite a sensation and was described as 'electrifying'.[968] A reporter in the *Minnesota Daily* commented:

jammed with fast choreography, *Sounddance* piled a tremendous amount of action into a short space of time. There was little chance to anticipate any movement, so the work was filled with surprises and necessitated the viewer to attempt watching several places on the stage at one time.[969]

According to Robert Greskovic:

> Nothing remained constant except the insistent re-grouping and dispersing ... A split-legged lift created a bridge for someone to run under; someone's turn attracted another dancer's attention and resulted in a new combination of dancers without further ado. As one dancer walked on all fours in a supine position, another rested on his torso as if reclining on a table.[970]

Arlene Croce enthused:

> *Sounddance...* emerged as a triumph, and the season's biggest hit ... lavishly exciting choreography ...The entrances and exits are made through a center slot in a draped curtain that extends the width of the stage. Each dancer appears, is immediately caught up in the vortex of the dance, and at the end is hurled by a centrifugal force back through the slot ... Tudor's *Toneburst* raises its energy level to volcanic fury.[971]

Jowitt remarked in 1977 that 'perhaps the music causes the dance to seem wilder than it is. And the lights. I see the dancers as playing with fierce energy on an empty shore at high noon.'[972] For Anna Kisselgoff, writing in 1977:

> It is ... the invention of the movement that makes *Sounddance* so rich ... Mr Cunningham bursts forth onto the stage. It is a startling image and this is a startling work ... The movement range is vibrant, even quirky ... The company performs its virtuoso leaps, kicks, turns, Mexican hat-dance steps, brush steps and weaving in-and-out-of clusters with true brilliance.[973]

And again in 1994: 'The crescendo of pure movement that makes *Sounddance* so exciting ... with its speed, off-balance look, innovative entanglements and complex clusters of dancers who constantly release tension, the overall effect is as exhilarating as ever'.[974]

From the moment the soloist enters by bursting through the curtain, there is a degree of release in this dance that is unusual in Cunningham. Once on stage, the dancers engage in extremely athletic movement, which is often evocative of acrobatics, or even a circus, such as the actions described by Greskovic (above). We see a great number of leaps and cartwheels, movements involving turning at high speeds (including a rotating movement, reminiscent of what was called 'buzzing' in my Dublin childhood, where two partners, facing each other, hold hands with crossed outstretched arms and rotate rapidly, pulling away from each other), and a considerable amount of pairwork exploring different ways of balancing through lifting and supporting movements. There is a sense of intense urgency and hidden significance in this frenetic expenditure of energy, arising from the concentration of the dancers and the quasi-ritualistic feel of some of the movement sequences, which involve producing three-dimensional shapes, where dance appears as a moving sculpture.

Sometimes it is as if groups of dancers form new organisms, particularly in one configuration that takes place upstage, partially obscured by dancers appearing in front. Here the dancers seem to burrow down towards one another – not unlike a rugby scrum – but their arms and legs are left free and move in wavy, undulating movements, evoking, perhaps, the tendrils of an underwater creature or an organism under a microscope. For a time, all the dancers attach themselves to this organism, but then they splinter off again and resume frenetic activities. There are a number of lifts that involve a frequent Cunningham motif, and variations on it, where a woman is held aloft at arm's length by two or more men, in a horizontal position (see Illustration 15) that is sometimes adjusted, as if she were a puppet. Despite the passivity of their roles in such lifts, as soon as the women rejoin the dance they participate in the seamless, athletic movement with equal autonomy. The lifts come across as performances of movement possibilities, without implications in terms of character or narrative, and the women dancers generally project as much energy and strength as the men do.

Torse (1976, film version 1977)[975] is a piece for ten dancers, with music by Maryanne Amacher and costumes by Mark Lancaster. A film of the dance, directed by Charles Atlas, was produced in 1977. In the film version, the dance is presented in two separate screens/frames, which appear side by side. It lasts for fifty-five minutes, and its structure was determined by chance procedures. Choreographed when Cunningham was 57, *Torse* is a remarkable work, classical both in relation to Cunningham's own work and in more general terms, in its assured, precise complexity and cool intensity. It is an extreme manifestation of discipline and of heightened tension, produced by a combination of complex, uneven weight distribution, bound flow, speed, and erratic, flexible use of space. Both the movements of individual dancers and the use of stage space are highly layered, with several different, contrasting movement events taking place at once, combining concentration on the present with a rhythmic dislocation of the moment, through the impossibility of registering all that is taking place in a single instant. Deborah Jowitt described *Torse* as 'a marathon of crisp, intricate footwork',

15. *Sounddance*, 1974. Left to right: Glen Rumsey, Frédéric Gafner, Jenifer
Weaver, Michael Cole

and continued that 'while the dancers' feet brush and hop, jump and turn, leap and tap, their torsos twist and bend – sometimes with odd and even dangerous disequilibrium with their feet'.[976]

The emphasis on weight is heightened in the film version by very audible footfalls. The frequency of asymmetrical movement, where gravity shifts from the centre of the body, produces a restlessness, in itself like an added, invisible layer of movement within movement. Holly Brubach recounted in 1977:

> He [Cunningham] insists that the dancer 'center the weight' each time the working leg returns the pelvis to first position ... Even in rapid *dégagés*, the dancer returns weight to the working foot as it closes. With his weight directly beneath him, the dancer is never caught off-guard, and Cunningham as choreographer has the option to surprise us with sudden changes in direction.[977]

There is indeed a sense of constant change, as speed, direction and configurations of dancers on stage keep shifting. Arlene Croce commented that 'the steps are utterly unforeseen permutations of academic combinations, and they come in such thick clusters that the audience is as winded as the dancers'.[978]

In her doctoral dissertation, Sharon Unrau stated that 'the 1970s Cunningham technique, as seen in *Torse* (1976), addresses change of direction, tilts, curves and twists of the back against the working leg, balances in hard-to-hold positions and relevés, leaps, and a great deal of allegro (very fast) footwork'.[979] Cunningham said that in *Torse* he focused on 'mainly the range of body movements corresponding to five positions of the back and backbone, positions with which I mostly work: upright, curve, arch, twist and tilt'.[980] He explained that this dance 'was done using chance operations so as to have the possibility of any formation of the dancers appearing'. He also said that 'each one of the dancers appears at some point as a soloist ... and though the general feeling throughout is that the dance remains a dance of ensembles, it is very individualised as well, each dancer at one point or another has a chance to appear outside the group'. The phrases were structured, not by time, but by weight changes: a weight change was equivalent to a count, but these could happen slowly or quickly. Cunningham decided the phrasing in advance, before the dancers came to rehearsal, using the *I Ching* and with the help of video. The number of phrases was 64, as in the *I Ching*, and the phrases from 1 to 64 had an equivalent number of weight changes. The combination of phrases, and the number of dancers who should perform them, were also decided using the *I Ching*. Exits and entrances, or the possibility of a duet, were decided by coin tossing.[981]

Jacqueline Lesschaeve remarked that putting a large group of dancers into a small part of the stage emphasised the space of the empty section, and commented that the constant shifting of the dancers ('flexible' use of space) created the impression that they were 'everywhere', as if in a 'flock'.[982] The use of space here exemplifies Cunningham's decision 'to open up the space to consider it equal, and any place, occupied or not, just as important as any other'. Cunningham continued: 'when I happened to read that sentence of Albert Einstein's, "There are no fixed points in space", I thought, indeed, if there are no fixed points, then every point *is* equally interesting and equally changing'. Without a central point of reference, 'you can constantly shift everything, the movement can be continuous, and numerous transformations can be imagined'.[983]

10. Intersubjective energies

On one level, these constant changes simply reflect what one can perceive in everyday life. 'But just think of a group of six people walking along on the sidewalk together. At any moment they can all walk off in different directions, in different rhythms.'[984] On another level, though, the pace of change, the complex layering of movement and the extreme alertness of the dancers do not represent a typical 'slice of life'. Rather, they are both an exaggeration and an aestheticisation of features of the everyday, especially in large cities. These features can be experienced as negative, even debilitating, but their enactment here by the dancers is exhilarating: nervous tension, time pressure, restlessness, anonymity in a crowd, constant change – all these characteristics are present, but are liberating rather than debilitating. Nervousness, speed and restlessness are inseparable from excitingly virtuosic, superbly controlled but unpredictable movement; and anonymity does not mean uniformity, but rather the freedom to remain separate and private while still interacting with the collective. According to Vernon Shetley, Cunningham's work evokes 'an image of a social contract based on the absolute irreducibility of the individual'.[985]

The complex treatment of space in Cunningham's choreography means that 'the dancers must ... cultivate an expanded awareness of the space around them, must be prepared to encounter a partner approaching from any direction, to avoid collisions as independent groups of dancers thread their ways through one another.'[986] Cunningham noted that his pieces develop the faculty of intersubjective awareness among the dancers, even when they cannot see each other, because the structure depends entirely on timing, rather than on reference to music:

You have to begin to know where the other dancer is, without looking. It has to do with the timing, the relationship with the timing. If you paid attention to the timing, then, even if you weren't facing them, you knew they were there. And that created a relationship.[987]

This relationship is not one of misplaced intimacy, as criticised by Sennett, leading us to believe that 'community is an act of mutual self-disclosure', but evokes rather the urban space of the city as a 'forum in which it becomes meaningful to join with other persons without the compulsion to know them as persons' (see above). These reconfigurations of individual and intersubjective energies are bodily processes, brought about through movement, not through words or through structures derived from other media. In the words of Tobi Tobias, discussing Cunningham: 'exploration of how bodies relate to each others' shape and weight ... makes you think about how the body's physical identity and language initiates emotional relationships ... perhaps movement is at the core, the body's response preceding the psyche's.'[988]

Robert Greskovic referred in 1984 to the 'sculptural concerns' in Cunningham's work, evidenced in his 'unquenchable fascination for working the full of the dancers' figure into every conceivable angle of space'.[989] This is a striking feature of *Fractions I*, made for video in 1977,[990] and subsequently remade for the stage. It lasts for thirty-three minutes and is for eight dancers. The dancers wear brightly coloured leotards and tights designed by Mark Lancaster, who also designed the set, consisting of two 6' by 4' painted panels. The music, *Equal Distribution* by Jon Gibson, is extremely spare and repetitive.

Fractions is very successful as a video dance – Arlene Croce described it as 'the finest piece of video choreography anyone has yet made'.[991] Cunningham himself has emphasised to an uncharacteristic extent the difficulties in making it: '*Fractions* was really difficult – terribly difficult to do', because 'there were so many variables'.[992] He took full account of the need to use space differently in video. In *Fractions* there was the added complication that monochrome TV monitors also appeared alongside 'live' dancers, showing parts of the dance not directly visible to the spectator, sometimes with truncated views of the dancers' bodies. This mode of presentation, as well as demanding 'polyattentiveness', draws the spectator's attention to the dance structure and to the process of viewing and its partiality. The small screens emphasise two-dimensionality, as opposed to the main image, which is shot to emphasise diagonals, perspectival depth and contrasts between dancers in the foreground and background. The skintight leotards also draw attention to three-dimensional body shape.

The presence of the monitors on stage is integral to the video version of the dance, and Cunningham incorporated similar elements into the stage version. As Croce says:

> *Fractions* may be the most successful of Cunningham's videodances because it's really about dancing, and 'television' is metaphorically present in its conception – a part of the real world of change which Cunningham believes in and makes dances about. Unlike *Westbeth*, a former video experiment, *Fractions* isn't fancy and self-conscious, with one eye on the lens; it's a natural happening.[993]

There are some extraordinary slow-motion duets with Karole Armitage and Robert Kovich, like moving sculpture, where pleasure in unexpected, virtuosic angles and shapes is indulged to the maximum as the movement almost – but not quite – stops for the eye to linger indefinitely.

A striking duet begins with Armitage standing with feet in a straight line, knees and heels touching (as in first position), arms by her sides, while Kovich approaches from behind, gently takes hold of her hands, and raises her arms alongside his own. From then on, he 'frames' all of her movements in a partnering that is at once intimate and separate. The dancers' energies are held in bound flow and confined to the sphere of their individual movements. Framed by Kovich, Armitage executes extremely sustained deep *pliés*, extensions, and poses resembling attitudes, with no moment of complete stillness. In an extraordinarily complex and sculptural quasi-pose (where movement never quite ceases), both dancers face the audience, with Armitage's supporting leg held straight, her working leg clearly elevated and bent behind, as in an 'attitude', with Kovich in *demi-plié*, his head crooked under Armitage's left shoulder, her left arm extending behind his left shoulder, and her right arm also extended parallel to Kovich's right arm, which he extends behind and above hers, and with his left hand clasping her left hand.

This 'pose' is repeated twice, first in a more closed position, with Kovich's left leg crossed behind and his left arm extended horizontally in front of both dancers. On the second repetition, there is a very slow opening up, with Kovich's right arm now rising into a vertical position and his left arm loosely curving in front (see Illustration 16), at the same time as the pace increases and the dancers very gradually disengage. These movements produce undecidable three-dimensional linear configurations that are never completely static, but are inhabited by an

16. *Fractions*, 1978. Karole Armitage and Robert Kovich

idea of stasis, evoking stillness at the heart of movement, and movement at the heart of stillness. They dramatise directional movements of widening and narrowing, sinking and rising, which accommodate to the partner's body in three-dimensional space, while also containing energy within individual boundaries.

By the 1980s, Cunningham had become 'establishment' (or rather, the establishment had 'gone Cunningham'), to the extent that his work began to seem almost classical to some. However, as Siegel commented in 1983, it was still 'different enough from everything else we see nowadays that it seems to come from another planet'. Concerning its relation to ballet, she continued:

> They [Cunningham dancers] do a lot of ballet steps ... yet they don't look balletic either ... [Cunningham] sees steps that are usually done in place, like arabesque and attitude, as part of a whole body rearrangement ... he'll use *tendus* or *développés*, not to show you a pointed foot or a stretched leg, but to create rhythmic punctuation. Jumps and other elevations ... are meant to redirect the line of travel or smash a group pattern that's forming.[994]

On Cunningham's relation to ballet, Arlene Croce remarked: 'Cunningham loves to skew classical standards ... Seeing legs whip back from a zigzag *fouetté* into *penchée arabesque* is like crossing a divide when the bridge is gone.'[995]

In 1991, when he began to use the computer program LifeForms in his choreographic process for the first time, Cunningham's work would move in another new direction, and a further fresh departure took place with the use of motion-capture technology in *BIPED* (1999). His own increasing immobilisation has also had a profound effect on his work. But the possibilities offered by new technologies, which Cunningham has exploited to extraordinary effect, are an extension (in the McLuhan sense of technology extending the senses) of his existing techniques, especially the use of chance. His recent work pushes further his exploration of vitalist energies that ultimately connect the activities of human beings to non-human 'life'. In the early twenty-first century, 'Merce' touches our profound cultural preoccupation with the role of technology and its effects on the boundaries of the human. As Tobi Tobias said of Cunningham's work in 1975:

> A sequence begins with a conglomerate of energy – individual dancers conglomerating into a group gestalt – in which you can still see, clearly, the individual workings ... something inevitable, inside nature, moves

like this ... this is the activity of molecules, the insides of intricate machines, fantasies of extraterrestrial entities.[996]

5: Kinesthetic imagination and changing economies of energy

A man is a two-legged creature – more basically and more intimately than he is anything else. And his legs speak more than they 'know'. *(Cunningham)*[997]

All media are extensions of some human faculty – psychic or physical. *(McLuhan and Fiore)*[998]

In this chapter, I revisit the concept of kinesthetic imagination and its relation to energy. Through analysis of the work of Wigman, Graham and Cunningham, I have observed the effects of kinesthetic imagination in terms of innovative movement techniques and choreographies, and their impact on spectators. But questions remain (to which I shall attempt partial answers) concerning kinesthetic imagination itself. How does it work? How does it relate to philosophical and critical accounts of relations between consciousness and the body, and between language and meaning? To what extent is it possible to resist dominant cultural tendencies through kinesthesia (i.e. what is the political role of kinesthetic imagination)? How does the role of kinesthetic imagination in transforming uses of energy relate to new technologies in dance, and what are its implications for economies of energy in dance, in the present and the emerging future?

1. Kinesthetic imagination and the spectator's body

In order to discuss how kinesthetic imagination works, we need first of all to examine the kinesthetic sense more closely. Through this sense, which is 'mediated by end organs located in muscles, tendons and joints and stimulated by body movements and tensions',[999] we experience movement sensations resulting from effort attitudes to space, weight, time and flow. Far from being peripheral to the established five senses of sight, sound, touch, taste and smell, kinesthesia is the ground for their operation and interaction. Writing about the sensory psychologist James Gibson, the dance artist and scholar Nigel Stewart affirms that: 'After Gibson, we can speak of kinesthesia in terms of its muscular, articular, vestibular, cutaneous, auditory, and visual modalities', and that 'kinesthesia is the ground to our consciousness'.[1000]

In a thorough and well-documented discussion, the scholar Jeffrey Longstaff points out that the distinction between proprioception (the detection of bodily events through the muscles, joints, and tendons) and exteroception (the detection of environmental events through the eyes, the ears and the skin) is invalid, as these dimensions interact in kinesthetic sensation. External stimuli, for instance, 'can induce perceptions of self-motion even in the absence of joint, muscle, tendon and vestibular stimulations'.[1001] Both in sensory psychology and in the phenomenological tradition of thought, kinesthetic awareness has been seen as foundational to all sensory experience and to consciousness itself.[1002] At the same time, kinesthetic awareness exists below the level of 'corporeal consciousness'. Although they are crucial to normal motor functioning, kinethestic sensations often go unnoticed, and we can perform movements without being aware of them. Cunningham is acutely aware of the microtextures of kinesthetic sensation, and recommends paying close attention to them.[1003]

Where spectators engage in virtual movement that re-enacts the dynamics observed in the perceived moving subject,[1004] they can experience something of what Laban called 'the bodily feel of the co-ordination of motion factors in complex efforts, and in sequences of them'.[1005] I discussed in previous chapters Theodor Lipps' notion of kinesthetic empathy as shared dynamism or 'inner mimesis', and John Martin's idea of a tension between recognition of familiar rhythms, which draw spectators in, and deviations from these rhythms, which expand spectators' existing kinesthetic experience. The degree to which spectators are able to recognise and respond to tensions/interactions between familiar and innovative patterns of energy depends largely on the extent of their movement awareness, as well as their specialist knowledge of dance and the extent to which performer and spectator share inculturated experience.

It is doubtless significant that explosions of new dance practices (notably in Germany before the World War I and in the USA and Europe in the 1960s) coincided with popular interest in the body and in movement which made for much more 'movement literate' spectators of dance. Recall Hans Brandenburg's comment, cited in chapter 2 above: 'One wants ... to transform the public from passive spectators into inner participants. But the spectator can only really participate actively when the most complete and most concentrated optical impressions urge him to inner participation, *provided that he also possesses a trained corporeal awareness*'.[1006] It is interesting that Brandenburg referred here to 'trained corporeal awareness' rather than to dance training, since the 'inner participation' of the spectator necessitates a shared kinesthetic awareness with the dancer that extends beyond familiarity with dance conventions. Our apparently spontaneous kinesthetic responses are derived from inculturated experience. The spectator's body, like that of the dancer, is a 'corporeity': a 'sensory ... imaginary network ... inseparable from an individual and collective history'.[1007]

In order for spectators to activate their kinesthetic imagination, they need to experience participation in the performer's movement rhythms. These rhythms also need to involve innovative and unexpected ways of using energy, which break habitual moulds. Through kinesthetic imagination, unforeseen movement possibilities are generated directly from kinesthetic events. As Cunningham has described his working process: 'In beginning to make a dance, I ordinarily begin alone, trying out movements in order to obtain a sense of what this particular dance might contain. Slips of the feet, rather then slips of the tongue'.[1008]

If a choreographer can proceed through 'slips of the feet', this undermines the notion that the dance is controlled by a sovereign subject. Indeed, kinesthetic imagination implies a decentred model of subjectivity. Within the discourse of philosophy, the writings of Maurice Merleau-Ponty support this view of kinesthetic imagination. Merleau-Ponty affirmed the centrality of kinesthesia to consciousness, and his thinking on the body and movement has close correspondences with Laban.[1009] Moreover, in his late writings, his exploration of embodied experience led him to critique immediacy and self-presence in ways that anticipated aspects of post-structuralist and particularly deconstructionist thought.[1010]

Merleau-Ponty discussed kinesthesia in terms of 'intentionality', or 'goal-directedness'. Goal-directed actions, specifically movement, situated the body in lived space/time. They could involve anticipated or virtual movement, and actions where the aim was given in the movement itself and was not fully transparent to the mover. For Merleau-Ponty, an attitude of openness towards a future movement was inseparable from a corporeal experience in the present, which he described as being neither a movement nor a mental representation of a movement, but rather 'an anticipation of, or arrival at, the objective ... *ensured by the body itself as a motor power, a "motor project" ... a "motor intentionality"'.*[1011] He saw potential movement as a never-ending process,[1012] which could be experienced in the body without involving actual displacement. 'The part of the body in question sheds its anonymity, is revealed, by the presence of a particular [kinesthetic] tension, as a certain *potential for action* within the framework of the anatomical apparatus.'[1013] More recently, Hubert Godard has argued that 'pre-movement', which is not under the conscious control of the subject,[1014] is crucial to all movements, and neuroscientists have shown how virtual or imagined movements themselves involve positive neural activity (see the Introduction).

In his late writings, Merleau-Ponty explored embodiment in relation
to movement and perception in ways that radically decentred the subject,
but which, unlike the psychoanalytic framework, were not tied to very
specific and arguably limiting models of the psyche. Already in
Phenomenology of Perception (1945), he had considered that corporeal
intentionality (my term, referring to his concept of actions whose aims
arise in the body and are not fully transparent to the agent) operated in
excess of conscious thought. The embodied subject was defined largely
through actions, or intended actions, and was therefore an 'agent'. At
the same time, the knowledge that underlay these actions was inseparable
from the actions themselves, and was not fully known by, or knowable to,
the doer. For instance, the act of modifying a gesture in response to a
change in circumstances could take place 'without any intervening
thought'.[1015] Paradoxically, then, despite being a 'body-subject' (a term
often used by commentators on Merleau-Ponty), the subject was also
transcended by his or her body.

Merleau-Ponty's description of corporeal intentionality applies to
action that is initiated in the body itself, and which carries a greater
density of information than the subject can consciously access. In
movement, this can take the form of innovative kinesthetic intentionality,
or kinesthetic imagination. Cunningham declared:

> I am no more philosophical than my legs, but from them I sense this
> fact: that they are suffused with energy that can be released in
> movement ... that the shape the movement takes is beyond the
> fathoming of my mind's analysis but clear to my eyes and rich to my
> imagination. A man is a two-legged creature – more basically and more
> intimately than he is anything else. And his legs speak more than they
> 'know'.[1016]

Cunningham is famous for telling his dancers that the only way to find
out how to do a movement is by doing it. For Cunningham, as for Merleau-
Ponty, 'we learn ... not by thinking about things, but by doing them'.[1017]

Acts of kinesthetic imagination comprise both virtual, imagined
movements and innovative effort actions that transform uses of energy
in habitual effort patterns. Projection beyond previous effort experience
implies a learning process of kinesthetic trial and error, where the body
itself provides feedback. Neuroscience shows that, when we make a
movement, 'the motor cortex in the brain sends out a command to the
appropriate muscles'. Almost immediately (within 60 milliseconds), 'a
message is sent back from the body's sensors to report back on how the

movement went ... Based on this information, the brain responds by sending an updated command to improve the movement, which generates yet more feedback.'[1018] Experts in movement, like dancers, learn to better predict the consequences of their movement commands, and to make corrections quickly, accurately, and without conscious thought. 'While strong muscles and flexibility might appear to make a good dancer, it is more likely their enhanced ability to deal with feedback which makes them unique.' Kinesthetic sensation produced by sensors within the body is the most efficient form of feedback. 'Visual information is processed far slower than proprioceptive information, reaching the brain approximately 70 milliseconds after the information from the body.'[1019] Movement imagery can have the effect of stimulating kinesthetic imagination, as in ideokinesiology, where imaging techniques are used in order to facilitate the body in modifying established patterns of neuromuscular co-ordination,[1020] and the conscious mind can contribute to re-educating the body into new patterns of energy usage.

2. Kinesthetic imagination:
Bourdieu's habitus and Derridean différance

Not only does kinesthetic imagination change uses of energy in movement, but these changes can produce effects of resistance to culturally normative practices and discourses that are incorporated in habitual effort patterns.

This argument is corroborated by aspects of the sociological thought of Pierre Bourdieu (1930–2002). What Bourdieu calls '*habitus*' can be described in terms of 'techniques of the body', which are 'acquired abilities' with biological, sociological and psychological dimensions.[1021] The *habitus* is 'constituted in the course of an individual history' and allows for a limited amount of invention, producing anticipations which are 'practical hypotheses based on past experiences'.[1022] Like Eugenio Barba's inculturated body (discussed in the Introduction), the *habitus* confounds the dualism of 'the self-transparent act of consciousness or the externally determined thing', being at once spontaneous and unconscious.[1023] As in Merleau-Ponty, in Bourdieu's 'practical sense',[1024] the relationship of consciousness to goals can be articulated through corporeal intentionality, where the aim of an action or movement is already given in the action or movement itself. Bourdieu's 'practical sense' is characterised by an excess of embodied action over epistemological agency, where the body can 'incorporate' strategies that are not fully known to the thinking subject. According to Bourdieu, 'it is because agents never know completely what they are doing that what they do has more sense than they know.'[1025]

Bourdieu's concept of the *habitus* as a 'self-correcting program',[1026] where the goal inheres in the action, can be compared to the process by which new movement techniques and choreographic ideas are elaborated, where they arise from the working process itself. Such kinesthetic innovations literally incorporate the past in the present, but also anticipate and project into the future,[1027] and can adapt to new and unforeseen situations. In Bourdieu's terms, these situations may bring about 'durable transformations of the *habitus*'.[1028] Similarly to inculturated effort patterns, Bourdieu's concept of the *habitus* is sociological as well as personal. As 'an intentionality without intention ... without rational computation and without the conscious positing of ends',[1029] the 'practical sense' works in opposition to the characteristics of 'instrumental reason'. What Bourdieu calls a 'feel for the game', a 'direction, an orientation, an impending outcome', or 'practical anticipation of the : "upcoming" future contained in the present',[1030] is directly motivated by, and subordinate to, the requirements for success in social 'fields', which are 'concrete social situations governed by a set of objective social relations'.[1031] However, I have argued that innovative uses of energy can in fact be motivated by resistance to culturally dominant effort patterns, conformity to which could be regarded as a requirement for success.

The dance critic and theorist Gay Morris has used Bourdieu's concepts to discuss Graham's work in relation to the dance 'field' of the 1940s. At this time, the configuration of the dance field presented difficulties for Graham, some of which I discussed in the previous chapter, notably a new generation of dancers, rising commercialism and the growing power of ballet. In order to succeed in this field, Graham needed to increase her accessibility while also reinforcing her vanguard standing. Her decision to produce works that 'took on elements of ballet form and to some degree technique, and which included narrative content', and to focus on 'myth and the unconscious, which connected her to the international avant-garde', can be seen as strategies adopted in response to the demands of the field, though, as Morris emphasises, 'following Bourdieu, such moves were not necessarily calculated on Graham's part'.[1032]

In Bourdieu's framework, then, art works are instrumentalised by being viewed as mere 'tools' or 'stakes' in struggles whose parameters are set by the demands of the 'field'.[1033] By contrast, I have argued that the works of the choreographers I have discussed resist normative uses of energy both within the 'field' of dance and in much broader contexts. From its inception, the sets of conventions or habits with which early modern dance engaged most directly were not those of ballet, nor those of other dance techniques, but rather the effort patterns experienced by embodied subjects in everyday life, patterns that can be altered by kinesthetic imagination. New uses of weight, space, time and flow in the action of walking, for instance, can profoundly modify habitual effort patterns.

At the beginning of their training, Duncan's dancers would spend several months focusing on walking. For Graham, the starting point for a whole new approach to movement was 'the simplest – walking, running, skipping, leaping ... Gradually, as I was able to force out the old, little new things began to grow.'[1034] Graham's emerging technique foregrounded the effort element of weight in movements of walking and running, accentuated by strong emphasis on downward thrust. As I described in Chapter 3, the walk in *Primitive Mysteries* was based on the dancers' re-activation of a muscular memory inculcated through repeatedly walking while thrusting the weight of their whole bodies against the surf at Long Island. In *Primitive Mysteries*, walking on a contraction greatly intensified the bound quality of the flow. I referred in the previous chapter to Cunningham's *RainForest*, where familiar elements of everyday movements, such as running, walking and skipping, were performed with unfamiliar attitudes to weight, space, time and flow. I also commented on how Cunningham's work explores group movements, focusing on similarities and differences between individuals in ways that clearly reference everyday interactions between people in crowds, yet with elements of velocity, off-balance weight, decentred space and bound flow that multiply differences and radically alter the everyday 'look'.

Dancers currently tend to be familiar with a wide variety of techniques, but they may also have worked extensively with one choreographer over a relatively long period of time, as is the case with the dancers of the works I have discussed in previous chapters. In time, these working processes can result in sedimentation of a new set of learned movement patterns. The acquisition of a new technique lays down a store of habitual movement, which the dancer can draw on. In Merleau-Ponty's words: 'We say that the body has understood and habit has been acquired when it [the body] has been penetrated by a new meaning.'[1035] This is the case, as Hubert Godard has argued, with choreographers 'who made something very strong emerge'. By way of example he names Cunningham, Trisha Brown and 'a few French choreographers'. Here, the movement style itself functions as a kind of 'philosophy', which the dancers literally incorporate. '[These choreographers] all have in common this immensely long period of work with the dancers: a daily working regime by means of which the philosophy of the dance gradually infiltrates the symbolic circuits, and passes into the deep strata of the non-verbal.'[1036]

The effects of kinesthetic imagination in dance, where it disrupts habitual and culturally normative uses of energy, can be compared with resistance to communicative norms in the language of avant-garde poetry and art, which was conceptualised by Julia Kristeva in terms of the 'semiotic' resisting the 'symbolic' code (see the Introduction). The rhythmic innovations in Cunningham's work can also be compared with key aspects of Jacques Derrida's *différance*.[1037] Like Kristeva, Derrida worked primarily with language and derived his theories from studying the workings of the sign in linguistic texts.[1038] The term '*différance*' is a Derridean neologism, combining ideas of 'differing' and 'deferring'. Derrida shows how, in texts, *différance* can disrupt meanings intended by the author.

Although it is generally used in analysis of linguistic texts, *différance* or 'spacing' (another Derridean concept, with which it is virtually synonymous) is predicated upon metaphors of movement in time and space. It is probably impossible to think this concept without reference to metaphors drawn from topology, and above all from movement, seen as a function of energy and intensity, which have a radically disruptive effect. *Différance* is characterised by Derrida in dynamic terms, as 'a *movement*, a displacement that indicates an irreducible alterity'. [1039] It introduces a kind of virtual movement into writing, a movement whose primary function is the dislocation of what Derrida calls binary oppositions. *Différance* resists binary oppositions, which are generally hierarchical (e.g. speech over writing, time over space) by insinuating otherness 'within the self-relation of a self-identical entity'. This renders each entity undecidable by preventing it 'from ever relating only to itself',[1040] thereby undermining its self-sufficiency. The production of intervals (differences and deferrals) brings about at once 'the insinuation of a space into the supposedly self-sufficient present', and the 'becoming-time of space',[1041] its displacement or dislocation into time.

Unlike the concepts of movement rhythm discussed in Chapter 1, which were based on 'natural', continuous, unbroken flow that implicitly privileged time over space, Cunningham's rhythms effect a form of *différance*, introducing effects of difference and deferral into rhythm itself. Constant shifts of spatial frameworks and 'cutting' of temporal flow produce a choreographical equivalent of 'spacing' that undermines binary oppositions of time and space and renders each 'undecidable'. For instance, stillness is evoked at the heart of movement, and movement at the heart of stillness, and off-balance moments appear to both maintain and displace equilibrium. Here we experience neither movement in time nor position in space separately, nor a unity of both (which is always 'deferred'), but rather the energy generated by non-teleological and non-hierarchical oscillation between them. Cunningham's choreographic 'spacing' opens up both space and time to their exterior, so that the spatio-temporal categories fundamental to Laban's concept of effort themselves become undecidable. Similarly, the complexity of relationships between movement events taking place simultaneously and that cannot be perceived at once produces effects of both difference (perception of diversity) and deferral (sequential rather than contemporaneous apprehension, preventing perception of the whole) which forcibly 'split open' the present.[1042]

3. Resistance and the risks of replication

To what extent can disruption of habitual uses of energy in movement resist cultural norms? The relationship between resistance and norm can never be straightforwardly oppositional, and necessarily involves varying degrees of complicity with, and replication of, the very norms that are being resisted. It is in the nature of resistance that it involves a degree of replication of dominant economies of energy, since it is necessary, in Norman Bryson's terms, to 'meet' the existing flow, in order to 'redirect' it.[1043] However, it is clear that this process involves risks. Unless kinesthetic imagination is combined with reflexive critiques of the insertion of dance practices into wider networks of power, innovative economies of energy are vulnerable to assimilation into dominant power structures.

Wigman lacked political acumen, and her dance offered no serious resistance to the encroachment of Nazi ideology. Her support came largely from critics with conservative leanings, and her life philosophy connections were regarded with suspicion on the political left. Her dances under fascism conformed increasingly to Nazi expectations. Susan Manning dates Wigman's turn towards fascism, which coincided with a turn away from her previous implicit feminism, from the staging of *Call of the Dead* [*Totenmal*] in 1930. Manning points out that this was a year of political crisis in Germany, and that the contradictory politics of *Totenmal*, which advocated both militarism and pacifism, 'projected the middle class desire not to have to choose between the extreme left and the extreme right. The staging of the war memorial obscured its contradictory politics, effacing the necessity of choice.'[1044] Apoliticism here furthered the cause of extremism. Paul Douglas, writing in *New Theatre* in 1934, criticised Wigman's mysticism and escapism, and argued that 'the social forces which caused this escape were neither understood nor was there an attempt made to cope with them'.[1045]

With respect to Graham, dancers on the left saw her as 'bourgeois' because, in the words of the critic Paul Douglas, writing in 1934, she 'seems to be seeking *external* values wholly unrelated to the dynamic struggle of existing social forces as a source for her material'.[1046] During the 1930s, critics did not recognise the feminist implications of Graham's uses of energy, seeing her work rather in purely 'modernist' terms, as depersonalised and abstract. Graham's celebration of virile strength and her refusal of feminine difference in her dances of the late 1920s and early 1930s are problematic in terms of radical feminism. Her declared lack of interest in the women's liberation movement was connected with her unwillingness to identify with women as a less powerful category than men, and she never in fact resolved the issue of how to deal with the 'feminine' in terms other than (stereotyped) extremes. In Marcia Siegel's words: 'For Graham, a traditional feminine stance can be adopted only as a weapon or a sign of weakness.'[1047]

Siegel considers Graham as a feminist nonetheless, and I have argued here for the strongly feminist implications of Graham's appropriation of 'virile' energies for women in her early work. By contrast, the critic Marianne Goldberg is highly suspicious of Graham's lack of political awareness in gender terms, the implications of which emerged clearly in her later work. In her 1984 production of the *Rite of Spring*, Graham 'presents the woman's sacrificial role as inevitable and natural – as if it were an immutable archetype of western culture'. Goldberg affirms that 'the "Rite of Spring" myth, in its supposed universality, denies that ideas and fantasies about sexuality are learned and constructed under particular historical structures of desire'. Graham accepted this pseudo-universality and did not address its historical contingencies. She even claimed that the 'chosen one' (the virgin victim of the sacrificial rite) could just as easily be a man as a woman, which, as Goldberg points out, 'reveals her lack of a political consciousness of what is involved in making art in patriarchal culture'.[1048]

Cunningham practises an apoliticism that is deliberate and self-conscious, and transposes political issues into his art. He has described his working method, according to which each individual operates separately and no one tells anyone else what to do, as 'political'.[1049] He has also described his approach as 'anarchic', and emphasised the autonomy and freedom of individuals and the lack of competition between them.[1050] I discussed in the previous chapter the role of technology in promoting a utopian view of the future, and the influence of Buckminster Fuller and Marshal McLuhan on Cunningham and Cage. In a famous article of 1957, Cage declared:

> Our intention is to affirm this life, not to bring order out of chaos nor to suggest improvements in creation, but simply to wake up to the very

life we're living which is so excellent once one gets one's mind and one's desires out of its way and lets it act of its own accord.[1051]

Cage did not pose the question, 'Excellent for whom?', and Cunningham's work has been criticised for not addressing difference in terms of unequal power relations. Susan Foster has argued that only physical differences are recognised and valued (in that Cunningham is interested in how each individual executes movements differently), while gender or ethnic identities are ignored. 'His approach presumed an absolute equivalence of male and female bodies, and black and white bodies.' According to Foster, the denial of racial difference is indicative of 'a tradition that presumed its own universality'.[1052]

In fact there are differences between the movement that Cunningham choreographs for male and for female dancers. Most obviously, lifting is strongly gendered, but there are sometimes also divergences in the effort qualities that the choreography calls for. In a documentary shown on BBC TV in 2000,[1053] Cunningham commented:

> I prefer to have the possibilities a woman gives in movement as well as the possibilities a man gives, and they are in one sense the same, but they are also different. Women so often to me have a kind of continuous quality, which can go on really for quite a long time. With the man so often it seems in spurts, up and down. There is a difference, and they do sort of complement each other.

This comment is juxtaposed with a remarkable passage from *Pond Way* (1998), where Banu Ogan crosses from downstage left to right with very sustained, free-flowing movement, barely punctuated by a weight change each time that she takes a step forward, when she is touched and held very lightly and fleetingly by a different man in the piece, before continuing on her way. Cunningham has not shown particular interest in exploring collective identities, but his approach does not presume 'absolute equivalence', in that the effort qualities which each dancer brings to the movement are inseparable from his or her individual, inculturated movement experiences. Jonah Bokaer, who has danced with the company since 2000, told me that he finds that the tremendous variety of backgrounds and nationalities in the current company 'has undoubtedly impacted the interpretation of Merce's rhythms'.[1054]

A further criticism of Cunningham might be that, although chance procedures apparently place everyone on the same level, his masterminding of their operation can create a significant gap between him and the dancers, all the more important now that there is a very considerable age difference between them. Also, as Cunningham is aware, when narrative is lacking, people are strongly motivated to discover 'stories' and interpretations. The difficulty for spectators of finding an intentional meaning and fixing an interpretation of events on stage even has parallels with (and risks replicating) the culture of secrecy discussed in the previous chapter, where the public struggles to make sense of, and is driven to personalise, recalcitrantly impersonal and highly complex bureaucratic systems. Interestingly, though, in *Split Sides* (2003) the chance process is made public for the first time, when dice are cast on stage by invited participants at the beginning of the performance, to decide which of two possible musical compositions, decors, costumes and lightings will come first or second. The choreography is also divided into two reversible parts, but this sequence is decided in advance, in order, as Cunningham explained to the audience, to give the dancers time to rehearse.[1055]

Frederic Jameson concluded a lecture given at the Whitney Museum in 1982 with an unanswered question concerning postmodernism's capacity for resistance to consumer capitalism:

> We have seen that there is a way in which postmodernism replicates or reproduces – reinforces – the logic of consumer capitalism; the more significant question is whether there is also a way in which it resists that logic. But that is a question we must leave open.[1056]

Jameson identified the break with memory and history, exemplified in the 'transformation of reality into images' and 'the fragmentation of time into a series of perpetual presents', as a characteristic of postmodernism that replicates 'late, consumer, or multinational capitalism'. Here the commodity exists in a present that has erased the traces of the labour that went into its production, and where the informational function of the media is to relegate the present to the past as quickly as possible, thereby helping us to 'forget, to serve as the very agents and mechanisms for our historical amnesia'.[1057]

Jameson described Cage's music as an example of postmodernist art; it is presented as a kind of auditory performance of forgetting: the enactment of forgetting in musical terms. 'The hearing of a single chord or note followed by a silence so long that memory cannot hold on to what went before, a silence then banished into oblivion by a new sonorous present which itself disappears.'[1058] This challenge to memory can be linked with McLuhan's description, cited in the previous chapter, of the effects of electronic technology on people's relationship to time. 'You now have everything at once. You don't move on from one thing at a time to the next thing. There is no more history; it's all here ... Speed, huge speed-up, means there's no more past.'[1059] John Cage affirmed that 'we are interested in not being bound by memory'.[1060]

Cunningham's dance, with its high speeds and fragmented, discontinuous flows, which interrupt linear progression in time, itself recalls key features of late capitalism. 'To increase their capacity for consumption, consumers must never be allowed to rest. They need to be kept forever awake and on the alert.'[1061] Like the consumer, the Cunningham dancer must be constantly alert. For the dancer, however, this alertness requires 'almost an emptying of the mind, not to receive more or less information, but to be able to be the movement'.[1062] The degree of choice open to the spectator of a Cunningham piece, where freedom to select what one watches coincides with the impossibility of seeing everything at once, also has certain parallels with the position of the consumer. Spectators can therefore connect with experience that is familiar in a different context, through which they have acquired skills of 'polyattentiveness' (Cage). Consumers frequently experience an excess of goods on offer as confusing and detrimental to decision-making, and even anguish-inducing (as argued recently by the psychologist and sociologist Barry Schwartz in *The Paradox of Choice*).[1063] However, the complexity and open-endedness of Cunningham's work resists consumerist logic by alerting spectators to multiple and unforeseen possibilities, while at the same time liberating them from pressures to make limiting choices.

4. New technologies

Recent experiments with the uses of digital technologies in dance have led to new ways of using energy that further expand the scope of kinesthetic imagination, including its reflexive potential. The affirmation of Laban and Lawrence, cited in Chapter 1, that machine effort should be regarded as 'an artificial extension of man's effort',[1064] can be compared with McLuhan's view that 'all media are extensions of some human faculty – psychic or physical' (see the epigraph to this chapter). In response to technological innovation, Laban and Lawrence argued that people were capable of learning 'new movements and combinations of efforts for which the human body engine does not seem to be adapted'. For instance, none of the combinations of positions or efforts required for landing from a parachute jump is natural, but people can be trained to get the feel of them and even to automatise their most salient features.[1065] This makes it possible to combine 'mechanical devices and human energy' as a 'complex unit, like the teamwork of several people, and not as the work of two separate entitites'.[1066] This would appear to anticipate later opportunities for 'interfacing' between the human body or psyche and new media, as happens with what are currently known as 'new technologies', which can be defined as 'electronic devices and applications that are based on the digital processing capabilities of the computer'.[1067]

Choreographies using new technologies are so diverse that it would be impossible to enumerate all the types of practice here. Examples include: use of computer programs such as DanceForms (formerly LifeForms) in the choreographing process (as discussed in the previous chapter on Cunningham); motion capture used to transfer data derived from real movements to a virtual character or 'avatar' (also made famous by Cunningham, with his *BIPED* of 1999, and by Bill T. Jones, with his *Ghostcatching* of the same year); telepresence (literally, achieving presence in distant places), of which a well-known example is Paul Sermon's *Telematic Dreaming* (1992), 'a live telematic video installation linking two sites';[1068] interactive performance spaces where 'the motion of the performer can directly influence the sonic or visual environment in the moment'[1069] (e.g. as seen in the work of 'half/angel', with Jools Gilson-Ellis and Richard Povall, or the interactive installation *Sensuous Geographies* by Sarah Rubidge and Alistair MacDonald); the integration of the body with inorganic matter by extending the body through machines, as practised by Australian performance artist Stelarc;[1070] and interactive digital dance, which can also be networked or webcast 'live'.

The multimedia dimension of new technologies allows kinesthetic imagination to expand and intensify its synesthesic interactions with other senses, notably sound, vision and tactility. For instance, in Rubidge's *Sensuous Geographies*,[1071] participants are sometimes 'performers' and sometimes watch other participants, who wear extraordinarily vividly colored, ritualistic costumes, which have been described as 'a cross between medieval gowns and burkas'.[1072] When wearing the costumes, participants cannot see, which heightens their awareness of the textured floorcloth and the mobile sound-world emanating from the speakers, to which their own movements in the performance space contribute. Moving together with, and touching, other participants while being unable to see also has the curious effect of blurring corporeal boundaries between self and other, opening up the intersubjective dimension of kinesthetic imagination.

It is not coincidental that many choreographers who use new technologies work in more than one medium or collaborate with artists in other media. New technologies can give greater responsibility to performers, and allow spectators to participate in ways that enable them to take partial responsibility for constructing works. Spectators can thereby become more involved in the activity of kinesthetic imagination and, as 'producers' themselves, less in danger of fetishising dance as spectacle. These recent uses of technology, through interactions with digital media, enable choreographers, performers and spectators to discover new dimensions to human movement. They mark a dramatic shift away from the strong opposition (discussed in Chapter 1) between organic and mechanical rhythms posited by early twentieth-century German thinkers and practitioners of body culture. It is also a shift away from the fear of 'uncanny' similarities between human and mechanical rhythms, epitomised in the views of Ludwig Klages, who believed that 'tools and machines make war on the realm of the living' and that 'the mechanization of nature, instead of enlivening, seizes all life at the roots'.[1073]

According to the theatre and dance scholar Kerstin Evert:

By contrast [with the early 1900s], interactive dance productions in the late 1900s situate body and technology in a system that is clearly under human control. This control, conditioned by the particularities of digital media, seems to reveal that man no longer feels subordinate to a dominant technical system, but rather that technology can serve man by allowing him to extend the reach of his body in new directions.[1074]

Evert also affirms that: 'the space that can be appropriated through the sense of touch and sight can ... be expanded electrically beyond the body's kinesphere[1075] and physical location, bringing about a technologically reinforced union of the human being with his world'.[1076] Indeed, Helmut Gottschild's idea, derived from Wigman, of an 'open' body, whose energy extends beyond the boundaries of the skin and interacts with the surrounding space, takes on new resonance in the light of digital technologies.

There are, of course, choreographers who are wary of technology and the danger that it might restrict and even replace the physical body. Furthermore, the issue of control cited by Evert is debatable. Technology's potential to extend pre-reflective sensory experience can affect kinesthetic imagination in ways that are unforeseen by the rational, transcendental subject. As I discussed in relation to Cunningham, with reference to chance operations, technology plays an important role in enabling choreographers to move beyond personal, subjective choices, by increasing the elements of choice and their unpredictability. Following a workshop on dance and technology held in 2001, documented in the book *Dance and Technology/Tanz und Technologie*, the British choreographer Wayne McGregor commented that 'the interface of computer or rather digital technology seems to provide some kind of impartiality, which frees up decisions and takes away many of the inhibitions about creating dance'. He also affirmed that 'new media interventions provide a strong motivation to actualise the virtual choreographic ideas – it does not lead to a more passive participation but *a radically altered, energised need to move.*'[1077] Many choreographers are keen to foster an interactive relationship with the technology they work with, where the technology plays an active role in stimulating their creative and performing processes. Choreographer and performance artist Kent de Spain wrote on the 'Dance-Tech' mailing list: 'I want the "systems" that I interact with (technology, other people) to require me to renegotiate my circumstances at any given moment.' More graphically, he declared, 'I want a system where that gigantic video image can jump off the screen and bite that artist in the butt.'[1078]

Analogous issues can arise for spectators/participants in interactive works, who sometimes feel that the success of their participation depends on their understanding of, and control over, the technology, whereas this might in fact limit their experience. The installation *Sensuous Geographies,* where the participants' influence on the sound environment is directly linked with the colour of the costume they put on, gave rise to an interesting discussion about how important it was for individuals to be able to identify their own sound effects. Some participants reported frustration at not being able to 'work it out', while others felt happy with this open-ended experience.[1079] From the production point of view, the user's degree of control over the technology is entirely relative to the latter's suitability for the purposes envisaged and the user's expertise (which may require a long learning process), not to mention the often very high costs of acquiring the necessary equipment, which limit its use, globally and socially. It is also important to retain awareness of the limitations of technology in relation to the biological body, for instance in controlling the aging process.

Digitally based technologies that can interface with humans are increasingly the object of cultural fantasies around the idea of the 'posthuman'.[1080] In the previous chapter, I cited Marshall McLuhan as declaring that 'all media are extensions of some human faculty – psychic or physical. The wheel ... is an extension of the foot. The book is an extension of the eye ... clothing, an extension of the skin ... electric circuitry, an extension of the central nervous system.'[1081] Recent manifestations of such 'extensions' have led to the term 'cyborg', which denotes a biotechnological life form. Steve Dixon discusses cyberneticist Gregory Bateson's question of whether a blind man's stick is part of the man. 'In epidermal biological terms it is not, but as far as cybernetic systems are concerned it is, as is a hearing aid, or Steven Hawking's voice synthesiser, since it constitutes part of a single information flow and feedback system.'

Dixon goes on to point out the implications of this approach. 'To fully embrace such radical theory may also involve accepting the proposition that one has become "posthuman"'. Posthuman theory places 'emphasis on cognition rather than embodiment ... with the body becoming a manipulable evolutionary prosthesis, as can be seen, for example, in the work of Stelarc'. He concludes his article with the affirmation that 'as performers increasingly virtualise and posthumanise themselves in digital manifestations, they too believe in, and are reliant upon this erasure of difference between live, recorded, physically present or telematically transmitted embodiments'.[1082] However, most choreographers strongly affirm the physical and kinesthetic reality of the body, and use technology not to erase differences between live and technologically mediated bodies, but rather to draw attention to the interfaces between them, which are based on differences as well as continuities. Further, technological 'extensions' can expand the possibilities of the human body, rather than rendering it obsolete (Stelarc's view of the body's obsolescence will be discussed below).

If used as an extension of a lived body, infused with its own intentionality and capacity to stimulate new uses of energy in movement (which are not wholly transparent to the consciousness of the rational subject), technology can itself extend the possibilities of kinesthetic imagination. For Merleau-Ponty, habitually using an object for a certain task can result in the object becoming integrated into the space of the lived body. Just as we do not consciously have to measure the size of our body against the space of a doorway in order to know whether we can pass through, a woman accustomed to wearing a feather on her hat, the driver of a car, or the user of a walking stick or a typewriter come to treat them as extensions of their own body space.[1083] Similarly, Cunningham commented on virtual dance figures: 'One could say, "They're not human", or "they're not this or that", but I have no sense about that. I'm sure that when the typewriter came in everybody said it wasn't human, and then of course you use it and it becomes human.'[1084]

Debates on the posthuman raised by new technologies are reminiscent of controversies over whether Oskar Schlemmer's experiments with the human form were anti-human or, as Schlemmer himself argued, had the effect of drawing attention to that 'which can *not* be mechanized'.[1085] Cunningham's view is comparable to Schlemmer's in that he is not interested in 'erasing' the human, but rather in playing on similarities and differences between the human and the technological. He has frequently joked about his work with LifeForms that on the computer screen he can make the head turn round several times, but that this doesn't interest him, because he wants to work with the limitations of the human body. At the same time, as a result of learning ways of moving that do not 'come naturally', but are derived from the computer, Cunningham's techniques and choreography, which were already very demanding, now place even greater demands on the dancers, requiring complex combinations of effort patterns.

In a panel discussion at a Merce Cunningham Study Day in London in 2002,[1086] Robert Swinston, the longest-standing member of the current company, was asked by an audience member whether the difficult movements ever felt comfortable. Swinston talked about the 'very fast and complicated' movement in *CRWDSPCR* (1993), and the need to learn the weight shifts and the movements for each part of the body separately. Because it's 'not organic', you have to 'repeat them until they become part of your body'. The movements did become 'natural', and 'homo-genized into your body', but this required 'fortitude' and 'pushing boundaries'. Swinston, like Derry Swan, a Cunningham dancer to whom I spoke about this,[1087] said that the younger dancers pick up the 'difficult' movement with a great deal less effort. (Cunningham has also commented on this phenomenon.) In response to the same question, former Cunningham dancer Emma Diamond emphasised the importance of the process of absorption into the 'muscle memory', which she described as 'extraordinary'.[1088] The use of computers to provide new models for organising uses of energy in movement has the potential to intensify for the dancer the experience described (in another panel discussion at the Study Day) by Cunningham dancer Daniel Squire. He commented in relation to dancing in *RainForest* (1968) that 'everyone is transported – becomes another creature than what they are – other than human', and that: 'the choreography does it to you, rather than you doing it to it'.

New technologies, then, can intensify the process whereby kinesthetic imagination generates new effort patterns and mobilises the parameters of the 'human'. For Cunningham, the natural world, and in particular the movements of animals and birds, have long been key sources of inspiration. (See his remarkable collection of drawings, *Other Animals: Drawings and Journals by Merce Cunningham*, New York: Aperture, 2002.) Rather than using rhythm as I discussed in Chapter 1, to distinguish the 'human' from the machine, the LifeForms computer program encouraged Cunningham to push non-human parameters further and to explore hybrid qualities of movement, including patterns derived from nature, notably in *Beach Birds* and *Beach Birds for Camera* (1991) and *Pond Way* (1998).[1089]

Since 1991, when he began to use LifeForms in his choreographing process, the movement qualities of Cunningham's dancers have become increasingly idiosyncratic. In *Beach Birds for Camera*, the quirky fragmentations of the body, the oddly angled limbs and, at times, a quasi-robotic rigidity and stiffness show the influence of LifeForms, which encouraged Cunningham to choreograph separately for different parts of the body. These movements also have undeniably birdlike as well as human qualities. The critic Leslie Kendall speaks of 'a whole vocabulary of familiar, angular motions: twitching, jerking, hopping, leg shaking, wing stretching, head cocking, group immobility, encroaching on one another's space for territory or pairing'.[1090] Cunningham always aims to hold open several different ways of looking at the same time, displacing fixed identities in an effect encapsulated in Clement Crisp's comment that the dancers in *Beach Birds* are 'like gulls and not like gulls'.[1091]

BIPED (1999) used motion-capture techniques, where effort qualities were transferred from live bodies onto avatars (although, to date, motion capture has been less effective at capturing weight than capturing other effort attitudes). Movement data was captured by cameras that tracked sensors placed on the bodies of live dancers, and was digitally mapped onto figures drawn by Shelley Eshkar, working in collaboration with Paul Kaiser, to create digital images, which were projected onto a scrim in front of the live dancers on stage. The interactions between the live dancers and the images animated by motion-capture data were both dramatic and moving. Many critics felt that the interaction enhanced the physicality of the live dancers. Deirdre Scarry commented, 'The dancers were sumptuously human, lengthening their limbs to full extension, fluidly moving through each phrase, and relating to each other onstage.'[1092]

Cunningham himself was most interested in the 'collision'[1093] between live and virtual dancers, and in the contrasts between the timings of the different sets of movement, which lead to 'a kind of doubling of the possibility of how you see and what you see'.[1094] Motion capture can also generate hybrid movement incorporating different effort qualities by combining digitised data from different sources. For instance, in *Fluid Canvas* (2002), motion-captured data from Cunningham's hands was combined with movement data drawn from animals, and spectators should be able to see a cat, a fish and a horse, this time in images projected at the back of the stage.[1095] In choreographer Ghislaine Boddington's words (addressing Cunningham): 'we can see fish movement through your hands – in the digital realm'. In response to this comment, Cunningham was keen to stress that 'it's adding something to our experience in just plain physical terms'.[1096]

In radically posthuman approaches to technology, it is envisaged that new, posthuman entities will replace the live performer. For Stelarc, the biological body is obsolete, unable to keep up with 'the complexity and quality of the information it has accumulated', and is 'intimidated by the precision, the speed and the power of technology' (a postmodern equivalent of the challenge to 'life' posed by conditions of modernity, as discussed in Chapter 1). The architecture of the body needs to be altered, thereby extending its consciousness of the world.[1097] Stelarc's performance experiments involve both extending the body through mechanical/robotic additions, such as a third hand, and using electronic technologies to interface robotic extensions and the biological body.

The body can be interfaced with its extensions, where electrodes convey internal signals to the added 'limbs', and with remote locations, from which externally produced signals are transmitted. In *Ping Body: an Internet Actuated and Uploaded Performance*, Stelarc 'interfaced his body with the Internet via electrodes, whose electrically charged involuntary movements were related to the stimulation caused by the Net traffic'. The unaccustomed overload of electronic stimulation 'shocks' the body and produces involuntary muscle action. In *ParaSite for Invaded and Involuntary Body*, the performer's body is again connected to the Internet, but in this performance 'a search engine selects random body images that act as optical stimulation and then the image jpg's are reprocessed as electricity for muscle stimulation. In this way the simulated visual body, or metabody, moves the actual body.'[1098]

According to Stelarc, predictable responses in the human body can be erased, 'as the neural pathways are not prepared for the additional electricity that shocks the body into spasms'. This will lead to the production of a body 'without memory, and without the thinging [sic] mind to contain it, and this is where the real fun begins'.[1099] Stelarc here asserts the necessity of (violently) erasing the body's memory, thereby destroying embodied subjectivity as we know it. However, as applied philosopher Fiona O'Neill observed at a recent performance by Stelarc at a workshop entitled *Homopolybots: Building modular humans*,[1100] it appeared that Stelarc himself had become accustomed to electronic stimuli, which had perhaps left memory traces in his body, and which were experienced quite differently by participating audience members.

I'd say that Stelarc still 'felt' the stimuli, obviously muscularly but also sensorily. However, he ignored or has become used to/accepting of, for the sake of performance/inured to, any pain sensations at the time of performance and subsequently. He does appear to be very fit, being both physically and mentally attuned to his art. Whereas the four participants in his lecture all felt some pain with the stimulus.[1101]

This indicates that the body does continue to learn and adapt, laying down new memories and energy 'pathways', which re-define the individuated subject.

Working with the body-technology interface can heighten reflexive awareness of one's body by producing increased sensitivity to kinesthetic sensations. Susan Kozel, who performed in Paul Sermon's installation *Telematic Dreaming*, declared that 'as a dancer, hearing anyone claim that virtual technology demonstrates the futility of the body makes me want to dig my heels in, theoretically and practically'.[1102] In this installation, where two remote locations were connected using video projectors and digital telephone (ISDN) lines, new technologies were used to enable interactions between subjects located in separate sites.

A double bed is located within both locations, one in a blacked out space and the other in an illuminated space. The bed in the light location has a camera situated directly above it, sending a live video image of the bed, and a person ('A') lying on it, to a video projector located above the other bed in the blacked out location. The live video image is projected down on to the bed with another person ('B') on it. A second camera, next to the video projector, sends a live video image of the projection of person 'A' with person 'B' back to a series of monitors that surround the bed and person 'A' in the illuminated location.[1103]

The image of Susan Kozel (person 'A') on her bed was projected onto a bed in a public room, where visitors had the option to join her. Video cameras in this public room transmitted the interactions between the visitor and Kozel's image back to her on monitors placed around her bed in her room upstairs. In turn, she was able to interact with the person on the bed downstairs by watching both of their images on the monitors. Kozel recounted, 'I was alone on my bed, moving my arms and legs in physical space as if in some sort of hypnotic ritual dance, yet in virtual space I carried on intense physical improvisation with other unknown bodies.' For her, the experience 'was one of extending my body, not losing or substituting it. My intuitive conviction that the virtual body is entwined with the fleshly body was reinforced by my experiences of intimacy and violence in *Telematic Dreaming*.' The performance made her even more aware of her physical body, especially its involuntary aspects. 'I became obsessed with the invisible side of my body: digestion, intestines, breathing.'

In this installation, visitors as well as performers needed to activate kinesthetic imagination to adapt their movement habits in order to allow them to navigate between three-dimensional and two-dimensional spaces. Paul Sermon, who also performed in the installation, commented, 'We move our hands around a three-dimensional object [the bed] but observe ourselves at the same time on a monitor that can only represent a two-dimensional image of this action.'[1104] As Söke Dinkla notes, 'digitally controlled spaces require a new understanding of one's body, which must be tested out both intellectually *and* physically'.[1105] Kozel recounted, 'Movement usually began in a hesitant way with hand contact taking on excessive importance. The impact of slow and small movement became enormous. Great care and concentration was required to make intricate web patterns with the fingers of a stranger, or to cause one fleshly finger to meet up with one video finger.'

Here, not only did spectators physically participate as 'visitors' to the work, but they also became actively involved in discovering new ways of moving with a virtual partner. Spectators had as much impact as Kozel on how the work developed in real time, and were in turn themselves deeply affected by the work.

> The mechanization or computerization of human experience is generally thought to diminish the physical and emotional sides of life, yet in the virtual world of *Telematic Dreaming*, questions of privacy, intimacy and identity were central. This was not just my experience as a performer, many members of the public were overwhelmed by their experiences on the other bed.

Interaction between real and virtual bodies also blurred the boundaries of 'self' and 'other'. At one point, Kozel, thinking that she was touching her partner's leg, discovered that it was her own.

> When I momentarily experienced my own body through my sense of touch it did not coincide with my body according to my sense of sight. The disorientation made me reassess what I took to be the frontier of my own body.

The erotically charged location of the bed also forced participants to confront issues of intimacy and power. As a performer, Kozel encountered both erotic intimacy and intimidating violence on the part of visitors. They could no longer remain passive, as they were responsible for making the work happen, and were confronted with the results of their actions, even if this simply meant encountering their own refusal to participate. Kozel recounted that 'some people simply froze, and fled the installation once they realized what it was about. When politicians or members of the Dutch royal family visited they did not even venture onto the bed for fear of being recorded in a compromising position.' This use of technology exploits the potential for open-ended reflexivity and awareness of issues of power to be built into the very functioning of the work, without the need for any didactic content or formal devices aimed at provoking a reflexive attitude.

In her remarkable study, *Dances That Describe Themselves: The Improvised Choreography of Richard Bull*, Susan Foster discusses how Michel Foucault, in his writings on power and the body, 'shows us just how hard it is to assess relations of domination and move outside them'.[1106] Foster describes rave dancing as 'an expenditure of energy for no productive purpose, an affront to Protestant and capitalist work ethics'. She explores the subversive potential of improvisation, which affirms 'the body's generative capacity to formulate new contestatory and critical stances towards the status quo'.[1107] However, she raises the 'nagging' question of whether, despite their contestational quality, even raves in fact continue to operate within the 'system', and in its interests. 'Do [raves] assist in controlling the populace by providing opportunities to unleash energies that might otherwise have been tapped for protest?'[1108] In his later work, dating from the late 1970s, Foucault advocated a critical attitude towards normalising structures, through a constant interrogation of what is apparently natural and inevitable in one's own identity. This would lead to the exploration of 'new forms of subjectivity through the refusal of [the] kind of individuality which has been imposed on us for several centuries'.[1109] Foster argues that rave dancing can be truly subversive only if the dancers 'find in a rave's events a critical reflection ... on the structures of behavior that discipline their lives'.[1110] Such critical reflexivity can be enhanced by the use of new technologies, as discussed in relation to Kozel's installation.

5. Resistance and expenditure:
Changing economies of energy

Laban conceptualised effort in terms of 'spending energy',[1111] and saw rhythm as a form of 'economy' of energy. Many post-structuralist thinkers have drawn parallels between the logic of capitalist economies and processes of producing meaning. Kristeva made connections between communicative and economic concepts of 'exchange', and argued that avant-garde texts pointed the way beyond capitalist economies of exchange. The theorist Georges Bataille was immensely influential in drawing on Marcel Mauss's essay on the 'gift' to propose a distinction between a 'general' economy, defined by 'the forces of expenditure', and a 'restricted' economy, defined by the forces of production.[1112] Jacques Derrida linked the restricted economy with the economy of the classical sign. In this economy, the individual sign is held to be dependent on the surrounding elements in the system to acquire meaning/value. Although the latter is never absolutely present (because of the context dependency), the lack of full presence is considered merely temporary, until full meaning is restored. For Derrida, then, 'the economy of the classical sign is based on a deferred presence, which is always regained ... and the restricted economy overpowers the general', marking the domination of Reason.[1113]

By contrast with the economy of the 'proper' (as in 'proper noun'), where everything returns to its rightful owner and the aim is to recuperate whatever is spent, and if possible to make a profit, Bataille proposes the concept of '*dépense*' (expenditure), which is 'spending of such an extreme nature that it approaches death'.[1114] *Dépense* is a unilateral gesture, epitomised in 'the effulgence of the sun, who dispenses energy – riches – without a counterpart'.[1115] It erupts as 'a continuous release of vital forces',[1116] and is 'a type of giving which is conceived beyond the limits of rationality'.[1117] It marks an attempt to 'project oneself, and something of oneself, *beyond the self*'.[1118] This is an instant of total surrender, which also leads beyond the self to a collective encounter. Michele Richman argues that '*dépense*' should be read as 'a critique of the quality of exchange and communication within contemporary culture'.[1119] The use of energy in *dépense*, which pits expenditure and loss against recuperation and profit, also resists recuperation of meaning and affirms instants of non-discursive communication.

Innovative uses of energy in dance can short-circuit habitual, inculturated effort patterns in a moment of *dépense* that interrupts the signifying chain and exceeds the accounting capacities of discursive communication. The dance works I have discussed in previous chapters resist subordination of energy to production of quantifiable goals (including discursive meanings), and instead celebrate dance itself as a source of energy, which they renew and intensify. They generate heightened energy levels, and amplify and intensify sensations of 'life' as material effects that are transmitted to spectators without calculation of recuperation into codifiable meanings, abstracted from the body.

6. Kinesthetic shocks

In *Disability and Contemporary Performance: New Technologies of Embodiment*, Petra Kuppers has discussed encounters with virtual physicalities on the Internet, where the participant engages in interactive movement with a figure on the computer screen through using a mouse. These encounters can trigger reflexive awareness based on the need to pay attention to one's own physical engagement with the technology, and to learn new modes of attention to and interaction with the 'other' body on the screen. She also recounts how her experience of straining to hear an unclear voice transmitted on the website of Contact 17 brought to mind a discussion of the 'grain of the voice' by the French theorist Roland Barthes (1915–90).[1120] Barthes compared what he called 'texts of bliss' with 'texts of pleasure', which could be enjoyed in comfort without unsettling 'historical, cultural, psychological assumptions' and without disturbing the 'consistency of [the subject's] selfhood'. Texts of bliss challenge these assumptions, 'unsettle ... the consistency of [the subject's] tastes, values, memories, bring to a crisis his relation with language',[1121] producing 'shock, disturbance, even loss'.[1122] 'Bliss' and the semiotic exceed the boundaries of the sayable, and are inaccessible to metalanguage. Here, the body speaks a non-expressive language, which Barthes describes as a 'vocal writing': it is an 'articulation of the body, of the tongue, not that of meaning, of language'. Barthes uses the example of the cinema, where the sound of speech can be captured 'close up' (the 'grain of the voice'), as if the actor's body were being 'thrown' into the listener's ear: 'it [sound] granulates, it crackles, it caresses, it grates, it comes: that is bliss'.[1123]

This experience of the intense materiality of the signifier can be both seductive and violent. Writing on photography, Barthes discusses what he calls the 'punctum', 'that mode of painful and compulsive pleasure that is not sought out but actively seeks out and *injures* the receiver'.[1124] The punctum has the effect of 'piercing' what Barthes sees as the falsity of a unitary self. Barthes identified the punctum specifically in photography, as a detail 'with a nagging, piercing quality', usually of the photographed subject's body, which is 'presented with an intense materiality (not as a sign) – a little boy's bad teeth, Tristan Tzara's hand, Andy Warhol's fingernails', and whose 'impact is on the spectator's body'. It produces 'a bodily shock of recognition', which is non-codifiable, and interrupts the signifying chain.[1125] Like the semiotic, the punctum interferes with culturally coded systems of communication. Working in different ways – the semiotic by breaking down coded structures and releasing their rhythmic differences, the punctum through the disproportionate impact on the whole of an intensely material, incongruous detail – these phenomena unsettle subjects' coherence and stability.

Similar effects can be produced when energy exceeds the effort patterns that normally regulate it. In dance, the punctum which pierces or jabs the spectator is felt kinesthetically, as a shock to established effort patterns, which directly affects the nervous system. This shock effect is unforgettable, persisting in memory and resisting the 'forgetting' endemic in consumer society where, in Zygmunt Bauman's words, 'the culture ... is mostly about forgetting, *not learning*'.[1126] Both structural linguistics and capitalism are systems that rely on the existence of stable formations, capable of regulating and binding the circulation of energy within the system. Moments of crisis occur when 'the very forms through which energy is rendered circulable ... cease to be able to harness that energy ... the regulator encounters energy that it cannot bind'.[1127] In the moment of performance, the communicative situation between dancer and spectator can be charged with 'a dimension of *force* that escapes the logic of the signifier: an excess of energy that symbolic exchange can never regulate'. This results in 'blockages (moments of stasis) in the circulation of energy, in the form of unexchangeable products'.[1128]

At such moments, dance is experienced through the nervous system as an energetic shock. Cunningham declared, 'Try looking at events another way and the whole world of gesture, the whole physical world in fact – is as if jabbed by an electric current.'[1129] Wigman spoke of 'the breakthrough of unconscious spiritual [*seelisch*] processes to a state of *corporeal consciousness*' (my emphasis),[1130] and many of her commentators used images of electrical force to convey the physical effects produced by her dance, which 'gripped' and '*electrified*' the spectator (see Chapter 2). Graham, too, aimed to address her spectators physically and aggressively, by impacting on the 'nervous system', which she saw as the primary instrument of experience.[1131] In a recent interview with me, Cunningham said of the impact of electronic music on dance: 'I call it simply [acting] on the nerves, because it's certainly not on the muscles ... it's brought through the nervous system, which doesn't count the way dancers do ordinarily ... in a sense it's the way all technology is going.'[1132]

Disruptions to habitual, inculturated patterns of effort cannot be exchanged for or translated into discursive units of meaning. Rather, they produce direct transmissions of kinesthetic energies between dancer and spectator, where the resulting shock can produce what Cunningham calls an 'abyss':

> An art, if it communicates anything, must have its communication in that place where the rational and the irrational do their intriguing and giddy duet ... I think that dance at its very best ... produces an indefinable and unforgettable abyss in the individual spectator – it is only an instant, and immediately following that instant the mind is busy questioning, deciding: the feelings are busy, agitating, confirming or denying. But there is that instant, and it does renew us.[1133]

Such dance communicates through a momentary punctum, where spectators are as if pierced by a kinesthetic shock that they cannot assimilate into habitual, culturally codified effort patterns. Without this moment, there cannot be any radical shift or reflection on uses of energy.

Conclusion

Acts of kinesthetic imagination are not motivated by rationally calculated, discursively articulated decisions, but rather by a desire to find new ways of using energy that emerge through the process of moving itself. The role of kinesthetic experience in grounding subjects, both on an individual level and in relation to cultural contexts, means that innovations in dance have implications that are not reducible to the effects produced by other art forms. Modifications to habitual effort patterns are context-specific, focusing on different effort elements according to the sets of pressures on embodied subjects in particular sets of circumstances. For instance, in the early twentieth-century 'body culture' contexts that I discussed, many people were attracted to the idea of intensifying 'life awareness' through movement, thereby resisting subordination of energy to the ends of commodity production. Rhythmic movement, in gymnastics as well as dance (especially when practised by women), was seen as having the function of intensifying vitality and freeing the body to become more expressive.

This context was crucial to the reception as well as the production of early modern dance. The degree to which spectators share kinesthetic experience and values with choreographers and dancers has a strong impact on how performances are received. Even responses that are intuitively felt to be spontaneous and natural cannot be separated from shared inculturation. In the case of reconstructions of older works, such as pieces by Graham, present-day audiences cannot have direct access to the effort experiences of contemporaries and their inculturated significance. Moreover, as has frequently been pointed out, the bodies of today's dancers are built differently, and this has an inevitable effect on effort qualities. In the case of works recorded on film or video, such as the dances by Wigman that I have discussed, the layers of mediation are even more complex. Whether for live, reconstructed performances or for filmed versions of dance works, historical inquiries can inform present-day spectators about relevant effort experiences and issues surrounding uses of energy for choreographers and spectators. This knowledge can enhance the kinesthetic effects of movement techniques and choreographies in the present. However, such research is necessarily partial, and ultimately, for spontaneous kinesthetic connections to occur, there has to be sufficient congruence with spectators' own experiences of movement.

Of the choreographers I have looked at, this issue is posed most frequently by Graham's work, since her technique has been extensively codified, and the Martha Graham Dance Company still performs her choreography. These performances continue to have a powerful effect on spectators of Western theatre dance, and draw superlative language from critics. According to the critic Ismene Brown, reviewing the Martha Graham Dance Company at London's Sadler's Wells theatre in November 2003: 'Martha Graham's dances may no longer be modern, but they make most choreographers of the past century look exhausted.' It may be that the work of the 1920s and 1930s, of which many pieces are now in the company repertory, has particular resonance today. This choreography still frequently produces strong feelings of empowerment for women. Brown declared with satisfaction that: 'every girl who has been cowed by raucous boys should go and see *Sketches from 'Chronicle'* and she'll come out raring and deadly'![1134]

I recently (April 2004) interviewed two dancers in the current Graham Company, Alessandra Prosperi and Maurizio Nardi, and was struck by how often the idea of power arose during our conversation. I asked them both about their first experiences of encountering Graham technique. Prosperi said that it hurt, but that she didn't mind, because it was 'powerful, liberating'. For Nardi, it felt like 'that's it': he had found a technique with 'viscerality' and 'power', where there was 'no half way', and which could 'project energy'. Prosperi commented that the Company was based on 'female power', and Nardi concurred, remarking that the 'men reinforce female power'. At the same time, it was a 'great technique' for men, because Graham 'knew male power'. Prosperi spoke of the attraction of 'intensity' and 'passion' in Graham's work, and its capacity to provoke a physical reaction in the spectator, as in *Cave of the Heart* (1946), where 'you shake with her [Medea]'. They both emphasised the popularity of *Sketches from 'Chronicle'* (1936), which 'everybody loves' (Prosperi) and which 'could have been created last month' (Nardi).

I also recently had the opportunity to ask Cunningham about the relative importance to him, as a spectator of his own work, of the kinesthetic and visual dimensions of his dance. He replied that kinesthesia was of 'the utmost importance' and that he felt movement kinesthetically, because 'that's what dancing is'. He declared: 'I realise that the work that I give is sometimes not a familiar kinesthetic way, but I quite firmly believe that as the dancers continue to do it, it becomes that way. So it can be added to the known kinesthetic possibilities. I just feel that very strongly.'[1135] This 'adding to the known kinesthetic possibilities' is the work of kinesthetic imagination. The Cunningham dancer Jonah Bokaer sees his choreography as a 'puzzle', which needs to be worked out and 'mapped' on both physical and mental levels. It also involves 'reprogramming the way different parts of the body co-ordinate', and becoming aware of different layers of perception. In this working-out of how to perform the movement, and in 'playing with the transitions' between movements, individual dancers give their own input into the work.[1136] Cunningham's increasing popularity (to the extent that he is now generally seen as mainstream rather than avant-garde) suggests that his mode of experimentation, which is constantly evolving, strikes a chord with many present-day spectators, who are themselves frequently familiar with activities of 'reprogramming'. The widespread use of digital technologies and the opportunities they offer (at the touch of a button) to change the way systems operate have fuelled interest in rapid transformations, whose parameters often exceed the grasp of a single individual.

The physical and mental work of kinesthetic imagination can result in radical transformations of the way dancers use energy, and new technologies, which extend the scope of kinesthetic imagination, can fuel energy expenditure of an extreme nature (*dépense*). The 'alternative economy' involved in Bataille's account of *dépense*, like Kristeva's semiotic and Barthes's punctum, brings into play a certain pleasure in risk-taking and an exhilaration in transgressing boundaries. However, this learning process requires physical work, and frequently a cost in terms of pain, on the part of the performer. Dance as an art form requires discipline and precision, even when transgressing habits and conventions. Moving away from organic, holistic rhythms towards more discrete, discontinuous uses of energy can greatly increase the wear and tear to the dancer's body, which, unlike its digital counterparts, cannot be replaced. China Laudisio, a former Cunningham dancer with whom I corresponded by email on this subject, recounted the pleasure she experienced in Cunningham's work before LifeForms:

> Before the computer, the movement – for me – was heavenly. I loved it. Lots of play with throwing the weight around, yet at the same time being in control. Every movement trying to be as big as possible, stepping beyond each step every time.[1137]

By contrast, Laudisio did not feel comfortable with the LifeForms work:

> I never had injury problems – yet the work became somehow painful . . . my mind and emotions rebelled against it, and physically it went against how I wanted to move . . . we had to jump and within the jump change our back '*x*' many times and change our arms '*x*' amount of

times, and then when we landed there were more changes . . . painful
because things were dissected and compartmentalized and there was
no freedom of flow.[1138]

The demands made on dancers by learning and executing movement
techniques and choreography that require far-reaching modifications to
habitual effort patterns mean that energy must be conserved to a
sufficient degree to safeguard their well-being and prevent injuries. This
is more difficult to achieve when the effort modifications that are involved
are extreme and interfere with the rest and recuperation function inherent
in organic rhythms. It requires respect for the limits of what is physically
desirable, which may fall short of what is possible. It also places
responsibilities on the dancers to manage their own energy expenditure.
Jonah Bokaer explained to me that he needs to 'economise' his energy in
accordance with the demands he can anticipate, and he wrote in *Dance
Umbrella News* that 'dancing with [Cunningham's] company . . . takes
dedication, an agile mind and a resilient commitment to taking care of
the body, which is often placed in extreme, unnatural circumstances'.[1139]

Extremes of expenditure involve extremes of consumption. In light of
the finitude of natural resources and the fragility of the ecosphere, whose
parts are closely integrated and where localised imbalances have been
seen to have far-reaching repercussions, post-industrial, predominantly
Western countries have seen increased awareness of the need to safeguard
equilibrium.

All modern economies are dependent on fixed stocks of non-renewable
material and energy resources. The Second Law of Thermodynamics
makes clear that they necessarily consume and degrade the very resource
base that sustains them. Our material economies treat other components
of the biosphere as resources, and all the products of economic activity
(that is, the by-products of manufacturing and the final consumer goods)
are eventually returned to the biosphere as waste. Thus, while we like to
think of our economics as dynamic, productive systems, the Second Law
states that, in thermodynamic terms, all material economic 'production'
is in fact 'consumption'.[1140] Excessive consumption depletes resources
and can cause long-term damage, the signs of which are by now
incontrovertible.

Medicine and biotechnologies are continuing to push forward the
boundaries of 'human' and 'natural' life, destabilising our certainties as
to what these categories may comfortably contain. This gives rise to ever-
spiralling ethical dilemmas and exposes new vulnerabilities, where 'life'
appears to be an ever more unstable, unidentifiable state. Moreover, the

combined factors of technology and terrorism mean that large parts of the Western world, which previously considered themselves inviolate, now feel exposed to risk of attack from unexpected sources. Cunningham commented on the effects of 9/11: 'We became vulnerable. We never thought we were before, but to have such a catastrophe happen, not with armaments, but with instruments we thought were simply to carry us from one place to another was ... horrible'. He continued by speaking of how impressively New Yorkers had reacted to the crisis, in the way that they 'gathered to help'.[1141]

It is difficult to identify issues at stake in uses of energy in dance during a period that is still being lived through; but in the light of this current awareness of finitude and climate of vulnerability, shared, intersubjective energies have undoubtedly taken on increased significance. Energy sharing in movement marks an increasing openness to interdependence and marks resistance to the values of separateness and autonomy that characterise individuation in Western societies, and which boost demand for consumer goods. In recent years, intersubjective elements have been given greater emphasis in some of Cunningham's work, in terms of eye contact between dancers, exchanged expressions, and interactions through touch. The critic Zoë Anderson writes of a duet between Holley Farmer and Daniel Squire in a performance of *Split Sides* (2003) at London's Barbican Theatre in October 2004:

> [they] move with marionette quickness ... then the dance slows ... these longer phrases glow with communicative warmth. Farmer's flicked feet seem conversational; she falls back against [Daniel] Squire, or stretches over his back. For all their physical closeness, they barely look at each other, *hardly need to.* At last, Farmer curls forwards, kicking her legs up behind as he lifts her. She's like a woman wading into surf, carried by the waves.[1142]

The use of shared energies in dance was developed to an unprecedented extent in contact improvisation, a dance form founded by Steve Paxton in 1972, which involved 'experimenting with partners giving and taking weight improvisationally'.[1143] In contact improvisation, dances are created collaboratively, with a great deal of mutual transference of weight between partners, requiring much physical contact and a high degree of trust. 'Dancers have to keep their energy freely flowing, abandoning self-control in favor of mutual trust and interaction'.[1144] The exchange of weight in 'give and take' and the strong emphasis on touch produce powerful resistance to economies of energy based on individuation.

Shared energies and physical trust are hallmarks of the work of the British choreographer Russell Maliphant. Maliphant's piece, *Torsion*, recently choreographed for George Piper Dances (Michael Nunn and William Trevitt), is a male duet that explores complex nuances of weight transferences, mutual support and interactive flow. It is a moving celebration of shared energies, which has been aptly described as an 'exercise in power-sharing' with 'a remarkable liquidity'.[1145] The movement vocabulary ranges from tango to arm-wrestling, and the frequent combination of strong interactive use of weight with free flow produces an extraordinary interface between physical aggression and extreme tenderness. At times the two men's bodies seem to oscillate between attempting to overpower the other, and participating in a single energy flow.

Almost in a reversal of the uses of energy discussed in relation to Cunningham's then iconoclastic new movement style in the 1940s and 1950s, where punctuality asserted the positivity of discreteness and discretion in defiance of a pseudo-personalisation of public space, here shared energies create rhythms in which the boundaries of individual subjects no longer appear fixed. These 'rhythmic subjects' move in and out of the state of individuation, not, as in Wigman's solos, through rhythmic exchanges with space, nor by establishing collective identities, but rather by constantly touching, exploring and renegotiating the boundaries of self and other. Similarly to Wigman, the privileging of separateness and containment is here undermined, in a move that recalls Merleau-Ponty's concept of dehiscence (see Chapter 2). Speaking of the world 'outside' the subject, Merleau-Ponty writes as follows:

> When I find the world, such as it is, under my hands, my eyes, against my body, I find much more than an object . . . this does not mean that between me and it, there is fusion, coincidence: on the contrary, this happens because a sort of dehiscence opens my body in two, and because between the world which is seen and which sees, the world which is touched and which touches, there is a covering, an encroaching, in such a way that we have to say that things pass into us as much as we pass into things.[1146]

For Merleau-Ponty, it is the 'otherness' of subjectivity which is primordial. 'I was first of all outside myself, in the world, with others.'[1147] The audience's encounter with uses of energy that exceed the boundaries of kinesthetic containment within individual effort patterns exposes dehiscence within and between subjects.

The use of new technologies in interactive works, where audiences participate in the performance, can catalyse confusion in the spectator/participant about the boundaries of one's own and others' bodies, causing oscillation between kinesthetic awareness of intersubjectivity and of individual uses of energy. (See the discussion in the previous chapter.) Writing on 'new technologies of embodiment', the performance theorist Petra Kuppers refers to 'a search for touch, intimacy and immersion', and describes intersubjectivity and individual embodiment as 'two poles of being', which can combine to 'keep options open, keep a sense of wonder at differences alive'.[1148] Some types of interactive work that use new technologies require the spectator/participant to physically move in the space, while others (e.g. digital dance that is responsive to manipulation of a mouse) involve the spectator largely through virtual movement, more akin to the conventional position of the seated spectator of theatre dance. While new ways of presenting dance and movement-based work will no doubt continue to proliferate, there is a specificity of theatre performance involving dancers and an audience that is certainly here to stay. This performance situation takes on a special significance, in the light of the current sensibilities I have just described, as a particular type of (temporary) community, with a greater or lesser degree of shared inculturated kinesthetic experience.[1149]

Here I have attempted to highlight the unique status of dance as an art form and the role of kinesthetic imagination for spectators as well as for choreographers and dancers. For my purposes I have mobilised relevant aspects of movement analysis, cultural commentary and theoretical discussion (philosophy, literary theory and sociology) along with the writings of choreographers, statements by dancers and commentaries by dance critics, which are anchored in contemporary cultural contexts. In order to investigate more fully the role of kinesthetic imagination in (re)structuring uses of energy in dance, and to ascertain how economies of energy work in the transmission of kinesthetic effects from performer to spectator, which constitutes the specificity of dance, one must look further in (at least) two directions, both requiring increased interdisciplinarity and also collaboration, which will complement my current approaches.

First, it will be necessary to examine the physiology of virtual movement in both dancer and spectator. For instance, how similar or different is virtual movement (in the sense of pre-movement/intentional movement) as experienced by dancers and as experienced by spectators as a result of kinesthetic empathy? This will require testing of both muscular and neural activity. In turn, how are these forms of activity similar to or different from those engaged in when movement is physically enacted?

Second, it will be necessary to engage, on a variety of levels, with diverse audience members in different locations (giving a much wider picture than that gained from reading dance critics, who constitute a restricted category of spectator), in order to conduct an ethnographic analysis of dance reception, which will need to be cross-referenced with the physiological data. If possible, it would be useful to conduct testing with 'atypical' audience members, who would not ordinarily attend dance performances. Obviously, such studies could be carried out relative to any type of dance performance, but they would be of most interest with dance that explores new ways of using energy, as I have discussed here, and I hope to begin this study by looking at Cunningham's work. Two well-known choreographers whom I have not discussed here, and whose work could also usefully be examined in this way, are Trisha Brown and William Forsythe – but there are of course many others.

I would like to conclude with a verbal 'choreography', spoken by Merce Cunningham and written, with slight adaptations and spatial layout, by Jonah Bokaer. Describing the 2004 performance of *Split Sides* referred to above, Zoë Anderson mentioned 'radical shifts of rhythm', and specifically a 'marvelous solo' by Jonah Bokaer, where he 'holds rigid poses, breaking them with sudden undulations'.[1150] This solo is indeed literally quite breathtaking. Bokaer has recounted that he worked with Cunningham for days 'to build and layer the material', and that 'he used some remarkably poetic language in staging it'.[1151] The result, as well as the solo, was a text whose imagery evokes the transformative effects of Cunningham's choreography, which 'punctures' time.

> Now Jonah.
> You're going to SLAM,
> pop, and then with this leg
> Drop. Think like breath on glass.
> Forget what's coming next –
> (To bust up Time, you see.)
> Tear up Time
> in your Head.
> Now with this leg slither –
> it's a Snake –
> right.
> Then turn your face Left and curve.
> Now –

CRUMBLE! That's it –
Brrhre aaahhp bumppp BAAAaaahhhh!
.......but make it uneven –
So the eye doesn't see what's coming
Next.
Think of
an Amoeba,
something moving
as one piece.
Each upon each upon each.
(All rhythm is, is cutting up Time, you see.)
Just decide
to forget what's coming
Next,
and if you do.......
Spontaneous Earth.[1152]

Glossary of specialised vocabulary

Theatre

downstage: towards or at the front of the stage
upstage: towards or at the rear of the stage
stage right/left: for the audience, 'stage right' is left, and vice versa

Laban

Forceful/strong attitude to weight: the prevailing effort is of muscular tension. Examples are pressing, pushing, wringing, pulling, punching, thrusting, slashing, hitting (hard), throwing, etc.

Light attitude to weight: the prevailing effort is of muscular relaxation. Examples are flicking, floating, dabbing, gliding. (See *Effort*, 60–62.)

Direct attitude to space: movement in a well-defined direction. A movement can be considered direct when the effort of unilateral tension prevails in it. Examples are dabbing, gliding, punching, thrusting, pressing.

Indirect/flexible attitude to space: the direction of the movement is constantly changing. A movement can be considered flexible when the effort of multilateral muscular function prevails in it. Examples are wringing, slashing, floating, flicking. (See *Effort*, 68–70.)

Sudden attitude to time: fast movement. A movement can be considered quick when the effort of an abrupt or sudden muscular function prevails in it.

Examples are punching, flicking, hitting, slashing, dabbing, jerking, thrusting.

Sustained attitude to time: slow movement. A movement can be considered sustained when the effort of continuous muscular function prevails in it. Examples are floating, pressing, wringing, gliding. (See *Effort*, 64–66.)

Bound flow: controlled movement, capable of being stopped and held without difficulty at any moment during the movement.

Free flow: loose movement, difficult to stop suddenly.

Many actions can be performed with either bound or free flow, e.g. wringing and dabbing. (See *Effort*, 56–58.)

Ballet

Arabesque: the body is balanced over one foot with the other leg extended fully behind, the arms extended, palms down, creating a long line of perfect symmetry from fingertips to toes.

Arabesque penchée: the extended leg is very high, causing the torso to lean well forward.

Attitude: a pose on one leg with the other leg lifted towards the back, well turned out, and bent at the knee. The bent knee is on a level with, or higher than, the foot.

Dégagé: a movement or position where the working leg is lifted off the floor.

Demi-plié: a half-bend of the knee. In a demi-plié, the feet never leave the floor.

Demi seconde: a position of the arms halfway between first and second. In first position, the arms are low and curved, with the palms facing the body. In second position, they are open to the side, with a slight curve downwards, the hands turned slightly to the floor.

Développé: the working foot is drawn up to the supporting knee and then the leg is unfolded to an open position.

First position: the legs are turned out from the hips, the heels and knees touching, the feet forming a straight line.

Fouetté: a whipping movement.

Plié: a bending movement of the knees.

Relevé: the act of rising to the ball of the foot.

Second position: the legs are turned out from the hips, and the heels are about twelve inches apart.

Tendu: stretched, held out, tight: a basic ballet position where the leg is extended straight out from the supporting leg with the toe fully pointed.

Third position en haut: the arm is raised, with the hand centred on the body, thus forming a half-circle.

Most of the ballet terms are in Sandra Noll Hammond, *Ballet Basics* (California: Mayfield, 1974).

Endnotes

1   Early examples include Sally Banes, *Terpsichore in Sneakers: Postmodern Dance* (Middletown, Connecticut: Wesleyan University Press [1977], 1987, revised edition), and Susan Foster's *Reading Dancing: Bodies and Subjects in Contemporary American Dance* (Berkeley: University of California Press, 1986).

2   Norman Bryson, 'Cultural studies and dance history', in *Meaning in Motion: New Cultural Studies of Dance*, ed. Jane C. Desmond (Durham: Duke University Press, 1997), 55 (55–77).

3   The following are examples that have been useful for my own work. Susan Manning's *Ecstasy and the Demon: Feminism and Nationalism in the Dances of Mary Wigman* (Berkeley: University of California Press) appeared in 1993, as did Sally Banes's *Greenwich Village 1963: Avant-Garde Performance and the Effervescent Body* (Durham, NC: Duke University Press). Sally Banes's *Writing Dancing in the Age of Postmodernism* (Middletown, CT: Wesleyan University Press) was published in 1994. 1995 saw the publication of Ramsay Burt's *The Male Dancer: Bodies, Spectacle, Sexualities* (London: Routledge); Ann Daly's *Done Into Dance: Isadora Duncan in America* (Bloomington: Indiana University Press); Susan Foster's edited collection (generated by the conference discussed by Bryson) *Choreographing History* (Bloomington: Indiana University Press); Mark Franko's *Dancing Modernism, Performing Politics* (Bloomington: Indiana University Press); and Helen Thomas's edited collection *Dance, Modernity and Culture* (London: Routledge). In 1996, Susan Foster's collection *Corporealities: Dancing Knowledge, Culture and Power* (London: Routledge) and Gay Morris's edited collection *Moving Words: Re-writing Dance* (London: Routledge) appeared. Ann Cooper Albright's *Choreographing Difference: The Body and Identity in Contemporary Dance* (Middletown, CT: Wesleyan University Press), Jane Desmond's edited collection *Meaning in Motion: New Cultural Studies of Dance* (Durham, NC: Duke University Press), Ellen Graff's *Stepping Left: Dance and Politics in New York City, 1928–1942* (Durham, NC: Duke University Press) and Karl Toepfer's *Empire and Ecstasy: Nudity and Body Movement in German Body Culture, 1910–1935* (Berkeley: University of California Press) were published in 1997. 1997 also saw the publication of an invaluable resource for Cunningham scholars, *Merce Cunningham: Fifty Years, a 'Chronicle and Commentary'* by David Vaughan (New York: Aperture). Sally Banes's *Dancing Women: Female Bodies on Stage* (London: Routledge), Ramsay Burt's *Alien Bodies: Representations of Modernity, 'Race' and Nation in Early Modern Dance* (London: Routledge), Felicia McCarren's *Dance Pathologies: Performance, Poetics, Medicine* (Stanford: Stanford University Press) and Randy Martin's *Critical Moves: Dance Studies in Theory and Politics* (Durham,

NC: Duke University Press) were published in 1998. In 1999, Sondra Fraleigh's and Penelope Hanstein's edited collection *Researching Dance: Evolving Modes of Enquiry* (London: Dance Books) and Linda Tomko's *Dancing Class: Gender, Ethnicity, and Social Divides in American Dance, 1890–1920* (Bloomington: Indiana University Press) appeared, and a new study on 'Ausdruckstanz' by Diana Howe, *Individuality and Expression: The Aesthetics of the New German Dance, 1908–1936* (Bern: Peter Lang) was also published.

4   Examples include Valerie Briginshaw, *Dance, Space and Subjectivity* (Basingstoke: Palgrave, 2001); *Moving History, Dancing Cultures: A Dance History Reader*, ed. Ann Cooper Albright and Ann Dils (Middletown, CT: Wesleyan University Press, 2001); *Dancing Many Drums: Excavations in African American Dance*, ed. Thomas F. deFrantz (Madison, WI: University of Wisconsin Press, 2002) and Helen Thomas' *The Body, Dance and Cultural Theory* (Basingstoke: Palgrave, 2003).

5   Roger Copeland, *Merce Cunningham: The Modernizing of Modern Dance* (London: Routledge, 2004), 24. Copeland himself sees these aesthetic values as linked with politics in Cunningham's work, in the classically modernist sense of a 'politics of *dis*engagement' and a 'politics of perception' (*Merce Cunningham*, 16). See my review in *Dance Research* (forthcoming).

6   Jane Desmond, 'Embodying difference: issues in dance and cultural studies', in *Meaning in Motion*, ed. Jane Desmond (Durham, NC: Duke University Press, 1997), 33 and 49–50 (29–54). This article was also published in *Cultural Critique* 26 (Winter 1993–94), 33–63.

7   *Dancing Modernism, Performing Politics* (London: Routledge, 1995), 54.

8   Wesleyan University Press, 1.

9   Wesleyan University Press, 227.

10   Stanford University Press.

11   Frederic H. Martini, *Fundamentals of Anatomy and Physiology* (New Jersey: Prentice Hall, 2001: 5th edition), 36 and 37.

12   Malcolm Slesser (general editor), *Dictionary of Energy* (London: Macmillan, 1982), 82. Dictionary definitions of 'economy' include 'All factors relative to the production, distribution and consumption of wealth in a human collectivity' (*Le Petit Robert, Dictionnaire*: Paris: Le Robert, 1991) and 'The management of the resources, finances, income and expenditure of a community, business enterprise etc' (*New Collins Concise Dictionary*). Throughout this book, all translations from texts whose titles are given in French or German are mine.

13   *The New Collins Concise Dictionary of the English Language* (London: Collins, 1982).

14   The term 'kinetic energy' is used in physics, to denote the energy of motion, and here it can also apply to objects, and can be quantified in terms of mass and speed. Physics also uses the terms 'potential energy', which is 'the stored energy of position possessed by an object', and 'mechanical energy', which is 'the energy acquired by the objects upon which work is done'. See Tom Henderson, 'The Physics Classroom':

www.glenbrook.k12.il.us/gbssci/phys/Class/energy/u5l1b.html.
Accessed 11 March 2004.

The words 'energy' and 'force' have overlapping areas of meaning and are often used interchangeably in non-scientific discourse. However, the relationship between energy and force in physics is complex. In the case of kinetic energy, energy can be defined as the force exerted multiplied by the distance moved. I am grateful to Stephen Pumfrey for this clarification.

15 *The New Collins Concise English Dictionary.* Links with the auditory sense mean that music is an important factor in the perception of movement. However, discussion of the role of music in the reception of dance is beyond the parameters of the present study; neither do I have space to examine in depth connections between dance and the visual arts.

16 Since I am not a dance practitioner, my approach to dance through uses of energy is inspired primarily by my experience as a spectator, and I recognise that my perspective is necessarily different from that of a trained dancer. However, I believe that theoretical reflection on movement should be based on physical practice, and so I have participated in a number of dance and movement-based activities: most importantly, a Summer School at the Laban Centre for Movement and Dance (now renamed 'Laban') in London, as well as Alexander technique, ballet classes and Iyengar Yoga. Alexander technique aims to change movement habits in everyday activities, releasing tension and increasing energy. It has been described as 'a life philosophy reduced to a practical application'. (Walter Carrington, cited in Elly D. Friedman, *Laban/Alexander/Feldenkreis: Pioniere bewusster Wahrnehmung durch Bewegungserfahrung* (Paderborn: Junfermann Verlag), 1989, 61.) My subtitle, 'Uses of energy', makes reference to Frederick Alexander's well-known book, *The Use of the Self* (1932). I am also a qualified massage therapist.

17 Cambridge University Press, 1995.

18 In phenomenology, intentional consciousness is consciousness directed towards an object: consciousness must be consciousness *of* something. The term 'corporeal intentionality' is my own.

19 Letter to Paul Demeny, 15 May 1871, in *Oeuvres de Rimbaud*, ed. Suzanne Bernard and André Guyaux (Paris: Garnier, 1981), 347.

20 Laban's writings are immensely complex and controversial, but I shall not engage with these controversies here. Laban has been criticised for a dubious political stance in relation to Nazism, which I discuss in Chapter 1. The mystical dimension of his thought has long been recognised. Carol-Lynne Moore has investigated the Rosicrucian basis of Laban's choreutic theories: see Carol-Lynne Moore, *Introduction to Movement Harmony* (Denver, CO: Cottage Industries, 2003). Laban was a Grand Master in a Masonic lodge from 1917–18. For a detailed discussion of his ideas, see Vera Maletic, *Body-Space-Expression: The Development of Rudolf Laban's Movement and Dance Concepts* (Berlin: Mouton de Gruyter, 1987). Maletic also contributed the informative

entries on Laban and Labanotation to the *International Encyclopedia of Dance* (Oxford University Press, 6 vols, 1998, vol.4), 89–104. On the background to Laban's early thought and for other details of his biography and extensive achievements, see Preston-Dunlop, *Rudolf Laban: An Extraordinary Life* (London: Dance Books, 1998). See also John Hodgson and Valerie Preston-Dunlop, *Rudolf Laban: An Introduction to his Work and Influence* (Plymouth: Northcote House, 1990).

[21] Rudolf Laban and F.C. Lawrence, *Effort* (London: Macdonald and Evans, 1947), xi. Laban's work with industry is documented by Valerie Preston-Dunlop, in *Rudolf Laban*. For the history of these ideas, see Vera Maletic, *Body-Space-*Expression, 93ff. Laban's ideas on Effort are also expounded at length in *Modern Educational Dance* (London: Macdonald and Evans [1948], 3rd edition, 1975), and in *The Mastery of Movement*, ed. Lisa Ullmann (London: Northcote House [1950], fourth edition, 1980).

[22] See Chapter 1.

[23] Laban, *Modern Educational Dance*, 26.

[24] Laban and Lawrence, *Effort*, xiv.

[25] See Laban, *Modern Educational Dance*, 54.

[26] Laban, *Rudolf Laban Speaks about Education and Dance*, ed. Lisa Ulmann (Surrey: Laban Art of Movement Centre, 1971), 23, 26 and 28.

[27] Laban, *Modern Educational Dance*, 10.

[28] Rudolf Laban, 'Dance in general', *Laban Art of Movement Guild Magazine*, 26 (May 1961), 16 and 17 (11–24).

[29] Cited in Maletic, *Body-Space-Expression*, 192.

[30] Laban and Lawrence, *Effort*, 58.

[31] *Ibid.*, 59.

[32] Laban, *Modern Educational Dance*, 24.

[33] Laban, Ibid, 102.

[34] Laban, Ibid, 6.

[35] Laban, 'Dance in general', 14.

[36] Laban, *Choreutics* (London: Macdonald and Evans, 1966), 49.

[37] 'The three 'R's of movement practice', *Laban Art of Movement Guild Magazine* 14 (March 1955), 13 (12–17).

[38] Cecily Dell, *A Primer for Movement Description using Effort-Shape and Supplementary Concepts* (New York: Dance Notation Bureau, 1970), 23, emphasis mine. See also Carol-Lynne Moore and Kaoru Yamamoto, *Beyond Words: Movement Observation and Analysis* (London: Gordon and Breach, 1988).

[39] Laban, *Modern Educational Dance*, 75.

[40] Laban, *Choreutics*, ed. Lisa Ullmann (London: Macdonald and Evans, 1966), 31.

[41] See Warren Lamb, *Posture and Gesture: An Introduction to the Study of Physical Behaviour* (London: Duckworth, 1965); Warren Lamb and Elizabeth Watson, *Body Code: The Meaning in Movement* (New Jersey: Princeton, 1979); and Marion North, *Personality Assessment through Movement* (Boston: Plays, Inc., 1975).

42   See Irmgard Bartenieff and Dori Lewis, *Body Movement: Coping with the Environment* (New York: Gordon and Breach, 1980); Cecily Dell, *A Primer for Movement Description*; and Cecily Dell, Aileen Crow and Irmgard Bartenieff, *Space Harmony: Basic Terms* (New York: Dance Notation Bureau, 1977). Disciplines that draw on Laban's ideas include psychology, psychotherapy, anthropology and ethnography, as well as notation, dance performance, choreography and teaching. There continues to be extensive debate over the appropriate use of terminology, such as 'Laban Movement Analysis', 'Labanalysis', 'Laban Movement Studies' and 'Laban Studies', and, until recently, UK and US developments of Laban's ideas have remained remarkably separate. For informed discussion of these complex issues, see the website of the New York Dance Notation Bureau, (http://dancenotation.org/DNB/theorybb/frame0.html) and follow the 'Names for what we do' thread. Accessed 12 March 2004.

43   Irmgard Bartenieff and Martha Davis, *Four Adaptations of Effort Theory in Research and Training* (New York: Dance Notation Bureau, 1970), 30. The Dance Notation Bureau was founded in 1940 by Ann Hutchinson Guest, Helen Priest Rogers, Eve Gentry and Janey Price. The concept of 'shaping' was brought to the US by Irmgard Bartenieff, who, together with Martha Davies and Forrestine Paulay, founded the Effort/Shape department at the Dance Notation Bureau in New York in 1965. In 1978, Bartenieff founded the Laban Institute of Movement Studies, which has now become the Laban/Bartenieff Institute of Movement Studies.

44   Bartenieff and Davies, *Effort-Shape Analysis of Movement: The Unity of Expression and Function* (New York: Albert Einstein College of Medicine, 1965, draft manuscript in the library of the Laban Centre, London), 33.

45   Ibid., 6 and 37.

46   Ibid., 12. For a discussion of the history of this evolution of Laban's ideas, see Vera Maletic, 'Laban concepts and Laban dialects: Issues of "shape" ', in *Laban Art of Movement Guild*, 77 (1978), 23–31.

47   Judith Kestenberg, *The Role of Movement Patterns in Development* (New York: Dance Notation Bureau, 1967), vol. 1, 88.

48   See Lisa Sandlos, 'Laban Movement Analysis: Unlocking the Mysteries of Movement'. www.xoe.com/LisaSandlos/lma.html. Accessed 8 March 2004. See also Bartenieff and Davis, *Four Adaptations*, 33. The different elements of LMA are not always grouped in the same categories. For a somewhat different account, see Carol-Lynne Moore and Kaoru Yamamoto, *Beyond Words: Movement Observation and Analysis* (Pennysylvania: Gordon and Breach, 1988), 181–205. Laban's work is constantly generating new ideas. Currently, for instance, a Laban-inspired project in Japan (MIDAS, or MIC Interactive Dance System) is seeking to correlate physical features of dance movement with categories of emotional image expression. 'In this system, we applied Rudolf Laban's dance theory to extract physical features of dance

movement from real-time video sequences and mapped this information to categories of emotional image expression. In this way, we can relate physical motion with mental emotion using multimedia.' 'MIDAS : MIC Interactive Dance System', www.mic.atr.co.jp/organization/dept3/papers/midas/Midas.html. Accessed 2 November 2004.

49   Kestenberg, *The Role of Movement Patterns*, vol. 1, 90. See also Janet Goodbridge, *Rhythm and Timing of Movement in Performance* (London: Jessica Kingsley Publishers, 1999), 34.

50   Kestenberg, *The Role of Movement Patterns*, 86.

51   See Bartenieff and Davis, *Four Adaptations of Effort Theory*, 35.

52   See Warren Lamb, 'The essence of gender in movement', *Laban Guild Movement and Dance Quarterly* 12, no.1 (Spring 1993), 1–3; 12, no. 2 (Summer 1993), 3 and 8; and 12, no. 3 (Autumn 1993), 7.

53   In 1965, Bartenieff and Forrestine Paulay carried out pioneering work with Alan Lomax in researching dance and work styles from different cultures, using selective Labanalysis. See *Folk Song Style and Culture*, ed. Alan Lomax (Washington, DC: American Association for the Advancement of Science), 1965, and a choreometrics discussion in Alan Lomax, *Folk song style and culture: a staff report* (Washington, DC, American Association for the Advance of Science, Publication no. 88, 1968). See also Chapter 10 of Bartenieff and Lewis, *Body Movement*, 'Ethnic studies'. For a recent example of detailed description of a non-Western dance form using Laban Movement Analysis, see Ciane Fernandes, 'Technique and Tradition: The Laban/Bartenieff System in the Learning of Indian Classical Dance (Bharatanatyam)'. www.cianefernandes.pro.br/ilabanindian.htm. Accessed 16 March 2004. LMA is used to analyse body movement in intercultural communication, for instance in TESOL (Teaching English to Speakers of Other Languages). See also discussion of Ness below.

54   Eugenio Barba, '*Le corps crédible*', in *Le Corps en jeu*, ed. Odette Aslan et al. (Paris: CNRS, 1993), 253 (251–61).

55   Laban, *The Mastery of Movement*, 169.

56   Laban and Lawrence, *Effort*, 1. Definitions of 'economy' include: 'efficient and concise use of nonmaterial resources (as effort, language, or motion)' (*Merriam-Webster's Collegiate Dictionary/Thesaurus*).

57   Ibid., 36.

58   Ibid., 18.

59   Ibid., 18.

60   Rudolf Laban, *Modern Educational Dance*, 53.

61   Laban and Lawrence, *Effort*, 6.

62   Laban, *Modern Educational Dance*, 26.

63   Ibid., 27.

64   Laban and Lawrence, *Effort*, 66.

65   Laurence Louppe, *Poétique de la danse contemporaine* (Bruxelles: Contredanse, 1996), 114.

66   Sally Ann Ness, *Body, Movement and Culture: Kinesthetic and Visual Symbolism in a Philippine Community* (Philadelphia: University of Pennsylvania Press, 1992), 4–5.

67   Ibid., 5–6.

68   Sally Ann Allen Ness, 'Being a body in a cultural way: Understanding the cultural in the embodiment of dance', in *Cultural Bodies: Ethnography and Theory*, ed. Helen Thomas and Jamilah Ahmed (Oxford: Blackwell, 2004), 129 and 131 (123–44).

69   *Ibid.*, 137.

70   Mary Wigman, *The Language of Dance*, ed. Walter Sorell (Middletown, CT: Wesleyan University Press, 1986), 40–42.

71   Michel Foucault, *Discipline and Punish: The Birth of the Prison* (London: Penguin [1975], 1991), 228 and 20.

72   Ibid., 222.

73   'Discipline' combines power (as in subjection) and knowledge (as in 'a branch of learning or instruction'): *The New Collins Concise English Dictionary*.

74   Michel Foucault, *Discipline and Punish*, 24.

75   The French term here is *assujettissement*, which combines these meanings.

76   Lois McNay, *Foucault, A Critical Introduction* (Oxford: Polity, 1994), 111.

77   McNay, *Foucault*, 111, emphasis mine.

78   France in the 1960s and 1970s saw a convergence of Marxism and psychoanalysis. Jean-Joseph Goux's *Freud, Marx: économie et symbolique* was published in 1973 (Paris: Seuil). The term 'libidinal economy' gained widespread currency through its use by Gilles Deleuze and Félix Guattari in *Anti-Oedipus* (New York: Viking [1972], 1977) and by Jean-François Lyotard in *Libidinal Economy* (Indiana University Press [1974],1992).

79   'Truth and Power', in *Michel Foucault, Power/Knowledge: Selected Interviews and Other Writings 1972–1977*, ed. Colin Gordon (New York: Harvester Wheatsheaf, 1980), 119 (109–133). (My emphasis.)

80   Derrida, *Writing and Difference* (London: Routledge and Kegan Paul [1967], 1978), 19–20.

81   The term '*différance*' ('*différence*' with an 'a') is discussed in Chapter 5.

82   New York: Norton.

83   Morag Shiach, *Hélène Cixous, A Politics of Writing* (London: Routledge, 1991), 22.

84   Subjectivity can be conceptualised in terms of economies of physical and psychical energies, which combine an open-ended 'energetic movement of life' with the restriction of energy to fixed pathways. See Teresa Brennan, *History after Lacan* (London: Routledge, 1993), 108. Kristeva's theory of the semiotic is based on Jacques Lacan's re-reading of Freud. Kristeva distinguishes what she calls the 'semiotic' from the 'symbolic', which, in Lacan, is a rule-bound category, 'an order of social and signifying relations, of law, language and exchange'. I quote here from Elizabeth Grosz's excellent account of the Kristevan 'semiotic'. 'The

symbolic is the domain of propositions and positions, the site for the creation of unified texts, cultural representations and knowledges; the semiotic is the undirected and uncontrolled input of the repressed impulses, energies and spasms of the infant in the first case, and later, of the subject in moments of crisis and psychical upheaval'. Elizabeth Grosz, 'Kristeva, Julia', in *Feminism and Psychoanalysis, A Critical Dictionary*, ed. Elizabeth Wright (Oxford: Blackwell, 1992), 195 (194–200).

[85] 'Only certain literary texts of the avant-garde ... reach the semiotic *chora*, which modifies linguistic structures'. Kristeva, *Revolution in Poetic Language* (New York: Columbia University Press [1974], 1984), 88.

[86] Ibid., 88.

[87] '[Freudian] drives are material, but they are not solely biological since they both connect and differentiate the biological and symbolic within the dialectic of the signifying body invested in a practice.' Kristeva, *Revolution in Poetic Language*, 167.

[88] In a summary of Godard's theory of tonic function, Kevin Frank compares Godard's view of diaphragmatic control and its release into a less cortically controlled action with Laban's 'bound' and 'free flow', ideas with which he became familiar through Godard's lectures. Kevin Frank, 'Tonic Function: A Gravity Response Model For Rolfing, Structural and Movement Integration'. www.somatics.de/KevinFrank/FrankKevin.htm. Accessed 18 February 2004.

[89] Laurence Louppe, "Singular, moving geographies', Hubert Godard interviewed by Laurence Louppe', in *Writings on Dance: The French Issue*, 15 (Winter 1996), 13 (12–21).

[90] Hubert Godard, '*Le geste et sa perception*', in Isaballe Ginot and Marchelle Michel, *La Danse au xxe siècle* (Paris: Larousse, 1998), 224 (224–229).

[91] 'Singular, moving geographies', 15.

[92] Michel Bernard, *Le Corps* (Paris: Delarge, 1976).

[93] Isabelle Launay, *A la recherche d'une danse moderne: Rudolf Laban, Mary Wigman* (Paris: Chiron, 1996), 8.

[94] 'Singular, moving geographies', 20.

[95] Isabelle Launay, *A la recherche d'une danse moderne*, 27.

[96] In Chapter 5 I discuss how participatory possibilities are expanding as a result of new technologies.

[97] Kevin Frank, 'Tonic Function'. The example cited is from E.S. Reed, *Applying the Theory of Action Systems to the Study of Motion Skills'* (Reprint of author, Dept. of Humanities and Communications, Drexel University, Philadelphia, PA, 53).

[98] Geoff Watts, presenter of 'Leading Edge', BBC Radio 4,Thursday 22 January, 2004, in discussion with the late Nick Davey, neuroscientist from Imperial College, London. Broadcast available at www.bbc.co.uk/radio4/science/leadingedge_20040122.shtml). Accessed 12 February, 2004.

[99] *Phenomenology of Perception*, 109, my emphasis. I have altered this translation slightly, from 'power of action' to 'potential for action', to

translate 'puissance d'action'. *Phénoménologie de la perception* (Paris: Gallimard, 1945), 126.

100 This was discussed by Professor Robert Winston, in 'The Human Mind, Programme 1 – Get Smart', BBC 1, 1 October 2003. A summary (which does not include this example) is available at www.bbc.co.uk/science/ humanbody/tv/humanmind/programme1.shtml .

101 See, for instance, Susan Foster's stimulating discussion in 'Kinesthetic empathies and the politics of compassion', in *Continents in Movement: Proceedings of the International Conference, 'The Meeting of Cultures in Dance History'*, ed. Daniel Tércio (Portugal: Faculdade de Motrididada Humana: Cruz Quebrada, 1999), 27–30. See also the discussion of Theodor Lipps in Chapter 1.

102 *Le Visible et l'invisible*, 74.

103 John Martin, *The Modern Dance* (New York: A.S. Barnes, 1933), 78. John Martin played a key role in the development of modern dance in the US. See Chapter 2.

104 John Martin, *America Dancing: The Background and Personalities of the Modern Dance* (New York: Dance Horizons [1936], 1968), 114–5.

105 Rudolf Bode (quoting Ludwig Klages), *Expression-Gymnastics* (New York: A. Barnes and Company, 1931), 15.

106 Fritz Giese, *Körperseele: Gedanken über persönliche Gestaltung* (Munich: Delphin Verlag, 1927), 174.

107 Matthew Jefferies, *Imperial Culture in Germany, 1871–1918* (New York: Palgrave Macmillan, 2003), 193.

108 There were significant parallels with the United States, and I shall discuss the US later, but it is not my intention here to examine cross-influences. On this topic, see Isa Partsch-Bergsohn, *Modern Dance in Germany and the United States: Crosscurrents and Influences* (Switzerland: Harwood Academic Publishers, 1994), and the discussion here in Chapter 2.

109 Matthew Jefferies comments on cultural pessimism that 'one of the most important aspects of the phenomenon was the way it became possible, for the first time, to be both conservative and *modern*' (*Imperial Culture in Germany*, 143). Jefferies refers here to *Deutsche Geschichte, 1866–1918*, by Thomas Nipperdey (2 vols., Munich: Beck, 1990–92).

110 See Karl Toepfer's fascinating *Empire of Ecstasy: Nudity and Movement in German Body Culture, 1910–1935* (Berkeley: University of California Press, 1997), 383, for reflections on this subject. I follow Toepfer in his historical delineation of this phenomenon and in his use of the adjective 'Germanic' rather than 'German': see Toepfer, 10. The existence of connections between this body culture and the later rise of National Socialism is a complex issue, which is beyond the scope of my study. See, for instance, Ramsay Burt, *Alien Bodies: Representations of Modernity, 'Race' and Nation in Early Modern Dance* (London: Routledge, 1998) and Susan Manning, *Ecstasy and the Demon: Feminism and Nationalism in the Dances of Mary Wigman* (Berkeley: University of California Press, 1993).

[111]   Georg Simmel, 'The Metropolis and Mental Life', 1903, in *Simmel on Culture: Selected Writings*, edited by David Frisby and Mike Featherstone (London: Sage, 1997), 174–5. On the rapid industrialization of Germany in the late nineteenth century, see Maurice Larkin, *Gathering Pace: Continental Europe 1870–1945* (London: Macmillan Education, 1978), 103ff.

[112]   The Frankfurt School is the name given to a group of researchers associated with the Institut für Sozialforschung (Institute for Social Research), founded in 1923 as an autonomous division of the University of Frankfurt. The Institute's first director, Carl Grünberg, set it up as a center for research in philosophy and the social sciences from a Marxist perspective. After Max Horkheimer took over as director in 1930, the focus widened. Leading members, such as Theodor Adorno (philosopher, sociologist and musicologist), Walter Benjamin (essayist and literary critic), and Herbert Marcuse (philosopher), influenced by aspects of psychoanalysis and existentialism, developed a version of Marxism known as 'critical theory.' They formulated influential aesthetic theories and critiques of capitalist culture. After a period of exile in the United States because of the Nazis, the Institute returned in 1949 to Frankfurt, where Jürgen Habermas became its most prominent figure. See 'Frankfurt School', www.encyclopedia.com, accessed 30 January 2003.

[113]   For an outline, see Rick Roderick, *Habermas and the Foundations of Critical Theory* (London: Macmillan,1986), 36 ff. See also Roger Brubaker, *The Limits of Rationality* (London: Allen and Unwin, 1984). I am grateful to Andrew Edgar for drawing my attention to this book.

[114]   Toepfer, *Empire of Ecstasy*, 10.

[115]   Cited in Toepfer, *Empire of Ecstasy*, 63.

[116]   Friedrich Nietzsche, *Thus Spoke Zarathustra*, (London: Penguin [1883–91], 1969), 62 and 135. Note, however, that Nietzsche is using the term 'dance' in a metaphorical sense.

[117]   Anson Rabinbach, *The Human Motor: Energy, Fatigue and the Origins of Modernity* (Berkeley: University of California Press, 1992), 46. I am extremely grateful to historian of science Roger Smith for drawing my attention to this book.

[118]   Rabinbach, *The Human Motor*, 55.

[119]   Rabinbach, Ibid., 53. Roger Smith has drawn my attention to the distinction made by physicists in the 1850s and early 1860s (but often ignored by non-physicists) between the definitions of energy as what is conserved (the First Law of Thermodynamics) and force as a mathematical function, a measure of the effect of energy (e.g. in work).

[120]   Ibid., 4. Helmholtz believed that the universe was capable of replenishing itself (62).

[121]   Cited in Teresa Brennan, *History after Lacan* (New York: Routledge, 1993), 203.

[122]   Brennan, *History after Lacan*, 208–9. 'The mixing in of labour-power means that there is an addition to the raw materials; it adds something

which was not there before. For Marx, it is precisely this energetic addition ... that means the labourer raises the use-values of the raw materials entering into the commodity, so that the finished commodity had a higher (more consumable) use-value than the raw materials required to produce it. *This energy addition characterizes all acts of labour.'* Brennan, *History after Lacan,* 204, emphasis mine.

123 Rabinbach, *The Human Motor,* 75.

124 Ibid., 240.

125 Ibid., 74.

126 Marx, *Capital,* cited in Rabinbach, *The Human Motor,* 74.

127 Rabinbach, *The Human Motor,* 6.

128 A.C. Seward, *Darwin and Modern Science.* www.bookrags.com/books/drwnm/PART23.htm. Accessed 22 February, 2004.

129 *The Twilight of the Idols,* cited in Rabinbach, *The Human Motor,* 20.

130 *Arbeit und Rhythmus,* 1896, cited in Karl Toepfer, *Empire of Ecstasy,* 15. See also discussion of Laban and Lawrence's Effort theories below.

131 Cited in Joan Janice Schall, 'Rhythm and Art in Germany 1900–1930' (Ph.D. dissertation, University of Austin, Texas, 1989), 17.

132 Hélène Cixous has related Freud's discussion of the uncanny in his famous essay of that name, which dates from 1919, to the doll in Hoffmann's story 'The Sandman', whose animation subverts the familiar border that divides life and death. See Dianne Chisholm, 'The Uncanny', in *Feminism and Psychoanalysis: A Critical Dictionary,* ed. Elizabeth Wright (London: Blackwell 1992), 437 (436–40). It is significant that the robot Maria in Lang's film is a woman. See Richard W. McCormick, *Gender and Sexuality in Weimar Modernity: Film, Literature and 'New Objectivity'* (New York: Palgrave, 2001), 29–30.

133 Critics of the Frankfurt School argued, in close agreement with Simmel, that the 'exchange principle' reduced 'the qualitatively different and non-identical' into 'the mould of quantitative identity'. Martin Jay, *Adorno* (London: Fontana, 1984), 37.

134 *The Portable Karl Marx,* ed. Eugene Kamenka (Harmondsworth: Penguin, 1983), 446–7.

135 Benjamin, *Charles Baudelaire, A Lyric Poet in the Era of High Capitalism* (New York: Verso, 1992), 166.

136 A malady attributed predominantly to the middle classes, neurasthenia was described as chronic fatigue that pathologically inhibited action, and was associated with excessive mental activity and the stresses of urban living. This concept, immensely influential in both the US and Europe, was introduced in 1869 by a New York electrotherapist named George Beard, whose book was translated into German in 1881. On neurasthenia, see Edward Shorter, *From Paralysis to Fatigue: A History of Psychosomatic Illness in the Modern Era* (New York: The Free Press, 1992), 220–32, and Rabinbach, *The Human Motor,* 153–78.

137 Thomas Rohkrämer, *Eine andere Moderne? Zivilizationskritik, Natur und Technik in Deutschland 1880–1933* (Munich: Schöningh, 1999), 121.

138   John Schikowski, *Der neue Tanz* (Berlin: Volksbühnen Verlag, 1924), 9–10.

139   Fischer, *Körperschönheit*, 209.

140   Wigman, cited in Hedwig Müller and Patricia Stöckemann, '… *Jeder Mensch ist ein Tänzer: Ausdruckstanz in Deutschland zwischen 1900 und 1945* (Giessen: Anabas Verlag, 1993), 36.

141   Compare the words of Ernst Schertel, cited earlier: 'what we call the self or personality or the soul is nothing but the conscious disclosure of transactions or displacements of tensions enacted inside our bodies'. Cited in Toepfer, *Empire of Ecstasy*, 63.

142   Cited in Chris Shilling, *The Body and Social Theory* (London: Sage, 1993), 158. Compare the discussion of Foucault in Chapter 5.

143   Bryan Turner, Introduction to Christine Buci-Glucksmann, *Baroque Reason: The Aesthetics of Modernity* (London: Sage, 1994), 20 (1–36). He situates this attitude in the period from Nietzsche and Freud to the Frankfurt School.

144   Grosz, *Volatile Bodies: Towards a Corporeal Feminism* (Bloomington: Indiana University Press, 1994), 37. In both Freud and Lacan, this libidinal investment gives meaning to the body, or what Lacan calls the 'imaginary anatomy'.

145   Ibid., 31.

146   See note 106. In his book of this name, Giese, who was strongly influenced by Klages and Bode and theories of empathy (these topics will be discussed later) called for 'a systematic cultivation of the body-soul' (152).

147   The writings of Wilhelm Reich (1857–97) are also relevant here. On Reich's views of energy, see R. Bruce Elder, *A Body of Vision: Representations of the Body in Recent Film and Poetry* (Waterloo, Ontario, Canada: Wilfrid Laurier University Press, 1997), 143–62.

148   Brennan, *History after Lacan*, 107 and 106.

149   Ibid., 107.

150   This was elaborated in his theory of the pleasure principle. See Henri F. Ellenberger, *Beyond the Unconscious*, introduced and edited by Mark S. Micale (Princeton: Princeton University Press, 1993), 100 ff. See also Frank J. Sulloway, *Freud, Biologist of the Mind* (London: Fontana, 1979), 63.

151   Sulloway, *Freud*, 63, 109 and 62.

152   Moira Gatens, *Imaginary Bodies: Ethics, Power and Corporeality* (London: Routledge, 1996), 11. Freud was profoundly influenced by his study with Charcot at the famous Salpêtrière clinic in Paris (1885–6), where Charcot regarded the movements of his 'hysterical' patients as 'a sign of motor-neurological distress'. Felicia McCarren, *Dance Pathologies: Performance, Poetics, Medicine* (Stanford: Stanford University Press, 1998), 171. The relationship between dance and madness is a fascinating and vast topic. Felicia McCarren's *Dance Pathologies* is an excellent study within this field. On dance, hysteria and hypnotism (especially in relation to the dancer known as 'Madeleine'), see Gabrielle

Brandstetter, '*Psychologie des Ausdrucks und Ausdruckstanz*', in *Ausdruckstanz: eine Mitteleuropäische Bewegung der ersten Hälfte des 20. Jahrhunderts*, ed. Gunhild Oberzaucher-Schüller et al. (Wilhelmshaven: Florian Noetzel, 1992), 199–211.

153   Teresa Brennan has argued that commodification represents a threat to living energies comparable to Freud's account of the 'hallucination', which 'traps psychical energy in a constructed, contained boundary that founds the subject' (Brennan, *History after Lacan*, 175). Like the hallucination, the commodity arouses a fantasy of 'instant gratification' but also delays it, and therefore similarly constitutes a 'point of resistance' which 'traps psychical energy' and binds 'living substances in forms which are inert, relative to the energetic movement of life' (Brennan, *History after Lacan*, 175).

154   Georg Simmel, 'On the concept and the tragedy of culture', in *Georg Simmel: The Conflict in Modern Culture and Other Essays*, introduced and translated by K. Peter Etzkorn (New York: Teachers College Press, 1968), 44.

155   Ibid., 46.

156   Walter Benjamin, *Charles Baudelaire*, 111 and 115.

157   Ibid., 132.

158   Matthew Jefferies, *Imperial Culture in Germany*, 193.

159   Nude-body culture, which emphasised the health-giving properties of light and air, as well as the beauty of the naked body, influenced the whole body-culture movement. Its first official organisation, the Bodyculture Association (*Verein für Körperkultur*), was founded in 1901. By the end of the Weimar Republic in 1933, membership of bourgeois naturist associations alone came to about 20,000. The *Bund Heimatschutz*, founded in 1904, with conservationist and environmentalist aims, won widespread support among the professional classes, and the *Deutscher Werkbund*, founded in 1907, with the aim of resolving the role of artists and craftsmen in an age of mass production, brought together architects and politicians, businessmen and industrialists. The German youth movement, whose focal point was the *Wandervogel* (youthful hiking societies), founded in 1901 and with a membership of 25,000 by 1914 (see Joan Janice Schall, *Rhythm and Art in Germany*, 29), shared the 'natural' values of the life reformers, and was critical of many aspects of official Wilhelmine culture. Its supporters emphasised in particular the need to emancipate the individual from stifling conventions and structures, which were seen as operating primarily through the body. For a thorough discussion of reform movements in Germany from 1871–1918, see Jefferies, *Imperial Culture in Germany*.

160   Elizabeth Grosz, *Volatile Bodies*, 37.

161   Cited in Toepfer, *Empire of Ecstasy*, 13.

162   Cited in Jefferies, *Imperial Culture*, 193.

163   Valerie Preston-Dunlop, *Rudolf Laban, An Extraordinary Life* (London: Dance Books, 1998), 72.

[164]   Cited in Rohkrämer, *Eine andere Moderne*, 154. On this topic, see also
        Donald E. Gordon, *Expressionism: Art and Idea* (New Haven: Yale
        University Press, 1987), 130.

[165]   'In the 19th century, new concerns about overpopulation, sexual
        psychopathy and degeneracy gave rise to the concept of "sexuality"
        and led to intensified efforts on many fronts to get a firmer intellectual
        grasp on a subject matter that rapidly seemed to grow ever more
        complex. Biological, medical, historical, and anthropological research
        by von Baer, Darwin, Mendel, Kaan, Morel, Magnan, Charcot, Westphal,
        Burton, Morgan, Mantegazza, Westermarck, Krafft-Ebing, Schrenck-
        Notzing, and others, laid the foundations of sex research in the modern,
        more specific sense. Finally, at the turn of the 20th century, the
        pioneering work of Havelock Ellis, Sigmund Freud, and Iwan Bloch
        established the investigation of sexual problems as a legitimate endeavor
        in its own right.' Erwin J. Haeberle, 'Introduction: The history and
        concept of sexology,' from *The Birth of Sexology: A Brief History in
        Documents*, 1983. www.sexuality.org/l/sex/sexohist.html, accessed 29
        October, 2004.

[166]   One of these was Monte Verità at Ascona, where a natural health
        sanatorium was founded in 1900, and which became an artists' colony
        and a centre for alternative living. Laban held summer schools here in
        1913 and 1914.

[167]   Jefferies, *Imperial Culture in Germany*, 224. See also discussion on p.221.

[168]   See, for instance, Steven E. Ascheim, *The Nietzsche Legacy in Germany*,
        1890–1999 (Berkeley: University of California Press, 1992).

[169]   Gabrielle Klein, *FrauenKörperTanz* (Munich: Wilhelm Hagen Verlag,
        1992), 155.

[170]   This 'duty' also had a national/racial dimension. Klein describes Bess
        Mensendieck's aim 'to bring women, especially "educated" women, to
        a realisation, in their own bodies, of their *national duty* to be healthy
        mothers' (Klein, *FrauenKörperTanz* ,152, my emphasis).

[171]   Rudolf Bode, cited in Klein, *Frauenkörpertanz*, 151. For more information
        on Bode, see Toepfer, *Empire of Ecstasy*, 127–29, and Marion Kant and
        Lillian Karina, *Hitler's Dancers: German Modern Dance and the Third Reich*
        (New York: Berghahn, 2003). Sexually liberated, creative and independ-
        ently minded women, such as Ida Hoffmann, one of the founders of
        the Monte Verità community at Ascona, saw a return to nature as aiding
        subversion rather than conservation of traditional hierarchies. In her
        1902 pamphlet, 'How do we women achieve harmonious and healthy
        conditions of existence?', Hoffmann attacked traditional religions as
        patriarchal, and advocated vegetarianism and nature cure for both
        sexes. See Martin Green, *Mountain of Truth: The Counterculture Begins,
        Ascona 1900–1920* (Hanover: University Press of New England, 1986),
        129.

[172]   Rudolf von Delius, *Das Erwachen der Frauen: Neue Ausblicke ins
        Geschlechtliche* (Dresden: Carl Reissner, 1924), 23 and 33.

[173]   Ibid., 23.

174   Ibid., 23, emphasis mine. It would be interesting to compare this with the views of the French feminist, Luce Irigaray, on the necessity for sexual difference to replace an apparently 'universal' but in fact male dominated world.

175   Ibid., 81.

176   Note that the activities denoted by the term '*Gymnastik*' usually excluded the use of apparatus, which was included under '*Turnen*'. Even before the end of the eighteenth century, the question of the neglect of physical exercise in education had become an issue in Germany. Initially attention was focused by figures such as GutsMuths (1759–1839), the grandfather of modern gymnastics and founder of the German Turner society, on improving physical strength and performance. Friedrich L. Jahn (1778–1852), who developed GutsMuths's '*Turnverein*' system into a worldwide programme, and Pehr H. Ling (1776–1839), who developed the famous Swedish Gymnastic system, were the originators of the major gymnastic exercise systems used for military training. Ling, however, was also instrumental in the development of gymnastics for health and in education. See Judith B. Alter, *Dancing and Mixed Media: Early Twentieth-Century Modern Dance Theory in Text and Photography* (New York: Peter Lang, 1994), 54, and Eva Wobbe, '*Die Gymnastik: Entwicklung der Bewegung bis zur Rhythmischen Gymnastik und deren Einfluss auf den Ausdruckstanz*', in *Ausdruckstanz*, ed. Gunhild Oberzaucher-Schüller et al., 26 (25–33). On this general topic, see also Nitschke, '*Der Kult der Bewegung: Turnen, Rhythmik und neue Tanz*', in *Jahrhundertwende. Der Aufbruch in die Moderne, 1880–1930*, ed. August Nitschke et al. (Rowohlt: Reinbek bei Hamburg, 1990), 258–85.

177   See Jack Spector, *Rhythm and Life: The Work of Emile Jaques-Dalcroze* (Stuyvesant, New York: Pendragon Press, 1990), 212. See also Rudolf Steiner, *A Lecture on Eurythmy* (London: Rudolf Steiner Press [1923], 1967).

178   According to Elly D. Friedmann, a congress on the subject of 'The Art of Movement', organized by the '*Neue Deutsche Schulreformer*', took place in Berlin in 1922, and brought together many different approaches to gymnastics and dance. See Elly D. Friedmann, *Laban/Alexander/ Feldenkrais: Pioniere bewusster Wahrnehmung durch Bewegungserfahrung* (Paderborn: Junfermann-Verlag, 1989), 21. However, I have been unable to find any further evidence of this congress.

179   Schikowski, *Der neue Tanz*, 9.

180   See Wigman, 'Tanz und Gymnastik', *Der Tanz* 1, no. 6 (April 1928), 6–7.

181   *The Mary Wigman Book*, ed. Walter Sorrell (Middletown, CT: Wesleyan University Press, 1975), 53. For more details, see Isabelle Launay, *A la recherche d'une danse moderne, Rudolf Laban, Mary Wigman* (Paris: Chiron, 1996), 255–6.

182   Wobbe, 'Die Gymnastik', 31.

183   Hans Fischer, *Körperschönheit und Körperkultur* (Berlin: Deutsche Buchgemeinschaft, 1928), 11.

[184]   Fischer, *Körperschönheit*, 169. There is an important difference between goal-oriented movement seen as 'directed from the brain', and 'intentionality without intention', which will be discussed in Chapter 5.

[185]   Fischer, *Körperschönheit*, 179.

[186]   Ibid., 232.

[187]   John Schikowski, *Der neue Tanz*, 10.

[188]   Inge Baxmann, 'Stirring up attitudes: Dance as a language and Utopia in the Roaring Twenties', *Ballett International*, 11 (February 1989), 13 (13–18).

[189]   The Delsarte system was imported into America by a young actor, Steele MacKaye, where it became known as the 'Delsarte System of Expression', and where it strongly influenced the development of modern dance, notably via Isadora Duncan (1877–1927), who paid tribute to Delsarte as 'the master of those principles of flexibility of muscles and lightness of body' (cited in Daly, *Done into Dance, Isadora Duncan in America* (Bloomington: Indiana University Press, 1995), 131), and via the Denishawn School, founded in 1915 by Ruth St Denis (1877–1968) and Ted Shawn (1891–1972).

[190]   Daly, *Done into Dance*, 124.

[191]   See Daly, *Done into Dance*, 128. Geneviève Stebbins published books in the 1890s that modified the Delsarte system by incorporating theories of breathing and rhythmic movement, producing 'harmonic gymnastics' for female students (Toepfer, *Empire of Ecstasy*, 147). Readers of Stebbins's manuals were assured that they were 'training the body easily to express a beautiful soul – or vice-versa'. Cited in Elizabeth Kendall, *Where She Danced* (New York: Alfred A. Knopf, 1979), 25. Stebbins drew on an eclectic collection of mystical and philosophical ideas in expounding her own version of 'vitalism'. See Gabrielle Brandstetter, *Tanz-Lektüren: Körperbilder und Raumfiguren der Avant-Garde* (Frankfurt-am-Main: Fischer Taschenbuch Verlag, 1995), 67. In 1906, Bess Mensendieck, a student of Stebbins based in Vienna, published an influential book, *Women's Body Culture* [*Körperkultur der Frau*]. Mensendieck's exercises were designed to help women perfect movement in the performance of everyday tasks. Hedwig Kallmeyer, another student of Stebbins and also influenced by Mensendieck, opened a school for girls in Berlin around 1905. Her students included Dora Menzler, who opened a Mensendieck-influenced school in Leipzig about 1908. Her 1924 book, *The Beauty of the Body* [*Die Schönheit des Körpers*], 'linked her teaching to feminist efforts to construct "a new ideal of woman"' (Toepfer, *Empire of Ecstasy*, 44).

[192]   For a detailed account of Dalcroze, see Jack Spector, *Rhythm and Life*.

[193]   See Spector, *Rhythm and Life*, 68.

[194]   Emile Jaques-Dalcroze, *Rhythm, Music and Education* (London: Dalcroze Society [1921], 1980), 166.

[195]   Cited in Susan Manning, *Ecstasy and the Demon*, 52.

[196]   Emile Jaques-Dalcroze, *Eurythmics, Art and Education*, 16–7, my emphasis.

197 Ibid., 5.
198 On American Delsartism and progressive education theory in the US at this time, see Nancy Lee Chalfa Ruyter, *Reformers and Visionaries: The Americanization of the Art of the Dance* (New York: Dance Horizons, 1979).
199 Jackson Lears, *No Place of Grace: Antimodernism and the Transformation of American Culture 1880–1920* (London: University of Chicago Press, 1981), 57.
200 See Gabrielle Brandstetter, *Tanz-Lektüren*, 67.
201 Cited in Toepfer, *Empire of Ecstasy*, 39.
202 Lears, *No Place of Grace*, 48.
203 Ibid., 50 and 53.
204 Daly, *Done into Dance*, 120.
205 Cited in Brandstetter, *Tanz-Lektüren*, 71. Duncan's text was originally published in 1903, based on a lecture given in Berlin that year. See Schall, 'Rhythm and Art in Germany', 49 and also Daly, *Done into Dance*, 223.
206 Isadora Duncan, *Isadora Speaks*, ed. Franklin Rosemont (San Francisco: City Lights, 1981), 48.
207 Duncan, *The Art of the Dance*, ed. Sheldon Cheney (New York: Theatre Arts Books, 1969), 63.
208 Ibid., 69.
209 Cited in Daly, *Done into Dance*, 120. By all accounts, men reacted equally positively, though it would be interesting to investigate possible gender differences.
210 Isadora Duncan, *The Art of the Dance*, 69.
211 Ibid., 68.
212 Ibid., 55.
213 Ibid., 99.
214 Frederick Burwick and Paul Douglass, 'Introduction', and Sanford Schwartz, 'Bergson and the politics of vitalism', in *The Crisis in Modernism: Bergson and the Vitalist Controversy*, edited by Frederick Burwich and Paul Douglass (Cambridge: Cambridge University Press, 1992), 9 and 279 (1–14 and 207–76).
215 The German Romantic poet, Novalis, for instance, saw all life as rhythm. See Klaus Lankheit, 'Die Frühromantik und die Grundlagen der gegenstandslosen Malerei', *Neue Heidelberger Jahrbucher* (1951), 65 (55–90). The Romantic painter Philipp Otto Runge regarded the world as process, as eternal becoming (Lankheit, 'Die Frühromantik', 69). See my *Symbolist Aesthetics and Early Abstract Art: Sites of Imaginary Space* (Cambridge, 1995), and also Schall, 'Rhythm and Art in Germany 1900–1930'.
216 Cited in Hans Kasdorff, *Ludwig Klages im Widerstreit der Meinungen* (Bonn: Bouvier Verlag, 1978), 108.
217 Giese, *Körperseele, Gedanken über persönliche Gestaltung* (Munich: Delphin Verlag, 1927), 153.

218   Delius, *Tanz und Erotik: Gedanken zur Persönlichkeitsgestaltung der Frau* (Munich: Delphinverlag, 1926), 23.

219   Delius, *Mary Wigman* (Dresden: Carl Reissner, 1925), 8.

220   Klein, *FrauenKörperTanz*, 188.

221   The term 'inner necessity' is also used by Lipps, and is a key term in Wassily Kandinsky's *On the Spiritual in Art* (1911). See Chapter 2.

222   Simmel, 'On the Concept and Tragedy of Culture', 28. As historian of science Roger Smith has pointed out to me, 'the idea of life controlling the future was projected biologically as heredity and especially the theory of the inheritance of acquired characteristics'.

223   Drost, *Die Lehre vom Rhythmus in der Heutigen Asthetik der Bildenden Künste* (Leipzig-Gausch: Merkur, 1919), 12.

224   Fischer, *Körperschönheit*, 168.

225   See Drost, *Die Lehre vom Rhythmus*, 15.

226   Ibid., 40.

227   I am very grateful to Thomas Rohkrämer for pointing out the connection between Klages and Bode and for indicating useful references on this topic.

228   Valerie Preston Dunlop, *Rudolf Laban: An Extraordinary Life* (London: Dance Books, 1998), 19. According to Michael Grossheim, however, 'the devaluation of corporeality is a fatal error in Ludwig Klages's philosophy'. Michael Grossheim, *Ludwig Klages und die Phänomenologie* (Berlin: Akademie Verlag, 1994), 200.

229   See Joan Janice Schall, *Rhythm and Art in Germany*, 148. Note also the influential and wide-ranging theories of rhythm of Wilhelm Wundt, as expounded in his *Grundzüge der physiologischen Psychologie* (1874) and *Völkerpsychologie* (1900–09). See Schall, *Rhythm and Art in Germany*, 44ff.

230   See Theodor Lipps, *Asthetik: Psychologie des Schönen und der Kunst* (Hamburg: Leopold Voss, 2 vols. [1903] 1923 and [1906] 1920), vol. 1, 441.

231   'Nachahmung': see Theodor Lipps, *Asthetik*, vol. 1, 120.

232   Theodor Lipps, *Asthetik*, vol. 1, 226.

233   Klages, cited in Grossheim, *Ludwig Klages*, 256–7.

234   Klages, cited in Grossheim, *Ludwig Klages*, 260.

235   Palagyi, cited in Grossheim, *Ludwig Klages*, 256.

236   Ludwig Klages, 'Das Wesen des Rhythmus' (1934) in *Ludwig Klages, Sämtliche Werke*, ed. Ernst Frauchiger et al. (Bonn: Bouvier Verlag, 1974), 511 (499–552). According to her biographer Hedwig Müller, Mary Wigman read Klages (see Chapter 2), and it has been suggested that Rudolf Laban also read him. See Martin Green, *Mountain of Truth*, 90.

237   Ascheim, *The Nietzsche Legacy in Germany*, 81.

238   Richard Hinton Thomas, 'Nietzsche in Weimar Germany – and the Case of Ludwig Klages', in *The Weimar Dilemma: Intellectuals in the Weimar Republic*, ed. Anthony Phelan (Manchester University Press, 1985), 81 (71–91).

239   Klages, '*Das Wesen der Rhythmus*', 526 and 528.

240   Rudolf Bode, *Der Rhythmus und Seine Bedeutung fur die Erziehung* (Jena: Eugen Diederichs, 1920), 8.

241   'Rhythm is a *qualitative*, *Takt* a *quantitative* principle.' Rudolf Bode, *Der Rhythmus*, 9.

242   Max Merz, '*Körperbildung und Rhythmus*', in *Tanz in dieser Zeit*, ed. Paul Stefan (Vienna: Universal Edition, 1926), 32 (29–32). In *Hitler's Dancers*, Liliana Karina describes Max Merz as 'a fanatical anti-Semite and Nazi' (33).

243   Rudolf Bode, *Expression-Gymnastics*, 15.

244   Ibid., 49.

245   Ibid., 42.

246   Ibid., 52.

247   Rudolf Bode, *Der Rhythmus*, 5.

248   See Laurence Louppe, *Poétique de la danse contemporaine* (Brussels: Contredanse, 1997), 158.

249   Emile Jaques-Dalcroze, *Eurythmics, Art and Education*, 54.

250   Rudolf Bode, *Der Rhythmus*, 31.

251   Ibid., 21. The characteristics attributed by Klages to rhythm were very close to those attributed by Henri Bergson to pure duration ('*durée*'). See Henri Bergson, *Time and Free Will: An Essay on the Immediate Data of Consciousness* (New York: Dover [1948], 2001), 100. For Bergson, duration, unlike spatial phenomena, was characterised by indivisible flow (the word 'rhythm' is etymologically related to the Greek *rhein*, meaning 'to flow'), and resisted scientific enquiry, whose principal object was 'to forecast and measure' (Bergson, *Time and Free Will*, 230). In 'graceful motion', movements anticipated movements to come, and 'each new direction is indicated in the preceding one', thereby holding the future in the present. Reality was movement, which was not fully accessible to the intellect. Bergson, *Creative Evolution* (London: Macmillan, 1911), 163–4.

252   New York: Berghahn Books.

253   Karina and Kant, *Hitler's Dancers*, 55.

254   Ibid., 171.

255   Ibid., 172.

256   Ann Daly, *Done into Dance*, 114–5.

257   Ibid., 220.

258   Ibid., 114.

259   Ann Daly, 'Isadora Duncan and the distinction of dance', *American Studies* 35, no. 1 (Spring 1994), 17 (5–23).

260   Ibid., 7.

261   See Hedwig Müller, *Mary Wigman, Leben und Werk der grössen Tänzerin* (Berlin: Quadriga, 1986), 46, and Karina and Kant, *Hitler's Dancers*, 91. Gay Morris has discussed how, in the US of the 1940s, black modern dancers such as Talley Beatty were identified with stereotypes of black rhythms as exhibitionist and excessively virtuosic, which relegated them to a marginal position within the white aesthetic canon. Gay Morris,

'Exhibitionism and the Black body in post-war American dance'. Paper presented at Symposium on 'Body, Dance, Performative Practices'. Goldsmiths College, University of London, 31 January 2004.

262   See Roger Smith, *The Fontana History of the Human Sciences* (London: Fontana, 1997), 531.

263   Rick Roderick, *Habermas and the Foundations of Critical Theory*, 34.

264   See Bryan S. Turner, 'Introduction' to Christine Buci-Glucksmann, *Baroque Reason*, 13. The term 'reason' is misleading in the sense that Weber believed that the capitalist drive for discipline, order and profit was in fact subtended by a highly irrational Calvinistic theology. As in Nietzsche (by whom he was influenced) and Freud, the Apollonian veneer of civilisation concealed darker Dionysian forces beneath. In Klages, by contrast, *Geist* is the controlling, Apollonian factor, while *Leben* is a more primal, Dionysian force.

265   Cited in August Nitschke, '*Der Kult der Bewegung*', 269.

266   Rabinbach, *The Human Motor*, 25.

267   Ibid., 172. This law was demonstrated by Auguste Chauveau in the 1880s. See Rabinbach, *The Human Motor*, 127. Marey is perhaps best known for his experiments with 'chronophotography'. Unlike the Anglo-American photographer, Eadweard Muybridge, who also experimented with the photographic representation of movement, Marey aimed to integrate time into space, and his work was very influential in the visual arts. His experiments were directly linked with the origins of cinema. (See Rabinbach, *The Human Motor*.) The relationship between cinema and early modern dance is an under-researched and very important topic.

268   See Rabinbach, *The Human Motor*, 175.

269   Ibid., 175–6.

270   See Burt, *Alien Bodies: Representations of Modernity, 'Race' and Nation in Early Modern Dance* (London: Routledge, 1998), 42 and 97.

271   Mel Gordon, cited in Burt, *Alien Bodies*, 97–8. In his famous essay of 1927, 'The mass ornament', the philosopher of culture Siegfried Kracauer (1889–1966) was highly critical of the abstract patterns produced by the synchronised movements of the Tiller Girls. (See Burt, *Alien Bodies*, 96.) These movements paralleled the processes of capitalist production, from which organic life was drained, and put into the foreground 'segments' rather than 'whole, autonomous bodies'. According to Kracauer, 'the hands in the factory correspond to the legs of the Tiller girls'. (Siegfried Kracauer, 'The mass ornament', in *New German Critique*, 5 (Spring 1975), 69 and 70 (67–76).) They exemplified a capitalist 'rationale', which '*does not encompass human beings*' and 'expunges life' ('The mass ornament', 72–4). Kracauer's critique focused on the same issues as did the 'life philosophers' and reformists. However, Kracauer did not believe that body culture and rhythmic gymnastics represented a valid mode of resistance to processes of capitalist production, because, instead of engaging with social and

political issues, they retreated into pseudo-mythologies that distracted attention away from the necessity for concrete change.

272 Rudolf Laban and F.C. Lawrence, *Effort* (London: Macdonald and Evans [1948], 1976), 39.

273 *Effort*, 65.

274 Laban, *Modern Educational Dance* (London: Macdonald and Evans, 6.

275 *Effort*, xv.

276 *Ibid.*, 5–6.

277 Laban, *Modern Educational Dance*, 8.

278 Ibid., 54.

279 See Glossary for explanation of the terms *direct/indirect, strong/light* and *sustained/sudden*.

280 Ibid., 76. Laban describes here the basic effort actions, including 'pressing' (60) and 'gliding' (74).

281 Laban, cited in Vera Maletic, *Body-Space-Expression: The Development of Rudolf Laban's Movement and Dance Concepts* (Berlin: Mouton de Gruyter, 1987), 94.

282 Fritz Böhme, 'Der neue Tanz', *Velhagen und Klasings Monatshefte* 39, no. 4 (vol. 2, 1924/5), 101 and 103 (97–104).

283 Laban and Lawrence, *Effort*, 66. Note the similarity with the ideas of Frederick Alexander.

284 Rudolf Laban, *A Vision of Dynamic Space*, compiled by Lisa Ullmann (London: The Falmer Press, 1984), 23.

285 Mary Wigman, '*Vom Studium des modernen Tanzes*' (Notebook, MWA, Berlin). 65Bl.hs. 83/73/1664.

286 This is the second section of Swinging Landscape, which comprises nine sections, all solos.

287 See the Glossary for explanation of this and other technical terms.

288 Wigman, *The Language of Dance* (Middletown, CT: Wesleyan University Press, 1966), 64–5. I cite from English translations of Wigman's writings where these are easily available.

289 Rudolf Bode, *Expression-Gymnastics* (New York: A.S. Barnes, 1931), 52.

290 John Schikowski, *Der neue Tanz* (Berlin: Volksbühnen Verlag, 1924), 9. The question of modern dancers' views of ballet is a wide and controversial topic, which I shall not discuss here.

291 Ibid., 9.

292 On this topic, see my 'Dancing free: Gendering movements in early modern dance', in *Modernism, Gender, Culture*, ed. Lisa Rado (New York: Garland, 1997), 247–79.

293 *Modern Dance in Germany and the United States: Cross Currents and Influences* (Switzerland: Harwood Academic Publishers, 1994), xviii.

294 See David Kuhns, *German Expressionist Theatre: The Actor and the Stage* (Cambridge University Press, 1997), n.74, 260. For an excellent discussion of *Ausdruckstanz* and its background, see the first two chapters of Dianne Sheldon Howe, *Individuality and Expression: The Aesthetics of the New German Dance, 1908–1936* (New York: Peter Lang, 1996). In addition to material on Wigman, Howe's book has chapters

on dancers beyond the scope of this study, including Valeska Gert. See also *Ausdruckstanz: eine Mitteleuropäische Bewegung der ersten Hälfte des 20. Jahrhunderts*, ed. Gunhild Oberzaucher-Schüller et al. (Wilhelmshaven: Florian Noetzel, 1992). It is important not to confuse the term 'expressive' with 'Expressionist': expressive dance was undoubtedly influenced by Expressionism, but the latter was a distinct movement.

295 Ann Daly, *Done Into Dance: Isadora Duncan in America* (Bloomington: Indiana University Press, 1995), 65.

296 Susan Manning, *Ecstasy and the Demon: Feminism and Nationalism in the Dances of Mary Wigman* (Berkeley: University of California Press, 1993), 61.

297 This was generally manifested in her more gloomy/sinister dances, unlike *Pastorale*, discussed in this chapter.

298 Preston-Dunlop, *Rudolf Laban: An Extraordinary Life* (London: Dance Books, 1998), 15.

299 Rudolf Laban, *Modern Educational Dance* (London: Macdonald and Evans [1948], third edition, 1975), 6.

300 John Martin, *The Modern Dance* (New York: A.S. Barnes, 1933), 59. Martin uses the term 'metakinesis' to describe dance where movement is entirely 'dictated' by 'the logic of the inner feeling', and is at the same time 'productive of an aesthetic reaction in an onlooker' (*The Modern Dance*, 60).

301 He discussed Lipps in *America Dancing, The Background and Personalities of the Modern Dance* (New York: Dance Horizons, 1936), 119ff.

302 Martin, *Introduction to the Dance* (New York: Dance Horizons [1939], 1965), 47–9.

303 Martin, *America Dancing*, 121–2.

304 Ibid., 117.

305 Martin, *Introduction to the Dance*, 51.

306 'What dancers think of the German dance', *The Dance Magazine of Stage and Screen* (May 1931): 64 and 14 (14–5, 52, 64).

307 See Manning, *Ecstasy and the Demon*, 149ff. Although Wigman portrayed herself as a victim of Nazism, the truth is in fact more complex.

308 Isa Partsch-Bergsohn, *Modern Dance in Germany and the United States: Crosscurrents and Influences* (Switzerland: Harwood Academic Publishers), 91.

309 John Martin, *Introduction to the Dance*, 235.

310 Manning, *Ecstasy and the Demon*, 264.

311 John Martin, *Introduction to the Dance*, 237. See also discussion in Manning, *Ecstasy and the Demon*, 257ff.

312 Karl Toepfer, *Empire of Ecstasy: Nudity in German Body Culture 1910–1935* (Berkeley: University of California Press, 1997), 107.

313 On Bodenwieser, see *Gertrud Bodenwieser and Vienna's Contribution to Ausdruckstanz*, ed. Bettina Vernon-Warren and Charles Warren (Amsterdam: Harwood Academic Publishers, 1999).

314   Maurice Larkin, *Gathering Pace: Continental Europe 1870–1945* (Basingstoke: Macmillan, 1969), 106.

315   Larkin, *Gathering Pace*, 96.

316   Hubert Godard, 'Le geste et sa perception', in Isabelle Ginot and Marcelle Michel, *La Danse au xxe siècle* (Paris: Larousse, 1998), 224 (224–9).

317   See Hedwig Müller, *Mary Wigman, Leben und Werk der grossen Tänzerin* (Berlin: Quadriga, 1986), 16.

318   Jack Anderson, *Art without Boundaries* (London: Dance Books 1997), 86.

319   Cited in Gabriele Fritsch-Vivié, *Mary Wigman* (Reinbek bei Hamburg: Rowohlt, 1999), 51.

320   Steven E. Ascheim, *The Nietzsche Legacy in Germany, 1890–1990* (Berkeley: University of California Press, 1992), 88–9.

321   Delius, *Tanz und Erotik: Gedenken zur Persönlichkeitsgestaltung der Frau* (Munich: Delphin Verlag, 1926), 12.

322   'The being of woman is appearance. She can never be grasped as pure interiority. Her soul first blossoms in form.' Rudolf von Delius, *Das Erwachen der Frauen: Neue Ausblicke ins Geschlechtliche* (Dresden: Carl Reissner, 1924), 81.

323   Delius, *Tanz und Erotik*, 8.

324   Ibid., 31.

325   Ibid., 11.

326   Delius, *Das Erwachen der Frauen*, 71.

327   Delius, *Tanz und Erotik*, 23.

328   Delius, Ibid., 29.

329   Ibid., 25.

330   Hedwig Müller, *Mary Wigman*, 27.

331   Preston-Dunlop, *Rudolf Laban*, 28.

332   Cited in Müller, *Mary Wigman*, 41.

333   On Laban and Kandinsky, see Valerie Preston-Dunlop, 'Laban, Schönberg, Kandinsky', in *Danses tracées, Dessins et notations des chorégraphes* (Paris: Dis-Voir, 1991), 133–48.

334   In fact, although Wigman became a close collaborator of Laban's in working out his theories of movement, and although she always recognised the enormous debt she and other dancers of the time owed to his inspiration, their paths would ultimately diverge, with Wigman going in the direction of artistic dance, while Laban's primary interest would remain in movement in a broader sense, and in involving ordinary people in what he called 'movement choirs'.

335   See Müller, *Mary Wigman*, 51.

336   See Fritsch-Vivié, *Mary Wigman*, 53. On connections with Dervish dances, see Ramsay Burt, *Alien Bodies: Representations of Modernity, 'Race' and Nation in Early Modern Dance* (London: Routledge, 1998), 179ff.

337   Cited in Colin Rhodes, 'The Body and the Dance', *Expressionism Reassessed*, ed. Shulamith Behr et al. (Manchester: Manchester University Press, 1993), 140 (133–46).

338 Kandinsky, *Complete Writings on Art*, 2 vols, ed. Kenneth Lindsay and Peter Vergo (London: Faber and Faber, 1982), 193. For material on Kandinsky and Graham, see Chapter 3.

339 Kandinsky, *Complete Writings*, 205–6.

340 Wigman, 'The philosophy of modern dance' in Selma Jeanne Cohen, *Dance as a Theatre Art: Source Readings in Dance History from 1581 to the Present* (New York: Dodd, Mead and Co., 1974), 153 (149–53).

341 Wigman, *The Language of Dance*, 50.

342 Howe, *Individuality and Expression*, 116.

343 Elizabeth Selden, 'New York soon will see Dance without Music', *New York Evening Post*, 12 January 1929, 2.

344 Müller, *Mary Wigman*, 89.

345 The *Neue Badische Landeszeitung*, March 1921, cited in Müller, *Mary Wigman*, 90.

346 John Schikowski, 'Sackgasse oder Atempause?', *Vorwärts*, No. 495, Berlin, 20 October 1925 (MWA, Berlin).

347 In 1922, Prinzhorn published *Bildnerei der Geisteskranken*, an analysis of art by mental patients at the Heidelberg Psychiatric Clinic, which remained the major work on the subject for many years. He acknowledged his debt to Klages's studies of the links between handwriting and character, and also to Freud and Jung. Prinzhorn regarded rhythm as 'the bearer of vital processes'. See Joan Janice Schall, *Rhythm and Art in Germany 1900–1930* (Ph.D. dissertation, University of Austin, Texas, 1989), 48.

348 Famous names associated with Ascona included Hermann Hesse, D.H. Lawrence and Carl Jung. On this subject, see Martin Green, *Mountain of Truth* (Hanover: University Press of New England, 1986), 117–55.

349 Müller, *Mary Wigman*, 71, emphasis mine.

350 See Müller, *Mary Wigman*, 203.

351 www.german.leeds.ac.uk/wmet/campus/things%20to%20know.htm. Accessed 26 December 2002.

352 Richard W. McCormick, *Gender and Sexuality in Weimar Modernity: Film, Literature and 'New Objectivity'* (New York: Palgrave, 2001), 61.

353 Eva Kolinsky, 'Non-German minorities, women and the emergence of civil society', in *The Cambridge Companion to Modern German Culture*, ed. Eva Kolinsky and Wilfried van der Will (Cambridge: Cambridge University Press, 1998), 122 (110–31).

354 Müller, *Mary Wigman*, 206.

355 See Hedwig Müller and Patricia Stöckemann, *'Jeder Mensch ist ein Tänzer': Ausdruckstanz in Deutschland zwischen 1900 und 1945* (Giessen: Anabas Verlag, 1993), 36.

356 Müller, *Mary Wigman*, 206.

357 See his *Geheimnisse der Entsiegelung, Zeichen der Seele: Zur Metaphysik der Bewegung* (Berlin: Kinetischer Verlag, 1920).

358 Valeska Gert, 'Mary Wigman and Valeska Gert', *Der Querschnitt*, 5 (1926): 361 (361–63). For a more in-depth discussion of Gert, see Ramsay Burt's excellent *Alien Bodies*.

359 Werner Suhr, *Der künstlerische Tanz* (Leipzig: Siegels Musikalien-bibliothek, 1922), 117.

360 McCormick, *Gender and Sexuality*, 50.

361 Ibid., 50 and 61.

362 Isabelle Launay, *A la recherche d'une danse moderne: Rudolf Laban, Mary Wigman* (Paris: Chiron, 1996), 191 and 202.

363 Frank Whitford, *Bauhaus* (London: Thames and Hudson, 1984), 142.

364 Magdalena Droste, *Bauhaus 1919–1933* (Cologne: Bauhaus Archiv/Benedikt Taschen Verlag, 1990), 58–60.

365 Cited in Will Grohmann, *Wassily Kandinsky, Life and Work* (London: Thames and Hudson, 1959), 187.

366 Magdalena Droste, *Bauhaus*, 101.

367 Cited in Hedwig Müller, *Mary Wigman*, 46.

368 *The Mary Wigman Book: Her Writings*, ed. Walter Sorell (Middletown, CT: Wesleyan University Press, 1984), 143.

369 Müller and Stöckemann, '... *Jeder Mensch ist ein Tanzer*', 40.

370 On Duncan's attitude to jazz, and racist implications, see Manning, *Ecstasy and the Demon*, 38–9.

371 August Nitschke, 'Der Kult der Bewegung: Turnen, Rhythmik und neue Tanz', in *Jahrhundertwende. Der Aufbruch in die Moderne, 1880–1930*, ed. August Nitschke et al. (Reinbek bei Hamburg: Rowohlt, 1990), 266 (258–85).

372 'Ich kann nicht Foxtrot tanzen', Gespräch mit Mary Wigman, *Nachtausgabe*, Berlin, 11 December 1925 (MWA, Berlin).

373 See Müller and Stöckemann, '... *Jeder Mensch*', 53.

374 Müller, *Mary Wigman*, 132–3.

375 Cited in Müller, *Mary Wigman*, 133.

376 Elizabeth Mauldon, 'Oskar Schlemmer – Rudolf Laban: Similarities and contrasts', *Laban Art of Movement Guild Magazine*, no.5 (May 1975): 10 (7–17).

377 Anna Kisselgoff, 'They created dance works at the Bauhaus, too', *New York Times*, Sunday 31 October 1982, 12 (12–14).

378 Ibid.

379 Cited in Kisselgoff, 'They created dance works', 13.

380 Oskar Schlemmer, 'Man and art figure', in *The Theater of the Bauhaus*, ed. Walter Gropius (Middletown, CT: Wesleyan University Press, 1961), 17 (17–48).

381 Magdalena Droste, *Bauhaus*, 101.

382 Schlemmer, 'Man and art figure', 25.

383 Ibid., 26. Schlemmer was inspired by the essay *On the Puppet Theatre*, by Heinrich von Kleist (1777–1811) and by E.T.A. Hoffmann's tale *The Sandman* (1817). He also referred to Gordon Craig's idea of the *Übermarionette*. See the translator's note in *The Theater of the Bauhaus*, 28.

384 Mauldon, 'Oskar Schlemmer', 12.

385 Ernest Scheyer, 'The shapes of space: The arts of Mary Wigman and Oskar Schlemmer', *Dance Perspectives* 41 (1970): 38 (7–48).

386 Cited in Müller and Stöckemann, ' ... *Jeder Mensch*', 40.

387 *The Mary Wigman Book*, 108.

388 Hans Brandenburg, 'Mary Wigman', *Die Fahne* 2, No. 4 (July 1921): no page numbers (MWA, Berlin).

389 Mary Wigman, '*Aus "Rudolf von Laban's Lehre vom Tanz"*', *Die neue Schaubühne*, 2/3 (February 1921): 33 (30–35).

390 Mary Wigman, 'Tänzerische Wege und Ziele', *Die Schöne Frau* 4, no. 9 (1928/29): 2 (1–2).

391 Frank Thiess, 'Der Tanz ohne Sinn', *Hannoverscher Anzeiger*, September 1922 (Archives, Laban Centre London: henceforth MWA, London).

392 'Der Neue Tanz', *Velhagen and Klasings Monatshefte* 2, no. 4 (1924/5): 103 (97–104).

393 Programme note, Munich, 28 April 1914 (MWA, Berlin).

394 'Von Mary Wigman's Zürcher Gastspiel wird viel geschrieben', anonymous, October 1923 (MWA, Berlin).

395 Anonymous, *Neue Freie Presse*, Vienna, 14 February 1924 (MWA Berlin).

396 Heinrich Gutmann, 'Mary Wigman, Tanzabend im Zentraltheater', *Neue Leipziger Zeitung*, August 1922 (MWA, London).

397 'Al Teatro Odescalchi – Le danze di Mary Wigman', Anonymous, *Il Messagiero*, Rome, 26 May 1925 (MWA, Berlin).

398 Eric Vogeler, 'Mary Wigman's Tanzdrama', *Berliner Tageblatt*, June 1923 (MWA, London).

399 'Der Polyphone Tanz: Mary Wigman's Heroische Variationen', *Vossische Zeitung*, Berlin, 28 September 1923 (MWA, Berlin). The article is attributed to A.M. but this is almost certainly Artur Michel, who was a regular correspondent for this paper.

400 Publicity leaflet dated January 1923, containing quotations from numerous reviews. Oskar Bie, *Börsen-Courier*; Fritz Böhme, *Deutsche Allgemeine Zeitung* (MWA, London).

401 A.M. Schumacher, 'Tanz als Urform: Versuch einer Entäusserung von der musikalischen Vorlage' (MWA, London).

402 Fritz Böhme, 'Mary Wigman', emphasis mine.

403 Fritz Böhme, 'Tanz als Weg zu neuer Volksgemeinschaft', *Deutsche Frauenkultur und Frauenkleidung* 34, no. 5 (1930): 1 1 (129–31), emphasis mine.

404 Janet Ward, *Weimar Surfaces: Urban Visual Culture in 1 20s Germany* (Berkeley: University of California Press, 2001), 95.

405 See Chapter 1.

406 Ward, *Weimar Surfaces*, 95.

407 See Ward, *Weimar Surfaces*, 123.

408 Rudolf von Delius, *Mary Wigman* (Dresden: Carl Reissner, 1925) 8, emphasis mine.

409 Victor Wittner, 'Mary Wigman's Tanzschöpfungen: Der Abend im Konzerthaus', *Neues 8–Uhr Blatt*, 18 December 1922, 2.

410 Rudolf Lämmel, *Der moderne Tanz* (Berlin: Peter J. Oestergaard, 1928), 106, emphasis mine.

411 Artur Jacob, 'Tanzabend von Mary Wigman', *Ruhr-Echo*, Dortmund, November 1922 (MWA, London).

412 Artur Michel, 'Der absolute Tanz', *Vossische Zeitung*, 5 February 1924 (MWA, Berlin), emphasis mine.

413 Wigman, (MWA, Berlin). 'Der Tänzer und das Theater', *Völkische Kultur*, Dresden (June 1933): 26–32.

414 Mary Wigman, 'Die natürliche Bewegung als Grundlage des Tanzes', lecture and demonstration given at Lessing Hochschule, Berlin, 6 May 1934, 22 (typescript, MWA, Berlin), emphasis mine.

415 Mary Wigman, 'Tanz', in Rudolf Bach, *Das Mary Wigman Werk* (Dresden: Carl Reissner Verlag, 1933), 19 (19–20), emphasis mine.

416 Rudolf Laban, 'Movement concerns the Whole Man', *Laban Art of Movement Guild Magazine* (November 1958): 12 (8–12).

417 Laban, *A Life for Dance* (London: Macdonald and Evans [1935] 1975), 178–9, emphasis mine.

418 John Schikowski, *Der neue Tanz*, 27.

419 Mary Wigman, 'Der Tanz als Kunstwerk', *Deutsche Allgemeine Zeitung* (Berlin, March 1921), MWA, Berlin (no page numbers).

420 Schikowski, *Der neue Tanz*, 24.

421 Mary Wigman, '*Der Tanz als Kunstwerk*'.

422 Hans Brandenburg, *Der Moderne Tanz* (München: Georg Müller [1913], 1917), 83, emphasis mine.

423 Mary Wigman, 'Ich kann nicht Foxtrot tanzen'.

424 Mary Wigman, 'Der Tänzer und das Theater'.

425 Mary Wigman, 'Tanz', 19.

426 'The three "R"s of movement practice', *Laban Art of Movement Guild Magazine* (March 1955): 13 (12–17).

427 Georg Fuchs, *Die Revolution des Theaters: Ergebnisse aus dem Münchener Künstlertheater* (Munich: Georg Müller, 1909), 54–5. On theatre, see also Schall, 'Rhythm and art in Germany', 71ff.

428 Wigman, 'Das Tanzerlebnis', *Die Musik* 11 (1933): 801–2.

429 Manning, *Ecstasy and the Demon*, 91. See also discussion of Wigman and Graham in Chapter 3.

430 See the epigraph to this chapter.

431 Wigman, 'Das Tanzerlebnis', *Die Musik*, 801.

432 Klaus Thora, 'Der Einfluss der Lebensphilosophie Rudolf von Laban's auf das tänzerische Weltbild', in *Ausdruckstanz*, ed. Gunhild Oberzaucher-Schüller, 156 (154–60).

433 Laban, cited in Thora, 'Der Einfluss', 158.

434 Mary Wigman, 'Aus "Rudolf von Laban's Lehre vom Tanz"' 30.

435 Ibid., 32.

436 'Mary Wigman, Tanzabend im Blüthner-Saal', *Vossische Zeitung*, Berlin, 27 April 1922 (MWA, Berlin). This review is attributed to A.M. (almost certainly Artur Michel).

437 See Rudolf Laban, *Choreutics*, ed Lisa Ullmann (London: Macdonald and Evans, 1966).

438 Michel, 'Der absolute Tanz'.

439   'Vom Studium des modernen Tanzes'.
440   Wigman, *Kompositionen* (Seebote: Uberlingen 1925), 17.
441   Fischer, *Körperschönheit und Körperkultur* (Berlin: Deutsche Buchgemeinschaft, 1928), 223.
442   Wigman, in Walter Sorell, *Mary Wigman: Ein Vermächtnis* (Wilhelmshaven: Florian Noetzel Verlag, 1986), 281.
443   Wigman, in Walter Sorell, *Mary Wigman,* 281–2.
444   Artur Michel, 'Der absolute Tanz'.
445   Rudolf Laban, *A Vision of Dynamic Space,* 54 and 23.
446   Kuhns, *German Expressionist Theatre,* 92.
447   *The Evolution of Wigman's Dance Technique,* 1986 (New York Public Library, Dance Collection: henceforth NYPL). Gottschild, who was Professor Emeritus of Dance at Temple University until 1996, studied with Wigman for 10 years.
448   Isa Partsch-Bergsohn, *Modern Dance in Germany and the United States,* 19.
449   Rudolf Laban, *A Vision of Dynamic Space,* 55.
450   Fritz Böhme, 'Der neue Tanz', 101.
451   *The Mary Wigman Book,* 120.
452   'Mary Wigman, 1886–1973: "When the Fire Dances between Two Poles"', Allegra Fuller Snyder and Annette Macdonald, Pennington, New Jersey: Dance Horizons, 1991.
453   Wigman, *The Language of Dance,* 39.
454   'As Mary Wigman dances'. Translated by Hallie Flanagan, courtesy of *Theatre Guild Magazine* (MWA, London).
455   By this I mean the use of devices within the work that draw attention to the construction of the performance situation itself, e.g. playing with costumes/props, or making the audience self-conscious about their role as spectator. Pina Bausch is an example of a choreographer whose work makes extensive use of such devices.
456   Wigman, *The Language of Dance,* 40–41, emphasis mine.
457   Brigitta Hermann, cited in Mary Anne Santos Newhall, 'Illuminating the dark heart: A re-creation of Mary Wigman's *Witch Dance II* (1926)', in *Proceedings, Society of Dance History Scholars,* Oregon, June 1998 (University of California Riverside: SDHS, 1998), 304 (301–8).
458   Wigman, *The Mary Wigman Book,* 120, emphasis mine.
459   Wigman, *The Language of Dance,* 98, emphasis mine.
460   *Deutsche Allgemeine Zeitung,* 3 October 1926, emphasis mine (MWA, Berlin).
461   Wigman, untitled lecture, given to the Hagen-Arnsberg union of women welfare workers, 25 November 1927, 9, emphasis mine (unpublished manuscript, MWA, Berlin).
462   Mary Wigman, 'Komposition', in Rudolf Bach, *Das Mary Wigman Werk,* 26 (25–6), emphasis mine.
463   Georg Stauth and Bryan S. Turner, *Nietzsche's Dance: Resentment, Reciprocity and Resistance in Social Life* (Oxford: Blackwell, 1988), 149.

464   Wigman, cited in Müller and Stöckemann, *Jeder Mensch*, 36 (my emphasis).

465   Rudolf Lämmel, 'Tanz und Seele', *Kölnische Ilustrierte Zeitung* no.42, 1052–3 (MWA, Berlin).

466   Martin Green, *The Mountain of Truth*, 194.

467   Cited in Manfred Kuxdorf, 'The New German Dance Movement', in *Passion and Rebellion: The Expressionist Heritage*, ed. Stephen Eric Bronner and Douglas Kellner (London, Croom Helm, 1983), 355 (350–60).

468   Fritz Böhme, 'Mary Wigman' (MWA, Berlin).

469   R. Windeck, cited in Müller, *Mary Wigman*, 132. This citation is not dated, but it occurs in the context of a discussion of the 1920s.

470   Unfortunately, I have not found any accounts by contemporary female spectators.

471   Arnim Knab, 'Mary Wigman: Visionen', *Schrifttanz*, August 1919, 55 (55–6).

472   Oskar Bie, 'Mary Wigman, Künstlerhaus', *Berliner Börsen-Courier*, 22 January 1921 (MWA, Berlin).

473   A critical view recounted by Delius, *Mary Wigman*, 18.

474   Delius, *Mary Wigman*, 32–3.

475   Renate Berger, 'Moments can change your life: Creative crises in the lives of dancers in the 1920s', in *Visions of the 'Neue Frau': Women and the Visual Arts in Weimar Germany*, ed. Marsha Meskimmon and Shearer West (Aldershot: Ashgate, 1995), 83 (77–95).

476   Cited in Müller, *Mary Wigman*, 229.

477   Manning, *Ecstasy and the Demon*, 168.

478   Cited in Manning, *Ecstasy and the Demon*, 167.

479   Cited in Manning, *Ecstasy and the Demon*, 202. See Manning for further discussion.

480   Produced and directed by Allegra Fuller Snyder, Dance Horizons, 1991. *Witch Dance* can also be seen on DVD, in *Envisioning Dance on Film and Video*, ed. Judy Mitoma (London: Routledge), 2003.

481   On 'New Objectivity', see Gordon, *Expressionism: Art and Idea*, 25, and on Wigman's style in this period see Partsch-Bergsohn, *Modern Dance in Germany and the United States*, 33.

482   Scheyer, 'The Shapes of Space', 38.

483   See Hans Kasdorff, *Ludwig Klages in Widerstreit der Meinungen: Eine Wirkungsgeschichte von 1895–1975* (Bonn: Bouvier Verlag Herbert Grundmann, 1978), 352.

484   Rudolf Bach, *Das Mary Wigman Werk*, 27–31.

485   Ibid., 27.

486   Ibid.

487   Snyder and Macdonald, *Mary Wigman 1886–1973* (video).

488   Wigman, *The Language of Dance*, 42.

489   Dianne Sheldon Howe, 'Manifestations of the German Expressionist Aesthetic as Presented in Drama and Art in the Dance and Writings of Mary Wigman' (D.Phil. thesis, University of Madison-Wisconsin, 1985), 153 and 152.

490   Ibid.
491   Irmgard Bartenieff and Martha Davies, *Effort-Shape Analysis of Movement* (New York: Albert Einstein College of Medecine), 1965, 8. See discussion of Effort-Shape in the Introduction.
492   Judith Kestenberg, *The Role of Movement Patterns in Development* (New York: Dance Notation Bureau Press, 1977), vol. 1, 89–90.
493   Kestenberg, *The Role of Movement Patterns*, 96.
494   Manning, *Ecstasy and the Demon*, 129.
495   Georg Fuchs, *Die Revolution des Theaters*, 54–5. ff.
496   Schikowski, 'Mary Wigman (Bach-Saal)', *Vorwärts*, no. 519, Berlin, 2 November 1927 (MWA, Berlin).
497   'Mary Wigman: Hamburger Bühne', *Hamburger Nachrichten*, Tuesday 11 November 1926, 1–2 (MWA, London).
498   Arnim Knab, 'Mary Wigman, Visionen'.
499   Bach, *Das Mary Wigman Werk*, 28.
500   'Städtische Oper und Schauspielhaus: Tanzabend von Mary Wigman', Anonymous, A.H. *Hannoversches Tageblatt*, 22 September 1922 (MWA, Berlin).
501   Review in *Bohemia* (Prague). (MWA, London.)
502   Felix Emmel, 'Tänzerische Verwirklichung', *Tanzgemeinschaft* 2 (1930, special issue on Mary Wigman), 4 (2–4). (MWA, London.)
503   See Manning, *Ecstasy*, 127–30; Burt, *Alien Bodies*, 179–81, Sally Banes, *Dancing Women: Female Bodies on Stage* (London: Routledge, 1998), 129–36.
504   Manning, *Ecstasy and the Demon*, 130.
505   Wigman, *The Language of Dance*, 41.
506   Ibid., 40.
507   R.Mk., 'Mary Wigman: Hamburger Bühne', *Hamburger Nachrichten*, Tuesday 11 November 1926, 1–2 (MWA, London).
508   Fritz Böhme, 'Mary Wigman: Die Feier', *Deutsche Allgemeine Zeitung*, Berlin, February 1927 (MWA, Berlin).
509   Arnim Knab, 'Mary Wigman: Visionen', 55 (55–6), and A.M. (probably Artur Michel), 'Theater und Musik. Mary Wigman's Tanzabend: Zum Ensemble-Gastspiel im Opernhaus', *Tagespost*, Graz, 19 February 1924 (MWA, Berlin).
510   Arnim Knab, 'Mary Wigman: Visionen', 55.
511   Rudolf von Delius, *Mary Wigman*, 7.
512   Bach, *Das Mary Wigman Werk*, 28.
513   John Schikowski, 'Mary Wigman: Bach-Saal' (MWA, Berlin).
514   Bach, *Das Mary Wigman Werk*, 27.
515   Ibid., 31.
516   Whitney Chadwick, *Women Artists and the Surrealist Movement* (London: Thames and Hudson, 1985), 74.
517   Wigman, *The Mary Wigman Book*, 120.
518   Delius, *Mary Wigman*, 21 and 32.
519   Vera Skoronel, 'Mary Wigman's Führertum', *Tanzgemeinschaft*, 4. This view of genius as 'universal' is itself problematic. In writing about her

own dance, Wigman was also adopting a conventionally 'masculine' role.

520   *Schwingende Landschaft*, sometimes also translated as 'Shifting Landscape'.

521   Fritz Böhme, 'Schwingende Landschaft: Neue Tänze von Mary Wigman', *Deutsche Allgemeine Zeitung*, Berlin, 11 November 1929 (MWA, Berlin).

522   *Dresdener Volksbühne*, 1 December 1929 (MWA, Berlin).

523   Wigman, *The Language of Dance*, 60.

524   Ibid., 53.

525   Ibid.

526   *The Role of Movement Patterns*, vol. I, 98.

527   'Her [Graham's] leg could fly out to the side and make a circular gesture, known as the "fan kick."' Alice Helpern, 'The technique of Martha Graham', *Studies in Dance History* 2 (1991), 14 (1–59).

528   Wigman, *Language of Dance*, 53.

529   The figure of Shiva as Nataraj (Lord of the Dance) is 'an exquisite study of balance and symmetry, of movement and at the same time of stillness', regarded by sculptor Auguste Rodin as 'the highest sculptural concept of body movement known to the world'. Rina Singha and Reginald Massey, *Indian Dances, Their History and Growth* (London: Faber and Faber, 1967), 32.

530   Wigman, *Language of Dance*, 53.

531   Ibid., 53 and 59.

532   Maurice Merleau-Ponty, *Le Visible et l'invisible* (Paris: Gallimard, 1964), 165.

533   Wigman, cited in Beverley Cassia Berman, *Martha Graham and Mary Wigman: Dance in counterpoint* (typescript in Dance Collection, NYPL, no date), 8.

534   Graham, cited in Adolphe W. Roberts, 'The Fervid Art of Martha Graham', *Dance Magazine* (August 1928), 65 (13 and 65).

535   Martha Graham, 'Graham 1937', in *Martha Graham, The Early Years*, ed. Merle Armitage (New York: Da Capo, 1978), 102–3 (96–110).

536   This is a section of *Sketches from Chronicle*, reconstructed by Graham and Terese Capucilli. It premiered in December 1936, with five sections. The reconstructed version comprises three sections: 'Dances Before Catastrophe', 'Dances After Catastrophe', and 'Prelude to Action (Unity – Pledge to the Future)'. The first two sections were divided into two further subsections, and 'Steps in the Street' was the first subsection of 'Dances After Catastrophe'. 'Chronicle' is often interpreted as being about the Spanish Civil War, but in fact it is not tied to any specific war. All three sections are dramatic and percussive, maintaining constant tension, with dynamic contrasts between soloist and group and between changing geometrical configurations formed by the dancers. I attended performances at the Edinburgh Festival in August 1996 and at the Barbican (London) in May 1999. My description is based on these performances and on the 1991 Paris performance included in the TV

documentary, Dancemakers: Martha Graham, presented by Judith Mackrell, broadcast on BBC 2 on 15 August 1992.

537 Henrietta Bannerman, 'The work (1935–1948) of Martha Graham (1894–1991): An analysis of her movement system' (Ph.D. dissertation, University of Surrey, UK, 1998), 86.

538 Original score by Wallingford Riegger, newly orchestrated in the reconstruction by Justin Dello Joio.

539 *Every Little Movement: A Book about François Delsarte* (New York: Dance Horizons, 1963).

540 'Through modern science we have mastered to a wonderful extent the use of things as tools for accomplishing results upon and through other things. The result is all but a universal state of confusion, discontent, and strife. The one factor which is the primary tool in the use of all these other tools – namely, ourselves – in other words, our own psycho-physical disposition, as the basic condition of our employment of all agencies and energies, has not even been studied as the central instrumentality' (from Dewey's Introduction to *Constructive Conscious Control of the Individual*, 1923). Dewey credited Alexander with discovering 'a technique which will enable individuals really to secure the right use of themselves' (from Dewey's introduction to Frederick Alexander's *The Use of the Self*, 1932).
See: www.alexandertechnique.com/articles/dewey. Accessed 27 February 2004.

541 Isa Partsch-Bergsohn, *Modern Dance in Germany and the United States* (Switzerland: Harwood Academic Publishers, 1994), 51. See also Janice Ross, *Moving Lessons: Margaret H'Doubler and the Beginning of Dance in American Education* (Madison, WI: University of Wisconsin Press, 2000).

542 Walter Terry, *Frontiers of Dance: The Life of Martha Graham* (New York: Thomas Y. Crowell Company, 1975), 63.

543 Don McDonagh, 'A conversation with Gertrude Shurr', *Ballet Review* 4, no.5 (1973), 3 and 12 (3–20).

544 *Dance Perspectives* 16 (1963), 'Composer/choreographer, Louis Horst', 6 (6–8).

545 Don McDonagh, 'A conversation with Gertrude Shurr', 13–14.

546 Ibid., 4.

547 Janet Mansfield Soares, *Louis Horst: Musician in a Dancer's World* (Durham, NC: Duke University Press), 1992, 51.

548 Graham, *Blood Memory* (New York: Doubleday, 1991), 98.

549 See Jowitt, *Time and the Dancing Image* (Berkeley: University of California Press, 1988), 176, where this parallel is described and illustrated.

550 See my *Symbolist Aesthetics and Early Abstract Art* (Cambridge: Cambridge University Press, 1995), 35. In Munich, Kandinsky lived in the same street as Laban.

551 On the implications for art of Albert Einstein's theory of relativity (1905) and Ernest Rutherford's experimental proof of subatomic particles (1903), see Donald E. Gordon, *Expressionism: Art and Idea* (New Haven: Yale University Press, 1987), 23.

552 Cited in E.J. Garte, 'Kandinsky's ideas on changes in modern physics and their implications for his development', in *Gazette des Beaux-Arts*, 110 (1987), 139 (137–44).

553 Kandinsky, *Cours du Bauhaus* (Paris: Denoël/Gonthier, 1975), 76.

554 Kandinsky, *Complete Writings on Art* (2 vols.), ed. K. Lindsay and P. Vergo (London: Faber and Faber, 1982), vol. 2, 770–1 and vol. 1, 402.

555 On this topic, see my *Symbolist Aesthetics*.

556 Martha Graham, souvenir programme 1936, *Imperial Gesture* (Dance Collection, New York Public Library for the Performing Arts at Lincoln Center; henceforth NYPL).

557 Martha Graham souvenir programme 1936, *Imperial Gesture*.

558 Ernestine Stodelle, 'Before yesterday. The first decade of modern dance: Martha Graham', *Dance Observer* 29 (January 1962), 5–7.

559 Deborah Jowitt, 'Paring down to the quick', *Village Voice*, 9 May 1974, 75 (75–79).

560 Clement Greenberg, 'Modernist painting', *Art and Literature* 4 (1965), 194 (193–201). On Graham and modernism, see Henrietta Bannerman, 'Thoroughly Modern Martha', in *Dance Theatre Journal* 17, no. 2 (2001), 32–36; Mark Franko, *Dancing Modernism, Performing Politics* (Bloomington: Indiana University Press, 1995); Helen Thomas, *Dance, Modernity and Culture* (London: Routledge, 1995), and my 'Dancing free: Women's movements in early modern dance', in *Modernism, Gender and Culture*, ed. Lisa Rado (New York: Garland, 1997), 247–79.

561 It is notoriously difficult to fit historical developments in dance into the categories of 'modernism' and 'postmodernism'. See discussion in my 'Dancing free: Women's movements in early modern dance', which refers to definitions of 'modernism' by Sally Banes, Nick Kaye and Susan Manning.

562 Greenberg, 'Modernist painting', 198.

563 Wassily Kandinsky, *Complete Writings on Art*, vol. 1, 369.

564 Ibid., 369.

565 *Phenomenology of Perception* (London: Routledge and Kegan Paul, 1962), 110.

566 Not surprisingly, Kandinsky was interested in dance, and collaborated with the composer Thomas von Hartmann and the dancer Alexander Sakharoff on a series of transpositions between media, involving painting, music and dance. Just before his death, he was planning a ballet for which he was to design the sets and Thomas von Hartmann was to compose the music. (See my *Symbolist Aesthetics*, 211.) In 1926 he produced a series of line drawings of Gret Palucca, a former student of Wigman's. In these drawings, Kandinsky depicted the 'precise stucturing of individual moments', the rhythmic structure produced by the intersecting forms delineated by Palucca's body at given moments in time. (See Kandinsky, *Complete Writings*, vol. 1, 320: drawings on pp. 319–23.) Palucca herself was attracted to abstract painting, and,

before dancing, she would relax in front of a diamond-shaped composition by Piet Mondrian (*Symbolist Aesthetics*, 266).

567   I shall designate the United States of America as 'America'.

568   Ann Douglas, *Terrible Honesty: Mongrel Manhattan in the 1920s* (New York: Noonday Press 1996), 172, 173, and 183.

569   Douglas, *Terrible Honesty*, 220.
      Marian Horosko, *Martha Graham: The Evolution of her Dance Movement and Training* (Florida: University Press of Florida [1991], 2002, revised edition), 37.

570   Graham, cited in Alice Helpern, *The Technique of Martha Graham*, 13.

571   Wanda M. Corn, *The Great American Thing: Modern Art and National Identity 1915–1935* (Berkeley: University of California Press, 1999), 244.

572   Douglas, *Terrible Honesty*, 35.

573   On this topic, see also my 'A technique for power: Reconfiguring economies of energy in Martha Graham's early work', in *Dance Research* 20, no. 1 (Summer 2002): 3–32, which dialogues with Gay Morris, 'Bourdieu, the body, and Graham's post-war dance', *Dance Research* 19, no. 2 (Winter 2001): 52–82.

574   Martha Graham, 'A modern dancer's primer for action', in *The Dance Anthology*, ed. Cobbett Steinberg (New York: The New American Library, 1980), 46 (44–52).

575   Terry Walter, 'Interview with Martha Graham: The early years' (1973), two audio cassettes (Dance Collection, NYPL).

576   Martha Graham, *Blood Memory*, 38 and 5.

577   Ibid., 42, 24, 25.

578   Ibid., 38.

579   Don McDonagh, *Martha Graham, A Biography* (New York: Popular Library, 1973), 13.

580   Ibid., 13.

581   See Martha Banta, *Imaging American Women: Idea and Ideals in Cultural History* (New York: Columbia University Press, 1987), 90–91.

582   Lois W. Banner, *American Beauty* (New York: Alfred A. Knopf, 1983), 276.

583   Deborah Jowitt, 'Martha Graham', *International Encyclopedia of Dance*, ed. Selma Jeanne Cohen et al. (Oxford: Oxford University Press, 1998), vol. 3, 210 (209–221). This is an excellent and succinct entry.

584   Jowitt in 'The early years: Martha Graham and Modernism' (videotapes in Dance Collection, NYPL), cassettes 26 and 27. Documentation of the festival, 'The early years: American modern dance from 1900 through the 1930s', hosted by SUNY College at Purchase, New York, 9–12 April 1981.

585   *Dance Observer* 27 (March 1960), 38.

586   See Jane Sherman and Norton Owen, 'Martha Graham and Ted Shawn', *Dance Magazine* (July 1965), 42–5.

587   Jowitt described this comment as as a 'harsh, if oblique, reference to Denishawn'. Deborah Jowitt, 'Martha Graham', *International Encyclopedia of Dance*, 210–11.

588 Doris Humphrey, *The Art of Making Dances* (London: Dance Books, 1987), 106.

589 Bannerman, 'Thoroughly Modern Martha', 34.

590 Shurr in 'The early years' (video).

591 Ibid. See also Don McDonagh, 'A conversation with Gertrude Shurr'.

592 Cited in Margaret Lloyd, *The Borzoi Book of Modern Dance* (Dance Horizons: New York 1974), 49–50.

593 Alice Helpern, *The Technique of Martha Graham*, 14.

594 Shurr in 'The early years'.

595 Gertrude Shurr, in Marian Horosko, *Martha Graham*, 38. The first sentence in fact comes last in the text.

596 Thea Nerissa Barnes, in 'Not just a somersault: Insights on aspects of Martha Graham technique 1938–1992' (videotape, Laban Centre for Movement and Dance, London 1993).

597 Walter Terry, *Frontiers of Dance*, 59.

598 Jane Dudley, 'Jane Dudley talks about the Schools of Wigman and Graham', *Dance and Dancers* 22, no. 5 (May 1971), 56 (54, 56).

599 Graham, in Joel Shapiro, 'Martha Graham at the Eastman School', *Dance Magazine* (July 1974), 56 (55–7).

600 The term 'choreography' was not yet in currency in the modern dance context, and Graham did not initially think of herself as a choreographer.

601 'Martha Graham: The dancer revealed' (videotape, co-production of WNET, New York, Caméras Continentales, La Sept/Arte, BBC, 1994). Distributed by KULTUR International Films Ltd.

602 'Martha Graham: The dancer revealed'.

603 Deborah Jowitt, *Dance Beat, Selected Views and Reviews 1967–1976* (Marcel Drekker: New York/Basel, 1977), 72.

604 Graham, *Blood Memory*, 114.

605 Jowitt, *Time and the Dancing Image*, 169.

606 On Graham's dance and left-wing politics, see Ellen Graff, *Stepping Left: Dance and Politics in New York City, 1928–1942* (Durham, NC: Duke University Press, 1997); Stacey Prickett, '"The People": Issues of identity within the revolutionary dance', in *Of, by and for the People: Dancing on the Left in the 1930s*, ed. Lynn Garafola, Studies in Dance History 5, no. 1 (1994), Madison, WI: Society of Dance History Scholars, 14–22; and Mark Franko, *Dancing Modernism, Performing Politics* (Bloomington: Indiana University Press, 1995), and *The Work of Dance: Labor, Movement and Identity in the 1930s* (Middletown, CT: Wesleyan University Press, 2002).

607 Douglas, *Terrible Honesty*, 18.

608 Prickett, 'The People', 16.

609 See Franko, *The Work of Dance*, 54–62. See also my closing discussion in Chapter 1.

610 Ibid., 53 and 76.

611 Ibid., 57 and 75–6.

612 Deborah Jowitt, *Dance Beat*, 72.

[613]   In Marian Horosko, *Martha Graham. The Evolution of her Dance Theory and Training*, 42.

[614]   Cecily Dell, 'Random Graham', *Dance Scope* (Spring 1966), 21 (21–26).

[615]   Dorothy Bird and Joyce Greenberg, *Bird's Eye View: Dancing with Martha Graham and on Broadway* (University of Pittsburgh Press, 1997), 34.

[616]   Mark Franko, *Dancing Modernism, Performing Politics*, 50 and 53.

[617]   Graham, 'The Dance in America', *Trend* 1, no.1 (March/April/May 1932), 7, emphasis mine (5–7).

[618]   Graham, *Blood Memory*, 10, my emphasis.

[619]   Graham, 'A modern dancer's primer for action', 45, emphasis mine.

[620]   Graham, *Blood Memory*, 13, emphasis mine.

[621]   Ibid., 176.

[622]   Franko, *The Work of Dance*, 66. Franko also makes an interesting connection between Graham and Mary Austin, author of *The American Rhythm* (1923), whose distinction between rhythms that 'produce an emotional *effect* and those that are spiritually *affective*' is strikingly close to his own distinction between emotion and affect.

[623]   Graham, *Blood Memory*, 89.

[624]   For anecdotes concerning her championing of blacks, see *Blood Memory*, 37 and 153.

[625]   Graham, 'The Dance in America', 6. Graham's praise for Indian dance echoes closely the views of composer and writer Dane Rudhyar, with whom she became friends in the mid-1920s. In his article, 'The Indian dances for power' (*Dance Observer* 5, August–September 1934: 64), Rudhyar argued that 'the Indian dances for power ... because he establishes deliberately a relationship between a primordial, elemental life current and his outer self or body'. For Rudhyar, the function of dance was to 'generate ... more vital power in soul, mind and body'.

[626]   Graham, 'A Modern Dancer's Primer for Action', 46.

[627]   Ibid., 45.

[628]   Corn, *The Great American Thing*, 241.

[629]   Cited in Corn, *The Great American Thing*, 241. On this topic, see also Franko, *Dancing Modernism*, 43ff.

[630]   Graham, 'A Modern Dancer's Primer for Action', 45.

[631]   Ibid.

[632]   Don McDonagh, *Martha Graham: A Biography* (New York: Popular Library, 1973).

[633]   Marcia Siegel, *Watching the Dance Go By* (Boston: Houghton Mifflin, 1977), 204.

[634]   Franko, *Dancing Modernism*, 44.

[635]   Graham *Blood Memory*, 25–6.

[636]   Lynn Dumenil, *The Modern Temper: American Culture and Society in the 1920s* (New York: Hill and Wang, 1995), 138.

[637]   Graham *Blood Memory*, 160.

[638]   See Nancy F. Cott, *The Grounding of Modern Feminism* (New Haven: Yale University Press, 1987), 166.

[639]   Graham, *Blood Memory*, 211.

640 Susan Ware, *Seven Women who Shaped the American Century* (Cambridge, Massachussetts: Harvard University Press, 1998), 242.

641 Her later work raises other issues that it is not possible to discuss here. See my 'Dancing free'.

642 Paula Bryant Pratt, *The Importance of Martha Graham* (San Diego: Lucent Books, 1995), 51.

643 See Corn, *The Great American* Thing, 59.

644 Henrietta Bannerman, 'Graham reviewed', *The Dancing Times* (October 1996), 28 (23, 25, 28).

645 McDonagh, *Martha Graham*, 68.

646 'Prejudice Purely', *The New Republic*, April 11th, no year given (Martha Graham Clipping Files, Dance Collection, NYPL). Kirstein later revised his judgment on Graham: see chapter in Armitage, *Martha Graham*. Compare his pronouncement on Wigman. 'Mary Wigman, despite her energy, or perhaps because of its blind drive, always remained Mary Wigman, the German blue-stocking with a female virginal egotism which could not be masked by soul-immersion in Nietzsche, dim readings of the Bhagavad Gita or in her half-controlled self-hypnotized projections of grief, passion, ecstasy or boredom'. Cited in Susan Manning, *Ecstasy and the Demon: Feminism and Nationalism in the Dances of Mary Wigman* (Berkeley: University of California Press, 1993, 22).

647 Bird, *Bird's Eye View*, 50–51.

648 Ibid., 51.

649 Ibid., 37.

650 Ibid., 34.

651 Julia Foulkes, *Modern Bodies: Dance and American Modernism from Martha Graham to Alvin Ailey* (Chapel Hill: University of North Carolina Press, 2002), 103.

652 Marcia Siegel, Forward to *Bird's Eye View*, xx.

653 *Bird's Eye View*, 47.

654 Henrietta Bannerman, 'The work (1935–1948) of Martha Graham (1894–1991)', 83, emphasis mine.

655 *Bird's Eye View*, 49.

656 Ibid., 52, emphasis mine.

657 Ibid., 75, emphasis mine.

658 Ibid., 10.

659 Ibid., 56. Note comparison with Wigman's use of mask, producing a 'split' subject.

660 Franko, *Dancing Modernism*, 52.

661 Graham, 'Seeking an American art of the dance', in Oliver M. Sayler, *Revolt in the Arts: A Survey of the Creation, Distribution and Appreciation of Art in America* (New York: Brentano's,1930), 249 (249–55).

662 Marcia Siegel, Foreword to *Bird's Eye View*, xvi.

663 'The early years: Martha Graham and Modernism' (video).

664 *Bird's Eye View*, 44.

665 Young, cited in Franko, *Dancing Modernism*, 38.

666 John Martin, in Merle Armitage, *Martha Graham*, 13.

667 Cited in Clive Barnes and Peter Williams, 'Two Looks at Lightning', *Dance and Dancers* (October 1963), 18 (12–22 and 39–40).

668 Marcia Siegel, *At the Vanishing Point: A Critic Looks at Dance* (New York: Saturday Review Press, 1972), 184, emphasis mine.

669 Gertrude Schurr in 'The early years' (video).

670 Terry Walter, 'Interview with Martha Graham: The Early Years', 1973 (audiocassette).

671 Bannerman, 'The Work (1935–1948) of Martha Graham', 264.

672 Graham, 'A modern dancer's primer for action', 50–51.

673 Graham, *Blood Memory*, 46.

674 Eileen Or, 'Body and Mind: The Yoga roots of Martha Graham's "contraction" and "release"', in *Proceedings, Society of Dance History Scholars*, Joint Conference with the Association for Dance in Universities and Colleges in Canada, Ryerson Polytechnic University, Toronto, Ontario, Canada (10–14 May 1995), 206 (203–13).

675 Pratt, *The Importance of Martha Graham*, 50.

676 Helpern, *The Technique of Martha Graham*, 23.

677 Programme note, Royal Opera House, Covent Garden, 19 July 1976 (Dance Collection, NYPL).

678 *Bird's Eye View*, 103.

679 Frederick J. Hoffman, *The 20s: American Writing in the Postwar Decade* (New York: The Free Press, 1962), 357.

680 Cited in Hoffman, *The 20s*, 358.

681 Julia L. Foulkes, *Modern Bodies*, 154.

682 Marcia Siegel, *Watching the Dance Go By*, 201.

683 Sophie Maslow in 'The early years' (video).

684 *Bird's Eye View*, 21.

685 Graham, 'Seeking an American art of the dance', in Sayler, *Revolt in the Arts*, 250.

686 Lynn Dumenil, *The Modern Temper*, 156. In this context, Dumenil discusses Carl Sandburg, Hart Crane and Charles Demuth. See also the discussion of Stieglitz below.

687 Cited in Deborah Jowitt, *Time and the Dancing Image*, 176.

688 Graham, 'The American dance', in *The Modern Dance*, ed Virginia Stewart and Merle Armitage (New York: Dance Horizons, 1970), 56 (53–58). Alfred Stieglitz and Paul Rosenfeld believed that 'the artist must stand critically outside industrial culture'. Corn, *The Great American Thing*, 14.

689 Graham, 'The dance in America', 5.

690 T.J. Jackson Lears, *No Place of Grace: Antimodernism and the Transformation of American Culture 1880–1920* (Chicago: University of Chicago Press, 1981), 223.

691 Dumenil, *The Modern Temper*, 150 and 154.

692 Douglas, *Terrible Honesty*, 245.

693 Ibid., 252.

694 Ibid., 247.

695 Dumenil, *The Modern Temper*, 202.

696 Corn, *The Great American Thing*, 298.

697 'The early years: Martha Graham and modernism' (video).

698 Untitled article by Graham, in *Federal Dance Magazine*, 193? (Martha Graham Clipping Files, 1925–33, Dance Collection, NYPL).

699 Corn, *The Great American Thing*, 314.

700 Ibid., 19 and 31.

701 Ibid., 14.

702 Cited in Corn, *The Great American Thing*, 24. Note connections with anxieties concerning blurring of boundaries between 'animate' and 'inanimate' discussed in Chapter 1.

703 Corn, *The Great American Thing*, 30.

704 Cited in Corn, *The Great American Thing*, 52.

705 Corn, *The Great American Thing*, 184.

706 Ibid., 175.

707 Ibid., 63. See Corn for a wide-ranging discussion of foreign artists working in New York in the 1920s.

708 Barbara Zabel, 'Gendered still life: Paintings of still life in the Machine Age', in *Modernism, Gender, Culture*, ed. Lisa Rado (New York: Garland 1997), 231 (229–246).

709 Graham, 'The American dance', 54.

710 Corn, *The Great American Thing*, 179.

711 Graham, 'The American Dance', 54–5. On links between the 'primitive' and the 'masculine', see Franko, *Dancing Modernism*, 55.

712 My comments are based on viewing the film, *Heretic*, danced by Martha Graham and Dance Group of Twelve, 1931 (film in Dance Collection, NYPL).

713 Deborah Jowitt, *Dance Beat*, 71.

714 Bannerman, 'The work (1935–1948) of Martha Graham', 108.

715 *Heretic*, danced by Takako Asakawa and Martha Graham Dance Company, 1986 (film in Dance Collection, NYPL).

716 Billie Lepczyk, 'Martha Graham's Movement Invention viewed through Laban Analysis', *Dance: Current Selected Research*, vol. 1, ed. Lynette Y. Overby and James H. Humphrey (New York: AMS Press, 1989), 47 (45–61).

717 Graham, *Blood Memory*, 114.

718 Danced by Martha Graham, 193?, presented by Pictorial Films (film in Dance Collection, NYPL).

719 Tobi Tobias, 'An interview with May O'Donnell', *Ballet Review* 9, no.1 (Spring 1981), 79 (64–81).

720 Marcia Siegel, *At the Vanishing Point*, 195–6.

721 Marcia Siegel, *The Shapes of Change: Images of American Dance* (Berkeley: University of California Press, 1985), 39.

722 Lepczyk, 'Martha Graham's Movement Invention', 52–3. The sagittal plane is the 'wheel' plane, as opposed to the horizontal ('table') and vertical ('door') planes.

723 Cited in Elinor Rogosin, *The Dance Makers: Conversations with American Choreographers* (New York: Walker and Company, 1980), 40. See the

outstanding photographs of this dance in Barbara Morgan, *Martha Graham: Sixteen Dances in Photographs* (Dobb's Ferry, New York, 1980).

724 Don McDonagh, 'A conversation with Gertrude Shurr', 20.

725 Cited in Russell Freedman, *Martha Graham: A Dancer's Life* (New York: Clarion Books, 1998), 69–70.

726 Jack Anderson, 'Some personal grumbles about Martha Graham', *Ballet Review* 2, no.1 (Spring 1967), 25 (25–30).

727 Tobi Tobias, 'Inner space', *New York Magazine*, 28 October, 1991, 80 (80–81).

728 My comments are based on viewing a film, danced by Yuriko Amamaya and Martha Graham Dance Company (produced and filmed By Dwight Godwin for Jerome Robbins Film Archive, 1964), Dance Collection, NYPL.

729 Ramsay Burt, *Alien Bodies* (London: Routledge, 1998), 185.

730 Bird, *Bird's Eye View*, 75.

731 Bannerman, 'The work (1935–1948) of Martha Graham', 56.

732 Don McDonagh, *Martha Graham*, 78. See McDonagh for an excellent and detailed description of this dance.

733 Manning has suggested a comparison between the relationship between the individual and the group in this dance and in Wigman's 'Scenes from a Dance Drama',1924. 'Tänzerinnen Weiblicher Geschichte: Mary Wigman und Martha Graham', in *Tanzdrama* 15 (1991), 10 (7–13). I have not discussed Wigman's group works here, partly because they are extensively analysed by Manning in *Ecstasy*, but also because they are not available on film or video.

734 Marcia Siegel, *Watching the Dance Go By*, 206.

735 Susan Manning, '*Tänzerinnen Weiblicher Geschichte*', 10.

736 Martha Graham, 'The dance in America', 6.

737 Cited in Brenda Dixon-Stowell, 'Ethnic and exotic aspects in the choreography of selected works by Ted Shawn and Martha Graham', in *Proceedings of the Seventh Annual SDHS Conference*, Goucher Colleage, Towson MD (17–19 February 1984), 26 (21–8).

738 Dixon-Stowell, 'Ethnic and Exotic Aspects', 6. Aspects of this style were almost certainly influenced by Stravinsky's 'Le sacre du printemps', in which Graham had danced the leading role.

739 Burt, *Alien Bodies*, 188–9.

740 Ibid., 182 and 185–6.

741 See Bonnie Bird in 'Not just a somersault' (video).

742 Judith Mackrell, *Dancemakers: Martha Graham* (TV documentary).

743 Cited in Armitage, *Martha Graham*, 108.

744 Laban, *Modern Educational Dance* (London: Macdonald and Evans [1948], 1976), 102.

745 Martha Graham, 'Affirmations', in Armitage, *Martha Graham*, 105 (96–110).

746 Graham's relationship with her dancers is a complex issue, which I cannot explore here. Note that the reflexivity of this dance is paralleled in *Heretic*, where the 'heresy' is also that of modern dance itself.

747 Martin, *Introduction to the Dance* (New York: Dance Horizons [1939], 1965), 239–40.

748 Anne Andrews Hindman, 'The myth of the frontier in American dance and drama 1930–1943', Ph.D. dissertation, University of Georgia, 1972 (UMI: Ann Arbor), microfilm, 6–7.

749 Hindman, 'The myth of the frontier', 1.

750 Dumenil, *The Modern Temper*, 96.

751 See the excellent discussion by Warren I. Susman, in *Culture as History: The Transformation of American Society in the Twentieth Century* (New York: Pantheon Books, 1984).

752 Hindman, 'The myth of the frontier', 254.

753 Walter Terry, *Frontiers of Dance*, 80.

754 Armitage, *Martha Graham*, 87.

755 See filmed extract in 'Martha Graham: The dancer revealed', and the outstanding photographs in Morgan, *Martha Graham*. I viewed a videotape of *Frontier*, danced by Martha Graham (filmed by Julien Bryan and Jules Bucher 1936–9, co-produced by the Martha Graham Center of Contemporary Dance, Inc., in association with the Teatro Municipale Romolo Valli, Reggio Emilia, Italy, for the Festival Graham, 1987), video in Dance Collection, NYPL.

756 'In Search of Design', *Dance Perspectives* 28 (Winter 1966), no page nos.

757 This pose is shown clearly in a wonderful photograph by Barbara Morgan (*Martha Graham*, 29).

758 Marcia Siegel, *The Shapes of Change*, 143.

759 Ibid.

760 Ibid.

761 On the social conditions of American women in the early colonial days, see Andrew Sinclair, *The Emancipation of the American Woman* (New York: Harper and Row, 1965). Space precludes further discussion here of the social relevance of Graham's early work. See, however, *Studies in Dance History* 5, no. 1 (1994) for articles on this topic.

762 Graham, *Blood Memory*, 224.

763 *Frontier* (A Connecticut College School of Dance Archive Film, produced and filmed by Dwight Godwin for Jerome Robbins Film Archive, 1964), film in Dance Collection, NYPL.

764 *Frontier* (filmed by Amra Nowack Associates for Jerome Robbins Film Archive at Brooklyn Academy of Music, 1975), film in Dance Collection, NYPL.

765 *Frontier* (videotaped in performance at the New York State Theater, 1985), video in Dance Collection, NYPL.

766 Graham, 'A modern dancer's primer for action', 46.

767 Marcia Siegel, 'Re-radicalizing Graham: Revivals or forgeries', *Hudson Review* 68, no. 1 (Spring 1995), 104 (101–7).

768 Cunningham, www.merce.org (accessed 16 August 2002). Compare Merce Cunningham, 'The function of a technique for dance', in *The*

Dance has Many Faces, Walter Sorell (Cleveland/New York: The World Publishing Company, 1951), 250 (250–5), emphasis mine.

[769]   Cunningham, cited by Susan Sontag, in 'Conversations on the dance', Merce Cunningham and Susan Sontag, recorded 3 March 1986 (audiocassette, Dance Collection at New York Public Library for the Performing Arts at Lincoln Center; henceforth NYPL).

[770]   In relation to *Biped*, Valerie Preston-Dunlop writes: 'What does fragmentation do to human movement? Ultimately, it dehumanises it.' *Dance and the Performative: A Choreological Perspective – Laban and Beyond* (London: Verve, 2002), 264.

[771]   The quality of undecidability is associated with Jacques Derrida's logic of *différance*. See discussion in Chapter 5.

[772]   'The dance was made in a series of chunks of movement, some chunks involving the whole company (6), and others as little as one or two. These chunks varied in length, but as first arranged added up to five-minute sections, five in all, the whole being twenty-five minutes. All the sections were to be done at any performance, but the order they were in could be shifted ... Christian Wolff's music exists in two versions: 'Music for Merce Cunningham' is for six or seven instruments; 'Duo for Pianists' is for two pianos ... Rauschenberg's costumes consisted of leotards and tights dyed in various shades of brown.' David Vaughan, *Merce Cunningham: Fifty Years* (New York: Aperture 1997), 117–8. These costumes had an 'autumnal feel'. David Vaughan, *Merce Cunningham: Fifty Forward* (CD Rom, New York: Cunningham Dance Foundation, 2005). My comments here are based on studying a videotape of the performance on 6 January 1998, viewed at the Archives of the Cunningham Dance Foundation. The camera is looking down on the stage and is sufficiently distant for the figures not to appear in great detail. Music by Christian Wolff: 'Or Four People' (1994). Sets and lighting by Mark Lancaster. Costumes by Mark Lancaster, Suzanne Gallo. Dancers: Holley Farmer, Maydelle Fason, Foofwa d'Imobilité, Banu Ogan, Glen Rumsey, Jeannie Steele. I also attended a performance at the Théâtre de la Ville, Paris (12 November,1999). 'Rune' will be discussed further later in this chapter.

[773]   Lancaster designed new costumes in 1982 and again in 1995.

[774]   See Glossary for ballet terms.

[775]   Sandra Noll Hammond, *Ballet Basics* (California: Mayfield, 1984), 75. The use of ballet terminology in relation to Cunningham's work is controversial, but the movements are frequently derived from (and dislocate) the ballet lexicon.

[776]   Foofwa d'Imobilité, performing what was originally Cunningham's part.

[777]   Henri Bergson, *Creative Evolution* (London: Macmillan, 1911), 163–4.

[778]   I use the past tense here because the challenges Cunningham introduced started to make an impact in the early 1940s.

779 Hubert Godard, interviewed by Laurence Louppe, in 'Singular, moving geographies', *Writings on Dance* 15, *The French Issue* (Winter 1996): 19 (12–21).

780 'Space, time and dance' (1952), in David Vaughan, *Merce Cunningham: Fifty Years* , 67 (66–7).

781 Valerie Preston-Dunlop, 'Dance dynamics – Focusing on the rhythmic form of the movement Itself' (Part II), *Dance Theatre Journal,* 13, no. 2 (Autumn/Winter 1996): 36 (34–38).

782 Merce Cunningham Study Day, The Place Theatre, London (16 September 2002).

783 Cited in Vaughan, *Merce Cunningham,* 89.

784 Jane Vranish, 'Moving for the moment', in *Pittsburgh Post-Gazette,* 23 September 1994, 2 (2 and 28).

785 Joan Acocella, 'Cunningham's recent work', in *Choreography and Dance* 4, no. 3, *Merce Cunningham: Creative Elements* (1997): 15 (3–15).

786 Merce Cunningham, 'The function of a technique for dance', 253, emphasis mine.

787 'Excerpts from lecture-demonstration given at Anna Halprin's Dance Deck (13 July 1957)', in David Vaughan, *Merce Cunningham,* 101 (100–01).

788 Merce Cunningham, 'The function of a technique for dance', 251.

789 Cunningham, 'The impermanent art', 1952, reproduced in David Vaughan, *Merce Cunningham,* 86 (86–7).

790 Mark Franko, *Dancing Modernism/Performing Politics* (Bloomington: Indiana University Press, 1995), 84. By contrast, he sees a fundamental shift in Cunningham's work from anti-expressivism in the fifties and early sixties to inexpressivity in the eighties and nineties.

791 Franko, *Dancing Modernism,* 80.

792 Gus Solomons, in David Vaughan, 'Cunningham and his dancers', *Ballet Review* 15, no. 3 (Fall 1987): 29 (19–40).

793 Sondra Fraleigh, cited in Preston-Dunlop, 'Dance dynamics', 38.

794 For full discussions of the political implications of the so-called 'aesthetic of indifference', see Moira Roth's seminal article, 'The aesthetic of indifference', *Art Forum* (1977): 46–53, and Moira Roth and Jonathan Katz, *Difference/Indifference: Musings on Postmodernism, Marcel Duchamp and John Cage* (Amsterdam: Gordon and Breach, 1998), 63.

795 Vaughan, *Merce Cunningham,* 246.

796 In 1945, the then rector of the college, Bob Wunsch, was arrested on the charge of 'crimes against nature'. Within the college, he had always concealed his sexual preferences, but the community offered him no support when he resigned, and he left alone, with no farewells, and subsequently 'disappeared'. See Martin Duberman, *Black Mountain College* (New York: E.P. Dutton and Co., 1972), 225–7. The publication in 1948 of Charles Kinsey's report on male sexual behaviour, which showed that a high percentage of the male population had engaged in homosexual practices, 'heightened acceptance but also increased fear and condemnation of homosexuality'. Susan Foster, 'Closets full of

dances: Modern dance's performance of masculinity and sexuality', in *Dancing Desires, Choreographing Sexualities on and off the Stage*, ed. Jane C. Desmond (Madison, WI: University of Wisconsin Press, 2001), 177 (147–207).

[797] Paul Griffiths, *Cage* (Oxford: Oxford University Press, 1981), 7.

[798] David Vaughan, *Merce Cunningham*, 27.

[799] Cited in David Vaughan, *Merce Cunningham*, 33–4. From the description given by Vaughan, this play is reminiscent of aspects of German expressionist drama.

[800] Daniel Belgrad, *The Culture of Spontaneity, Improvisation and the Arts in Postwar America* (Chicago: University of Chicago Press, 1998), 145.

[801] Cited in Belgrad, *The Culture of Spontaneity*, 147, emphasis mine. Goodman taught at Black Mountain College in 1950, and is perhaps best known as the co-author, with Fritz Perls and Ralph Hefferline, of *Gestalt Therapy*, published in 1951.

[802] David Vaughan, *Merce Cunningham*, 88 and 117.

[803] David Riesman, *The Lonely Crowd: A Study of the Changing American Character* (New Haven: Yale University Press, 1950), 15 and 25.

[804] Ibid., 217.

[805] Ibid., 373.

[806] Ibid., 261.

[807] Riesman, *The Lonely Crowd*, 21–2.

[808] Paul Goodman, *Growing Up Absurd: Problems of Youth in the Organized Society* (New York: Vintage Books, 1966), 10 and 91.

[809] New York: Doubleday.

[810] William Whyte, *The Organization Man* (London: Jonathan Cape, 1957), 7.

[811] Ibid., 362.

[812] Richard Sennett, *The Fall of Public Man* (London: Faber and Faber [1974], 1986), 4–5.

[813] Ibid., 339.

[814] Ibid., 338–340, emphasis mine.

[815] Ibid., 267.

[816] Peter Knight, *Conspiracy Culture, from Kennedy to the X-Files* (New York: Routledge, 2000), 28.

[817] Timothy Melley, *Empire of Conspiracy: The Culture of Paranoia in Postwar America* (Ithaca: Cornell University Press, 2000), 7.

[818] Ibid., 2.

[819] Cunningham, 'The impermanent art', 1952, 86.

[820] This quote is in fact by Laura Kuhn, quoting John Cage, quoting John Rahn, to Cunningham, whose response was 'Oh, that's wonderful'. 'Laura Kuhn in conversation with Merce Cunningham', in *Art Performs Life: Merce Cunningham/Meredith Monk/Bill T. Jones's* (Minneapolis: Walker Art Center, 1998), 43 (22–43).

[821] Vernon Shetley, 'Merce Cunningham', *Raritan* 8, no. 3 (1989): 87 (72–90). Shetley's article, published in 1989, takes account of work after

the period I am discussing, but his comments are also relevant to earlier work.

822 Merce Cunningham, 'Two Questions and Five Dances', *Dance Perspectives* 34 (Summer 1968), 47(46–53).

823 See Marcia Siegel, *The Shapes of Change: Images of American Dance* (Boston: Houghton Mifflin, 1979), 294.

824 Vernon Shetley, 'Merce Cunningham', 87.

825 'Excerpts from Lecture-Demonstration', 101.

826 'Entretien avec Merce Cunningham: Montrer et laisser les gens se faire une opinion', in *Danse et Utopie: Mobiles I* (Paris: l'Harmattan, 1999), 207 (199–208), translation mine.

827 An edited version of this interview was published in *Dance Theatre Journal* 20, no.2 (2004), 38–43.

828 Susan Hapgood, in *Neo-Dada: Redefining Art 1958–62*, ed. Susan Hapgood (New York: The American Federation of Arts, 1994), 11 (11–66).

829 Ibid.,16.

830 'Every current history of Fluxus makes a deep bow to Cage.' Jill Johnson, 'Dada and Fluxus', in *Neo-Dada*, 93. Cage himself, however, knew little of Fluxus, and was also very sceptical about the label 'neo-Dadaist'.

831 John Cage in conversation with Daniel Charles, *For the Birds* (London: Marion Boyars [1976], 1981), 222.

832 Daniel Belgrad, *The Culture of Spontaneity*, 161.

833 Cited in Belgrad, *The Culture of Spontaneity*, 154.

834 See his *Merce Cunningham*, and 'Beyond expressionism: Merce Cunningham's critique of the "natural"', in *Dance History: An Introduction*, ed. Janet Adshead-Lansdale and June Layson (London: Routledge, 1983), 182–97. Copeland does note that Graham's early work, despite its narrative content, was markedly minimalist, and featured the 'nervous angular' quality which Copeland attributes to George Balanchine, whom he sees as more 'modern' than Graham.

835 Daniel Belgrad, *The Culture of Spontaneity*, 159.

836 As reported by Belgrad in *The Culture of Spontaneity*, 162.

837 Cited in Belgrad, *The Culture of Spontaneity*, 161.

838 Charles Atlas, 'Merce Cunningham, a lifetime of dance'. Directed by Charles Atlas. BBC TV Channel 2, broadcast 26 August 2000.

839 Jane Vranish, 'Moving for the moment', 2.

840 Marianne Simon, in Earle Brown, Remy Charlip, Marianne Simon, David Vaughan, 'The Forming of an Aesthetic: Merce Cunningham and John Cage', in *Ballet Review* 13, no. 3 (Fall 1985), 40 (23–40).

841 Merce Cunningham Study Day, The Place Theatre, London (16 September 2002).

842 Cunningham, http://www.merce.org (accessed 16 August 2002). However, Cunningham's current use of computers in choreographing (see chapter 5 below) means that his relationship to the dancers' bodies can be mediated by virtual bodies.

843 Marianne Simon, in Earle Brown et al., 'The forming of an aesthetic: Merce Cunningham and John Cage', 29.

844 Remy Charlip, in Earle Brown et al., 'The forming of an aesthetic', 29.

845 Carolyn Brown, cited in Mark Franko, *Dancing Modernism*, 171.

846 Carolyn Brown, in David Vaughan, 'Cunningham and his dancers', 28–9.

847 Ibid., 28.

848 Marcia Siegel, *At the Vanishing Point: A Critic Looks at Dance* (New York: Saturday Review Press [1968], 1972), 236.

849 Cited in David Vaughan, *Merce Cunningham*, 137.

850 Cited in Laura Kuhn, 'Cunningham and Cage', *Ballet Review* 26, no. 3 (1998), 81 (80–98). See also David Vaughan, *Merce Cunningham: Fifty Years*, 29–30. Cunningham's comment about the predominance of fear in his life at this time (1944) may or may not be related to the climate of homophobia referred to above.

851 Cunningham, cited in David Vaughan, *Merce Cunningham*, 30.

852 Cited in David Vaughan, *Merce Cunningham*, 30.

853 Kuhn, 'Cunningham and Cage', 81–2.

854 Cited in David Vaughan, *Merce Cunningham*, 29.

855 Margaret H'Doubler, 'A question of values and terms', *Dance Observer* 12 (Aug-Sept 1945), 83.

856 Arlene Croce, 'An interview with Merce Cunningham', 3.

857 John Cage, 'Grace and clarity', *Dance Observer* 11 (November 1944), 108 (108–9).

858 'Martha Graham and Dance Company, National Theatre, May 7–14, 1944', *Dance Observer* 11 (June–July 1944), 63 (63).

859 Robert Sabin, 'Martha Graham and Dance Company, National Theatre, week of May 14, 1945', *Dance Observer* 12 (June–July 1945): 69 (69–70).

860 Robert Sabin, 'Dance at the Coolidge Festival', *Dance Observer* 11 (December 1944), 120 (120–1).

861 *Dance Observer* 14 (July 1947), 64.

862 Richard Lippold, 'Martha Graham and Dance Company, Plymouth Theatre, January 21–February 2, 1946', *Dance Observer* 13 (March 1946), 34 (34–6).

863 See my 'Displacing "humans": Merce Cunningham's crowds', *Body, Space and Technology Journal* (e-journal), 1 (2000). www.brunel.ac.uk/depts/pfa/bstjournal

864 *Dance Observer* 13 (June–July 1946), 74 (74–5).

865 Robert Sabin, 'Merce Cunningham, John Cage: Studio Theatre, April 5, 1944', *Dance Observer* 11 (May 1944), 57 (57–8).

866 Cited in David Vaughan, *Merce Cunningham*, 29.

867 Carolyn Brown, in David Vaughan, 'Cunningham and his dancers', 36 (19–40).

868 John Cage, *For the Birds*, 43.

869 David Vaughan, *Merce Cunningham*, 58.

870 Remy Charlip, in Earle Brown et al., 'The forming of an aesthetic', 33.

871 Cited in Janet Goodridge, *Rhythm and Timing of Movement in Performance: Drama, Dance and Ceremony* (London: Jessica Kingsley, 1999), 121.

872 'Merce Cunningham in conversation' (The Place Theatre, London, 20 September 2002).

873 Merce Cunningham, 'Choreography and the dance', in *The Dance Anthology*, ed. Cobbett Steinberg, 59.

874 In Earle Brown et al., 'The forming of an aesthetic', 28, emphasis mine.

875 Miwa Nagura, 'Cross-cultural differences in the interpretation of Merce Cunningham's choreography', in *Moving Words: Re-Writing Dance*, ed. Gay Morris (London: Routledge, 1996), 271 (270–87).

876 Roger Copeland, 'Beyond expressionism', 189.

877 Cited in David Vaughan, *Merce Cunningham*, 58.

878 David Vaughan, *Merce Cunningham*, 64. This is often compared with Duchamp's exhibiting of 'readymades' as art works. However, 'readymades' were not simply everyday objects, but rather mass-produced objects. See Wanda M. Corn, *The Great American Thing: Modern Art and National Identity, 1915–1935* (Berkeley: University of California Press, 1990), 72.

879 Cited in David Vaughan, *Merce Cunningham*, 70.

880 In *Story* (1963), 'the choreography itself offered the dancers a certain amount of freedom: given phrases of movement, the dancers were free to vary them in the space, direction, order of continuity, speed and dynamics ... In one section, the dancers were given direction and level, and length of time in the direction and level, but the movement was completely of the dancers' own devising, with just one "rule": the dancer had to remain attached to one place in the space with at least one foot throughout the time span (which varied) except once, when the dancer was allowed to move into another area by a body's length and continue'. Carolyn Brown, cited in John Percival, *Experimental Dance* (London: Studio Vista, 1971), 43–4. In *Field Dances* (1963), 'the dancers made their own choices of movements, and their own decisions as to how many times they would do a given movement or phrase, at what tempo, and where in the space'. David Vaughan, *Merce Cunningham*, 129–30.

881 David Vaughan, *Merce Cunningham*, 8.

882 Cunningham, cited in 'Zen and the art of dance', Deborah Jowitt, *The Village Voice* 17 (January 1977), 49 (48–9).

883 Cunningham interviewed by Michael Seaver, *The Irish Times*, 6 May 2002.

884 'Space, Time and Dance', 1952, 67.

885 Riesman, *The Lonely Crowd*, 212.

886 'Interview with Roger Reynolds' (1961), in *John Cage*, ed. Robert Dunn (New York: Henmar Press, 1962), 50 (45–52).

887 Cited in David Vaughan, *Merce Cunningham*, 84–5.

888 Cited in David Vaughan, *Merce Cunningham*, 189, emphasis mine. Some further examples cited by Vaughan are *Fielding Sixes* (1980), where 'chance operations gave the continuity' (Cunningham, cited 213);

Gallopade (1981), where 'the gestures are removed from context, and further fragmented by using chance to find the continuity' (Cunningham, cited 217), and *Fabrications* (1987), where 'the continuity of the phrases was determined by chance' (232).

[889] Charlip in Earle Brown et al, 'The forming of an aesthetic', 33.

[890] I shall discuss this process below in relation to Derridean *différance*.

[891] Vernon Shetley, 'Merce Cunningham', 83.

[892] Roger Copeland, 'Genre and style', in *What is Dance? Readings in Theory and Criticism*, ed. Roger Copeland and Marshall Cohen (Oxford: Oxford University Press, 1983), 321 (307–24).

[893] Vaughan, *Merce Cunningham*, 57.

[894] John Cage in conversation with Daniel Charles, *For the Birds*, 91.

[895] Ibid., 199.

[896] Extract from Francine du Plessix Gray's diary, recording one of Cage's conversations on Zen. Duberman, *Black Mountain*, 349.

[897] John Cage in conversation with Daniel Charles, *For the Birds*, 201.

[898] 'LifeForms' is a special computer program designed for creating choreographic elements by simulating choreographic work processes. The user can animate a figure by entering it on the timeline in pre-defined positions/single images. The computer then calculates the intermediate transitions (interpolation) and generates the finished animated figure, or choreography. Alternatively, the user can also model positions/single images on a basic figure first and then insert this figure into the timeline. See Glossary, in *Dance and Technology, Moving Towards Media Productions*, ed. Söke Dinkla and Martina Leeker (Berlin: Alexander Verlag, 2002), 430. LifeForms has been renamed as DanceForms. See www.credo-interactive.com (accessed 20 April 2004).

[899] Merce Cunningham, 'The impermanent art', 86.

[900] Remy Charlip, in 'The forming of an aesthetic', 37–8.

[901] Marianne Simon, in 'The forming of an aesthetic', 37.

[902] Cunningham, 'The impermanent art', 86.

[903] Cited in Nagura, 'Cross-cultural differences', 272.

[904] Cunningham, 'The impermanent art', 86.

[905] Cunningham, www.merce.org, accessed 16 August 2002.

[906] Cunningham, 'The impermanent art', 86.

[907] Carolyn Brown, 'On chance', *Ballet Review* 2, no. 2 (Summer 1968), 16–17 (7–25).

[908] Belgrad, *The Culture of Spontaneity*, 120–1.

[909] The openness to unpredictability that remains at the heart of Cunningham's aesthetic does not fit neatly into the categories of modernism and postmodernism, and I have deliberately not engaged here with the polemic concerning Cunningham's position in this regard.

[910] Belgrad, *The Culture of Spontaneity*, 161.

[911] Cited in Belgrad, *The Culture of Spontaneity*, 127.

[912] Sennett, *The Fall of Public Man*, 330.

[913] Merce Cunningham, 'The function of a technique for dance', 252.

914   Merce Cunningham Study Day, The Place Theatre, London (16 September 2002).

915   Cunningham, 'The Function of a Technique for Dance', 252–3.

916   Earle Brown, in Earle Brown et al., 'The forming of an aesthetic', 40.

917   For details, see Vaughan, *Merce Cunningham: Fifty Years.*

918   Cage, cited in Martin Duberman, *Black Mountain,* 350.

919   Michael Kirby, 'The New Theatre', *Tulane Drama Review* 10, no. 2 (Winter 1965), 29 (23–43).

920   Johnson, 'Dada and Fluxus', 98.

921   London: Penguin Books, 1967, 119.

922   John Cage in conversation with Daniel Charles, *For the Birds* (London: Marion Boyars [1976], 1981), 77.

923   John Cage, *A Year from Monday: New Lectures and Writings by John Cage* (London: Calder and Boyars [1963], 1968), ix.

924   John Cage, *For the Birds*, 213.

925   Cited in *The Buckminster Fuller Reader*, ed. James Meller (London: Pelican Books [1970], 1972), 11.

926   'Loops' is now also the title of a digital abstract portrait of Cunningham's hands, by Paul Kaiser, Shelley Eshkar and Marc Downie.

927   *The Buckminster Fuller Reader*, 36.

928   John Cage in conversation with Daniel Charles, *For the Birds*, 108.

929   Richard Kostelanetz, *The Theatre of Mixed Means*, (London: Pitman [1967], 1970), 255.

930   John Cage, *A Year from Monday*, ix.

931   McLuhan and Fiore, *The Medium is the Massage* (London: Penguin, 1967), 26–40.

932   Cage, in Richard Kostelanetz, *The Theatre of Mixed Means,* 52.

933   Richard Kostelanetz, *The Theatre of Mixed Means*, 42.

934   Marshall McLuhan, *Forward Through the Rearview Mirror: Reflections On and By Marshall McLuhan*, ed. Paul Benedetti and Nancy DeHart (Prentice-Hall Canada Inc, 1997),184. For a very stimulating discussion of McLuhan as a postmodern 'actor', see Glenn Willmott, *McLuhan, or Modernism in Reverse* (Toronto: University of Toronto Press, 1996).

935   Elinor Rogosin, *The Dance Makers: Conversations with American Choreographers* (New York: Walker and Co., 1980), 67.

936   Arlene Croce, 'An interview with Merce Cunningham', *Ballet Review* 1, no. 4 (Winter 1966), 4 (3–5). See also Carolyn Brown, 'McLuhan and the dance', *Ballet Review* 1, no.4 (Winter 1966), 13–20.

937   See also an excerpt in *Merce Cunningham, A Lifetime of Dance.*

938   Vaughan, *Merce Cunningham,* 89.

939   Cited in David Vaughan, *Merce Cunningham*, 88.

940   'Space, Time and Dance', in Vaughan, *Merce Cunningham,* 66. This description is strikingly relevant to Kandinsky. See my discussion of Kandinsky in *Symbolist Aesthetics and Early Abstract Art: Sites of Imaginary Space* (Cambridge University Press, 1995).

941   *Watching the Dance Go By* (Houghton Mifflin: Boston 1977), 289.

942   Shetley, 'Merce Cunningham', 77.

943   James Waring, 'Maker of dances in a style eloquently his own', *The Village Voice*, January 2, 1957 (clippings file, Cunningham Dance Foundation, no page numbers).

944   *Watching the Dance Go By* (Houghton Mifflin: Boston) 1977, 289.

945   Edwin Denby, 1944, in Edwin Denby, *Dance Writings and Poetry*, ed. Robert Cornfield (New Haven: Yale University Press, 1998), 117.

946   'I had become interested in not having a fixed order to a piece. *Rune* ... reflected this for the first time.' Vaughan, *Merce Cunningham*, 117.

947   Cunningham Dance Foundation. Film version made in Hamburg, July 1966; produced by Studio Hamburg, direction by Arne Arnbom. The comments that follow are based mainly on this version.

948   Cunningham, cited in Vaughan, *Merce Cunningham, Fifty Years*, 150.

949   See John Percival, *Experimental Dance*, 41.

950   Noel Goodwin, 'Cage without bars', *Dance and Dancers* 18, no. 2 (February 1967), 39 (38–39).

951   Interestingly in this respect, Siegel commented that 'there was a certain pleasant camaraderie between the dancers and the presiding technicians in the first version of *Variations V*, at Philharmonic Hall ... Now, in *Canfield* [1969], with the arrogant competence of Rocket Control, they are running the show.' Siegel, *At the Vanishing Point*, 141–2.

952   Cited in Noel Goodwin, 'Cage without bars', 39.

953   Don McDonagh, *The Rise and Fall of Modern Dance* (New York: E.P. Dutton, 1970), 62.

954   Kerstin Evert, 'Dance and technology at the turn of the last and present centuries', in *Dance and Technology*, ed. Söke Dinkla and Martina Leeker (Berlin: Alexander Verlag, 2002), 42–4 (30–65).

955   McDonagh, *The Rise and Fall of Modern Dance*, 62.

956   Clive Barnes, 'Places and planets', *Dance and Dancers* 18, no. 3 (March 1967), 30 (30–31).

957   My discussion here is based on studying a recording made of the first performance of *RainForest*, on 9 March 1968 at the State University College at Buffalo, New York, as part of the 2nd Buffalo Festival of the Arts, featuring Merce Cunningham, Carolyn Brown, Barbara Lloyd, Sandra Neels, Albert Reid and Gus Solomons, Jr. I also viewed a version made at the Holland Festival in June 1970, in black and white with no sound, and featuring Carolyn Brown, Merce Cunningham, Meg Harper, Sandra Neels, Chase Robinson and Jeff Slayton, with music by David Tudor (*Rainforest*), décor by Andy Warhol and lighting by Richard Nelson. (Videos viewed at Archives of Cunningham Dance Foundation.) I have also attended several performances of this piece.

958   See Copeland, *Merce Cunningham*, 33, for an account of the influence of space imagery on the late-1960s *Zeitgeist*. On 16 March 1966, Neil Armstrong and Dave Scott were launched in Gemini 8 to conduct the first linkup in space, docking with an Agena target satellite. A spacewalk had been planned for Scott, but this was prevented by technical

problems. After watching the television footage of the Moon landing in 1969, Cunningham's manager, Jean Rigg, told him that 'the lighting effects on the Moon were exactly what he had been trying for in *Canfield* [1969]. Merce Cunningham replied: "Yes. And the sound too"'. Marcia Siegel, *At the Vanishing Point*, 243.

959   Except for Cunningham himself, each of the six dancers performed his or her role, then left the stage and did not return.

960   Siegel, *At the Vanishing Point*, 239.

961   See Laban, *Modern Educational Dance* (London: Macdonald and Evans [1948], 3rd edition, 1976), 71.

962   Cunningham, cited in Vaughan, *Merce Cunningham*, 186.

963   Sharon Unrau, 'Children's dance: An exploration through the techniques of Merce Cunningham' (Ph.D. dissertation, Ohio State University, 2000), 113.

964   Cited in Vaughan, *Merce Cunningham*, 196.

965   Cited in Vaughan, *Merce Cunningham*, 193.

966   I have viewed video recordings at the Cunningham Dance Foundation of two performances of this piece. 'Merce Cunningham Dance Foundation presents Merce Cunningham, 60 Years of Dancing' (Brooklyn Academy of Music, 19 September 1997), and 'A Lifetime of Dance: Merce Cunningham Dance Company' (City Center, 21 July 1999). Music: David Tudor, *Untitled* (1975/94). Design and lighting, Mark Lancaster. Staged by Chris Komar and Meg Harper. Dancers: Robert Swinston, Jeannie Steele, Koji Minato, Thomas Caley, Jean Freebury, Banu Ogan, David Kulick, Glen Rumsey, Cheryl Therrien and Lisa Boudreau.

967   Cunningham, quoted in David Vaughan, *Merce Cunningham*, 194.

968   Paul Walsh, 'Merce Cunningham Dance Co: "We're not trying to say anything"', *New Times* 6, no. 29 (9–15 April 1975) (Clipping file, Cunningham Dance Foundation, no page numbers).

969   K. Filas, *Minnesota Daily*, 4 April 1975 (clippings file, Cunningham Dance Foundation, no page nos.).

970   'Merce Cunningham and Dance Company, Roundabout Theatre', *The Soho Weekly News*, 11 December 1975 (clippings file, Cunningham Dance Foundation, no page numbers).

971   Arlene Croce, 'Dancing: Notes on a natural man', *The New Yorker*, 7 February 1977 (clippings file, Cunningham Dance Foundation, no page numbers).

972   Deborah Jowitt, 'Merce: Enough electricity to light up Broadway', *The Village Voice*, 7 February 1977 (clippings file, Cunningham Dance Foundation, no page numbers).

973   'Dance: A classic by Cunningham', *The New York Times*, 21 January 1977. Deborah Jowitt, 'Merce: Enough electricity to light up Broadway', *The Village Voice*, 7 February 1977 (clippings file, Cunningham Dance Foundation, no page numbers).

974   'A burst of life's energy long pent-up', *The New York Times*, 7 March 1994.

975 Cunningham Dance Foundation. Dancers: Karole Armitage, Louise Burns, Ellen Cornfield, Morgan Ensminger, Lisa Fox, Meg Harper, Chris Komar, Robert Kovich, Julie Roess-Smith and Jim Self.

976 Deborah Jowitt, 'Merce: Enough electricity to light up Broadway'.

977 Cited in Unrau, 'Children's dance', 26.

978 Cited in Unrau, 'Children's dance', 26.

979 Unrau, 'Children's dance', 25.

980 *The Dancer and the Dance: Merce Cunningham in Conversation with Jacqueline Lesschaeve* (New York: Marilyn Boyars, 1991), 22.

981 See *The Dancer and the Dance*, 19–24.

982 *The Dancer and the Dance*, 22.

983 Ibid., 18.

984 Ibid., 19.

985 Veron Shetley, 'Merce Cunningham', 88.

986 Ibid., 81.

987 *The Dancer and the Dance*, 23.

988 Tobi Tobias, 'Notes for a piece on Cunningham', *Dance Magazine* (September 1975), 42 (40–42).

989 Robert Greskovic, 'Cunningham as sculptor', *Ballet Review* 11, no. 4 (Winter 1984), 93 (89–95).

990 Cunningham Dance Foundation, directed by Charles Atlas.

991 Arlene Croce, *Going to the Dance* (New York: Albert Knopf, 1982), 122.

992 Peter Z. Grossman, 'Talking with Merce Cunningham about video', *Dance Scope* 13, nos 2/3 (Winter–Spring 1979), 66 (57–68).

993 Croce, *Going to the Dance*, 123.

994 Marcia Siegel, 'Strangers return', *Ballet International* 6 (1983), 19 (16–21).

995 Croce, *Going to the Dance*, 124.

996 Tobi Tobias, 'Notes for a piece on Cunningham', 40.

997 Cunningham, 'The Impermanent Art', 1952, reproduced in David Vaughan, *Merce Cunningham: Fifty Years* (New York: Aperture, 1997), 86 (86–7).

998 Marshall McLuhan and Quentin Fiore, *The Medium is the Massage* (London: Penguin Books, 1967), 26–41.

999 *Merriam Webster's Collegiate Dictionary/Thesaurus* (Dallas: Zane Publishing, Inc. 1997, 1996).

1000 Nigel Stewart, 'Re-languaging the body: Phenomenological description and the dance image', *Performance Research* 3, no. 2, *On Place* (Summer 1998): 44 (42–53). Gibson's work is discussed in this article.

1001 Jeffrey Longstaff, 'Cognitive Structures of Kinesthetic Space: Reevaluating Rudolf Laban's Choreutics in the Context of Spatial Cognition and Motor Control' (D.Phil. thesis, City University/Laban Centre, London, 1996), 35.

1002 The phenomenological thinker Algis Mikunas argues that 'the kinesthetic modality underlies all perceptual fields ... it is possible to translate one field of experience into another in terms of a common denominator: the kinesthetic awareness ... it is possible to speak of kinesthetic awareness as a basic process of knowing, which sub-tends all bodily actions, and synthesizes them ... the kinesthetic awareness ... underlies all fields of experience.' Algis Mikunas, 'The primacy of movement', *Main Currents in Modern Thought* 31, no. 1 (September–October 1974), 8–9 (8–12).

1003 Cunningham speaking to dance students, in 'Merce Cunningham, A lifetime of dance'. Directed by Charles Atlas. BBC2 TV, broadcast 26 August 2000.

1004 Lipps also talks about empathy with objects, but I am confining my discussion to moving subjects.

1005 Laban and Lawrence, *Effort*, 18.

1006 Hans Brandenburg, *Der Moderne Tanz* (München: Georg Müller [1913], 1917), 83, emphasis mine.

1007 Isabelle Launay, *A la recherche d'une danse moderne: Rudolf Laban, Mary Wigman* (Paris: Chiron, 1996), 8.

1008 'Merce Cunningham, A lifetime of dance'.

1009 On the close correspondences between Merleau-Ponty and Laban, see Vera Maletic, *Body-Space-Expression: The Development of Rudolf Laban's Movement and Dance Concepts* (Berlin: Mouton de Gruyter, 1987), 189ff.

1010 This discussion is beyond the scope of my study. For a very well-informed and wide-ranging discussion of Merleau-Ponty, including his relationship to post-structuralism, see Jack Reynolds, 'Merleau-Ponty (1908–1961)', *The Internet Encyclopedia of Philosophy*, 2001. www.iep.utm.edu/m/merleau.htm. Accessed 12 November, 2004.

1011 *Phenomenology of Perception*, 110 (emphasis mine).

1012 Ibid., 233.

1013 *Phenomenology of Perception*, 109 (emphasis mine). See the note on my translation of this passage in the Introduction. Virtual movement can take place in response to rhythmic stimuli. I have argued elsewhere that rhythmic structures show a tendency towards spatialisation of time and temporalisation of space, re-articulating our spatio-temporal experience through kinesthetic awareness. See my *Symbolist Aesthetics and Early Abstract Art: Sites of Imaginary Space* (Cambridge: Cambridge University Press, 1995) and more concisely in my 'Rhythmic structures and imaginary space in Rimbaud, Mallarmé, Kandinsky and Mondrian', in *Word and Image Interactions*, ed. Martin Heusser (Basel: Wiese Verlag, 1993), 143–56.

1014 'Only by changing perception, emotion, or the meaning of the situation can we change the setting of the gravity response.' Kevin Frank, 'Tonic function: A gravity response model for Rolfing structural and movement integration', 1995. www.somatics.de/KevinFrank/FrankKevin.htm (accessed 23 October 2004).

1015 *Phenomenology of Perception*, 111.

1016 Cunningham, 'The impermanent art', 86.

1017 Nick Crossley, *The Social Body: Habit, Identity and Desire* (London: Sage, 2001), 128.

1018 Deborah Bull, 'The Science of proprioception'. This text appears on the BBC TV website for 'The dancer's body: A machine that dances', written and presented by Deborah Bull (broadcast on BBC2, September and October 2003). www.bbc.co.uk/music/dancersbody/body/proprioception.shtml (accessed 16 July, 2004).

1019 Ibid.

1020 On ideokinesiology and somatic disciplines, see Eric Franklin, *Dynamic Alignment Through Imagery* (Champaign, Illinois: Human Kinesics, 1996). Compare Kuppers's account of the effects of visualisation and movement, which she links with Laban's belief that 'the mind and body are constituted as a continuity'. Petra Kuppers, *Disability and Contemporary Performance: Bodies on Edge* (New York: Routledge, 2003), 129–30.

1021 See Marcel Mauss, 'Techniques of the body', in *Incorporations: Zone 6*, ed. Jonathan Crary and Sanford Kwinter (New York: Urzone, 1992), 455–477. Bourdieu also uses the term 'techniques of the body', e.g. in *The Logic of Practice*, 69.

1022 Ibid., 54–7.

1023 Bourdieu, *The Logic of Practice*, 56.

1024 *In Other Words: Essays Towards A Reflexive Sociology* (Cambridge: Polity, 1990), 108.

1025 Bourdieu, *The Logic of Practice*, 69.

1026 Bourdieu, *Sociology in Question* (London: Sage, 1993), 87.

1027 Bourdieu, *The Logic of Practice*, 54.

1028 Bourdieu, *Sociology in Question*, 87.

1029 Bourdieu, *In Other Words*, 108.

1030 Bourdieu, *The Logic of Practice*, 66.

1031 Randal Johnson, 'Editor's introduction: Pierre Bourdieu on art, literature and culture', in Pierre Bourdieu, *The Field of Cultural Production: Essays on Art and Literature* (Cambridge: Polity, 1993), 6.

1032 Gay Morris, 'Bourdieu, the body, and Graham's post-war dance', in *Dance Research* 19, no. 2 (Winter 2001), 60–61 (52–82). See also my 'A technique for power: Reconfiguring economies of energy in Martha Graham's early work', in *Dance Research* 20, no. 1 (Summer 2002), 3–32.

1033 'The impetus for change ... resides in the struggles that take place in the corresponding field of production. These struggles, whose goal is the preservation or transformation of the established power relationships in the field of production, obviously have as their effect the preservation or transformation of the structure of the field of works, which are the tools and stakes in these struggles.' Bourdieu, *The Field of Cultural Production*, 183.

1034 Cited in Margaret Lloyd, *The Borzoi Book of Modern Dance* (Dance Horizons: New York, 1974), 49–50.

1035 *Phenomenology of Perception*, 146. I have changed the translation slightly.

1036 Hubert Godard, interviewed by Laurence Louppe, 18.

1037 Jacques Derrida (1930–2004) is best known in the Anglo-Saxon world as the architect of 'deconstruction'. For an account of Derrida's thought, see, for instance, Rodolphe Gasché, *The Tain of the Mirror: Derrida and the Philosophy of Reflection* (London: Harvard University Press, 1986).

1038 He was strongly influenced by the Swiss linguist Ferdinand de Saussure, who argued that meaning in language is produced by a system of codified differences, rather than by direct relations between a 'signifier' and a 'signified'.

1039 Derrida, cited in Gasché, *The Tain of the Mirror*, 200.

1040 *Ibid.*, 199.

1041 *Ibid.*, 198.

1042 See the discussion of Cunningham's dances in the previous chapter, especially of *Rune* and *Fractions*. The process of *différance* in Cunningham's choreography is more developed in his post-computer work. See my 'Displacing 'humans': Merce Cunningham's crowds', *Body, Space and TechnologyJournal* (e-journal) 1, no.1 (2000). www.brunel.ac.uk/depts/pfa/bst (accessed 25 October 2004).

1043 Compare Norman Bryson, 'Semiology and visual interpretation', in *Visual Theory*, ed. Norman Bryson, Michael Ann Holly and Keith Moxey (Cambridge: Polity, 1991), 71 (61–73).

1044 Manning, *Ecstasy and the Demon: Feminism and Nationalism in the Dances of Mary Wigman* (Berkeley: University of California Press, 1993), 159–60.

1045 Paul Douglas, 'Modern dance forms' (1935), in Mark Franko, *Dancing Modernism, Performing Politics* (Bloomington: Indiana University Press, 1995), 138 (137–42).

1046 Ibid., 140.

1047 Marcia Siegel, 'The harsh and splendid heroines of Martha Graham', in *Moving History/Dancing Cultures: A Dance History Reader*, ed. Ann Dils and Ann Cooper Albright (Middletown, CT: Wesleyan University Press, 2001), 311.

1048 Marianne Goldberg, '"She who is possessed no longer exists outside": Martha Graham's *Rite of Spring*', in *Women and Performance* 3, no.1 (1986), 21, 22 and 26 (17–27).

1049 'Entretien avec Merce Cunningham: Montrer et laisser les gens se faire une opinion', in *Danse et Utopie: Mobiles* (Paris: l'Harmattan, 1999), 207 (199–208), translation mine.

1050 Merce Cunningham, 'Two questions and five dances', *Dance Perspectives* 34 (Summer 1968), 47 (46–53).

1051 'In this Day', *Dance Observer* 24 (January 1957), 10.

1052 Susan Foster, 'Closets full of dances: Modern dance's performance of masculinity and sexuality', in *Dancing Desires: Choreographing Sexuality on and off the Stage*, ed. Jane C. Desmond (Madison, WI: University of Wisconsin Press, 2001), 174 and 175 (147–207).

[1053] ' Merce Cunningham, a lifetime of dance', directed by Charles Atlas (co-produced in 2000 by La Sept ARTE, INA, Thirteen/WNET, BBC and NPS).

[1054] Email, 23 December 2004. He also made the very interesting point that the kind of music dancers listen to influences their rhythmic sense (conversation of 15 October 2004).

[1055] I refer here to the performances of *Split Sides* at the Barbican Theatre in London, 5–9 October 2004.

[1056] Frederic Jameson, 'Postmodernism and consumer society', in *Postmodern Culture*, ed. Hal Foster (London: Pluto Press, 1985), 125 (111–25).

[1057] Ibid., 125.

[1058] Ibid., 121.

[1059] Marshall McLuhan, *Forward Through the Rearview Mirror: Reflections On and By Marshall McLuhan*, ed. Paul Benedetti and Nancy DeHart (Toronto: Prentice-Hall Canada Inc., 1997), 184.

[1060] Cited in *Newsweek*, 11 January 1954 (clippings file, Merce Cunningham Dance Foundation, no page number).

[1061] Bauman, *Globalization: The Human Consequences* (Cambridge: Polity Press, 1998), 83.

[1062] Jonah Bokaer, email of 23 December 2004.

[1063] *The Paradox of Choice: Why More is Less* (London: Ecco/Harper Collins, 2004).

[1064] Laban and Lawrence, *Effort*, 82.

[1065] Ibid., 74–5.

[1066] Laban and Lawrence, *Effort*, 83.

[1067] Kerstin Ewart, 'Dance and technology at the turn of the last and present centuries', in *Dance and Technology, Moving Towards Media Productions*, ed. Söke Dinkla and Martina Leeker (Berlin: Alexander Verlag, 2002), 58 (30–65).

[1068] Oliver Grau, *Virtual Art, From Illusion to Immersion* (Cambridge, Massachusetts: MIT Press, 2003), 274.

[1069] Richard Povall, 'A little technology is a dangerous thing', in *Moving History/Dancing Cultures*, 455. A very early example of this process can be seen in Cunningham's *Variations V*, 1965 (see the previous chapter).

[1070] See Stelarc's website: www.stelarc.va.com.au/index2.html (accessed 15 July, 2004).

[1071] *Sensuous Geographies* is a collaboration between Sarah Rubidge (choreographer/digital installation artist) and Alistair MacDonald (composer) with Maggie Moffatt (costumes), Maria Verdicchio and Sébastien Besse (installation environment).
See www.sensuousgeographies.co.uk (accessed 16 July 2004). See also Rubidge's account of her choreographic process in 'Identity in flux: A practice-based interrogation of the ontology of the open art work', in Valerie Preston-Dunlop and Ana Sanchez-Colberg, *Dance and the Performative, A Choreological Dimension: Laban and Beyond* (London: Verve, 2002) 135–63.

1072 Review by Mark Brown in *The Guardian* Thursday 6 February , 2003. See http://www.sensuousgeographies.co.uk (accessed July 16 2004).

1073 Klages, cited in Thomas Rohrkrämer, *Eine andere Moderne? Zivilisationskritik, Natur und Technik in Deutschland 1880–1933* (Munich: Schöningh, 1999), 191.

1074 Kerstin Evert, 'Dance and Technology at the Turn of the Last and Present Centuries', *Dance and Technology*, 54 (30–65).

1075 In Laban, this is the body's reach space.

1076 Evert, 'Dance and technology at the turn of the last and present centuries', 46.

1077 *Dance and Technology*, 338 (emphasis mine).

1078 Incorporated in messages from David Vaughn posted 23 May 2003 and 20 May 2003 to dance-tech@dancetechnology.org. For information on this list, which is part of the Dance and Technology Zone, see www.art.net/~dtz (accessed 23 October 2004).

1079 Symposium held at University College Chichester (UK), 12 June 2004.

1080 Clearly there are also older technologies, notably video, that have had a significant impact on dance, but space does not permit me to discuss these separately here.

1081 Marshall McLuhan and Quentin Fiore, *The Medium is the Massage* (London: Penguin Books), 26–41.

1082 *Theory and Contexts: Ontologies of Online Theatre – Facts and Fallacies of Cyberspatial Theatre*, www.mdx.ac.uk/www/epai/presencesite/html/dixontol01.html (accessed 16 July 2004).

1083 *Phenomenology of Perception*, 144–5.

1084 Cited in Kent de Spain, 'Dance and technology: A *pas de deux* for post-humans', in *Dance Research Journal* 32, no. 1 (Summer 2000): 12–13 (2–23).

1085 Oskar Schlemmer, 'Man and art figure', in *The Theatre of the Bauhaus*, ed. Walter Gropius (Middletown, CT: Wesleyan University Press, 1961), 17 (17–48).

1086 16 September, The Place Theatre, London (organised by Dance Umbrella).

1087 This conversation took place before Swan left the Cunningham Company, in July 2004.

1088 16 September 2002, 'Merce Cunningham Study Day', The Place Theatre, London.

1089 Interestingly, designers of robots often take inspiration from animals: this is known as 'biomimesis'.

1090 Leslie Kendall, 'Cunningham dancers focus on pure movement at the Pillow', *The Daily Gazette*, 8 July 1993 (Archives of Cunningham Dance Foundation).

1091 'Pierrot's journey is still marvellous', *Financial Times*, 8 June 2000, 18.

1092 Siobhan Scarry, 'In step with digital dance', *Wired News*, 26 April 1999. www.wired.com/news (accessed 15 October 2000). Valerie Preston-Dunlop, on the other hand, finds this difficult movement 'dehumanised'. 'In this dance [the dancers] move their heads more independently of the rest of the body than ever before. Faces are uptipped: they turn, lean, twist, jump, land, with heads tilted backwards, an incredibly difficult and disorientating feat.' *Dance and the Performative*, 264. On this topic, see also my 'Displacing "humans": Merce Cunningham's crowds'.

1093 Scarry, 'In step with digital dance'.
1094 Cited in Kent de Spain, 'Dance and technology', 14.
1095 Décor by Marc Downie, Paul Kaiser and Shelley Eshkar.
1096 'Virtual Incarnations', symposium at Institute of Contemporary Arts, London, 14 September 2002.
1097 Stelarc, '*Vers le post-humain, du corps esprit au système cybernétique*' ('Towards the post-human, from body spirit to cybernetic system'), in *Nouvelles de danse*, '*Danse et nouvelles technologies*', 40–41 (Autumn–Winter 1999), 83 and 84 (80–98).
1098 Marc Fernandes, 'The body without memory: An interview with Stelarc'. www.ctheory.net/text_file.asp?pick=354 (accessed 23 October 2004).
1099 Marc Fernandes, 'The body without memory: An interview with Stelarc'.
1100 Publicity for this event provided by O'Neill:
      'A workshop titled *Homopolybots: Building Modular Humans* will take place at the University's Conference Centre, Room 3, on May 9th [2003] from 9am to 4pm. The Homopolybots workshop aims to bring together University Researchers and Artists to discuss particular problems and questions associated with creating modular humans and will explore such questions as: Can we create enhanced humans using modular prosthetic devices? How does a mechanical body differ from a human body, if at all? When does an object become a "part of" a human body?'
1101 Email from O'Neill.
1102 'Spacemaking: Experiences of a virtual body', by Susan Kozel. www.art.net/resources/dtz/kozel.html (accessed 23 October 2004). A longer version of this article appeared in *Dance Theatre Journal* 11, no. 3 (Autumn 1994). All quotes from Kozel from here on are taken from this site.
1103 Paul Sermon, 'Telematic dreaming'. www.artdes.salford.ac.uk/sermon/dream/dream.html (accessed 16 July 2004).
1104 'Interview with Paul Sermon', *Dance and Technology, Moving Towards Media Productions*, ed. Söke Dinkla and Martina Leeker (Berlin: Alexander Verlag, 2002), 254 (244–67).
1105 Söke Dinkla, 'Towards a rhetoric and didactics of digital dance', *Dance and Technology*, 24 (15–29).
1106 (Middletown, CT: Wesleyan University Press, 2002), 233.
1107 *Ibid.*, 224.
1108 *Ibid.*, 228.
1109 Foucault, 'The subject and power', cited in Lois McNay, *Foucault, A Critical Introduction* (Oxford: Polity, 1994), 121.
1110 Foster, *Dances That Describe Themselves*, 227–8.

[1111] Laban, *The Mastery of Movement*, ed. Lisa Ullmann (London: Northcote House [1950] ,1980), 169.

[1112] Michele H. Richman, *Reading Georges Bataille: Beyond the Gift* (Baltimore: Johns Hopkins University Press, 1982), 38.

[1113] Richman, *Reading Georges Bataille*, 142.

[1114] Ibid., 3.

[1115] Bataille, cited in Richman, *Reading Georges Bataille*, 17.

[1116] *Ibid., 22.*

[1117] Richman, *Reading Georges Bataille*, 30.

[1118] Bataille, cited in Richman, *Reading Georges Bataille*, 34.

[1119] Richman, *Reading Georges Bataille*, 152.

[1120] *Disability in Contemporary Performance*, 116. The site in question is www.goAccess.de, run by Contact 17, a Germany-based group of disabled and non-disabled performers.

[1121] Roland Barthes, *The Pleasure of the Text* (New York: Hill and Wang, 1975), 14. I have changed the verbs from singular to plural form.

[1122] Barthes, *The Pleasure of the Text*, 19.

[1123] Ibid., 66–7.

[1124] Cited by Elaine Aston, in 'Gender as sign-system: the feminist spectator as subject', in *Analyzing Performance: A Critical Reader*, ed. Patrick Campbell (Manchester: Manchester University Press, 1996), 58 (56–69) (emphasis mine).

[1125] Michael Moriarty, *Roland Barthes* (Cambridge: Polity, 1991), 203–4.

[1126] Zygmunt Bauman, *Globalization*, 82, emphasis mine.

[1127] Jean-François Lyotard, *Political Writings* (Minnesota: University of Minnesota, 1993), 64–5.

[1128] Ibid., 64.

[1129] Cunningham, 'The impermanent art', 87.

[1130] Wigman, cited in Hedwig Müller and Patricia Stöckemann, '... *Jeder Mensch ist ein Tänzer': Ausdruckstanz in Deutschland zwischen 1900 und 1945* (Giessen: Anabas Verlag, 1993), 36.

[1131] Graham, 'A modern dancer's primer for action', in *The Dance Anthology*, ed. Cobbett Steinberg (New York: The New American Library, 1980), 46 (44–52).

[1132] '"The possibility of variety"': Dee Reynolds phones Merce Cunningham', *Dance Theatre Journal* 20, no. 2 (2004), 42 (38–43).

[1133] Cunningham, cited in David Vaughan, 'Merce Cunningham and the Northwest', in *Society of Dance History Scholars Conference Proceedings* (University of California, 1989), 123 (111–25).

[1134] Ismene Brown, reviewing the Martha Graham Dance Company at Sadler's Wells, London, November 2003, wrote in the *Daily Telegraph*: 'In the awesome, rabble-rousing 1936 *Sketches from "Chronicle"*, Graham's oratorical power is Churchillian. The women's tautly curved arms and faces become stark, skeletal crescents, and even their skirts become messengers of a terrifying, apocalyptic magic. Unmissable.' ('Sensuality unleashed', 20 November 2003, www.telegraph.co.uk/arts; accessed 9 August 2004.)

[1135]   Unpublished section of my interview with Merce Cunningham in April 2004, of which an edited version was published as '"The possibility of variety": Dee Reynolds phones Merce Cunningham', *Dance Theatre Journal* (20:2, 2004), 38-43.

[1136]   Interview with Bokaer, 7 April 2004.

[1137]   Email 7 September 2002.

[1138]   Email 11 September 2002.

[1139]   Conversation of 16 October 2004, and 'New York giants', *Dance Umbrella News* (Autumn Edition, 2004), no page numbers.

[1140]   www.geocities.com/combusem. Accessed 2 August 2004.

[1141]   Unpublished section of my interview with Merce Cunningham.

[1142]   Zoë Anderson, ''Split Sides', Barbican, London', *The Independent*, Review Section, 8 October 2004, 35 (emphasis mine).

[1143]   Cynthia Jean Cohen Bull, 'Looking at movement as culture: Contact improvisation to disco', in *Moving History/Dancing Cultures, A Dance History Reader*, ed. Ann Dils and Ann Cooper Albright (Middletown, CT: Wesleyan University Press, 2001), 405 (404-13).

[1144]   *Ibid.*, 406.

[1145]   Debra Craine, 'Russell Maliphant/George Piper', *The Times*, 27 April 2002, 23.

[1146]   *Le Visible et l'invisible*, 165.

[1147]   Ibid., 74.

[1148]   Petra Kuppers, *Disability and Contemporary Performance: Bodies on Edge* (New York: Routledge, 2003), 120–1.

[1149]   On a similar topic, see Randy Martin, 'Dance and Its others, theory, state, nation and socialism', in *Of the Presence of the Body: Essays on Dance and Performance Theory*, ed. André Lepecki (Middletown, CT: Wesleyan University Press, 2004), 47–63.

[1150]   Zoë Anderson, '*Split Sides*', 35.

[1151]   Bokaer, 'New York Giants'.

[1152]   Merce Cunningham, 'Staging a DanceForms™ 1.0 solo', during the creation of *Split Sides* (2003).

Bibliography

1) Books and Articles

Acocella, Joan. "Cunningham's Recent Work." *Choreography and Dance 4*, no. 3 (1997): 3-15. Special issue, *Merce Cunningham: Creative Elements*.

Albright, Ann Cooper. *Choreographing Difference: The Body and Identity in Contemporary Dance*. Middletown, CT: Wesleyan University Press, 1997.

Albright, Ann Cooper, and Ann Dils, eds. *Moving History, Dancing Cultures: A Dance History Reader*. Middletown, CT: Wesleyan University Press, 2001.

Alexander, Frederick. *The Use of the Self*. New York: E.P.Dutton and Co, 1932.

Alter, Judith B. *Dancing and Mixed Media: Early Twentieth-Century Modern Dance Theory in Text and Photography*. New York: Peter Lang, 1994.

Anderson, Jack. *Art without Boundaries*. London: Dance Books 1997.

_____. "Some Personal Grumbles about Martha Graham." *Ballet Review* 2, no.1 (1967): 25-30.

Anderson, Zoë. "'Split Sides', Barbican, London." *The Independent*, Review Section (Friday 8 October), 2004: 35.

Armitage, Merle, ed. *Martha Graham, The Early Years*. New York: Da Capo, 1978.

Ascheim, Steven E. *The Nietzsche Legacy in Germany, 1890-1999*. Berkeley: University of California Press, 1992.

Aston, Elaine. "Gender as sign-system: the feminist spectator as subject." In *Analyzing Performance: A Critical Reader*, edited by Patrick Campbell, 56-69. Manchester: Manchester University Press, 1996.

Balcom, Lois. "Martha Graham and Dance Company, National Theatre, May 7-14, 1944." *Dance Observer* 11, no. 6 (June-July 1944): 63.

Banes, Sally. *Dancing Women: Female Bodies on Stage*. London: Routledge, 1998.

_____. *Greenwich Village 1963: Avant-Garde Performance and the Effervescent Body*. Durham, N.C.: Duke University Press, 1993.

_____. *Terpsichore in Sneakers: Postmodern Dance*. Middletown, CT: Wesleyan University Press, 1977 and revised edition, 1987.

_____. *Writing Dancing in the Age of Postmodernism*. Middletown, CT: Wesleyan University Press, 1994.

Banner, Lois W. *American Beauty*. New York: Alfred A. Knopf, 1983.

Bannerman, Henrietta. "Graham Reviewed." *The Dancing Times* (October 1996): 23, 25, 28.

_____. "Thoroughly Modern Martha." *Dance Theatre Journal* 17, no. 2 (2001): 32-36.

_____. "The Work (1935-1948) of Martha Graham (1894-1991): An Analysis of her Movement System". Ph.D. diss., University of Surrey (UK), 1998.

Banta, Martha. *Imaging American Women: Idea and Ideals in Cultural History*. New York: Columbia University Press, 1987.

Barba, Eugenio. "Le corps crédible." In *Le Corps en jeu*, edited by Odette Aslan et al. Paris: CNRS 1993, 251-61.

Barnes, Clive. "Places and Planets." *Dance and Dancers* 18, no. 3 (March 1967), 30-31.

Barnes, Clive, and Peter Williams. "Two Looks at Lightning." *Dance and Dancers* (October 1963): 12-22 and 39-40.

Bartenieff, Irmgard, and Aileen Crow. *Space Harmony: Basic Terms.* New York: Dance Notation Bureau, 1977.

Bartenieff, Irmgard, and Dori Lewis. *Body Movement: Coping with the Environment.* New York: Gordon and Breach, 1980.

Bartenieff, Irmgard, and Martha Davies. *Effort-Shape Analysis of Movement.* New York: Albert Einstein College of Medecine, 1965. Draft manuscript in library of Laban Centre, London.

Barthes, Roland. *The Pleasure of the Text.* New York: Hill and Wang, 1975.

Bauman, Zygmunt. *Globalization: The Human Consequences.* Cambridge: Polity Press, 1998.

Baxmann, Inge. "Stirring up Attitudes: Dance as a Language and Utopia in the Roaring Twenties." *Ballett International*, 11 (February 1989): 13-18.

Belgrad, Daniel. *The Culture of Spontaneity: Improvisation and the Arts in Postwar America.* Chicago: University of Chicago Press, 1998.

Benedetti, Paul, and Nancy DeHart, eds. *Forward Through the Rearview Mirror: Reflections On and By Marshall McLuhan.* Prentice-Hall Canada Inc, 1997.

Benjamin, Walter. *Charles Baudelaire, A Lyric Poet in the Era of High Capitalism.* New York: Verso, 1992.

Berger, Renate. "Moments can change your life: Creative crises in the lives of dancers in the 1920s." In *Visions of the "Neue Frau": Women and the Visual Arts in Weimar Germany*, edited by Marsha Meskimmon and Shearer West, 77-95. Aldershot: Ashgate, 1995.

Bergson, Henri. *Creative Evolution.* London: Macmillan 1911.

——————. *Time and Free Will: An Essay on the Immediate Data of Consciousness.* New York: Dover (1948), 2001.

Bird, Dorothy, and Joyce Greenberg. *Bird's Eye View: Dancing with Martha Graham and on Broadway.* Pittsburgh: University of Pittsburgh Press, 1997.

Bode, Rudolf. *Expression-Gymnastics.* New York: A. Barnes and Company (1925), 1931.

——————. *Der Rhythmus und Seine Bedeutung für die Erziehung.* Jena: Eugen Diederichs, 1920.

Böhme, Fritz. "Der neue Tanz." *Velhagen und Klasings Monatshefte* 2, no. 4 (1924/5): 97-104.

——————. *Geheimnisse der Entsiegelung, Zeichen der Seele: Zur Metaphysik der Bewegung.* Berlin: Kinetischer Verlag, 1920.

——————. "Tanz als Weg zu neuer Volksgemeinschaft." *Deutsche Frauenkultur und Frauenkleidung* 34, no. 5 (1930): 129-131.

Bokaer, Jonah. "Gnosticism." *Movement Research Performance Journal* 27/28, 'Then and Now' (Spring 2004; 25th Anniversary Double Issue, ed. Clarinda MacLow). B3-5.

_____. "New York Giants." *Dance Umbrella News,* Autumn Edition (2004): no page nos.

Bourdieu, Pierre. *In Other Words: Essays Towards A Reflexive Sociology.* Cambridge: Polity, 1990.

_____. *The Logic of Practice.* Cambridge: Polity, 1990.

_____. *Sociology in Question.* London: Sage, 1993.

Brandenburg, Hans. *Der Moderne Tanz.* Munich: Georg Müller (1913), 1917.

Brandstetter, Gabrielle. "Psychologie des Ausdrucks und Ausdruckstanz." In *Ausdruckstanz: eine Mitteleuropäische Bewegung der ersten Hälfte des 20. Jahrhunderts,* edited by Gunhild Oberzaucher-Schüller et al., 199-211. Wilhelmshaven: Florian Noetzel, 1992.

_____, *Tanz-Lektüren: Körperbilder und Raumfiguren der Avant-Garde.* Frankfurt-am-Main: Fischer Taschenbuch Verlag, 1995.

Brennan, Teresa. *History after Lacan.* London: Routledge, 1993.

Briginshaw, Valerie. *Dance, Space and Subjectivity.* Basingstoke: Palgrave, 2001.

Bronner, Stephen Eric and Douglas Kellner, eds. *Passion and Rebellion: The Expressionist Heritage.* London, Croom Helm, 1983.

Brown, Carolyn. "On Chance." *Ballet Review* 2, no. 2 (1968): 7-25.

_____. "McLuhan and the Dance." *Ballet Review* 1, no. 4 (1966): 13-20.

Brown, Earle, Remy Charlip, Marianne Simon and David Vaughan. "The Forming of an Aesthetic: Merce Cunningham and John Cage." *Ballet Review* 13, no. 3 (Fall 1985): 23-40.

Brown, Louise. "What Dancers Think of the German Dance." *The Dance Magazine of Stage and Screen* (May 1931): 14-15, 52, 64.

Brubaker, Roger. *The Limits of Rationality.* London: Allen and Unwin, 1984.

Bryson, Norman. "Cultural Studies and Dance History." In *Meaning in Motion: New Cultural Studies of Dance,* edited by Jane C. Desmond, 55-77. Durham, N.C.: Duke University Press 1997.

_____. "Semiology and Visual Interpretation." In *Visual Theory,* edited by Norman Bryson, Michael Ann Holly and Keith Moxey, 61-73. Cambridge: Polity, 1991.

Bull, Cynthia Jean Cohen. "Looking at Movement as Culture: Contact Improvisation to Disco." In *Moving History/Dancing Cultures, A Dance History Reader,* edited by Ann Dils and Ann Cooper Albright, 404-413. Middletown, CT: Wesleyan University Press, 2001.

Burt, Ramsay. *Alien Bodies: Representations of Modernity, "Race" and Nation in Early Modern Dance.* London: Routledge, 1998.

_____. *The Male Dancer: Bodies, Spectacle, Sexualities.* London: Routledge, 1995.

Burwick, Frederick and Paul Douglass. "Introduction" to *The Crisis in Modernism: Bergson and the Vitalist Controversy,* edited by Frederick Burwich and Paul Douglass, 1-14. Cambridge: Cambridge University Press, 1992.

Cage, John. "Grace and Clarity." *Dance Observer* 11, no. 9 (November 1944): 108-9.

"In this Day." *Dance Observer* 24 (January 1957): 10.

_____. "Interview with Roger Reynolds." In *John Cage*, edited by Robert Dunn, 45-52. New York: Henmar Press, 1962.

_____. *A Year from Monday: New Lectures and Writings by John Cage*. London: Calder and Boyars (1963), 1968.

Cage, John, and Daniel Charles. *For the Birds*. London: Marion Boyars, (1976), 1981.

Chadwick, Whitney. *Women Artists and the Surrealist Movement*. London: Thames and Hudson, 1985.

Chisholm, Dianne. "The Uncanny." In *Feminism and Psychoanalysis: A Critical Dictionary*, edited by Elizabeth Wright, 436-440. London: Blackwell 1992.

Conley, Verena Andermatt. *Hélène Cixous*. New York: Harvester Wheatsheaf, 1992.

Copeland, Roger. "Beyond Expressionism: Merce Cunningham's Critique of the 'Natural'." In *Dance History: An Introduction*, edited by Janet Adshead-Lansdale and June Layson, 182-197. London: Routledge, 1983.

_____. "Genre and Style." In *What is Dance? Readings in Theory and Criticism*, edited by Roger Copeland and Marshall Cohen, 307-24. Oxford: Oxford University Press, 1983.

_____. *Merce Cunningham: The Modernizing of Modern Dance*. London: Routledge, 2004.

Corn, Wanda. *The Great American Thing: Modern Art and National Identity 1915-1935*. Berkeley: University of California Press, 1999.

Cott, Nancy F. *The Grounding of Modern Feminism*. New Haven: Yale University Press, 1987.

Craine, Debra. "Russell Maliphant/George Piper." *The Times*, 27th April 2002, 23.

Croce, Arlene. *Going to the Dance*. New York: Albert Knopf, 1982.

Crossley, Nick. *The Social Body: Habit, Identity and Desire*. London: Sage, 2001.

Cunningham, Merce. "Choreography and the Dance." In *The Dance Anthology*, edited by Cobbett Steinberg, 52-62. New York: New American Library, 1980.

_____. *The Dancer and the Dance: Merce Cunningham in Conversation with Jacqueline Lesschaeve*. New York: Marilyn Boyars, 1991.

_____. "Entretien avec Merce Cunningham: Montrer et laisser les gens se faire une opinion." Isabelle Ginot. In *Danse et Utopie: Mobiles*, 199-208. Paris: l'Harmattan, 1999.

_____. "Excerpts from Lecture-Demonstration given at Anna Halprin's Dance Deck (13 July 1957)." In David Vaughan, *Merce Cunningham: Fifty Years, Chronicle and Commentary*, 100-101. New York: Aperture, 1997.

_____. "The Function of a Technique for Dance." In *The Dance has Many Faces*, edited by Walter Sorell, 250-255. Cleveland/New York: The World Publishing Company, 1951.

_____. "The Impermanent Art." In David Vaughan, *Merce Cunningham Fifty Years*, 86. New York: Aperture 1997.

_____. "An Interview with Merce Cunningham." Arlene Croce. *Ballet Review* 1, no. 4 (1966): 3-5.

_____. "Laura Kuhn in conversation with Merce Cunningham." In *Art Performs Life: Merce Cunningham/ Meredith Monk/ Bill T. Jones*, 22-43. Minneapolis: Walker Art Center, 1998.

_____. "'The Possibility of Variety': Dee Reynolds phones Merce Cunningham." *Dance Theatre Journal* 20, no.2 (2004): 38-43.

_____. "Space, Time and Dance" (1952). In David Vaughan, *Merce Cunningham: Fifty Years*, 66-7. New York: Aperture, 1997.

_____ . "Two Questions and Five Dances." *Dance Perspectives* 34 (Summer 1968): 46-53.

Daly, Ann. *Done Into Dance: Isadora Duncan in America*. Bloomington: Indiana University Press, 1995.

_____. "Isadora Duncan and the Distinction of Dance". *American Studies* 35, no. 1 (Spring 1994): 5-23.

Dance Perspectives no. 28 (Winter 1966). *In Search of Design*.

DeFrantz, Thomas F., ed. *Dancing Many Drums: Excavations in African American Dance*. Wisconsin: University of Wisconsin Press, 2002.

Delius, Rudolf von. *Das Erwachen der Frauen: Neue Ausblicke ins Geschlechtliche*. Dresden: Carl Reissner, 1924.

_____. *Mary Wigman*. Dresden: Carl Reissner, 1925.

_____. *Tanz und Erotik: Gedanken zur Persönlichkeitsgestaltung der Frau*. Munich: Delphinverlag, 1926.

Dell, Cecily. *A Primer for Movement Description using Effort-Shape and Supplementary Concepts*. New York: Dance Notation Bureau, 1970.

_____. "Random Graham." *Dance Scope* (Spring 1966): 21-26.

Denby, Edwin. *Dance Writings and Poetry*, edited by Robert Cornfield. New Haven: Yale University Press, 1998.

Derrida, Jacques. *Writing and Difference*. London: Routledge and Kegan Paul (1967), 1978.

Desmond, Jane, ed. *Meaning in Motion: New Cultural Studies of Dance*. Durham, N.C.: Duke University Press, 1997.

_____. "Embodying Difference: Issues in Dance and Cultural Studies." In *Meaning in Motion*, edited by Jane Desmond, 29-54. Durham, N.C.: Duke University Press, 1997.

De Spain, Kent. "Dance and Technology: A *Pas de Deux* for Post-humans." *Dance Research Journal* 32, no. 1 (Summer 2000): 2-23.

Dinkla, Söke. "Towards a Rhetoric and Didactics of Digital Dance." In *Dance and Technology, Moving Towards Media Productions*, edited by Söke Dinkla and Martina Leeker, 15-29. Berlin: Alexander Verlag, 2002.

Douglas, Ann. *Terrible Honesty: Mongrel Manhattan in the 1920s*. New York: Noonday Press, 1996.

Douglas, Paul. "Modern Dance Forms" (1935). In Mark Franko, *Dancing Modernism, Performing Politics*, 137-42. Bloomington: Indiana University Press, 1995.

Drost, Willy. *Die Lehre vom Rhythmus in der Heutigen Asthetik der Bildenden Künste*. Leipzig-Gausch: Merkur, 1919.

Droste, Magdalena. *Bauhaus 1919-1933*. Cologne: Bauhaus Archiv/ Benedikt Taschen Verlag, 1990.

Duberman, Martin. *Black Mountain College*. New York: E.P.Dutton and Co, 1972.

Dudley, Jane. "Jane Dudley talks about the Schools of Wigman and Graham." *Dance and Dancers* 22, no. 5 (May 1971): 54, 56.

Dumenil, Lynn. *The Modern Temper: American Culture and Society in the 1920s*. New York: Hill and Wang, 1995.

Duncan, Isadora. *The Art of the Dance*, edited by Sheldon Cheney. New York: Theatre Arts Books, 1969.

_____. *Isadora Speaks*, edited by Franklin Rosemont. San Francisco: City Lights, 1981.

Elder, R. Bruce. *A Body of Vision: Representations of the Body in Recent Film and Poetry*. Waterloo, Ontario, Canada: Wilfrid Laurier University Press, 1997.

Ellenberger, Henri F. *Beyond the Unconscious*, introduced and edited by Mark S. Micale. Princeton: Princeton University Press, 1993.

Evert, Kerstin. "Dance and Technology at the Turn of the Last and Present Centuries." In *Dance and Technology*, edited by Söke Dinkla and Martina Leeker, 30-65. Berlin: Alexander Verlag, 2002.

Fischer, Hans. *Körperschönheit und Körperkultur*. Berlin: Deutsche Buchgemeinschaft, 1928.

Foster, Susan. "Closets Full of Dances: Modern Dance's Performance of Masculinity and Sexuality." In *Dancing Desires, Choreographing Sexualities on and off the Stage*, edited by Jane C. Desmond, 147-207. Madison, Wisconsin: University of Wisconsin Press, 2001.

_____. *Dances that Describe Themselves: The Improvised Choreography of Richard Bull*. Middletown, CT: Wesleyan University Press, 2002.

_____. "Kinesthetic Empathies and the Politics of Compassion." In *Continents in Movement: Proceedings of the International Conference, "The Meeting of Cultures in Dance History"*, edited by Daniel Tércio, 27- 30. Portugal: Faculdade de Motrididada Humana: Cruz Quebrada, 1999.

_____. *Reading Dancing: Bodies and Subjects in Contemporary American Dance*. Berkeley: University of California Press, 1986.

Foster, Susan, ed. *Choreographing History*. Bloomington: Indiana University Press, 1995.

_____. *Corporealities: Dancing Knowledge, Culture and Power*. London: Routledge, 1996.

Foucault, Michel. "Body/Power", in *Michel Foucault, Power/Knowledge*, edited by Colin Gordon, 55-62. London: Harvester, 1980.

_____. *Discipline and Punish: The Birth of the Prison.* (London: Penguin (1975), 1991.

_____. "Truth and Power", in *Michel Foucault, Power/Knowledge: Selected Interviews and Other Writings 1972-1977*, edited by Colin Gordon, 109-133. New York: Harvester Wheatsheaf, 1980.

Foulkes, Julia. *Modern Bodies: Dance and American Modernism from Martha Graham to Alvin Ailey.* Chapel Hill: University of North Carolina Press, 2002.

Fraleigh, Sondra and Penelope Hanstein, eds. *Researching Dance: Evolving Modes of Enquiry.* London: Dance Books, 1999.

Franklin, Eric. *Dynamic Alignment Through Imagery.* Champaign, Illinois: Human Kinesics, 1996.

Franko, Mark. *Dancing Modernism, Performing Politics.* Bloomington: Indiana University Press, 1995.

_____. *The Work of Dance: Labor, Movement and Identity in the 1930s.* Middletown, CT: Wesleyan University Press, 2002.

Freedman, Russell. *Martha Graham: A Dancer's Life.* New York: Clarion Books, 1998.

Friedmann, Elly D. *Laban/Alexander/Feldenkrais: Pioniere bewusster Wahrnehmung durch Bewegungserfahrung.* Paderborn: Junfermann-Verlag, 1989.

Fritsch-Vivié, Gabriele. *Mary Wigman.* Reinbek bei Hamburg: Rowohlt, 1999.

Fuchs, Georg. *Die Revolution des Theaters: Ergebnisse aus dem Münchener Künstlertheater.* Munich: Georg Müller, 1909.

Garte, E.J. "Kandinsky's Ideas on Changes in Modern Physics and their Implications for his Development." *Gazette des Beaux-Arts* (1987): 137-44.

Gasché, Rodolphe. *The Tain of the Mirror: Derrida and the Philosophy of Reflection.* Cambridge, Massachussetts: Harvward University Press, 1986.

Gatens, Moira. *Imaginary Bodies: Ethics, Power and Corporeality.* London: Routledge, 1996.

Gert, Valeska. "Mary Wigman and Valeska Gert." *Der Querschnitt*, 5 (1926): 361-63.

Giese, Fritz. *Körperseele: Gedanken über persönliche Gestaltung.* Munich: Delphin Verlag, 1927.

Godard, Hubert. "Le geste et sa perception." In *La Danse au xxe siècle*, edited by Isaballe Ginot and Marcelle Michel, 224-229. Paris: Larousse, 1998.

_____. "'Singular, Moving Geographies': Hubert Godard interviewed by Laurence Louppe." In *Writings on Dance, The French Issue*, 15 (Winter 1996): 12-21.

Goldberg, Marianne. "'She Who Is Possessed No Longer Exists Outside': Martha Graham's 'Rite of Spring'". In *Women and Performance* 3, no.1 (1986): 17-27.

Goodman, Paul. *Growing Up Absurd: Problems of Youth in the Organized Society.* New York: Vintage Books, 1966.

Goodridge, Janet. *Rhythm and Timing of Movement in Performance: Drama, Dance and Ceremony.* London: Jessica Kingsley, 1999.

Goodwin, Noël. "Cage without Bars." *Dance and Dancers* 18, no. 2 (February 1967): 38-39.

Gordon, Donald E. *Expressionism: Art and Idea.* New Haven: Yale University Press, 1987.

Goux, Jean-Joseph. *Freud, Marx: économie et symbolique.* Paris: Seuil, 1973.

Graff, Ellen. *Stepping Left: Dance and Politics in New York City, 1928-1942.* Durham, N.C.: Duke University Press, 1997.

Graham, Martha. "The American Dance." In *The Modern Dance*, edited by Virginia Stewart and Merle Armitage, 53-58. New York: Dance Horizons, 1970.

_____. *Blood Memory.* New York: Doubleday, 1991.

_____. "The Dance in America." *Trend* 1, no.1 (March/April/May 1932): 5-7.

_____. "Graham 1937." In *Martha Graham, The Early Years*, edited by Merle Armitage, 96-110. New York: Da Capo, 1978.

_____. "A Modern Dancer's Primer for Action." In *The Dance Anthology*, edited by Cobbett Steinberg, 44-52. New York: The New American Library, 1980.

_____. "Seeking an American Art of the Dance." In Oliver M. Sayler, *Revolt in the Arts: A Survey of the Creation, Distribution and Appreciation of Art in America*, 249-55. New York: Brentano's, 1930.

Grau, Oliver. *Virtual Art, From Illusion to Immersion.* Cambridge, Massachusetts: MIT Press, 2003.

Green, Martin. *Mountain of Truth: The Counterculture Begins, Ascona 1900-1920.* Hanover: University Press of New England, 1986.

Greenberg, Clement. "Modernist Painting." *Art and Literature* 4 (1965): 193-201.

Greskovic, Robert. "Cunningham as Sculptor." *Ballet Review* 11, no. 4 (Winter 1984): 89-95.

Griffiths, Paul. *Cage.* Oxford: Oxford University Press, 1981.

Grohmann, Will. *Wassily Kandinsky, Life and Work.* London: Thames and Hudson, 1959.

Gropius, Walter, ed. *The Theater of the Bauhaus.* Middletown, CT: Wesleyan University Press, 1961.

Grossheim, Michael. *Ludwig Klages und die Phänomenologie.* Akademie Verlag: Berlin, 1994.

Grossman, Peter Z. "Talking with Merce Cunningham about Video." *Dance Scope* 13, nos. 2/3 (Winter-Spring 1979): 57-68.

Grosz, Elizabeth. "Kristeva, Julia." In *Feminism and Psychoanalysis, A Critical Dictionary*, edited by Elizabeth Wright, 194-200. Oxford: Blackwell, 1992.

_____. *Volatile Bodies: Towards a Corporeal Feminism.* Bloomington: Indiana University Press, 1994.

Hammond, Sandra Noll. *Ballet Basics.* California: Mayfield, 1984.

Hapgood, Susan, ed. *Neo-Dada: Redefining Art 1958-62.* New York: The American Federation of Arts, 1994.

H'Doubler, Margaret. "A Question of Values and Terms." *Dance Observer* 12, no. 7 (Aug-Sept 1945): 83.

Helpern, Alice. *The Technique of Martha Graham.* New York: Morgan and Morgan, 1994.

Hindman, Anne Andrews. "The Myth of the Frontier in American Dance and Drama 1930-1943." Ph.D. diss., University of Georgia, 1972. UMI: Ann Arbor, microfilm.

Hodgson, John and Valerie Preston-Dunlop. *Rudolf Laban: An Introduction to his Work and Influence.* Plymouth: Northcote House, 1990.

Hoffman, Frederick J. *The 20s: American Writing in the Postwar Decade.* New York: The Free Press, 1962.

Horosko, Marian. *Martha Graham: The Evolution of Her Dance Theory and Training.* Florida: University Press of Florida, revised edition (1991), 2002.

Horst, Louis, et al. *Dance Perspectives* 16 (1963). Special issue, *Composer/Choreographer, Louis Horst.*

Howe, Diana. *Individuality and Expression: The Aesthetics of the New German Dance, 1908-1936.* Bern: Peter Lang, 1999.

Humphrey, Doris. *The Art of Making Dances.* London: Dance Books, 1987.

International Encyclopedia of Dance. Oxford: Oxford University Press, 6 vols., 1998.

Jameson, Frederic. "Postmodernism and Consumer Society." In *Postmodern Culture,* ed. Hal Foster, 111-125. London: Pluto Press, 1985.

Jaques-Dalcroze, Emile. *Rhythm, Music and Education.* London: Dalcroze Society (1921), 1980.

Jay, Martin. *Adorno.* London: Fontana, 1984.

Jefferies, Matthew. *Imperial Culture in Germany, 1871-1918.* Basingstoke: Palgrave Macmillan, 2003.

Johnson, Randal. "Editor's Introduction: Pierre Bourdieu on Art, Literature and Culture." In Pierre Bourdieu, *The Field of Cultural Production: Essays on Art and Literature,* 1-28. Cambridge: Polity, 1993.

Jowitt, Deborah. *Dance Beat, Selected Views and Reviews 1967-1976.* Marcel Drekker: New York/Basel, 1977.

_____. "Martha Graham." *International Encyclopedia of Dance,* edited by Selma Jeanne Cohen et al. Oxford University Press, 1998, vol. 3: 209-221.

_____. "Paring Down to the Quick." *Village Voice,* 9 May 1974: 75-79.

_____. *Time and the Dancing Image.* Berkeley: University of California Press, 1988.

_____. "Zen and the Art of Dance." *The Village Voice,* 17 January 1977: 48-9.

Kamenka, Eugene, ed. *The Portable Karl Marx*. Harmondsworth: Penguin, 1983.

Kandinsky, Wassily. *Complete Writings on Art*, 2 vols., edited by Kenneth Lindsay and Peter Vergo. London: Faber and Faber, 1982.

——————. *Cours du Bauhaus*. Paris: Denoël/Gonthier, 1975.

Kant, Marion and Lillian Karina. *Hitler's Dancers: German Modern Dance and the Third Reich*. New York: Berghahn, 2003.

Kasdorff, Hans. *Ludwig Klages im Widerstreit der Meinungen*. Bonn: Bouvier Verlag, 1978.

Kendall, Elizabeth. *Where She Danced*. New York: Alfred A. Knopf, 1979.

Kestenberg, Judith. *The Role of Movement Patterns in Development*, 2 vols. New York: Dance Notation Bureau Press, 1977 and 1979.

Kirby, Michael. "The New Theatre." *Tulane Drama Review* 10, no. 2 (Winter 1965): 23-43.

Kisselgoff, Anna. "They Created Dance Works at the Bauhaus, Too." *New York Times*, Sunday 31 October, 1982, 12-14.

Klages, Ludwig. *Ludwig Klages, Sämtliche Werke*, edited by Ernst Frauchiger et al. Bonn: Bouvier Verlag, 1974.

Klein, Gabrielle. *FrauenKörperTanz*. Munich: Wilhelm Hagen Verlag, 1992.

Knight, Peter. *Conspiracy Culture, from Kennedy to the X-Files*. New York: Routledge, 2000.

Kolinsky, Eva. "Non-German Minorities, Women and the Emergence of Civil Society." In *The Cambridge Companion to Modern German Culture*, edited by Eva Kolinsky and Wilfried van der Will, 110-131. Cambridge: Cambridge University Press, 1998.

Kostelanetz, Richard, ed. *The Theatre of Mixed Means*. London: Pitman, (1967), 1970.

Kracauer, Siegfried. "The Mass Ornament." In *New German Critique*, 5 (Spring 1975): 67-76.

Kristeva, Julia. *Revolution in Poetic Language*. New York: Columbia University Press (1974), 1984.

——————. *Sèméiotikè, Recherches pour une sémanalyse*. Paris: Seuil, 1969.

Kuhn, Laura. "Cunningham and Cage." *Ballet Review* 26, no. 3 (1998): 80-98.

Kuhns, David. *German Expressionist Theatre: The Actor and the Stage*. Cambridge University Press, 1997.

Kuppers, Petra. *Disability and Contemporary Performance: Bodies on Edge*. London: Routledge, 2003.

Kuxdorf, Manfred. "The New German Dance Movement." In *Passion and Rebellion: The Expressionist Heritage*, edited by Stephen Eric Bronner and Douglas Kellner, 350-360. London: Croom Helm, 1983.

Laban, Rudolf. *Choreutics*, edited by Lisa Ulmann. London: Macdonald and Evans, 1966.

——————. "Dance in General." *Laban Art of Movement Guild Magazine* 26 (May 1961): 11-24.

——————. *A Life for Dance*. London: Macdonald and Evans, 1975.

_____. *The Mastery of Movement*, edited by Lisa Ullmann. London: Northcote House (1950) 1980.

_____. *Modern Educational Dance*. London: Macdonald and Evans (1948) 1976.

_____. *Rudolf Laban Speaks about Education and Dance*. Edited by Lisa Ulmann. Surrey: Laban Art of Movement Centre, 1971.

_____. "The Three 'R's of Movement Practice." *Laban Art of Movement Guild Magazine* 14 (March 1955): 12-17.

_____. *A Vision of Dynamic Space*, compiled by Lisa Ullmann. London: The Falmer Press 1984.

Laban, Rudolf and F.C. Lawrence. *Effort*. London: Macdonald and Evans, 1947.

Lamb, Warren. "The Essence of Gender in Movement." *Laban Guild Movement and Dance Quarterly* 12, no.1 (Spring 1993): 1-3; 12, no. 2 (Summer 1993), 3 and 8; and 12, no. 3 (Autumn 1993), 7.

_____. *Posture and Gesture: An Introduction to the Study of Physical Behaviour*. London: Duckworth, 1965.

Lamb, Warren, and Elizabeth Watson. *Body Code: The Meaning in Movement*. New Jersey: Princeton, 1979.

Lämmel, Rudolf. *Der moderne Tanz*. Berlin: Peter J. Oestergaard, 1928.

Larkin. Maurice. *Gathering Pace: Continental Europe 1870-1945*. London: Macmillan Education (1969), 1978.

Launay, Isabelle. *A la recherche d'une danse moderne, Rudolf Laban, Mary Wigman*. Paris: Chiron 1996.

Lears, Jackson. *No Place of Grace: Antimodernism and the Transformation of American Culture 1880-1920*. London: University of Chicago Press, 1981.

Lepczyk, Billie. "Martha Graham's Movement Invention viewed through Laban Analysis." *Dance: Current Selected Research*, vol. 1, edited by Lynette Y. Overby and James H. Humphrey, 45-61. New York: AMS Press, 1989.

Lippold, Richard. "Martha Graham and Dance Company, Plymouth Theatre, January 21-February 2, 1946." *Dance Observer* 13, no. 6 (March 1946): 34-6.

Lipps, Theodor. *Asthetik: Psychologie des Schönen und der Kunst*, 2 vols. Hamburg: Leopold Voss, (1903) 1923 and (1906) 1920.

Lloyd, Margaret. *The Borzoi Book of Modern Dance*. Dance Horizons: New York 1974.

Lomax, Alan. *Folk Song Style and Culture*. Washington DC: American Association for the Advancement of Science, 1965.

_____ *Folk song style and culture: a staff report*. Washington, D.C: American Association for the Advancement of Science, Publication no. 88, 1968.

Longstaff, Jeremy. "Cognitive Structures of Kinesthetic Space: Reevaluating Rudolf Laban's Choreutics in the Context of Spatial Cognition and Motor Control." D.Phil Thesis, City University/Laban Centre, London, 1996.

Louppe, Laurence. *Poétique de la danse contemporaine*. Bruxelles: Contredanse, 1996.

Lyotard, Jean-François. *Libidinal Economy.* Bloomington: Indiana University Press (1974), 1992.

_____. *Political Writings.* Minnesota: University of Minnesota, 1993.

McCarren, Felicia. *Dancing Machines: Choreographies of the Age of Mechanical Reproduction.* Stanford: Stanford University Press, 2003.

Maletic, Vera. *Body-Space-Expression: The Development of Rudolf Laban's Movement and Dance Concepts.* Berlin: Mouton de Gruyter, 1987.

_____. "Laban Concepts and Laban Dialects: Issues of 'shape'." *Laban Art of Movement Guild Magazine* 77 (1978): 23-31.

Mallarmé, Stéphane. "Ballets." In *What is Dance? Readings in Theory and Criticism*, edited by Roger Copeland and Marshall Cohen, 111-115. Oxford: Oxford University Press, 1983.

_____. "Ballets", translated by Evlyn Gould. *Performing Arts Journal* 15, no. 1 (January 1993): 106-110.

_____. "Crayonné au théâtre", in *Oeuvres complètes*, 2 vols., edited by Bertrand Marchal, 160-213. Paris: Gallimard, Bibliothèque de la Pléiade, vol.2, 2003.

Martin, John. *America Dancing: The Background and Personalities of the Modern Dance.* New York: Dance Horizons, 1968.

_____. *Introduction to the Dance.* New York: Dance Horizons, 1939.

_____. *The Modern Dance.* New York: A.S. Barnes, 1933.

Martin, Randy. *Critical Moves: Dance Studies in Theory and Politics.* Durham, N.C.: Duke University Press, 1998.

_____. "Dance and Its Others, Theory, State, Nation and Socialism." In *Of the Presence of the Body: Essays on Dance and Performance Theory*, edited by André Lepecki, 47-63. Middletown, CT: Wesleyan University Press, 2004,

Martini, Frederic H. *Fundamentals of Anatomy and Physiology*, 5th edition. New Jersey: Prentice Hall, 2001.

Marx, Karl. *The Portable Karl Marx*, edited by Eugene Kamenka. Harmondsworth: Penguin, 1983.

Mauldon, Elizabeth. "Oskar Schlemmer – Rudolf Laban: Similarities and Contrasts." *Laban Art of Movement Guild Magazine*, no.5 (May 1975): 7-17.

Mauss, Marcel. *The Gift.* New York: Norton (1926), 1967.

_____. "Techniques of the Body." In *Incorporations: Zone 6*, edited by Jonathan Crary and Sanford Kwinter, 455-477. New York: Urzone 1992.

McCarren, Felicia. *Dance Pathologies: Performance, Poetics, Medecine.* Stanford: Stanford University Press, 1998.

McCormick, Richard W. *Gender and Sexuality in Weimar Modernity: Film, Literature and "New Objectivity".* Basingstoke: Palgrave, 2001.

McDonagh, Don. "A Conversation with Gertrude Shurr." *Ballet Review* 4, no. 5 (1973): 3-20.

_____. *Martha Graham, A Biography.* New York: Popular Library, 1973.

_____. *The Rise and Fall of Modern Dance.* New York: E.P. Dutton, 1970.

McLuhan, Marshall. *Forward Through the Rearview Mirror: Reflections On and By Marshall McLuhan,* edited by Paul Benedetti and Nancy DeHart, Toronto: Prentice-Hall Canada Inc, 1997.

McLuhan, Marshall, and Quentin Fiore. *The Medium is the Massage.* London: Penguin, 1967.

McNay, Lois. *Foucault, A Critical Introduction.* Oxford: Polity, 1994.

Meller, James, ed. *The Buckminster Fuller Reader.* London: Pelican Books (1970), 1972.

Melley, Timothy. *Empire of Conspiracy: The Culture of Paranoia in Postwar America.* Ithaca: Cornell University Press, 2000.

Merleau-Ponty, Maurice. *Phenomenology of Perception.* London: Routledge and Kegan Paul (1945),1962.

_____. *Le Visible et l'invisible.* Paris: Gallimard, 1964.

_____. *The Visible and the Invisible.* Evanston: Northwestern University Press, 1968.

Merriam-Webster's Collegiate Dictionary/Thesaurus.

Merz, Max. "Körperbildung und Rhythmus." In *Tanz in dieser Zeit,* edited by Paul Stefan, 29-32. Vienna: Universal Edition, 1926.

Mikunas, Algis. "The Primacy of Movement". In *Main Currents in Modern Thought* 31, no. 1 (September-October 1974), 8-12).

Mitoma, Judy, ed. *Envisioning Dance on Film and Video.* London: Routledge, 2003.

Moore, Carol-Lynne. *Introduction to Movement Harmony.* Denver, Colorado: Cottage Industries, 2003.

Moore, Carol-Lynne and Kaoru Yamamoto. *Beyond Words: Movement Observation and Analysis.* London: Gordon and Breach, 1988.

Morgan, Barbara. *Martha Graham: Sixteen Dances in Photographs.* Dobb's Ferry, New York: 1980.

Moriarty, Michael. *Roland Barthes.* Cambridge: Polity, 1991.

Morris, Gay. "Bourdieu, the Body, and Graham's Post-War Dance." *Dance Research* 19, no. 2 (Winter 2001): 52-82.

Morris, Gay, ed. *Moving Words: Re-writing Dance.* London: Routledge, 1996.

Müller, Hedwig. *Mary Wigman, Leben und Werk der grössen Tänzerin.* Berlin: Quadriga 1986.

Müller, Hedwig, and Patricia Stöckemann. *". . . Jeder Mensch ist ein Tänzer": Ausdruckstanz in Deutschland zwischen 1900 und 1945.* Giessen: Anabas Verlag, 1993.

Nagura, Miwa. "Cross-Cultural Differences in the Interpretation of Merce Cunningham's Choreography." In Gay Morris, ed., *Moving Words: Re-Writing Dance,* 270-287. Routledge: London, 1996.

New Collins Concise Dictionary of the English Language. London: Collins, 1982.

Ness, Sally Ann. *Body, Movement and Culture: Kinesthetic and Visual Symbolism in a Philippine Community*. Philadelphia: University of Pennsylvania Press, 1992.

Newhall, Mary Anne Santos. "Illuminating the Dark Heart: A Re-Creation of Mary Wigman's 'Witch Dance II' (1926)." *Proceedings, Society of Dance History Scholars*, Oregon, June 1998, 301-8. University of California Riverside: SDHS, 1998.

Nietzsche, Friedrich. *Thus Spoke Zarathustra*. London: Penguin (1883-91), 1969.

Nitschke, August. "Der Kult der Bewegung: Turnen, Rhythmik und neue Tänze." In *Jahrhundertwende. Der Aufbruch in die Moderne, 1880-1930*, edited by August Nitschke et al., 258-85. Reinbek bei Hamburg: Rowohlt, 1990.

North, Marion. *Personality Assessment through Movement*. Boston: Plays, Inc., 1975.

Oberzaucher-Schüller, Gunhild, et al., eds. *Ausdruckstanz: Eine Mitteleuropäische Bewegung der ersten Hälfte des 20. Jahrhunderts*. Wilhelmshaven: Florian Noetzel, 1992.

Or, Eileen. "Body and Mind: The Yoga Roots of Martha Graham's 'Contraction' and 'Release'". *Proceedings, Society of Dance History Scholars*, Joint Conference with the Association for Dance in Universities and Colleges in Canada, Ryerson Polytechnic University, Toronto, Ontario, Canada, 10-14 May 1995: 203-13.

Partsch-Bergsohn, Isa. *Modern Dance in Germany and the United States: Crosscurrents and Influences*. Switzerland: Harwood Academic Publishers, 1994.

Percival, John. *Experimental Dance*. London: Studio Vista, 1971.

Le Petit Robert, Dictionnaire. Paris: Le Robert, 1991.

Povall, Richard. "A Little Technology is a Dangerous Thing," In *Moving History/Dancing Cultures*, edited by Ann Dils and Ann Cooper-Albright, 455-458. Middletown, CT: Wesleyan University Press, 2001.

Pratt, Paula Bryant. *The Importance of Martha Graham*. San Diego: Lucent Books, 1995.

Preston-Dunlop, Valerie. "Dance Dynamics – Focusing on the Rhythmic Form of the Movement Itself" (Part II). *Dance Theatre Journal* 13, no. 2 (Autumn/Winter 1996): 34-38.

_____. "Laban, Schönberg, Kandinsky." In *Danses tracées, Dessins et notations des chorégraphes*, 133-148. Paris: Dis-Voir, 1991.

_____. *Rudolf Laban, An Extraordinary Life*. London: Dance Books, 1998.

Prickett, Stacey. "'The People': Issues of Identity within the Revolutionary Dance." In *Of, By and For the People: Dancing on the Left in the 1930s*, edited by Lynn Garafola, 14-22. Studies in Dance History 5, no. 1, Madison, Wisconsin: Society of Dance History Scholars, 1994.

Rabinbach, Anson. *The Human Motor: Energy, Fatique and the Origins of Modernity.* Berkeley: University of California Press, 1992.

Reynolds, Dee. "The Dancer as Woman: Loïe Fuller and Stéphane Mallarmé". In *Impressions of French Modernity: Art and Literature in France 1850-1900,* edited by Richard Hobbs, 155-172. Manchester: Manchester University Press, 1998.

_____. "Dancing Free: Gendering Movements in Early Modern Dance." In *Modernism, Gender, Culture,* edited by Lisa Rado, 247-279. New York: Garland, 1997.

_____. "Displacing 'Humans': Merce Cunningham's Crowds." *Body, Space and Technology Journal* (e-journal), 1 (2000). <http://www.brunel.ac.uk/depts/pfa/bstjournal>

_____. "The Kinesthetics of Chance: Mallarmé's 'Un coup de Dés' and Avant-garde Choreography". In *Symbolism, Decadence and the "fin-de-siècle",* edited by Patrick McGuinness, 90-104. Exeter: University of Exeter Press, 2000.

_____. "'Le mouvement pur et le silence déplacé par la voltige': Mallarmé and Dance, from Symbolism to Post-modernism." In *Situating Mallarmé,* edited by David Kinloch and Gordon Millan, 33-49. Bern: Peter Lang, 2000.

_____. "Rhythmic Structures and Imaginary Space in Rimbaud, Mallarmé. Kandinsky and Mondrian." In *Word and Image Interactions,* ed. Martin Heusser, 143-56. Basel: Wiese Verlag, 1993.

_____. *Symbolist Aesthetics and Early Abstract Art: Sites of Imaginary Space.* Cambridge: Cambridge University Press, 1995.

_____. "A Technique for Power: Reconfiguring Economies of Energy in Martha Graham's Early Work." *Dance Research* 20, no. 1 (Summer 2002): 3-32.

Richman, Michele H. *Reading Georges Bataille: Beyond the Gift.* Baltimore: Johns Hopkins University Press, 1982.

Riesman, David. *The Lonely Crowd: A Study of the Changing American Character.* New Haven: Yale University Press, 1950.

Rimbaud, Arthur. *Oeuvres de Rimbaud,* edited by Suzanne Bernard and André Guyaux. Paris: Garnier, 1981.

Roberts, Adolphe W. "The Fervid Art of Martha Graham." *Dance Magazine* (August 1928): 13 and 65.

Roderick, Rick. *Habermas and the Foundations of Critical Theory.* London: Macmillan, 1986.

Rogosin, Elinor. *The Dance Makers: Conversations with American Choreographers.* New York: Walker and Company, 1980.

Rohkrämer, Thomas. *Eine andere Moderne? Zivilizationskritik, Natur und Technik in Deutschland 1880-1933.* Munich: Schöningh, 1999.

Ross, Janice. *Moving Lessons: Margaret H'Doubler and the Beginning of Dance in American Education.* Madison Wisonsin: University of Wisconsin Press, 2000.

Roth, Moira. "The Aesthetic of Indifference." *Art Forum* (1977): 46-53.

Roth, Moira and Jonathan Katz. *Difference/Indifference: Musings on Postmodernism, Marcel Duchamp and John Cage.* Amsterdam: Gordon and Breach, 1998.

Rubidge, Sarah. "Identity in Flux: A Practice-Based Interrogation of the Ontology of the Open Art Work." In *Dance and the Performative, A Choreoloogical Dimension: Laban and Beyond,* edited by Valerie Preston-Dunlop and Ana Sanchez-Colberg, 135-163. London: Verve, 2002.

Rudhyar, Dane. "The Indian Dances for Power." *Dance Observer* 5 (August-September, 1934), 64.

Ruyter, Nancy Lee Chalfa. *Reformers and Visionaries: The Americanization of the Art of the Dance.* New York: Dance Horizons, 1979.

Sabin, Robert. "Dance at the Coolidge Festival." *Dance Observer* 11, no. 10 (December 1944): 120-1.

_____. "Martha Graham and Dance Company, National Theatre, week of May 14, 1945." *Dance Observer* 12, no. 6 (June-July 1945): 69-70.

_____. "Merce Cunningham, John Cage: Studio Theatre, April 5, 1944". *Dance Observer* 11, no. 5 (May 1944): 57-8.

Schall, Joan Janice. "Rhythm and Art in Germany 1900-1930." Ph.D. diss., University of Austin, Texas, 1989.

Scheyer, Ernest. "The Shapes of Space: The Arts of Mary Wigman and Oskar Schlemmer." *Dance Perspectives* 41 (1970): 7- 48.

Schikowski, John. *Der neue Tanz.* Berlin: Volksbühnen Verlag, 1924.

Schlemmer, Oskar. "Man and Art Figure." In *The Theatre of the Bauhaus,* edited by Walter Gropius, 17- 48. Middletown, CT: Wesleyan University Press, 1961.

Schwartz, Barry. *The Paradox of Coice: Why More is Less.* London: Ecco/HarperCollins, 2004.

Schwartz, Sanford. "Bergson and the Politics of Vitalism." In *The Crisis in Modernism: Bergson and the Vitalist Controversy,* edited by Frederick Burwich and Paul Douglass, 207-276. Cambridge: Cambridge University Press, 1992.

Selden, Elizabeth. "New York soon will see Dance without Music." *New York Evening Post* (12 January 1929): 2.

Sennett, Richard. *The Fall of Public Man.* London: Faber and Faber (1974), 1986.

Sermon, Paul. "Interview with Paul Sermon." In *Dance and Technology, Moving Towards Media Productions,* edited by Söke Dinkla and Martina Leeker, 244-267. Berlin: Alexander Verlag, 2002,

Shapiro, Joel. "Martha Graham at the Eastman School." *Dance Magazine* (July 1974): 55-7.

Shawn, Ted. *Every Little Movement: A Book about François Delsarte.* New York: Dance Horizons, 1963.

Sherman, Jane, and Norton Owen. "Martha Graham and Ted Shawn." *Dance Magazine* (July 1965): 42-5.

Shetley, Vernon. "Merce Cunningham." *Raritan* 8, no. 3 (1989): 72-90.

Shiach, Morag. *Hélène Cixous, A Politics of Writing.* New York: Routledge, 1991.

Shilling, Chris. *The Body and Social Theory.* London: Sage, 1993.

Shorter, Edward. *From Paralysis to Fatigue: A History of Psychosomatic Illness in the Modern Era.* New York: The Free Press, 1992.

Siegel, Marcia. *At the Vanishing Point: A Critic Looks at Dance.* New York: Saturday Review Press, 1972.

_____. "The Harsh and Splendid Heroines of Martha Graham." In *Moving History/Dancing Cultures: A Dance History Reader*, edited Ann Dils and Ann Cooper Albright, 307-314. Middletown, CT: Wesleyan University Press, 2001.

_____. "Re-Radicalizing Graham: Revivals or Forgeries." *Hudson Review* 68, no. 1 (Spring 1995): 101-7.

_____. "Strangers Return." *Ballet International* 6 (1983): 16-21.

_____. *The Shapes of Change: Images of American Dance.* Berkeley: University of California Press, 1985.

_____. *Watching the Dance Go By.* Boston: Houghton Mifflin, 1977.

Sinclair, Andrew. *The Emancipation of the American Woman.* New York: Harper and Row, 1965.

Simmel, Georg. *The Conflict in Modern Culture and Other Essays*, introduced and translated by K. Peter Etzkorn. New York: Teachers College Press, 1968.

_____. "The Metropolis and Mental Life", 1903. In *Simmel on Culture: Selected Writings*, edited by David Frisby and Mike Featherstone, 174-185. London: Sage, 1997.

Singha, Rina, and Reginald Massey. *Indian Dances, Their History and Growth.* London: Faber and Faber, 1967.

Slesser, Malcolm, general editor. *Dictionary of Energy.* London: Macmillan, 1982.

Smith, Roger. *The Fontana History of the Human Sciences.* London: Fontana 1997.

Soares, Janet Mansfield. *Louis Horst: Musician in a Dancer's World.* Durham, N.C.: Duke University Press, 1992.

Sorrell, Walter. *Mary Wigman: Ein Vermächtnis.* Wilhelmshaven: Florian Noetzel Verlag, 1986.

Sorrell, Walter, ed. *The Mary Wigman Book.* Middletown, CT: Wesleyan University Press, 1975.

Spector, Jack. *Rhythm and Life: The Work of Emile Jaques-Dalcroze.* Stuyvesant, New York: Pendragon Press, 1990.

Stauth, Georg, and Bryan S. Turner. *Nietzsche's Dance: Resentment, Reciprocity and Resistance in Social Life.* Oxford: Blackwell, 1988.

Steiner, Rudolf. *A Lecture on Eurythmy.* London: Rudolf Steiner Press (1923), 1967.

Stelarc. "Vers le post-humain, du corps esprit au système cybernétique." *Nouvelles de danse, "Danse et nouvelles technologies"*, 40-41 (Autumn-Winter 1999): 80-98.

Stewart, Nigel. "Re-Languaging the Body: Phenomenological Description and the Dance Image." *Performance Research* 3, no. 2, *On Place* (Summer 1998): 42-53.

Stodelle, Ernestine. "Before Yesterday. The First Decade of Modern Dance: Martha Graham." *Dance Observer* 29 (January 1962): 5-7.

Suhr, Werner. *Der künstlerische Tanz.* Leipzig: Siegels Musikalienbibliothek, 1922.

Sulloway, Frank J. *Freud, Biologist of the Mind.* London: Fontana, 1979.

Susman, Warren I. In *Culture as History: The Transformation of American Society in the Twentieth Century.* New York: Pantheon Books, 1984.

Ter-Arutunian, Rouben. "In Search of Design." *Dance Perspectives* 28 (Winter 1966): no page nos.

Terry, Walter. *Frontiers of Dance: The Life of Martha Graham.* New York: Thomas Y. Crowell Company, 1975.

Thomas, Helen. *The Body, Dance and Cultural Theory.* Basingstoke: Palgrave, 2003.

_____. *Dance, Modernity and Culture.* London: Routledge, 1995.

Thomas, Richard Hinton. "Nietzsche in Weimar Germany – and the Case of Ludwig Klages." In *The Weimar Dilemma: Intellectuals in the Weimar Republic,* edited by Anthony Phelan, 71-91. Manchester: Manchester University Press, 1985.

Tobias, Tobi. "An Interview with May O'Donnell." *Ballet Review* 9, no. 1 (Spring 1981): 64-81.

_____. "Inner Space." *New York Magazine,* 28 October, 1991: 80-81.

_____. "Notes for a Piece on Cunningham." *Dance Magazine* (September 1975): 40-42.

Toepfer, Karl. *Empire and Ecstasy: Nudity and Body Movement in German Body Culture, 1910-1935.* Berkeley: University of California Press, 1997.

Tomko, Linda *Dancing Class: Gender, Ethnicity, and Social Divides in American Dance, 1890-1920.* Bloomington: Indiana University Press, 1999.

Turner, Bryan. "Introduction." Christine Buci-Glucksmann, *Baroque Reason: The Aesthetics of Modernity,* 1-36. London: Sage, 1994.

Unrau, Sharon. "Children's Dance: An Exploration through the Techniques of Merce Cunningham". Ph.D. diss., Ohio State University, 2000.

Vaughan, David. "Cunningham and his Dancers." *Ballet Review* 15, no. 3 (Fall 1987): 19-40.

_____. "Merce Cunningham and the Northwest." In *Society of Dance History Scholars Conference Proceedings.,* 111-125. University of California, 1989.

_____. *Merce Cunningham: Fifty Forward.* CD Rom, New York: Cunningham Dance Foundation, 2005.

_____. *Merce Cunningham: Fifty Years, Chronicle and Commentary.* New York: Aperture, 1997.

Vernon-Warren, Bettina, and Charles Warren, eds. *Gertrud Bodenwieser and Vienna's Contribution to Ausdruckstanz.* Amsterdam: Harwood Academic Publishers, 1999.

Vranish, Jane. "Moving for the Moment." *Pittsburgh Post-Gazette*, 23 September 1994: 2 and 28.

Ward, Janet. *Weimar Surfaces: Urban Visual Culture in 1920s Germany.* Berkeley: University of California Press, 2001.

Ware, Susan. *Seven Women who Shaped the American Century.* Cambridge, Massachussetts: Harvard University Press, 1998.

Whitford, Frank. *Bauhaus.* London: Thames and Hudson, 1984.

Whyte, William. *The Organization Man.* New York: Doubleday, 1956.

Wigman, Mary. "Aus 'Rudolf Laban's Lehre vom Tanz'." *Die neue Schaubühne* 2/3 (February 1921): 30-35.

_____. "Komposition." In Rudolf Bach, *Das Mary Wigman Werk,* 25-6. Dresden: Carl Reissner Verlag, 1933.

_____. *Kompositionen.* Seebote: Uberlingen 1925.

_____. *The Language of Dance.* Middletown, CT: Wesleyan University Press, 1966.

_____. *The Mary Wigman Book: Her Writings,* edited by Walter Sorell. Middletown, CT: Wesleyan University Press 1984.

_____. "The Philosophy of Modern Dance." In *Dance as a Theatre Art: Source Readings in Dance History from 1581 to the Present,* edited by Selma Jeanne Cohen, 149-53. New York: Dodd, Mead and Co. 1974.

_____. "Tanz." In Rudolf Bach, *Das Mary Wigman Werk,* 19-20. Dresden: Carl Reissner Verlag, 1933.

_____. "Das Tanzerlebnis." *Die Musik,* vol.11 (1933): 801-2.

_____. "Tanz und Gymnastik." *Der Tanz* 1, no. 6 (April 1928): 6-7.

_____. "Tänzerische Wege und Ziele." *Die Schöne Frau* 4, no. 9 (1928/29): 1-2.

Willmott, Glann. *McLuhan, or Modernism in Reverse.* Toronto: University of Toronto Press, 1996.

Wittner, Victor. "Mary Wigman's Tanzschöpfungen: Der Abend im Konzerthaus." *Neues 8-Uhr Blatt,* 18 December 1922, 2.

Wobbe, Eva. "Die Gymnastik: Entwicklung der Bewegung bis zur Rhythmischen Gymnastik und deren Einfluss auf den Ausdruckstanz." In *Ausdruckstanz: Eine Mitteleuropäische Bewegung der ersten Hälfte des 20 Jahrhunderts,* edited by Gunhild Oberzaucher-Schüller, 25-33. Wilhelmshaven: Florian Nutzel Verlag, 1992.

Zabel, Barbara. "Gendered Still Life: Paintings of Still Life in the Machine Age." In *Modernism, Gender, Culture,* edited by Lisa Rado, 229-246. New York: Garland 1997.

2) AUDIOVISUAL DOCUMENTS
(NYPL = New York Public Library at Lincoln Center)

"Conversations on the Dance." Audiocassette. Merce Cunningham and Susan Sontag, recorded 3 March 1986. Dance Collection, NYPL.

"Dancemakers: Martha Graham." Television program. London: BBC TV Channel 2, 15 August 1992. Presented by Judith Mackrell.

"The Early Years: Martha Graham and Modernism." Videotapes. Cassettes 26 and 27, 1981. Dance Collection, NYPL.

"The Evolution of Wigman's Dance Technique." Videotape. Helmut Gottschild, 1986. Dance Collection, NYPL.

"Fractions I." Videotape. Choreographed by Merce Cunningham, directed by Charles Atlas, 1977. Dancers: Karole Armitage, Louise Burns, Graham Conley, Ellen Cornfield, Meg Eginton, Lisa Fox, Chris Komar, Robert Kovich. Cunningham Dance Foundation.

"Frontier." Choreographed by Martha Graham (1925) and danced by Martha Graham. Filmed by Julien Bryan and Jules Bucher 1936-39, and co-produced by the Martha Graham Center of Contemporary Dance, Inc., in association with the Teatro Municipale Romolo Valli, Reggio Emilia, Italy, for the Festival Graham, 1987. Video in Dance Collection, NYPL.

_____. Reconstructed by Martha Graham and danced by Ethel Winter. A Connecticut College School of Dance Archive Film, produced and filmed by Dwight Unwin for Jerome Robbins Film Archive, 1964. Film in Dance Collection, NYPL.

_____. Choreographed by Martha Graham and danced by Janet Eilber. Filmed by Amra Nowack Associates for Jerome Robbins Film Archive at Brooklyn Academy of Music, 1975). Film in Dance Collection, NYPL.

_____. Choreographed by Martha Graham and danced by Peggy Lyman. Videotaped in performance at the New York State Theater, 1985. Video in Dance Collection, NYPL.

"Heretic." Choreographed by Martha Graham, 1929. Danced by Martha Graham. Outtakes discovered by Barry Fischer in the Fox Movietone News collection at the University of South Carolina, Columbia. Video in Dance Collection, NYPL.

_____. Choreographed by Martha Graham, 1929. Danced by Takako Asakawa and Martha Graham Dance Company, 1986. Videotaped in performance in Williamsburg, Virginia, or in Jacksonville, Florida, in 1986. Video in Dance Collection, NYPL.

"Interview with Martha Graham: The Early Years." 2 audio cassettes. Walter Terry, 1973. Dance Collection, NYPL.

"Lamentation." Choreographed by Martha Graham, 1930. Danced by Martha Graham, 193? presented by Pictorial Films. Film in Dance Collection, NYPL.

"Martha Graham: The Dancer Revealed." Videotape. Co-production of WNET, New York, Caméras Continentales, La Sept/Arte, BBC, 1994. Distributed by KULTUR International Films Ltd.

"Mary Wigman, 1886-1973: 'When the Fire Dances between Two Poles.'" Videotape. Produced and directed by Allegra Fuller Snyder. Pennington New Jersey, Dance Horizons, 1991.

"Merce Cunningham, A Lifetime of Dance." Television programme. Directed by Charles Atlas. BBC TV, Channel 2, broadcast 26 August 2000.

"Not Just a Somersault: Insights on Aspects of Martha Graham Technique 1938-2992." Videotape. Laban Centre for Movement and Dance, London 1993.

"Primitive Mysteries." Choreographed by Martha Graham, 1931. Reconstructed by Martha Graham. Danced by Yuriko and members of the Martha Graham Company. A Connecticut College School of Dance Archive Film, produced and filmed by Dwight Godwin, 1964. Film in Dance Collection, NYPL.

"Torse." Videotape. Choreographed by Merce Cunningham, directed by Charles Atlas. Cunningham Dance Foundation, 1977. Dancers: Karole Armitage, Louise Burns, Ellen Cornfield, Morgan Ensminger, Lisa Fox, Meg Harper, Chris Komar, Robert Kovich, Julie Roess-Smith, Jim Self.

"Variations V." Film. Choreographed by Merce Cunningham. Hamburg, July 1966. Directed by Arne Arnbom, produced by Studio Hamburg, Cunningham Dance Foundation.

Index